FROMMER'S
EasyGuide
TO
Montréal & Québec City

By
Leslie Brokaw, Erin Trahan & Matthew Barber

Easy Guides are ✦ **Quick To Read** ✦ **Light To Carry**
✦ **For Expert Advice** ✦ **In All Price Ranges**

W9-BRX-250

FrommerMedia LLC

Published by
FROMMER MEDIA LLC

Copyright © 2016 by Frommer Media LLC. All rights reserved. No part of this publication may be repro-
duced, stored in a retrieval system, or transmitted in any form or by any means, electronic, mechanical,
photocopying, recording, scanning, or otherwise, except as permitted under Sections 107 or 108 of the
1976 United States Copyright Act, without the prior written permission of the Publisher. Requests to the
Publisher for permission should be addressed to support@frommermedia.com.

Frommer's is a registered trademark of Arthur Frommer. Frommer Media LLC is not associated with any
product or vendor mentioned in this book.

ISBN 978-1-62887-190-6 (paper), 978-1-62887-191-3 (e-book)

Editorial Director: Pauline Frommer
Editor: Melinda Quintero
Production Editor: Kelly Dobbs Henthorne
Cartographer: Roberta Stockwell
Photo Editor: Meghan Lamb
Cover Design: Howard Grossman

Frommer Media LLC also publishes its books in a variety of electronic formats. Some content that
appears in print may not be available in electronic formats.

Manufactured in the United States of America

5 4 3 2 1

FROMMER'S STAR RATINGS SYSTEM

Every hotel, restaurant and attraction listed in this guide has been ranked for quality and value. Here's
what the stars mean:

★   Recommended
★★   Highly Recommended
★★★   A must! Don't miss!

AN IMPORTANT NOTE

The world is a dynamic place. Hotels change ownership, restaurants hike their prices, museums
alter their opening hours, and busses and trains change their routings. And all of this can occur
in the several months after our authors have visited, inspected, and written about, these hotels,
restaurants, museums and transportation services. Though we have made valiant efforts to keep
all our information fresh and up-to-date, some few changes can inevitably occur in the periods
before a revised edition of this guidebook is published. So please bear with us if a tiny number
of the details in this book have changed. Please also note that we have no responsibility or liabil-
ity for any inaccuracy or errors or omissions, or for inconvenience, loss, damage, or expenses suffered by anyone as a result of assertions in this guide.

CONTENTS

ABOUT THE AUTHORS

Leslie Brokaw has co-authored a dozen Frommer's guides since 2006. She teaches at Emerson College and is an editor at "MIT Sloan Management Review." She has a newfound appreciation for what it takes to explore Montréal with an infant and a stroller.

Erin Trahan writes about movies and travel from her home north of Boston and teaches at Montserrat College of Art. She edits "The Independent," an online film magazine, and posts other writing at www.erintrahan.com. This is her fifth Frommer's guide to Québec.

Matthew Barber is a freelance writer who has contributed to three previous Frommer's guides. He is a correspondent for the food section of the Boston Globe. He lives in Boston with his wife, Leslie Brokaw, and their son and dog.

ABOUT THE FROMMER TRAVEL GUIDES

For most of the past 50 years, Frommer's has been the leading series of travel guides in North America, accounting for as many as 24 percent of all guidebooks sold. I think I know why.

Although we hope our books are entertaining, we nevertheless deal with travel in a serious fashion. Our guidebooks have never looked on such journeys as a mere recreation, but as a far more important human function, a time of learning and introspection, an essential part of a civilized life. We stress the culture, lifestyle, history, and beliefs of the destinations we cover and urge our readers to seek out people and new ideas as the chief rewards of travel.

We have never shied from controversy. We have, from the beginning, encouraged our authors to be intensely judgmental, critical—both pro and con—in their comments, and wholly independent. Our only clients are our readers, and we have triggered the ire of countless prominent sorts, from a tourist newspaper we called "practically worthless" (it unsuccessfully sued us) to the many rip-offs we've condemned.

And because we believe that travel should be available to everyone regardless of their incomes, we have always been cost-conscious at every level of expenditure. Although we have broadened our recommendations beyond the budget category, we insist that every lodging we include be sensibly priced. We use every form of media to assist our readers and are particularly proud of our feisty daily website, the award-winning Frommers.com.

I have high hopes for the future of Frommer's. May these guidebooks, in all the years ahead, continue to reflect the joy of travel and the freedom that travel represents. May they always pursue a cost-conscious path, so that people of all incomes can enjoy the rewards of travel. And may they create, for both the traveler and the persons among whom we travel, a community of friends, where all human beings live in harmony and peace.

Arthur Frommer

THE BEST OF MONTRÉAL & QUÉBEC CITY

I f the province of Québec had a tagline, it could be: "Any excuse for a party." An enormous *joie de vivre* pervades the way that Montréal and Québec City go about their business. The calendars of both cities are packed with festivals and events that bring out locals and guests from around the world year-round.

Montréal is planning big celebrations in 2017 for its 375th birthday (**www.375mtl.com**), but even as it highlights its rich history, it's still a modern city focused on the present, with pizzazz at every turn. The city's creative inhabitants provide zest to the ever-changing neighborhoods of Plateau Mont-Royal, Mile End, and Quartier des Spectacles, which have arts venues, boutiques, cafes, and miles of restaurants—many of which are unabashedly clever and stylish. Vieux-Montréal (Old Montréal) is the beautifully preserved historic district, and downtown features skyscrapers that come in unexpected shapes and non-corporate colors. A subway system (the Métro) is swift and dependable.

Québec City is more traditional and more French, although it is fast replacing its former conservatism with sophistication and playfulness. With an impressive location above the St. Lawrence River and carefully tended 18th- and 19th-century houses in its historic *quartier,* this city is almost impossibly romantic—and unlike any other in North America.

MONTRÉAL'S best AUTHENTIC EXPERIENCES

o **Enjoy an Afternoon or Evening of Jazz:** In downtown, Quartier des Spectacles, Vieux-Montréal, and the Plateau, jazz is a favorite musical form for locals and visitors—especially in June and July, during the renowned Festival International de Jazz. See p. 239.

o **Savor Gourmet Meals at Affordable Prices:** Experience all of French cuisine's interpretations—traditional, haute, bistro, Québécois—the way the locals do: by ordering the table d'hôte specials. You'll get to indulge in two or more courses for a fixed price that is only slightly more than the cost of a single main course. Most restaurants offer the option. See p. 80.

o **Explore Vieux-Montréal:** The city's oldest quarter has an overwhelmingly European flavor. Place Jacques-Cartier is the central outdoor square, and in every direction from there you'll find museums, bistros, and art galleries worth savoring. A revitalized waterfront just adjacent also inspires strolling or biking. A walking tour of the neighborhood is on p. 142.

QUÉBEC CITY'S best
AUTHENTIC EXPERIENCES

o **Linger at an Outdoor Cafe:** Tables are set out at Place d'Armes in Upper Town, in the Quartier du Petit-Champlain in Lower Town, and along the Grande-Allée just outside the old city's walls. It's a quality-of-life innovation the French and their Québécois brethren have perfected. See chapter 13.

o **Soak Up Lower Town:** Once all but abandoned to the grubby edges of the shipping industry, the riverside neighborhood of Basse-Ville/Vieux-Port has been reborn. Chic boutique hotels, high-end restaurants, and a smattering of antiques shops now fill rehabilitated 18th- and 19th-century buildings. See p. 253 for a walking tour.

Le Château Frontenac and the Terrasse Dufferin in Québec City

Every narrow street, leafy plaza, sidewalk cafe, horse-drawn *calèche*, pitched roof, and church spire gives off the air of France's provincial towns. But to get the full Québec City treatment, amble those streets in the evening and find a bench on Terrasse Dufferin, the promenade alongside the Château Frontenac. The river below will be the color of liquid mercury in the moon's glow, and on a clear night, you'll see a sky full of stars. Faint music from the *boîtes* in Lower Town is a possibility. Romance is a certainty.

o **Get Serious about Terroir:** The best Québécois cuisine highlights local, seasonal fare. Duck, deer, and mackerel are on many menus for that reason, as are Québec-made cheeses, microbrews, and dishes with maple syrup. The practice of going local isn't limited to traditional recipes, either. Nearly every recommended restaurant in this book embraces Québec's *terroir*— and if a menu doesn't broadcast its origins, it's probably being modest. Just ask. Chances are the menu has at least one local star.

MONTRÉAL'S best RESTAURANTS

o **Europea,** 1227 rue de la Montagne (© **514/398-9229**): For the full treatment, order the 10-taste *menu degustation.* You'll see why chef Jérôme Ferrer, whose roots are in France and Spain, is a designated "Grand Chef" of the esteemed Relais & Châteaux community of restaurants and hotels. See p. 74.

o **Brasserie T,** 1425 rue Jeanne-Mance (© **514/282-0808**): At a more moderate price point, Brasserie T is the little sister of chef/owner Normand Laprise's **Toqué!**, another top choice (p. 83). But Brasserie T is more casual and has a fun patio overlooking the Quartier des Spectacles plaza (complete with dancing waters in warm months). See p. 77.

QUÉBEC CITY'S best RESTAURANTS

o **Le Saint-Amour,** 48 rue Sainte-Ursule (© **418/694-0667**): This romantic, epicurean mecca has an old-world elegance. A 2008 visit by Sir Paul McCartney left a vegetarian legacy at this otherwise thoroughly Québécois (meaning meat-centric) restaurant. Whatever your tastes, dining here is unforgettable. See p. 201.

o **Panache,** 10 rue St-Antoine (© **418/692-1022**): It's romance all the way, from the fireplace and velvet couches to the wrought-iron staircase leading to hideaway attic corners and French-Canadian cuisine with a kick, inside

Québec City's Panache Restaurant

the knockout **Auberge St-Antoine.** For cheaper options, look for Panache's two mobile food trucks and casual outdoor **Café de la Promenade** in the warmer months. See p. 205.

MONTRÉAL'S best HOTELS

o **Hôtel Gault,** 449 rue Ste-Hélène (© **866/904-1616** or 514/904-1616): Other hotels have more amenities, but for an experience that is uniquely Montréal, the sleek and minimalist Gault, with exposed brick walls, enveloping beds, and slightly tucked away location, provides a romantic getaway option. See p. 64.

o **Le Saint-Sulpice Hôtel Montréal,** 414 rue St-Sulpice (© **877/785-7423** or 514/288-1000): Saint-Sulpice offers first-class service just short of full luxury in the heart of Vieux-Montréal. All rooms here are suites, so they're big in addition to modern and

Hôtel Gault, Montréal

chic—especially important for families that need a little more room. The hotel also has a fine in-house restaurant with a beautiful hidden terrace. Thorough, professional, and affordable. See p. 67.

QUÉBEC CITY'S best HOTELS

o **Auberge St-Antoine,** 8 rue St-Antoine (✆ **888/692-2211** or 418/692-2211): Sure, you could stay at Château Frontenac, looming on the cliffs above, the very symbol of the city. But for a more intimate visit, stay in Basse-Ville (Lower Town). This romantic luxury hotel has grown into one of Québec's most desirable lodgings, with an arresting lounge and a top restaurant (**Panache;** see Québec City's Best Restaurants, above) to boot. See p. 188.

o **Hôtel Le Germain-Dominion,** 126 rue St-Pierre (✆ **888/833-5253** or 418/692-2224): An anchor in the successful redevelopment of the once-dreary Vieux-Port, the Dominion has bedding so cozily enveloping that you may not want to go out. Do, though—for the fireplace, croissants, and café au lait in the lobby, if nothing else. See p. 189.

MONTRÉAL'S best HISTORICAL LANDMARKS

o **Pointe-à-Callière (Montréal Museum of Archaeology and History),** 350 Place-Royale (✆ **514/872-9150**): A first visit to Montréal might best begin here. This strikingly modernistic structure at the edge of Vieux-Montréal marks the spot where the first European settlement put down roots. It stands atop extensive excavations that unearthed not only remains of the French newcomers, but also of the First Nations that preceded them. Wind your way through the subterranean complex on the self-guided tour. See p. 113.

o **Musée du Château Ramezay,** 280 rue Notre-Dame est (✆ **514/861-3708**): This house, in Vieux-Montréal, was built in 1705. It became the local headquarters to the American Continental Army in 1775 when revolutionary forces took control of the city from the British; Benjamin Franklin even stayed here when he was trying to get the Québécois to side with the Americans in their revolt against the British (his effort failed). See p. 113.

Pointe-à-Callière, the Montréal Museum of Archaeology and History

QUÉBEC CITY'S best
HISTORICAL LANDMARKS

o **Château Frontenac,** 1 rue des Carrières (© **866/540-4460**): About 36 tons (or 80,000 lb.) of stunning copper cover the rooftops and spires of this landmark hotel. Its signature silhouette, erected at the end of the 19th century, inspired other grand buildings, such as Gare du Palais (Québec City's train station) to follow its architectural lead. See p. 218.

o **Basilique Cathédrale Notre-Dame de Québec,** 20 rue Buade (© **418/694-0665**): The staying power of this vast Catholic institution is evident in both the basilica's structure (dating back as early as 1647 and rebuilt several times since) and its spirit. The basilica is home to the Notre-Dame de Québec parish, which celebrated its 350th anniversary in 2014. See p. 217.

MONTRÉAL'S best MUSEUMS

o **Musée des Beaux-Arts,** 1380 rue Sherbrooke ouest (© **514/285-2000**): Canada's first museum devoted exclusively to the visual arts opened in 1912 and is now the most glorious in the province. A 2011 expansion opened an important pavilion devoted to Québécois and Canadian Art. A new four-level pavilion devoted to the Old Masters is in the works and slated to open by 2017, to coincide with Montréal's 375th anniversary celebrations. See p. 105.

o **Musée McCord,** 690 rue Sherbrooke ouest (© **514/398-7100**): The half-dozen or so exhibits here are compact, making for a satisfying trip. Permanent shows explore the history of Montréal and the role of clothing to establish identity among members of First Nations. Temporary exhibits have focused topics as varied as actress Grace Kelly, "queer baroque" ceramics works, and the costumes of Cirque du Soleil. See p. 107.

QUÉBEC CITY'S best
MUSEUMS

o **Musée de la Civilisation,** 85 rue Dalhousie (© **866/710-8031** or 418/643-2158): Here is that rarity among museums: a collection of cleverly mounted temporary and permanent exhibitions that both children and adults find engrossing, without talking down or metaphysical maunderings. Make time for "People of Québec . . . Then and Now," a permanent, sprawling examination of Québec history. See p. 211.

o **Musée National des Beaux-Arts du Québec,** Parc des Champs-de-Bataille (© **866/220-2150** or 418/643-2150): Referred to simply as Musée du Québec, this museum highlights modern art (Québec surrealist Jean-Paul Riopelle especially) and has a large collection of Inuit art, much produced in the 1980s and 1990s. See p. 223.

MONTRÉAL'S best FREE THINGS TO DO

o **Walk up Mont Royal, the City's Namesake Mountain:** If you take the most direct (and steepest) route, it only takes an hour to walk up and back down Mont Royal, going from the downtown entrance to the chalet at the top, which has spectacular views of the city. Most people, though, set a more leisurely pace—strolling the broad pedestrian-only chemin Olmsted and lingering by the lake and outdoor sculptures en route. City buses can take you one direction or the other. See p. 158 for a suggested walking tour.

o **Hover around the Edges of Festivals:** Montréal's calendar packs in over 100 festivals throughout the year (see p. 130 for some highlights). Most, including the internationally famous jazz festival and the Just for Laughs comedy festival (both held in summer), feature free performances right on the city streets and plazas. Check out what's happening at the Quartier des Spectacles as a first step. See p. 131.

QUÉBEC CITY'S best FREE THINGS TO DO

o **Ooh over Pyrotechnics:** In August, crowds gather along the Vieux-Québec port to watch the international fireworks competition **Les Grand Feux Loto-Québec.** The event runs on select Wednesday and Saturday nights, and nations compete to produce the biggest, loudest, or most creative fireworks displays. See p. 237.

o **Soak in the Ambiance of Place-Royale:** One of the most beautiful and historic public plazas, the small Place-Royale is where you linger, gaze at the surrounding stone homes and jaunty roofs, and feel the European charm promised by all the travel guides (yes, including this one). See p. 214.

MONTRÉAL'S best OF THE OUTDOORS

o **Bike the City:** Montréalers' enthusiasm for bicycling has spurred an ongoing development of bicycle paths that wind through downtown areas and out to the countryside. Rentals are available from shops (for day trips) and the BIXI network (for short trips). See p. 126.

o **Traverse the Lachine Canal:** First constructed in the early 1800s to detour around the rapids of the same name, the canal reopened for recreational use in 1997 after much renovation. You can explore the canal and its surroundings on foot, on a rented bicycle, or on kayaks or pedal boats (available for rental from H2O Adventures, located right on the canal near the Marché Atwater; see p. 127).

QUÉBEC CITY'S best OF OUTDOORS

o **Take a Walking Tour:** Combine immersion in Québec's rich history with a good stretch of the legs among the battlements and through the storied city's cobblestoned streets. Follow the walking tours in chapter 16 or go on a group tour. See p. 243 and p. 253.

o **Drive to Montmorency Falls:** North of the city by 11km (6¾ miles) is the impressive Montmorency Falls—higher than Niagara Falls, although far narrower. It's a spectacular cascade in all four seasons. An easy path leads to the base of the falls, and both stairs and a cable car go to the top. A footbridge crosses the water where it flows over the cliff, for those with nerves of steel. See p. 264.

MONTRÉAL'S best FOR FAMILIES

o **Visit the Biodôme de Montréal:** Perhaps the most engaging attraction in the city for younger children. The Biodôme houses replications of four ecosystems: a Laurentian forest; the St. Lawrence marine system; a polar environment; and, most appealingly, a tropical rainforest. See p. 119.

o **Spend a Day at the Centre des Sciences de Montréal:** Running the length of a central pier in Vieux-Port, this science center for children and pre-teens has a handful of permanent interactive displays as well as appealing special exhibits (past shows have included the history of video games, sex, and the archeological adventures of Indiana Jones). It's also home to a popular IMAX theater. See p. 111.

QUÉBEC CITY'S best FOR FAMILIES

o **Watch the Changing of the Guard: La Citadelle** is the fortress built by the British to repel an American invasion that never came. It's still an active military post, and the colorful ceremonial Changing of the Guard is just the right length of time to hold the attention of the youngest spectators. See p. 219.

o **Celebrate Summer (or Winter, Spring, or Fall): Festival d'Eté** (Summer Festival), **Carnaval de Québec,** or any number of festivals hosted throughout the calendar year, cater especially to families. Free activities abound and special guests like Bonhomme (an enormous snow figure) pop in for a skate, or to help reach that tippy-top spot of the snow sculpture. See p. 235.

MONTRÉAL'S best NON-TOURIST DESTINATIONS

o **Food Shop the Marché Jean-Talon:** We're not saying there won't be out of towners here, at one of Montréal's pre-eminent fruit, vegetable, and food markets, but there will be fewer than at **Marché Atwater,** simply by virtue of Jean-Talon's location at the northern end of Mile End, beyond where most casual visitors wander. See p. 119.

o **Groove with Les Tam-Tams du Mont-Royal:** Sundays from early May to late September, a friendly crowd gathers on the eastern edge of Parc Mont-Royal for drumming, dancing, and snacking from food trucks. Hundreds of drummers, hippies, and fantasy combatants join in at each session, along with an audience that just takes it all in. Bring a blanket and a picnic and sprawl out on the grassy lawns. Find it at the monument to Sir George-Étienne Cartier near avenue du Parc at the corner of rue Rachel. See p. 125.

QUÉBEC CITY'S best NON-TOURIST DESTINATIONS

o **Hang Out in St-Roch:** This neighborhood has been up and coming for over a decade, but it doesn't get the busloads of tourists that other neighborhoods do. Along rue St-Joseph you'll find coffee shops, *boulangeries,* secondhand stores, high-end clothing by Québécois designers, and an eclectic mix of nightlife from experimental bistros to ethnic cuisine. See p. 224 and p. 242.

o **Stroll Rue St-Jean outside the Gate:** Some of the city's finest food purveyors are just outside the St-Jean Gate of the wall enclosing the old Upper Town, in a neighborhood called Faubourg St-Jean. Walk 1.5km (9/10 mile) along rue St-Jean to get to avenue Cartier and turn left. The route flows through the heart of the non-touristy Montcalm neighborhood, flush with eateries, clothing boutiques, and city-dwellers. See p. 222.

A Note About English & French in This Book

Like the Québécois themselves, this guidebook goes back and forth between using the French names and the English names for areas and attractions. Most often, we use French. Québec's state-mandated language is French, and most signs, brochures, and maps in the region appear in French. However, we use the English name or translation as well, if that makes the meaning clearer. *Bon voyage!*

SUGGESTED ITINERARIES

2

While some suggestions here are best for warm weather, most of the recommendations are appropriate for all seasons—just remember to bundle up in wintertime. Public transportation in Montréal is excellent, and Québec City is compact, so unless noted, you won't need a car for these tours.

THE BEST OF MONTRÉAL IN 1 DAY: HISTORIC MONTRÉAL

This overview of historic Montréal allows time for random exploring, shopping, or lingering in sidewalk cafes. If you're staying only one night, book a room in a Vieux-Montréal boutique hotel. Many first-time visitors find themselves drawn to the plazas and narrow cobblestone streets of this 18th- and 19th-century neighborhood, so you might as well be based there. *Start: Vieux-Montréal, at Place d'Armes.*

---

1 Place d'Armes

Begin your day in this outdoor plaza, the heart of **Vieux-Montréal ★★★**, at the site of the city's oldest building, the **Vieux Séminaire de St-Sulpice** (p. 109), built by priests who arrived in 1657. Next to it is the **Basilique Notre-Dame ★★★** (p. 110), an 1824 church with a stunning interior of intricately gilded rare woods. Its acoustics are so perfect that the late, famed opera star Luciano Pavarotti performed here several times.

Consider taking the walking tour of Vieux-Montréal on p. 142, which takes you past every historic structure in this historic neighborhood and eventually to our next stop. Or, to go to Pointe-à-Callière directly, walk down the slope from the Basilica on either side street.

2 Pointe-à-Callière ★★★

The **Pointe-à-Callière (Museum of Archaeology and History)** is our favorite museum for a full immersion into Québec history. Its underground tunnels have remnants of Amerindian camps and early French settlements. See p. 113.

3 Olive et Gourmando ☕ ★★★
This funky cafe is a city highlight.
Eat in or take out if the weather's
right for a picnic lunch by the river.
The Cuban sandwich is a popular
choice. See p. 86.

Unless you're a very ambitious walker,
take a cab, the Métro to Guy-Concordia,
or a BIXI rental bike to get to:

4 Musée des Beaux-
Arts ★★★
This is the city's glorious fine-
arts museum. Temporary shows,
especially, are dazzling. See
p. 105.

5 Rue Crescent
From the museum, walk south

The Basilique Notre-Dame in Montréal

on rue Crescent. If you're in a
shopping mood, Ste-Catherine, 2 blocks down, is the nexus for department stores and mid-priced shopping (turn left and head east). Rue Crescent itself is a touristy strip for drinking and people-watching. If it's
warm, grab a seat on one of the large terraces.

6 Sir Winston Churchill Pub ☕ ★
Epicenter of the rue Crescent scene for years, this pub fills with people of all
ages. It's a good spot to nurse a pint while taking in the passing pedestrian
parade. See p. 137.

For dinner options downtown or in other neighborhoods, see the listings in chapter 6.

THE BEST OF MONTRÉAL IN 2 DAYS: A RICH FRENCH HERITAGE

With the absolute essentials of historic Old Montréal and downtown Anglophone cultural institutions under your belt on Day 1, take a journey into
French Montréal on your second day. Residents here spend time outdoors all
times of the year, and this itinerary nudges you in the same direction. *Start:
Viau Métro station.*

1 Jardin Botanique ★★★
These lush, romantic, year-round botanical gardens comprise 75 hectares
(185 acres) of plants and flowers with 10 exhibition greenhouses. They
offer up sophistication and relaxation to start the day. See p. 120.

Take the Métro to Sherbrooke and walk 1 block west to rue St-Denis, turning right (north).

2

SUGGESTED ITINERARIES

The Best of Montréal in 2 Days: a Rich French Heritage

11

Montréal's Place des Arts, a cultural center for ballet, opera, and symphony

2 Rue St-Denis & Plateau Mont-Royal

Rue St-Denis is one central artery of Francophone Montréal, thick with cafes, bistros, offbeat shops, and lively nightspots. As you head north into Plateau Mont-Royal, famous for its outdoor winding staircases, there are no must-see sights, so wander at will and surrender to the heart of French Montréal's color and vitality. Maybe set a cafe as a destination: One good option is **Boulangerie Première Moisson,** a bakery of delectables at 860 av. Mont-Royal est (at rue St-André). There, more than the half the 50 staff hail from France.

See chapter 6 for more eating options in the Plateau. Take the Métro to Place des Arts for evening options.

3 Quartier des Spectacles

What to do tonight? The Quartier des Spectacles is the entertainment district of the city. It's walking distance from both Vieux-Montréal and downtown and includes the **Place des Arts** plaza. Ballet, opera, and symphony orchestras are all here, as are many of the festivals that take place year round. Even if you don't speak French, consider getting tickets for a French-language show for a fully immersive experience. Regular priced and same-day discount tickets are available at the high-tech ticketing center **La Vitrine,** 2 Ste-Catherine est (© **866/924-5538** or 514/285-4545). Last-minute bargains are also posted online at www.lavitrine.com.

Whether you get tickets or not, this area is still a good spot for finding a meal or strolling. If a festival is going on, chances are more than good that parts of it will be spilling over, for free, right here.

THE BEST OF MONTRÉAL IN 3 DAYS: THE GREAT OUTDOORS

If you've followed the above itineraries on Days 1 and 2, you've already visited Montréal's primary must-see sights. Today, take in the great parks and waterways of the city. *Start: Peel Métro station (if you're in the mood for a hike) or a taxi ride to Lac des Castors at the top of Parc du Mont-Royal.*

1 Parc du Mont-Royal ★★

The hill that rises behind downtown is the small mountain, Mont Royal, which gives the city its name. This crest became a public park somewhat according to plans by architect Frederick Law Olmsted. Throngs of people come for its woods, paths, and meadows in all four seasons. You can join them with a stroll up from Peel station (see p. 158 for a walking tour). Otherwise, take a taxi ride to Lac des Castors (Beaver Lake) at the top or hop on bus #11, which runs between Métro stations Mont-Royal and Chemin de la Côte-des-Neiges. See p. 125.

After some time at the city's highest point, make your way either by bus and Métro, or by taxi, to the waterways at the southern end of the city.

2 Vieux-Port ★★★

The Old Port at the edge of Vieux-Montréal has been transformed into a broad, vibrant park. Principal among the attractions is the **Centre des Sciences de Montréal** (p. 111), on quai (pier) King Edward. The center contains interactive exhibits that enthrall most everyone's inner geek.

In the warm months, glass-enclosed **Le Bateau-Mouche** (www. bateaumouche.com; © **800/361-9952** or 514/849-9952), reminiscent of the boats on the Seine in Paris, take passengers on a route inaccessible by traditional vessels and providing sweeping views of the city and nearby islands. See p. 123.

You can also rent **bicycles** and **in-line skates** by the hour or day from here, and then head out to the peaceful **Lachine Canal,** a nearly flat 11km (6.8-mile) bicycle path that's open year round. See p. 126. The **St-Ambroise brewpub** (www.mcauslan.com; © **514/939-3060**) is right along the canal, and its terrace makes a good destination in warm months. Its Pub Annexe St-Ambroise, inside, is open year round.

3 Le Jardin Nelson 🍴 ★★

Vieux-Montréal has plenty of good restaurants, and one of the most popular is **Le Jardin Nelson,** on the main square, Place Jacques-Cartier. It's open in the warm months and has a back terrace where jazz musicians perform during the day and evening. The menu offers a roster of main-course and dessert crepes. See p. 138.

DON'T BE shy, GIVE BIXI A TRY

I love the BIXI concept—take a bike, ride it around, drop it anywhere—but I had to wonder: Are those gray-and-red cruisers really for anyone, even little ole non-Montréaler me? The answer: *Mais oui!* A visit to www.bixi.com showed the BIXI bike stations closest to where I was staying. At the station, I planned my route and drop-off point using the large posted map (and I took note of the bike lanes that are everywhere). I put my bag into BIXI's iron-clad front rack and bungee, which could secure a barrel of daredevils plunging down Niagara Falls. One swipe of a credit card, and off

I careened—I was in Montréal, on a bike!

I'm comfortable with urban biking, but I'll admit to wobbling my first few BIXI kilometers. By design, the bikes are unisex and supersturdy, and I am neither. As I watched one neighborhood roll into the next, I realized my feet could barely reach the pedals. Seat height is adjustable, so I took a break and lowered it, *pas de problème*. When the sun is shining down the Main, there's really no better way to get from croissant to bagel. (For more on BIXI, see p. 126.)

—Erin Trahan

A ROMANTIC DAY IN MONTRÉAL

Romance is in the eyes of the beholder, which makes this a tricky tour to propose. Sitting hand in hand on a quiet park bench might be all you need for a moment to be luminous—while your best friend might dream of dropping C$300 on a luxurious dinner in a sky-high restaurant. You can have both. Options here range from the modest to the opulent. This day starts in Plateau Mont-Royal then moves to Vieux-Montréal and stays there. *Start: Mont-Royal Métro station.*

1 Stroll Parc La Fontaine ★

Start at the park's northern end, along rue Rachel est. This park in Plateau Mont-Royal is one of the city's most popular. Half is landscaped in a formal French manner, half in a more casual English style. You can rent ice skates to glide across the frozen central lake in winter, while in summer you can rent rowboats, walk the paths, and cuddle up lakeside. See p. 125 (Alternatively, if you haven't been yet, head to **Jardin Botanique,** the city's lush, year-round botanical gardens. See "The Best of Montréal in 2 Days," above.)

Travel back to Vieux-Montréal, where the rest of this itinerary takes place. To get there, hop a BIXI bike or take the Métro to Place d'Armes.

2 Take the Waters ★

Do like the Swedish do to relax and hit the baths. Vieux-Montréal has two options: **Scandinave Les Bains** and **Bota Bota.** At Scandinave Les Bains, visitors (in bathing suits) have the run of the complex that includes a warm bath the size of a small swimming pool with jets and a waterfall and a steam room thick with the scent of eucalyptus oil. A transformed ferryboat docked in Vieux-Port houses Bota Bota, which offers a similar circuit of dry saunas, steam rooms, and Jacuzzis, two of which are outside. See p. 114 and p. 110.

3 Find Some Sweets for Your Sweet

Perhaps cupcakes from the cute bakery **Les Glaceurs** in Vieux-Montréal (453 rue St-Sulpice)? Or maybe treats by local chocolatier **Les Chocolats de Chloé,** which spices up offerings with cardamom, pistachio, and Earl Grey tea? (The chocolates are sold in their shop at 546 rue Duluth est in the Plateau and at the Vieux-Montréal restaurant **Olive et Gourmando;** see p 86.)

4 Check into Auberge du Vieux-Port ★★

Exposed brick and stone walls, massive beams, and polished hardwood floors define the hideaway bedrooms. The intimate roof top terrace offers a prime place to enjoy drinks (and has views of the fireworks over the harbor from June to August during **L'International des Feux Loto-Québec**, an annual fireworks competition). See p. 64 and p. 133.

5 Savor a Dinner Cruise on Le Bateau-Mouche

This glass-enclosed vessel is reminiscent of those on the Seine in Paris. It's a floating restaurant and terrasse, and the dinner is a chichi affair. The staff is outfitted in black-tie and women will be comfortable in cocktail dresses. If you coordinate your trip with the summer fireworks festival, the pyrotechnics will explode right above you. See p. 123.

The dinner cruise on Le Bateau-Mouche comes with spectacular river views.

THE BEST OF QUÉBEC CITY IN 1 DAY: STEP BACK INTO THE 17TH & 18TH CENTURIES

With an ancient wall surrounding the oldest part of the city, Québec City sustains the look of a provincial European village that keeps watch over the powerful St. Lawrence River. For a short visit, book a hotel in the Old City, either within the walls of the Haute-Ville (Upper Town) or in the quieter Basse-Ville (Lower Town). *Start: Château Frontenac.*

1 Château Frontenac ★★★

As soon as you're done unpacking, head to **Château Frontenac** (p. 218)—its peaked copper roofs are visible from everywhere. The hotel's posh bar and pretty cafe are great for a splurge. The long promenade alongside the hotel, the **Terrasse Dufferin,** offers panoramic views of the St. Lawrence River and of the city's **Basse-Ville (Lower Town).** In winter, an old-fashioned toboggan run takes over the steep staircase at the south end.

Head down to Basse-Ville either by the *funiculaire,* the glass-encased outdoor elevator, or the staircase called L'escalier du Casse-Cou. They're right next to each other. Both routes end at the top of rue du Petit-Champlain, a touristy pedestrian street of shops and restaurants. Save that for later, and instead walk ahead on rue Sous-le-Fort and make the first left turn to reach:

2 Place-Royale ★★★

Restored 17th- and 18th-century houses surround this small but picturesque square, the site of the first European colony in Canada. The **church** on one side was built in 1688. A visit to the **Musée de la Place Royale** is an option here. See p. 214.

Past the Musée de la Place Royale, at the end of rue Notre-Dame, turn around to view a *trompe l'oeil* **mural** depicting citizens of the early city. Continue past the mural and turn right to walk toward the river. Turn left on rue Dalhousie and walk to:

3 Musée de la Civilisation ★★★

A city highlight. This ambitious museum, filled with fascinating exhibits, can easily fill 2 or 3 hours. Don't miss the permanent exhibition "People of Québec . . . Then and Now," which explores the province's roots as a fur-trading colony and gives a rich sense of Québec's daily life over the generations. See p. 211.

Leaving the museum, turn left on rue Dalhousie, left on rue St-Paul, and walk to rue du Sainte-au-Matelot.

4 A Bounty of Bistros ☕

Within a block of the corner of rues St-Paul and du Sault-au-Matelot is a strong selection of bistros and casual eateries. Almost any of them will do for a snack

Rue St-Paul in Old Town Québec City

or a meal, but one favorite choice is **L'Échaudé, ★**. It offers classic French dishes and puts out sidewalk tables in summer. See p. 204.

5 **Rue St-Paul & Antiquing**

The northern end of the short street rue St-Paul is great for browsing for antiques and collectibles.

Turn right at rue St-Thomas and cross rue St-André.

6 **Marché du Vieux-Port ★★**

This large market is open year round, and offers regional produce and other agricultural products for sale. Look for *vin de cidre* (cider wine), cassis from the Île d'orléans company Cassis Monna et filles, or maple syrup items (*sirop d'érable*). See p. 216.

7 **Drink it All In**

To close out a day back in time, dine at one of the many restaurants that are steeped in Québec history and food specialties. **Initiale ★★★** guarantees an impeccable meal, while **Aux Anciens Canadiens ★★** offers traditional Québécois cuisine. For a more modern take on provincial sophistication, **Le Clocher Penché Bistrot ★★★** is one of the best bistros in a town that specializes in them. See p. 203, p. 197, and p. 209 respectively.

THE BEST OF QUÉBEC CITY IN 2 DAYS: MILITARY HISTORY THAT RESOUNDS TODAY

During repeated conflicts with the British in the 18th century, the residents of New France moved to the top of the cliffs of Cap Diamant. Over the years, they created fortifications with battlements and artillery emplacements that eventually encircled the city. Most of the defensive walls remain, although many have been restored repeatedly. For your second day in Québec City, these historic mementos are the centerpiece of your tour. *Start: Terrasse Dufferin.*

1 Promenade des Gouverneurs ★

Walk south to the end of Terrasse Dufferin. At the end, go up the staircase to the **Promenade des Gouverneurs.** This path was renovated in 2007 and skirts the sheer cliff wall, climbing up and up past Québec's military **Citadelle,** a fort built by the British army between 1820 and 1850 that remains an active military garrison. The promenade/staircase ends at the grassy **Parc des Champs-de-Bataille,** about 15 minutes away. See p. 246.

From here, walk around the rim of the fortress.

2 La Citadelle ★

The Citadelle has a low profile, dug into the land, instead of rising above it. A ceremonial changing of the guard takes place daily at 10am in summer (June 24 to the first Mon of Sept) and can be viewed from here. See p. 251.

Walk down the hill toward the road. Grande-Allée passes through the city walls at porte (gate) St-Louis, our next destination.

3 Porte St-Louis & the Walls ★

After Grande-Allée passes through the large gate called **porte St-Louis,** it becomes rue St-Louis, a main road through Old Town. The long greenway on the inside of the walls here is **Parc l'Esplanade.** Stroll along it and down a steep hill to another main gate in the wall, **porte St-Jean** (a 20th-century re-creation). Nearby is the **Parc de l'Artillerie,** where you can view an officer's mess and quarters and an old iron foundry. See p. 251.

Walk west on rue St-Jean through the gate. This is Place d'Youville, a plaza with hotels, a concert hall, and restaurants. Many of the city's festivals, in both summer and winter, set up outdoor stages here.

4 Ristorante il Teatro 🍵

A good bet for lunch or dinner, with sidewalk seating in warm weather. The menu offers Italian comfort food in a snazzy setting, with pasta and risotto specialties. The restaurant is part of Le Capitole, a hotel-theater complex.

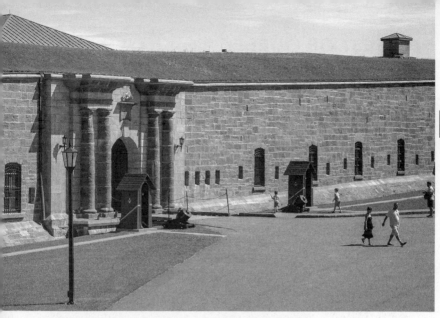
Entrance to the historic Citadelle in Québec City, still in use today

Walk back through the gate to browse along:

5 Rue St-Jean

An ever-updated variety of shops, pubs, and restaurants line rue St-Jean, one of the liveliest of Vieux-Québec's streets. Chapter 14 lists some of the shopping possibilities here.

At the end of rue St-Jean, bear right up Côte de la Fabrique. At the end is:

6 Basilique Cathédrale Notre-Dame de Québec ★★★

In 2014, the Basilica celebrated 350 years as the mother parish to all of North America. What with bombardments, fires, and repeated rebuilding, this oldest Christian parish north of Mexico is nothing if not perseverant. Parts of it, including the bell tower, survive from the original 1647 building, but most of what remains is from a 1771 reconstruction. Step inside to see the blindingly bright gold leaf. See p. 217.

Leaving the church, walk left along rue du Buade and turn right onto the narrow pedestrian alley rue du Trésor. Artists set up here and sell etchings, drawings, and watercolors. Rue du Trésor ends at the central plaza of Upper Town, Place d'Armes. Château Frontenac is directly across the plaza.

7 Outdoor Cafe Dining ☕

If it's warm, snag an outdoor table at any of the restaurants on rue Ste-Anne. One favorite is **Le Pain Béni ★**, the restaurant at the **Auberge Place d'Armes** (p. 200). The food here is adventurous: Québécois classics with modern twists. Options include medium-sized portions for sharing, tapas-style.

THE BEST OF QUÉBEC CITY IN 3 DAYS: FRESH ARTS & FRESH AIR

While the romance of the capital is largely contained within Vieux-Québec's Lower and Upper Towns, outside the Old City offers much to experience in its own right. On your third day, try to make time for at least one or two of the following attractions, toward the western end of Parc des Champs-de-Bataille (Battlefields Park). ***Start: Musée des Beaux-Arts.***

1 Musée National des Beaux-Arts du Québec ★★★
Inside **Parc des Champs-de-Bataille** (**Battlefields Park,** which contains the Plains of Abraham) is the capital's most important art museum. It focuses on Inuit sculpture and the works of Québec-born artisans. The original 1933 museum connects with a newer structure via a glass-roofed pavilion with a reception area, museum shop, and cafe. See p. 223.

Walk outside into:

2 Parc des Champs-de-Bataille ★★★
Get some fresh air with a stroll through the 108 hectares (267 acres) that comprise Canada's first national urban park and the city's playground.

Strolling through Parc des Champs-de-Bataille

Within its rolling hills are two Martello towers, cylindrical stone defensive structures built between 1808 and 1812, as well as cycling paths and picnic grounds. See p. 228.

Head back to the main street, Grand-Allée, and cross over to the perpendicular street:

3 Avenue Cartier

Just a few blocks from the museum, avenue Cartier is part of the laid-back residential Montcalm district with many intriguing shops and restaurants.

4 Café Krieghoff ☕ ★★★

This cheerful cafe has an outdoor terrace a few steps up from the sidewalk. On weekend mornings, artsy locals of all ages pack the tables piled high with bowls of café au lait and huge plates of eggs, sweet pastries, or classics like steak frites.

5 Grande-Allée

Walk back to Grande-Allée and turn left to get back to the Old City. There's a gentle downhill slope. After about 3 blocks, you'll find a stretch of shoulder-to-shoulder cafes and clubs. The Old City is another 10-minute walk ahead.

A ROMANTIC DAY IN QUÉBEC CITY

We'll acknowledge for a second time that one person's definition of romance might be different from another's (see "Romantic Montréal," above) but this endearing city has so many charms, we wanted to provide a few ideas for how to unlock them. *Start: Château Frontenac.*

1 Let a Horse be Your Guide

Hiring a **horse-drawn carriage** (or *calèche*) may sound like a romantic cliché, but how many times have you actually done it? There's no better place, or perhaps time, to try. Carriages will pick you up or can be hired from locations throughout the city, including at Place d'Armes. A 40-minute ride costs C$90, plus tip, for four people maximum. See p. 226.

If your trip ends at Château Frontenac, take rue Fort (pass Place d'Armes on your left), turn left on rue de Buade, and then right on Côte de la Fabrique, where at no. 2 you can:

2 Embrace the French Language

There's a reason so many English-speakers associate the French language with romance—it truly slides off the tongue. Québec is deeply proud of its Francophone past, present, and future. Better acquaint yourself with all three at **Musée de l'Amérique Francophone ★★**. While you're at it, why not memorize a few phrases to take home. How about: *Tu es ma joie de vivre.* (You are the joy of my life.) Too sappy? *Attache ta tuque* means Get, ready, let's go! (Or more literally, Put on your winter hat.) See p. 220.

From here, turn left on rue de Buade, grab your partner's hand, and keep going down the steep grade of the curved Côte de la Montagne, where you'll find stairs to:

3 Amble Down rue de Petit-Champlain

You can't leave town without a stroll down the old-world, amiable rue de Petit-Champlain, especially after dark, when the shops are lit from within. You'll find a few of them listed in chapter 14. Wintertime is especially magical here, when much of the street is lit by small Christmas lights.

Take a moment to bask in the enchanting backdrop, and then do what most travelers do, plan your next meal. If you want, you can:

A calèche ride through Québec City

4 Celebrate a Milestone & Join the Party

Whether you are falling in love, marking an anniversary, or simply thrilled at your first-ever horse-drawn carriage ride, it doesn't matter—you name the milestone, and then make like the Québécois, and celebrate! This city loves its **festivals** and there's likely a festival party underway somewhere that you can throw yourself into (see chapter 15 for a list).

5 Romantic Table for Two, Please

To top off a romantic day, consider a meal at the legendary **Le Saint-Amour** restaurant in Upper Town. Or, venture off the central tourist grid to the St-Roch neighborhood. For a classy, contemporary bistro experience, book a table for two at **Le Clocher Penché Bistrot ★★★**. If a perfect bottle of wine and tapas is more your style, head for **Le Cercle ★★★**. See p. 201, 209, or 208.

MONTRÉAL & QUÉBEC CITY IN CONTEXT

M ontréal and Québec City, the twin cities of the province of Québec, have a stronger European flavor than Canada's other municipalities. French is the first language of most residents and the official language of the province, and a strong affiliation with France continues to be a central facet of the region's personality.

The defining dialectics of Canadian life are culture and language, and both are thorny issues that have long threatened to tear the country apart. Many Québécois have long believed that making Québec a separate, independent state is the only way to maintain their rich French culture in the face of the Anglophone—English speaking—ocean that surrounds them. On the other hand, the popularity of the political party that represents this point of view, Parti Québécois, waxes and wanes, and today is viewed by many as too extreme to be taken seriously. Even though secession is nearly completely unlikely, as Montréal celebrates its 375 birthday (in 2017), Québec's role within the Canadian federation continues to be one of the most debated and volatile topics of conversation in Canadian politics.

A multitude of reasons account for the festering intransigence, of course—about 250 years' worth. After France lost power in Québec to the British in the 18th century, a kind of linguistic exclusionism developed, with wealthy Scottish and English bankers and merchants denying French-Canadians access to upper levels of business and government. This bias continued well into the mid-20th century.

Many in Québec stayed committed to the French language and culture after the imposition of British rule. Even with later waves of other immigrant populations pouring into the cities, a bedrock of French loyalty guarded the province's Gallic roots. France may have relinquished control of Québec to Great Britain in 1763, but France's influence, even 150 years after its rule, remains powerful. Many Québécois continue to look across the Atlantic for inspiration in fashion, food, and the arts. Culturally and linguistically, it is that tenacious French connection that gives the province its special character.

Two other important cultural phenomena have emerged over the past two decades. The first is an institutional acceptance of gay rights. By changing the definition of "spouse" in 39 laws and regulations in 1999, Québec's government eliminated all legal distinctions between same-sex and heterosexual couples and became Canada's first province to recognize the legal status of same-sex civil unions. Gay marriage became legal in all of Canada's provinces and territories in 2005. Montréal, in particular, has transformed into one of North America's most welcoming cities for gay people.

The second phenomenon is the continuing influx of a wide variety of immigrants into the province's melting pot. That has led to a not-insignificant amount of angst over the so-called reasonable accommodation of minority religious practices, particularly those of Muslims and Orthodox Jews. "The identity inherited from the French-Canadian past is perfectly legitimate and it must survive," a 2008 national report said, "but it can no longer occupy alone the Québec identity space." Immigrants, together with aboriginal people from 11 First Nation tribes who live in the province, help make the region as vibrant and alive as any on the continent.

THE CITIES TODAY

What makes both Montréal and Québec City special is the way they meld the very old and very new. In Québec City, the centuries-old walls that provided military protection are still in place, and the streets and lanes within their embrace have changed little, preserving for posterity the heart of New France. But the city's St-Roch neighborhood has a youthful pop and an influx of new technology and media companies, that have brought with them trendy restaurants and bars.

Montréal has shifted personas over the decades, and today is one of the most cosmopolitan and "European" cities in North America. It has mostly shaken off the racy image it developed when the U.S. was "dry" during U.S. Prohibition from 1920 to 1933. In those years, American bootleggers, hard drinkers, and prostitutes flocked across the border, much to the distress of much of Montréal's citizenry. In the 1950s, a cleanup began alongside a boom in high-rise construction. Restoration also began in the old port area, which had become dilapidated and rundown. In 1967, Montréal welcomed international audiences to Expo 67, the World's Fair.

The renaissance of much of the oldest part of the city, Vieux-Montréal, blossomed in the 1990s and continues today. A newly (and seemingly continually) renovated Quartier des Spectacles arts district, walking distance from the major parts of the city, gives the city a new flair. It's where many of the celebrations throughout 2017 for the city's 375th birthday will likely be taking place (details about the celebrations are at **www.375mtl.com**).

Quartier des spectacles, a hub for design creativity in Montréal

To understand the province's unique politics, you need to back up about 50 years. A phenomenon later labeled the Quiet Revolution began bubbling in the 1960s. The movement focused on transforming the largely rural, agricultural province into an urbanized entity. French-Canadians, long denied access to the upper echelons of desirable corporate careers, started to insist on equal opportunity with the powerful Anglophone minority. In 1968, Pierre Trudeau, a bilingual Québécois, became Canada's prime minister, a post he held for 18 years. More flamboyant and brilliant than any of his predecessors, he devoted much time to trying to placate voters on both sides of the French-English issue.

Also in 1968, the Parti Québécois was founded by René Lévesque, and a separatist movement began in earnest. (See "The Fight to Keep Québec's French Heritage," p. 28.) The question of whether Québec would stay part of Canada was an underlying issue for decades, and during the 1990s especially it led to an unsettled mood in the province. Large businesses left town, anxious that if the province actually did secede, they would find themselves based outside of Canada proper. Economic opportunities were limited.

Things began to change after the turn of the century. The Canadian dollar began to strengthen. Unemployment, long in double digits, shrank to less than 6%. Crime in Montréal, which was already one of the continent's safest cities, hit a 20-year low. The rash of FOR RENT signs that disfigured Montréal in the 1990s was replaced by a welcome shortage of retail and office space. In 2002, the 28 towns and cities on the Island of Montréal merged into one megacity with a population that's now about 1.9 million.

As significantly, the proportion of foreign-born Québec citizens continued to grow. In 2006, foreign-born nationals made up 20% of Canada's population, with Montréal, Toronto, Vancouver, and Calgary their prime destinations. The province of Québec welcomed over 50,000 permanent residents in 2010, with over 46,000 of them settling in Montréal, and another 2,600 in Québec City.

Immigrants have made Montréal their own. Food author Ruth Reichl has written, for instance, that when she lived there in the 1960s, the streets inhabited by Montréal's Eastern-European Jewish community "were rich with the scent of garlic, cloves, and allspice emanating from the mountains of pickles and deliciously rich smoked meat that I spied each time a restaurant door swung open." Those rich aromas of the world's cuisines remain a defining feature of the city and its neighborhoods.

LOOKING BACK: MONTRÉAL & QUÉBEC CITY HISTORY

First Immigrants

The region's first settlers were the Iroquois, who spent time in what's now called Québec long before the Europeans arrived. The Vikings landed in Canada more than 1,000 years ago, probably followed by Irish and Basque fishermen. English explorer John Cabot stepped ashore briefly on the east coast in 1497, but it was the French who managed the first meaningful European toehold.

When Jacques Cartier sailed up the St. Lawrence in 1535, he recognized at once the tremendous strategic potential of Québec City's Cap Diamant (Cape Diamond), the high bluff overlooking the river. But he was exploring, not empire building, and after stopping briefly on land, he continued on his trip.

Montréal, at the time, was the site of a fortified Iroquois village called Hochelaga, composed of 50 longhouses. Cartier was on a sea route to China but was halted by the fierce rapids just west of what is now the Island of Montréal. (In a demonstration of mingled optimism and frustration, he dubbed the rapids "La Chine," assuming that China was just beyond them. Today, they're still known as the Lachine.) Cartier visited the Indian settlement in what's now Old Montréal before moving on.

Samuel de Champlain arrived 73 years later, in 1608, motivated by the burgeoning fur trade, obsessed with finding a route to China, and determined to settle the territory. He was perhaps emboldened after the Virginia Company founded its fledgling colony of Jamestown, hundreds of miles to the south, just a year before. Called Kebec, Champlain's first settlement grew to become Québec City's Basse-Ville, or Lower Town, and spread across the flat riverbank beneath the cliffs of Cap Diamant. In 2008, Québec City hosted major celebrations of the 400th anniversary of this founding.

Champlain would make frequent trips back to France to reassure anxious investors that the project, which he said would eventually "equal the states of greatest kings," was going apace. In truth, the first years were bleak. Food was scarce, and scurvy ravaged many of the settlers. Demanding winters were far colder than in France. And almost from the beginning, hostilities raged, first between the French and the Iroquois, then between the French and the British (and later, the Americans). At issue was control of the lucrative trade of the fur of beavers, raccoons, and bears, and deer hides, as the pelts were shipped off to Paris fashion houses. The commercial battle lasted nearly a century.

To better defend themselves, the settlers in Québec City built a fortress at the top of the cliffs. Gradually, the center of urban life moved to inside the fortress walls.

The French and British struggle for dominance in the new continent focused on their explorations, and in this regard, France outdid England. Far-ranging French fur trappers, navigators, soldiers, and missionaries opened up not only Canada, but also most of what eventually became the United States, moving all the way south to the future New Orleans. Frenchmen mapped or settled at least 35 of the subsequent 50 U.S. states and left behind thousands of city names to prove it, including Detroit, St. Louis, Duluth, and Des Moines.

Paul de Chomedey, Sieur de Maisonneuve, arrived at what is now the Island of Montréal in 1642 to establish a colony and to plant a crucifix atop the rise he called Mont Royal. He and his band of settlers came ashore and founded Ville-Marie, dedicated to the Virgin Mary, at the spot now marked by Place-Royale in the old part of the city. They built a fort, a chapel, stores, and houses. Pointe-à-Callière, the terrific Montréal Museum of Archaeology and History, is built on the site of the original colony's establishment.

Life was no easier here than it was to the north in Kebec. The Iroquois in Montréal had no intention of giving up land to the Europeans. Fierce battles raged for years. Today, at Place d'Armes, a statue of de Maisonneuve marks the spot where the settlers defeated the Iroquois in bloody hand-to-hand fighting.

Still, the settlement prospered. Until the 1800s, Montréal was contained in the area known today as Vieux-Montréal. Its ancient walls no longer stand, but its colorful past is preserved in the streets, houses, and churches of this oldest part of the city.

England Conquers New France

In the 1750s, the struggle between Britain and France escalated. The latest episode was known as the French and Indian War (an extension of Europe's Seven Years' War), and strategic Québec became a valued prize. The French appointed Louis Joseph, Marquis de Montcalm, to command their forces in the town. The British sent an expedition of 4,500 men in a fleet under the command of a 32-year-old general, James Wolfe. The British troops surprised the French by coming up and over the cliffs of Cap Diamant, and the ensuing skirmish for Québec, fought on September 13, 1759, became one of the most important battles in North American history: It resulted in a continent that would be under British influence for more than a century.

Fought on Québec City's Plains of Abraham, today a beautiful and much-used city park, the battle lasted just 18 to 25 minutes, depending on whose account you read. It resulted in more than a thousand deaths and serious injuries, and both generals died from wounds received. English general Wolfe lived just long enough to hear that the British had won. Montcalm died a few hours later. Today, a memorial to both men overlooks Terrasse Dufferin in Québec City and uniquely commemorates both victor and vanquished of the same battle. The inscription—in neither French nor English, but Latin—is translated as, simply, "Courage was fatal to them."

The capture of Québec determined the war's course, and the Treaty of Paris in 1763 ceded all of French Canada to England. (In a sense, this victory was a bane to Britain: If France had held Canada, the British government might have been more judicious in its treatment of the American colonists. As it was, the British decided to make the colonists pay the costs of the French and Indian War, on the principle that it was their home being defended. Britain slapped so many taxes on all imports that the infuriated U.S. colonists openly rebelled against the crown.)

George Washington felt sure that French-Canadians would want to join the American revolt against the British crown, or at least be supportive, but he was mistaken on both counts. The Québécois detested their British conquerors, but they were also devout Catholics and saw their contentious American neighbors as godless republicans. Only a handful supported the Americans, and three of Washington's most competent commanders came to grief in attacks against Québec and were forced to retreat.

Thirty-eight years later, during the War of 1812, the U.S. army marched up the banks of the Richelieu River where it flows from Lake Champlain in what's now northern Vermont to the St. Lawrence in Québec. Once again, the French-Canadians stuck by the British and drove back the Americans. The war ended essentially in a draw, but it had at least one encouraging result: Britain and the young United States agreed to demilitarize the Great Lakes and to extend their mutual border along the 49th parallel to the Rockies.

The Fight to Keep Québec's French Heritage

In 1867, the British North America Act created the federation of the provinces of Québec, Ontario, Nova Scotia, and New Brunswick. The edict was a kind of independence for the region from Britain, but was unsettling for many French-Canadians, who wanted full autonomy. In 1883, *"Je me souviens"*—a defiant, proud "I remember"—became the province's official motto. From 1900 to 1910, 325,000 French-Canadians emigrated to the United States, many settling in the northeast states.

Viéux-Montréal has an unmistakably French feel.

In 1968 René Lévesque founded the Parti Québécois, and a movement to create a separate, French-centric state began in earnest. One attempt to smooth ruffled Francophones—French speakers—was made in 1969, when federal legislation stipulated that all services across Canada were henceforth to be offered in both English and French, in effect declaring the nation bilingual. That didn't assuage militant Québécois, however. They undertook to guarantee the primacy of French. To prevent dilution by newcomers, the children of immigrants were required to enroll in French-language schools, even if English or a third language was spoken in the home.

The inevitable radical fringe signaled its intentions by bombing Anglophone businesses. The FLQ (Front de Libération du Québec, or Québec Liberation Front), as it was known, was behind most of the terrorist attacks. Most Québécois separatists, of course, were not violent, but the bombings fueled passions and contributed to a sense that big changes were coming.

Secession remained a dream for many Québécois. In 1977, Bill 101 passed, all but banning the use of English on public signage. The bill funded the establishment of enforcement units, a virtual language police who let no nit go unpicked. The resulting backlash provoked the flight of an estimated 400,000 Anglophones—English speakers—to other parts of Canada.

In 1987, Canadian Prime Minister Brian Mulroney met with the 10 provincial premiers at a retreat at Québec's Meech Lake to cobble together a collection of constitutional reforms. The Meech Lake Accord, as it came to be known, addressed a variety of issues, but most important to the Québécois was that it recognized Québec as a "distinct society" within the federation.

MARCH OF THE LANGUAGE police

When the separatist Parti Québécois took power in the province in 1976, it wasted no time in attempting to make Québec unilingual. Bill 101 made French the provincial government's sole official language and sharply restricted the use of other languages in education and commerce. While the party's fortunes have fallen and risen and fallen, the primacy of Française has remained.

In the early days, agents of L'Office de la Langue Française, the French Language Police, fanned out across the territory, scouring the landscape for linguistic insults to the state and her people. MERRY CHRISTMAS signs were removed from storefronts. About 20% of the population spoke English as a primary language, and they instantly felt like second-class citizens. Francophones responded that it was about time they knew what second-class citizenship felt like.

Affected, too, was the food world. By fiat and threat of punishment, hamburgers became *hambourgeois* and hot dogs were rechristened *chiens chaud*. And Schwartz's Montréal Hebrew Delicatessen, one of the city's fixtures since 1928? Its exterior sign now reads "Chez Schwartz: Charcuterie Hébraïque de Montréal."

Manitoba and Newfoundland, however, failed to ratify the accord by the June 23, 1990, deadline. As a result, support for the secessionist cause burgeoned in Québec. An election firmly placed the Parti Québécois in control of the provincial government again. A 1995 referendum on succession from the Canadian union lost by a mere 1% of the vote.

Since that 1995 referendum, the issue has continued to divide families and dominate political discourse. Conversations with ordinary Québécois suggest they're weary of the argument, although French speakers do have sincere concerns about losing their culture. In 2014, Pauline Marois, then the Québec Premier and the leader of the Parti Québécois, overstepped her reach: Confident about gaining a parliamentary majority, she called for elections. During the campaign, heated conversation focused around Marois' proposed "charter of values," which would have restricted headscarves worn by Muslim public employees, among other provisions. Another prominent PQ candidate declared his focus on the independence of Québec. These two things proved to be a self-destructive one-two punch, and the party was trounced in its worst defeat since 1970. The Liberal party, which is strongly anti-secession, took power and Philippe Couillard became the province's new premier.

Today, Montréal may well be the most bilingual city in the world. Most residents speak at least a little of both French and English. The Québécois, it must be said, are exceedingly gracious hosts. Most Montréalers switch effortlessly from one language to the other as the situation dictates. Telephone operators go from French to English the instant they hear an English word, as do most store clerks, waiters, and hotel staff. English is less used in country villages and in Québec City, but for visitors, virtually any problem can be solved with a few French words, some expressive gestures, and a little goodwill.

Political Power for the First Nations

The French colonialists eventually came to realize that it was only through trade, alliances, and treaties—rather than force—that relations between native peoples and themselves could develop. From early on, formal alliances were part of the texture of their uneasy relationship.

Assimilation of natives into European identity was once perceived as a positive goal but has since been repudiated by natives, who are collectively known today as First Nations. The 1876 Indian Act established federal Canadian authority over the rights and lands of "Indians" and Indians who wanted full rights as Canadians had to relinquish their legal Indian status and renounce their Indian identity. Participation in traditional dances, for instance, became punishable by imprisonment.

Those laws changed slowly. It was only in 1985 that the law was modified so that an Indian woman who married a non-Indian would not automatically lose her Indian status. In 2007, the United Nations General Assembly adopted the Declaration on the Rights of Indigenous Peoples, recognizing the right of aboriginals to self-determination. Canada only endorses the declaration as a "non-legally-binding aspirational document."

In 2015, the Canadian Truth and Reconciliation Commission issued a report based on six years of interviews and public meetings that branded as "kidnapping" and "cultural genocide" a government-mandated system of residential schools for native children. The report documented physical, sexual, and cultural abuse at prison-like schools, which were financed by the government and run primarily by churches. The report concluded that "The Canadian government pursued this policy of cultural genocide because it wished to divest itself of its legal and financial obligations to aboriginal people and gain control over their lands and resources." The report offered 94 recommendations for reconciliation — including full adoption of that 2007 United Nations declaration on indigenous rights.

The interests of native peoples are today represented by the Assembly of the First Nations, which was established in 1985. Economic interests are represented in part by Tourisme Autochtone, the aboriginal tourism corporation (www.tourismeautochtone.com).

ART & ARCHITECTURE

Classic European art and architectural influences meet with an urbane, design-heavy aesthetic in Montréal and Québec City. Here are some art highlights.

Château Frontenac

An American architect, Bruce Price (1845–1903), is responsible for the most iconic building in the entire province of Québec: Château Frontenac (p. 218), Québec City's visual center. "The Château" opened as a hotel in 1893, and with its castlelike architecture, soaring turrets, and romantic French-Renaissance

LONG MAY THEY WAVE: THE flags OF CANADA

With a relatively small population spread over a territory larger than the continental U.S., Canadians' loyalties have always tended to be directed to the cities and regions in which they live, rather than to the nation at large. Part of this comes from the semicolonial relationship the nation retained with England after the British North America Act made it self-governing in 1867. Part comes from the fact that Canada has two official languages. Canadians didn't even have an official national anthem until *O Canada* was given the honor in 1980.

Local loyalties are reflected in the flags. Québécois began asserting themselves and declaring their regional pride after World War II and officially adopted their national flag, the Fleurdelisé, in 1950. It employs blue-and-white crossbars with four fleurs-de-lis (one in each resulting quadrant) and is flown prominently in Québec City.

In 1965, the red-and-white maple leaf version of the Canadian flag was introduced across all of Canada, replacing a previous ensign that featured a Union Jack in the upper-left corner.

In the face of decades of hurt and outright hostilities between French and English Canada, there must be occasional sighs of longing in some quarters for the diplomatic display of the flag of Montréal. Adopted way back in 1832, it has red crossbars on a white background. The resulting quadrants have depictions of a rose, a fleur-de-lis, a thistle, and a shamrock. They stand, respectively, for the founding groups of the new nation—the English, French, Scots, and Irish.

mystery, it achieved its goal of becoming the most talked-about accommodation in North America. Today this high-end property is managed by the Fairmont chain. Find photos at the hotel website, www.fairmont.com/frontenac-quebec/media/photos.

The Château was one of many similar-styled hotels commissioned by the Canadian Pacific Railway in the late 19th century during construction of Canada's first transcontinental railway. As part of the same Canadian Pacific Railway project, Price also designed Montréal's Windsor Station; the Dalhousie Station in Montréal; the façade of Royal Victoria College in Montréal; and the Gare du Palais train station in Québec City, whose turrets echo those of the Château Frontenac. As the leading practitioner of the château style, Price is sometimes credited with having made it the national look of Canada.

Cutting Edge Architecture

In 1967, Montréal hosted the World's Fair, called Expo 67. The event was hugely successful—62 nations participated, more than 50 million people visited, and Montréal became a star overnight. With its avant-garde vision on display, it was viewed as a prototype for a 20th-century city.

One of the most exhilarating buildings developed for the event was **Habitat 67,** a 158-unit housing complex on the St. Lawrence River. Designed by

Habitat 67, designed by local architect Moshe Safdie for the 1967 World's Fair in Montréal

Montréal architect Moshe Safdie (b. 1938), it still is arresting: It looks like a collection of modular concrete blocks all piled together. The vision was to show what community housing could be. The complex is still full of residents and is not open to the public for touring. You can view it across the water from the western end of Vieux-Port and online at Safdie's website, at www.msafdie. com/#/projects/habitat67.

Palais des Congrès (Convention Center), at the northern edge of Vieux-Montréal, is an unlikely design triumph, too. Built between 2000 and 2002 as part of a renovation and extension of the center, the building's transparent glass exterior walls are a crazy quilt of pink, yellow, blue, green, red, and purple rectangles. You get the full effect when you step into the inside hallway—when the sun streams in, it's like being inside a kaleidoscope. It's the vision of Montréal architect Mario Saia.

"Design Montréal"

Montréal is one of North America's most stylish cities. Much of its most playful design is in the form of creative reuse of older buildings and materials. The municipality encourages and promotes that creativity in citywide design competitions, with completed new works listed online at **www.mtlunescodesign. com/en**. They include "light therapy" video projections in the Quartier des Spectacles, pop-up stores featuring Montréal designers and publishers, and proposals to improve urban construction sites. In 2006, UNESCO (the United

geography 101: MOUNTAINS & MOLEHILLS

Montréal is an island that's part of the Hochelaga Archipelago. The island is situated in the St. Lawrence River near the confluence with the Ottawa River.

At Montréal's center is a 232m (761-ft.) mountain. Called Mont Royal, it's the geographic landmark from which the city takes its name.

Real mountains rise nearby. The Laurentides, also called the Laurentians, comprise the Canadian Shield and the world's oldest range. They are the playground of the Québécois and tourists. Their highest peak, Mont-Tremblant, is 968m (3,176 ft.) and a skiing mecca. Also, the Appalachians' northern foothills separate Québec from the U.S. and add to the beauty of the bucolic Cantons-de-l'Est region. This area was once known as the Eastern Townships and is where many Montréalers have country homes.

Nations Educational, Scientific, and Cultural Organization) designated Montréal a UNESCO City of Design for "its ability to inspire synergy between public and private players." Montréal joined Buenos Aires and Berlin, other honorees, as a high-style city worth watching.

First Nation's Art

The region's most compelling artwork is indigenous, and that includes work by members of the province's First Nations. An annual First Peoples Festival (**www.nativelynx.qc.ca**), held for week in late July and early August, highlights Amerindian and Inuit cultures by way of film, video, visual arts, music, and dance.

The province's most important museums feature rich collections of First Nations' work, including, in Montréal, both the Musée McCord (with an appealing permanent exhibition, "Wearing Our Identity: The First People's Collection") and the Musée des Beaux-Arts (which has a dedicated pavilion of Québécois and Canadian Art that includes 500 Inuit works and 180 Amerindian artifacts displayed on six levels).

In Québec City, the Musée National des Beaux-Arts du Québec is home to an important Inuit art collection assembled over many years by Raymond Brousseau. Also in Québec City, a permanent exhibition at the Musée de la Civilisation, "Our Story: First Nations and Inuit in the 21st Century," looks at the 11 Aboriginal nations whose members inhabit Québec today.

Those External Staircases

Stroll through Montréal's Plateau Mont-Royal and Mile End neighborhoods, and one of the first things you'll notice are the exterior staircases on the two- and three-story houses. Many are wrought iron, and most have shapely, sensual curves. Two theories exist above their provenance: Some say they were first designed to accommodate immigrant families who wanted their own front doors, even for second-floor apartments. Others suggest they were the idea of the landlords, who put the stairs outside to cut down on common interior space that wouldn't count toward rental space.

The Catholic Church, ever a force in the city, was originally all for the stairs because they allowed neighbors to keep an eye on each other. After the aesthetic tide turned, however, brick archways called loggia were built to hide the stairways. But the archway walls created ready-made nooks for couples to linger in, and the church helped push through legislation banning new exterior staircases entirely. That ban was lifted in the 1980s so that citywide efforts to maintain and renovate properties could keep the unique features intact.

MONTRÉAL & QUÉBEC CITY IN POPULAR CULTURE

BOOKS & THEATER The late Jewish Anglophone Mordecai Richler (1931–2001) is perhaps the most well-known Montréal-based writer outside the province. He inveighed against the excesses of Québec's separatists and language zealots in a barrage of books and critical essays in newspapers and magazines. Richler wrote from the perspective of a minority within a minority and set most of his books in the working-class Jewish neighborhood of St. Urbain of the 1940s and 1950s, with protagonists who are poor, streetwise, and intolerant of the prejudices of other Jews, French-Canadians, and WASPs from the city's English-side Westmount neighborhood. His most famous book is *The Apprenticeship of Duddy Kravitz* (1959), which in 1974 was made into a movie of the same name starring Richard Dreyfuss. In 2010, a film version of his *Barney's Version* starred Dustin Hoffman and Paul Giamatti.

Michel Tremblay (b. 1942), an important dramatist, grew up in Montréal's Plateau Mont-Royal neighborhood and uses that setting for much of his work. His *Les Belles-Sœurs* (*The Sisters-in-Law*), written in 1965, introduced the lives of working-class Francophone Québécois to the world. His novel *The Fat Woman Next Door Is Pregnant* is also set among post-WWII working-class denizens of the Plateau.

Contemporary works set in Montréal include *Lullabies for Little Criminals* by Heather O'Neill; *Nikolski*, by Nicolas Dickner; and *Bottle Rocket Hearts*, by Zoe Whittall.

MUSIC Montréal has a strong showing of innovative musicians who hail from its clubs. Singer-songwriter Leonard Cohen (b. 1934) is the best known internationally. He grew up in the Westmount neighborhood and attended McGill University. In addition to his music, he has written two novels set in Montréal: 1963's *The Favorite Game* and 1966's *Beautiful Losers*.

Singer-songwriter Rufus Wainwright (b. 1973), son of folk great, and Montréal native, Kate McGarrigle, grew up in Montréal. Rock bands Arcade Fire and Wolf Parade are both from the city. (The band Of Montréal, however, is from Athens, Georgia.)

Québécois films—made in the province, in French, for Québec audiences—can be difficult to track down outside the region. The Cinémathèque Québécoise (www.cinematheque.qc.ca; ℘ **514/842-9763**) is a good resource. It's located at 335 boul. de Maisonneuve est in Montréal's Quartier Latin.

Recent notable features made by Québécois filmmakers include *Rebelle* (*War Witch*) by Kim Nguyen (b. 1974), *Monsieur Lazhar* by Philippe Falardeau (b. 1968), and *Incendies* by Denis Villeneuve (b. 1967)—all three competed in the U.S. Academy Awards as Canada's representative in the Best Foreign Language Film category. Montréal native Xavier Dolan (b. 1989), is one of the hot actors and filmmakers of the moment. To find other recent Canadian films, many of which are made in Québec, look for winners of Canada's national Canadian Screen Awards (**www.academy.ca**) or winners of Québec's provincial Jutra Awards (**www.lesjutra.ca**).

Alanis Obomsawin (b. 1932) is an important documentarian. A member of the Abenaki Nation who was raised on the Odanak Reserve near Montréal, she began making movies for the National Film Board of Canada (www.nfb.ca) in 1971 and has produced more than 40 documentaries about the hard edges of the lives of aboriginal people. In 2008, "the first lady of First Nations film"—as the commissioner of the National Film Board called her—received the Governor General's Performing Arts Award for Lifetime Artistic Achievement.

EATING & DRINKING

"Classic" Montréal and Québec City cuisine is a spin on French food that highlights local Québec ingredients such as root vegetables, maple syrup, and game. Today, many restaurants also focus on the cooking styles of the world's immigrants who now make their homes in the cities. The food scene includes both comfort food and plates that are adventurous and playful, and both entice travelers to visit and indulge.

Restaurants are colloquially called "restos," and they range from moderately priced bistros and ethnic joints to swank luxury epicurean shrines.

Menu Basics

Always look for **table d'hôte** meals. These are fixed-price menus of three- or four-courses for little more than the price of an a la carte main course. (See the sidebar on p. 80 in chapter 6 for details.)

Many higher-end establishments offer **tasting menus,** with an array of small dishes for a sampling of the chef's skills. You might see **surprise menus,** also called "chef's whim," where you don't know what you're getting until it's in front of you. Fine restaurants often offer wine pairings with meals, where the sommelier selects a glass (or half glass, if you ask) for each course.

Local Food Highlights

Be sure to try regional specialties. A Québécois favorite is **poutine:** French fries doused with gravy and cheese curds. It's ubiquitous in winter. Other tasty comfort foods are listed on p. 92 in chapter 6.

Game is popular, including goose, caribou, and wapiti (North American deer). Many menus feature emu and lamb raised north of Québec City in Charlevoix. Mussels and salmon are also standard.

Québec cheeses deserve attention, and many can be sampled only in Canada because they are often unpasteurized, made of *lait cru* (raw milk), and therefore subject to strict export rules. Better restaurants will offer them as a final course. Of the more than 500 varieties available, consider these favorites: Valbert St-Isidor (similar to Swiss in texture), Ciel de Charlevoix (a blue cheese, hence the name "sky of Charlevoix"), and Le Chèvre Noire (a sharp goat variety covered in black wax). Québec cheeses pick up prizes each year in the American Cheese Society competition, North America's largest (www. cheesejudging.org). The *fromages de pays* label represents solidarity among artisanal producers who are members of Solidarité Rurale du Québec, a group devoted to revitalizing rural communities. Find some listed at www.fromage duquebec.qc.ca. Many artisanal cheese makers produce their cheeses on Île d'Orléans, an excellent day trip from Québec City (p. 260).

Beer & Wine

Alcohol is heavily taxed, and imported varieties even more so than domestic versions, so if you're looking to save a little, buy Canadian. That's not difficult when it comes to beer, thanks to the many regional breweries from Montréal powerhouse Molson to microbreweries that produce delicious products. Among the best local options are Belle Gueule and Boréal. The sign BIERES EN FUT means "beers on draft." The annual Montréal beer festival, the Mondial de la bière (www.festivalmondialbiere.qc.ca), is a giddy five-day event in June where typically over 100 breweries present their wares. Among the local brewpubs is the **St-Ambroise brewpub** (www.mcauslan.com; **©** **514/939-3060**), which in the summertime has a beautiful terrace right along the Lachine Canal.

Canada does not produce significant quantities of wine due to a climate generally inhospitable to the ever essential grapes. But you might try bottles from the vineyards of the Cantons-de-l'Est region (just east of Montréal). Sample, too, the sweet "ice wines" and "ice ciders" made from grapes and apples after the first frost; many decent ones come from vineyards and orchards in the same Cantons-de-l'Est region, just an hour's drive from Montréal. One popular winery is Vignoble de L'Orpailleur (www.orpailleur.ca). *L'orpailleur* refers to someone who mines for gold in streams—the idea being that trying to make good wine in Québec's cold climate requires a similar leap of faith in the ability to defy the odds.

WHEN TO GO

High season in the province of Québec is summer, from the holiday of June 24 (Jean-Baptiste Day) through early September (Labour Day). Festivals listed in chapters 8 and 15 give you a peek at some of the back-to-back options. In Québec City, the period from Christmas to New Year's and February weekends during the big winter Carnaval are especially busy, too. Celebrating the winter holidays is a particular treat in Québec City, banks of snow are almost certain along the streets and nearly every ancient building sports wreaths, decorated fir trees, and glittering white lights. Just north of Montréal, the Laurentian Mountains do big ski business late November to late March (see our day trip, "Skiing at Mont-Tremblant", in chapter 10), and the same holds true north of Québec City, in Charlevoix (see our day trip, "Skiing at Le Massif", in chapter 17). Hotels are most likely to be full and charge their highest rates in these periods.

Low season is during March and April, with fewer scheduled events and winter sports start to be iffy. The late-fall months of October and November are also slow due to their all-but-empty social calendars. But autumn is still a lovely time to visit: walks in the cities' parks are a refreshing tonic, the trees still have their fall color, and the roads are less crowded for day trips into the countryside from either city.

Weather

Temperatures are usually a few degrees lower in Québec City than in Montréal. Spring, short but sweet, arrives around the middle of May. Summer (mid-June through mid-September) tends to be humid in Montréal, Québec City, and other communities along the St. Lawrence River, and drier at the inland resorts of the Laurentides and the Cantons-de-l'Est. Intense, but usually brief, heat waves mark July and early August, although temperatures rarely remain oppressive in the evenings.

Autumn (Sept–Oct) is as short and changeable as spring, with warm days and cool nights. It's during this season that Canadian maple trees blaze red and orange.

Bracing for the Canadian Winter

Québécois who live through half-year-long winters know how to dress for the cold. Layers are essential and practicality trumps fashion. A dark wool or down coat can serve both gods, but sporty ski clothes also work throughout the province. Pack a hat, gloves, scarf, thermal socks, and waterproof boots with traction. Umbrellas can be practical on snowy days if it's not too windy. Long underwear is probably only needed for outdoor activities. A second pair of shoes, if the primary ones get soaked, can save a vacation.

Winter brings dependable snow for skiing outside Montréal in the Lauren-tides and Cantons-de-l'Est and, north of Québec City, in Charlevoix. Snow and slush are present in the city from November to March.

Weather forecasts from the Canadian government are at **weather.gc.ca**.

Average Monthly Temperatures (°C/°F)

MONTRÉAL

	JAN	FEB	MAR	APR	MAY	JUNE	JULY	AUG	SEPT	OCT	NOV	DEC
High (°C)	–6	–4	1	10	18	22	26	24	18	12	5	–2
High (°F)	21	24	35	51	65	73	79	76	66	54	41	27
Low (°C)	–13	–12	–6	1	8	13	16	15	10	3	–1	–10
Low (°F)	7	10	21	35	47	56	61	59	50	39	29	13

QUÉBEC CITY

	JAN	FEB	MAR	APR	MAY	JUNE	JULY	AUG	SEPT	OCT	NOV	DEC
High (°C)	–6	–4	1	10	18	22	26	24	18	12	5	–2
High (°C)	–8	–6	0	7	16	21	24	23	17	10	2	–5
High (°F)	18	21	32	46	62	71	76	74	63	50	37	23
Low (°C)	–16	–15	–8	0	6	11	12	13	7	2	–3	–12
Low (°F)	2	5	16	31	43	53	58	56	46	36	25	9

Holidays

Canada's important public holidays are New Year's Day (Jan 1); Good Friday and Easter Monday (Mar or Apr); Victoria Day (the Mon preceding May 25); St-Jean-Baptiste Day, Québec's own "national" day (June 24); Canada Day (July 1); Labour Day (first Mon in Sept); Canadian Thanksgiving Day (sec-ond Mon in Oct); and Christmas (Dec 25).

SETTLING INTO MONTRÉAL

4

M ontréal is the most eclectic of Canada's cities: Impressively bilingual in French and English, the island metropolis hosts international events such as the summer jazz fest (Festival International de Jazz de Montréal), delights culinary crowds with innovative French-Canadian cuisine, and exudes a sophisticated Euro-heritage in revitalized historic neighborhoods. Montréal's global population is a diverse microplanet of French, Scottish, Chinese, Haitian, Arabic, Eastern European, Italian, Portuguese, Filipino, and Greek immigrants. All this is wrapped up in a vibrant arts and culture scene and energized by an exuberant university community.

It's easy to take in the city like a local. Hop on a public BIXI bike to pedal from neighborhood to neighborhood. Maybe you'll wind your way up Mont Royal, the central landmark that gives Montréal its name, and then fly downhill to the Old Port for a visit along the canal. Cafes invite leisurely people watching, and restaurants in the postcard-pretty neighborhood of Vieux-Montréal offer authentic old-world ambience and stylish European flair. Evenings in Plateau Mont-Royal, Mile End, and Little Burgundy have a younger exuberance and a greater ratio of locals to visitors.

ESSENTIALS
Arriving
Served by highways, transcontinental trains and buses, and several airports, Montréal is easily accessible from within Canada, the U.S., or overseas.

BY PLANE
Most of the world's major airlines fly into the **Aéroport International Pierre-Elliott-Trudeau de Montréal** (airport code YUL; www.admtl.com; ② **800/465-1213** or 514/394-7377), more commonly known as Montréal-Trudeau Airport.

Tip: Save time and hassle by arranging flights so that your Customs entry takes place at your final Canadian destination. For instance, if you are flying from the U.S. and have to make one or

Festival International de Jazz de Montréal, just one of the city's blockbuster annual events

more stops en route, try to transfer in the U.S. Otherwise, when you make your first stop in Canada you'll have to collect your bags, pass through Customs, and then check your bags again to continue to your final destination.

Montréal-Trudeau is 21 km (13 miles) from downtown. The airport is well served by **Express Bus 747,** which operates 24 hours a day, 7 days a week, and runs between the airport and the Berri-UQAM Métro station (the city's main bus terminal, located east of Downtown in the Latin Quarter, or "Quartier Latin"). Its 11 designated stops are mostly along downtown's boulevard René-Lévesque. A trip takes 45 to 60 minutes, depending on traffic, and buses leave every 20 to 30 minutes. One-way tickets are sold at the airport for C$10 from machines at the international arrivals level. The ticket is good for 24 hours on all subways and buses. In the city, tickets to the airport are available at Métro stations and at the Stationnement de Montréal street parking pay stations (for use within 2 hours). You can also pay with cash on the bus (coins only, exact change). The schedule of stops is at **www.stm.info/info/747.htm.**

A taxi trip to downtown Montréal costs a flat fare of C$40, plus tip (C$4–$C6). Call ⓒ **514/394-7377** for more information or visit **www.admtl.com/en/access/taxis-limousines.**

BY BUS

Montréal's central bus station, called **Gare d'autocars de Montréal** (www.gamtl.com; ⓒ **514/842-2281**), is at 1717 rue Berri, near the corner of rue Ontario est. It replaced the city's old bus station in 2011. Connected to the terminal is one of the city's major Métro stations, **Berri-UQAM Station.** Several Métro lines pass through the station. UQAM—pronounced

"*Oo*-kahm"—stands for Université de Québec à Montréal, a public university which has a large urban campus here. **Taxis** usually line up outside the terminal building.

BY CAR

The drive from Toronto to Montréal is about 5 hours. Most of the route is on the 401 highway (Macdonald-Cartier Hwy.), which you'll take until you reach "the 20" (Autoroute du Souvenir) at the Ontario-Québec border. From there it's about an hour to downtown Montréal.

Driving north to Montréal from the U.S., the entire journey is on expressways. From New York City, all but about the last 64km (40 miles) of the 603km (375-mile) trip are within New York State on Interstate 87. I-87 links up with Canada's Autoroute 15 at the border, which goes straight to Montréal. From Boston, the trip is 518km (322 miles).

The drive from Montréal to Québec City takes about 3 hours. You have two options: Autoroute 40, which runs along the St. Lawrence's north shore, and Autoroute 20, on the south side (although not hugging the water at all).

Québec became the first province to mandate that residents have **radial snow tires** on their cars in winter. Visitors and their cars are exempt, but the law does give an indication of how harsh winter driving is and how treacherous the roads can be. Seriously consider using snow tires when traveling in the region from November through March.

For more information on driving rules in Canada and the province of Québec, see p. 271.

BY TRAIN

Montréal is a major terminus on Canada's **VIA Rail** network (www.viarail.ca; ℂ **888/842-7245** or 514/989-2626). Montréal's train station, **Gare Centrale,** is located in a busy, safe part of downtown, at 895 rue de la Gauchetière ouest (ℂ **514/989-2626**). The station is adjacent to the Métro subway stop **Bonaventure Station.** (The older Gare Windsor, is the city's former train station. It's down the block and still on some city maps. The castlelike building is now used for offices.)

VIA Rail trains are comfortable—all major routes have Wi-Fi, and some trains are equipped with dining and sleeping cars.

If you're coming from Toronto, you'll board the train at Union Station, which is downtown and accessible by subway.

The U.S. train system, **Amtrak** (www.amtrak.com; ℂ **800/872-7245**), has one train per day to Montréal from New York City's Penn Station that makes

Fill Up Before Crossing Over

Gasoline in Canada is expensive, at least by U.S. standards. Gas is sold by the liter, and 3.78 liters equals 1 gallon. Prices fluctuate, but count on at least C$1.12 per liter, which is the equivalent to about US$4.25 per gallon. If you're driving from the U.S., fill up before crossing the border.

MONTRÉAL: WHERE THE sun RISES IN THE SOUTH

For the duration of your visit to Montréal, you'll need to accept local directional conventions, strange as they may seem. The boomerang- or croissant-shaped island city borders the St. Lawrence River, and as far as locals are concerned, the river is south, with the U.S. not far off on the other side. Never mind that the river, in fact, runs almost north and south at this section. Don't fight it: Face the river. That's south. Turn around. That's north. Because of this convention, Montréal is the only city in the world where the sun rises in the south.

Directions given throughout the Montréal chapters of this book conform to this local directional tradition. Prominent thoroughfares, such as rue Ste-Catherine and boulevard René-Lévesque, run "east" (*est*) and "west" (*ouest*). The dividing line is boulevard St-Laurent, which runs "north" and "south." However, the maps in this book do have a true compass on them.

intermediate stops. Called the *Adirondack,* it's very slow: 11 hours if all goes well, although delays aren't unusual. Its scenic route passes along the Hudson River's eastern shore and west of Lake Champlain.

The train ride between Montréal and Québec City takes about 3 hours.

BY BOAT

Both Montréal and Québec City are stops for cruise ships that travel along the St. Lawrence River (in French, Fleuve St-Laurent). The Port of Montréal, where ships dock, is part of the lively Vieux-Port (Old Port) neighborhood and walking distance from restaurants and shops.

Visitor Information

The main tourist center in downtown Montréal is the large **Infotouriste Centre,** at 1255 rue Peel (© **877/266-5687** or 514/873-2015; info@bonjour quebec.com; Métro: Peel). It's open daily year round, and the bilingual staff can provide suggestions for accommodations, dining, car rentals, and attractions. The office has Wi-Fi for visitors and an office for changing money. In Vieux-Montréal is the teeny **Tourist Welcome Office** at 174 rue Notre-Dame est, corner of Place Jacques-Cartier (Métro: Champ-de-Mars). It's open May through early November, typically daily 10am to 6pm. The office closes in winter, but is open during the Montréal High Lights Festival in February.

The city of Montréal maintains a terrific website at **www.tourisme-montreal.org**. Its blog is packed with great specialty itineraries and up-to-the-minute suggestions.

City Layout

BASIC LAYOUT   At the southern end of the city is Vieux-Port (along the St. Lawrence River) and Vieux-Montréal, or Old Montréal. Just north of

Vieux-Montréal are Quartier International, where the convention center is located, and then Quartier des Spectacles, where Places des Arts (a complex of fine arts facilities) is located. Downtown is west of there, and the Plateau Mont-Royal and Mile End are both north.

The north-south artery boulevard St-Laurent (also known as The Main) serves as the line of demarcation between east and west Montréal. Most of the areas featured in this book lie west of boulevard St-Laurent.

In earlier days, Montréal was split geographically along cultural lines. English speakers lived mainly west of boulevard St-Laurent, while French speakers were concentrated to the east. Things still do sound more French as you walk east, as street names and Métro stations change from the British Peel and Atwater to the French Papineau and Beaudry.

In addition to the maps in this book, neighborhood street plans are available at www.tourisme-montreal.org and from the information centers listed above.

FINDING AN ADDRESS Boulevard St-Laurent, which runs from the south of the city up to the north, is the dividing point between east and west (*est* and *ouest*) in Montréal. *Pay attention:* **Numbers go east and west in both directions from boulevard St-Laurent.** For east-west streets, the numbers start at St-Laurent and then get higher in both directions. That means, for instance, that the Vieux-Montréal restaurants Chez l'Épicier, at 311 rue St-Paul est, and Marché de la Villette, at 324 rue St-Paul ouest, are 1km (about a half mile, or 13 short blocks) from each other—not directly across the street. **Make sure you know if your address is east or west** and confirm the cross street for all addresses.

There's no equivalent division for north and south (*nord* and *sud*). Instead, the numbers start at the river and climb from there, just as the topography does.

Neighborhoods in Brief

PRIMARY AREAS OF THE CITY

DOWNTOWN (CENTRE-VILLE) This area contains the Montréal skyline's most dramatic elements and includes most of the city's large luxury and chain hotels, prominent museums, corporate headquarters, main transportation hubs, and department stores.

The principal east-west streets include boulevard René-Lévesque, rue Ste-Catherine, boulevard de Maisonneuve, and rue Sherbrooke. The north-south arteries include rue McGill and boulevard St-Laurent (aka The Main), which serves as the line of demarcation between east and west Montréal. The district is loosely bounded by rue Sherbrooke to the north, boulevard René-Lévesque to the south, boulevard St-Laurent to the east, and rue Drummond to the west.

Within this neighborhood is the area called "the Golden Square Mile," an Anglophone district once characterized by dozens of mansions erected by the wealthy Scottish and English merchants and industrialists who dominated the city's political life well into the 20th century. Many of those stately homes were torn down when skyscrapers began to rise here after World War II, but some remain.

Rue Crescent, at the western side of downtown, is one of Montréal's major nightlife streets. While the northern end of the street houses luxury boutiques in Victorian brownstones, its southern end holds bars, clubs, and restaurants of all styles. The party atmosphere spills over onto neighboring streets. In warm weather, cafes and balcony terraces take over the sidewalks.

At downtown's northern edge is the urban campus of prestigious McGill University, an English-language school.

VIEUX-MONTRÉAL & VIEUX-PORT The city was born here in 1642, by the river at Pointe-à-Callière, the museum of archaeology and history. Today, especially in summer, many people converge around Place Jacques-Cartier, where cafe tables line narrow terraces. This is where street performers, strolling locals, and tourists congregate.

The main thoroughfares are rue St-Jacques, rue Notre-Dame, and rue St-Paul. The waterfront road that hugs the promenade bordering the St. Lawrence River is rue de la Commune.

The neighborhood is larger than it might seem at first. It's bounded on the north by rue St-Antoine, and its southern boundary is the Vieux-Port (Old Port), now dominated by a well-used waterfront promenade that provides welcome breathing room for cyclists, in-line skaters, and picnickers. To the east, Vieux-Montréal is bordered by rue Berri, and to the west, by rue McGill.

The neighborhood was declared an historic site in 1964, and celebrated the 50th year of its renaissance in 2014. A video showing before and after photos, along with information (in French) about the important role of urban planners in its revitalization, is online at www.youtube.com/watch?v=sxC972ufXD8.

Historic buildings house several small but intriguing museums here, and the district's architectural heritage has been substantially preserved. Restored 18th- and 19th-century structures have been adapted for use as shops, boutique hotels, galleries, cafes, bars, offices, and apartments. In the evening, many of the finer buildings are beautifully illuminated. In the summer, sections of rue St-Paul turn into pedestrian-only streets for strolling. The neighborhood's official website is www.vieux.montreal.qc.ca.

QUARTIER DES SPECTACLES This newly-vibrant area just north of Vieux-Montréal and east of Downtown is home to the Place des Arts (a plaza with the city's large concert halls and restaurants) and the Musée d'Art

Biking along the Montréal riverfront

Contemporain de Montréal, and is the city's cultural heart. This is where people flock for opera, music concerts, many of the popular indoor and outdoor festivals, comedy shows, digital art displays, and more. For the past few summers, an interactive installation of swings that light up and play music, called 21 Balançoires ("21 Swings") has delighted visitors of all ages. The neighborhood seems like it's under continual construction, and a C$34-million project set to be completed in 2018 will rework the esplanade into a giant outdoor stage and add two large pools with fountains. A vibrant website, at www.quartier desspectacles.com, lists festivals and other events taking place in its streets. The Quartier is bounded by boulevard René-Lévesque, rue Sherbrooke, City Councillors, and rue St-Hubert. Its eastern side overlaps with the Quartier Latin (below).

PLATEAU MONT-ROYAL & MILE END "The Plateau" is where many Montréalers feel most at home—away from downtown's chattering pace and the more touristed Vieux-Montréal. It's where many locals dine, shop, play, and live. In recent years it's also become home to a wave of young French ex-pats, who now make up an estimated 20% of Plateau residents giving the neighborhood the nickname *La Nouvelle-France.*

Bounded roughly by rue Sherbrooke to the south, boulevard St-Joseph to the north, avenue Papineau to the east, and rue St-Urbain to the west, the Plateau has a vibrant ethnic atmosphere that fluctuates and shifts with each new immigration surge.

Rue St-Denis runs the length of the district from south to north and for decades has been the thumping central artery of Francophone Montréal, as central to French-speaking Montréal as boulevard St-Germain is to Paris. Although its energy has waned in recent years, rue St-Denis is still thick with bistros, offbeat shops, and lively nightspots. It's still a good street to stroll and find a terrace cafe to relax at over a bowl-sized mug of café au lait.

Boulevard St-Laurent, running parallel to rue St-Denis, has a more polyglot flavor. Known as "The Main," St-Laurent was the boulevard first encountered by foreigners tumbling off ships at the waterfront. They simply shouldered their belongings and walked north, peeling off into adjoining streets when they heard familiar tongues or smelled the drifting aromas of food reminiscent of the old country. Without its gumbo of languages and cultures, St-Laurent would be something of an urban eyesore. It's not pretty in the conventional sense. But a collage of shoes and pastries and aluminum cookware, curtains of sausages, and the daringly far-fetched garments of designers on the forward edge of Montréal's active fashion industry fill the ground-floor windows of this neighborhood. Many warehouses and former tenements in the Plateau have been converted to house this panoply of shops, bars, and high- and low-cost eateries.

Other major streets are avenue du Mont-Royal, a destination for shopping and eating, and the swanky avenue Laurier.

Mile End, the neighborhood that adjoins Plateau Mont-Royal at its northwest corner, is contained by boulevard St-Joseph on the south, rue Bernard in the north, rue St-Denis on the east, and avenue du Parc on the west. It has designer boutiques, shops specializing in household goods, and some great restaurants (including some listed in this book).

Mile End also has pockets of ethnic mini neighborhoods, including Italian, Hassidic, and Portuguese. The area some still call Greektown, for instance, runs along avenue du Parc and is thick with restaurants and taverns.

PARC DU MONT-ROYAL Not many cities have a mountain at their core. Montréal is named for this small outcrop—Mont Royal, or "Royal Mountain." The park here is a soothing urban pleasure. With trails for hiking and cross-country skiing, it's well used by Montréalers, who refer to it simply and affectionately as "the Mountain." Buses travel through the park, and if you're in moderately good shape you can walk to the top in a couple hours from downtown, traveling along a popular pedestrian-only bridle path. See p. 158 for a suggested walking tour.

On its northern slope are two cemeteries, one that used to be Anglophone and Protestant, the other Francophone and Catholic—reminders of the city's historic linguistic and religious division.

JULY 1: citywide MOVING DAY

Montréal is an island of renters, and some 100,000 people move from old apartments to new ones every July 1. Rental leases used to be required to start on that day, chosen in part so that it doesn't fall within the school year. It's no longer a mandate, but most leases still start and end then. July 1 also coincides with Canada's National Day, ensuring that separatist-minded Francophone Québécois won't have time to celebrate that national holiday.

All but certain to be miserably hot and humid, Moving Day is a trial that can, nevertheless, be hilarious to observe. See families struggle to get bedroom sets and large appliances down narrow outdoor staircases! Watch sidewalks become obstacle courses of baby cribs, bicycles, and overflowing cardboard boxes! Listen to the cacophony of horns as streets become clogged with every serviceable van, truck, and SUV! Visitors can take advantage of numerous garage sales and trash picking, although you'll certainly want to avoid driving in residential areas on that day. The whole process provides a good excuse for partying when it's all over.

OTHER AREAS OF THE CITY

These neighborhoods, islands, and *quartiers* are mentioned less frequently in this book, but each has a special character and an appeal for particular visitors.

OLYMPIC PARK A 20-minute drive east of downtown on rue Sherbrooke (and an easy subway ride away) is Olympic Park, named for Stade Olympique (Olympic Stadium), the 1976 Olympic Stadium. Four other attractions here make up the recently branded "Espace Pour la Vie" (Space for Life): the city's spectacular Jardin Botanique (Botanical Garden) and three venues of special interest to children: Biodôme de Montréal, Insectarium de Montréal, and the Rio Tinto Alcan Planétarium (see p. 119).

LITTLE BURGUNDY About a 20-minute walk west of Vieux-Montréal is a neighborhood called Little Burgundy. It's a small stretch along rue Notre-Dame ouest (from about rue Guy to avenue Atwater) that is a new destination for its quirky boutiques, chichi bars, and—especially—its eateries. This small neighborhood is included in the restaurant and nightlife chapters.

GRIFFINTOWN Label this neighborhood "up and coming": Griffintown used to be a little-used neighborhood of parking lots and industrial buildings just west of Vieux-Montréal. In the past few years it has been under constant construction, and is on its way to being built up with stylish condos and a smattering of restaurants. As of this writing the neighborhood still didn't have much to draw tourists, but that may change quickly.

QUARTIER INTERNATIONAL To build Route 720, the expressway that runs underground through a section of the city, more than 850 homes and businesses were demolished in the early 1970s. That created atop the underground tunnel a desolate swath of empty space in prime real estate, smack-dab between downtown and Vieux-Montréal. This area has since become a business center, with office buildings (notably agencies or businesses with an interfnational focus, hence the name "International Quarter"), and, most prominently, the Palais des Congrès (Convention Center). The convention center is a design triumph, as unlikely as that seems. The transparent glass exterior walls are a crazy quilt of pink, yellow, blue, green, red, and purple rectangles. Step inside for the full effect—when the sun streams in, it's like being inside a huge kaleidoscope.

The Quartier is bounded, more or less, by rue St-Jacques on the south, avenue Viger on the north, rue St-Urbain on the east, and rue University on the west.

Olympic Park

THE VILLAGE Also known as the Gay Village (really), Montréal's gay and lesbian enclave is one of North America's largest. It's a compact but vibrant district with cafes, clothing stores, dance clubs, and antiques shops. It runs along rue Ste-Catherine est from rue St-Hubert to rue Papineau and onto side streets. Its Beaudry Métro station, on rue Ste-Catherine in the heart of the neighborhood, includes exterior columns in rainbow colors.

In recent years, the city has made the length of rue Ste-Catherine in the Village pedestrian-only for the entire summer. Bars and restaurants build ad-hoc terraces into the street, and a summer-resort atmosphere pervades.

PARC JEAN-DRAPEAU Connected by two bridges, the two small islands Île Ste-Helene and Île Notre-Dame make up Parc Jean-Drapeau (www.parcjeandrapeau.com), which is almost entirely car-free and accessible by Métro.

Ile Ste-Helene, or St. Helen's Island, was altered extensively to become the site of Expo 67, Montréal's very successful World's Fair in 1967. In the four years before the Expo, construction crews doubled its surface area with landfill, and then went on to create Île Notre-Dame beside it. When the World's Fair was over, the city preserved the site and a few of its exhibition buildings.

Today, the park is home to La Ronde amusement park (operated by the U.S. chain Six Flags), the popular summertime Aquatic Complex, and the Casino de Montréal. It's also where the three-day Grand Prix auto race takes place every June—a major event on the city's social calendar.

QUARTIER LATIN The southern end of rue St-Denis runs near the concrete campus of the Université du Québec à Montréal (UQAM). This is the Latin Quarter and decidedly student-oriented, rife with the messiness that characterizes student and bohemian quarters. Loud music pours out of cheap bars, grubby panhandlers ask for cash, and young adults travel by skateboard while plugged into iPhones. Locals seem nonplussed by the numbers of drug addicts around the Berri-UQAM Métro entrances, but outsiders may find the atmosphere intimidating.

THE UNDERGROUND CITY During Montréal's cold winters and sultry summers, life slows above ground on the streets of downtown as people escape into *la ville souterraine,* an extensive year-round subterranean universe. Here, in a controlled climate that recalls an eternal spring, it's possible to arrive at the railroad station, check into a hotel, shop for days, and go out for dinner—all without stepping outdoors.

The city's tourism industry calls it the "underground pedestrian network," but most locals still use the colloquial name "underground city." It got its start when major downtown developments—including as Place Ville-Marie (designed by I.M. Pei, before he created the Pyramid at the Louvre in Paris), Place Bonaventure, Complexe Desjardins, Palais des Congrès, and Place des Arts—put their below-street-level areas to profitable use, leasing space for shops and other enterprises. Over time—in fits and starts, and with no master plan—these spaces became connected with Métro stations, and then with each other through underground tunnels. It slowly became possible to travel much of downtown through a maze of corridors, tunnels, and plazas. Today, some 1,000 retailers and eateries are in or connected to the network.

The term "underground city" is not 100% accurate: Parts of the network are well above ground. In Place Bonaventure, for instance, passengers can exit the Métro and find themselves peering out a window several floors above the street.

Natural light is let in wherever possible, which drastically reduces the feeling of claustrophobia. However, the underground city covers a vast area without the convenience of a logical street grid, so it can be confusing.

GETTING AROUND

By Foot, Wheelchair, & Stroller

Montréal is a terrific city to experience outdoors. All the neighborhoods listed in this book are compact enough to be easily experienced by foot. Other transportation—Métro, bus, bike, taxi, car—will generally only be necessary when traveling from one neighborhood to another.

When walking, cross only at street corners and only when you have a green light or a walk sign. City police sometimes issue tickets to jaywalkers in an attempt to cut down on the number of accidents involving pedestrians.

Travelers in wheelchairs or using strollers will find the city alternately accommodating and maddening. Many sidewalks have curb cuts for easy passage onto the streets, but many buildings and Métro stops are not accessible. See p. 51 for more information about navigating the city with wheels.

By Métro

For speed and economy, nothing beats Montréal's **Métro system,** operated by the **STM (Société de transport de Montréal).** The stations are marked on the street by blue-and-white signs that show a circle enclosing a down-pointing arrow. The Métro is relatively clean, and quiet trains whisk passengers through a decent network. It runs from about 5:30am to 12:30am, Sunday through Friday, and until about 1am on Saturday night (technically Sun morning). Information is available online at www.stm.info/en or by phone at ✆ **514/786-4636.**

The Montréal Métro makes for easy navigation of the city's neighborhoods

Fares are set by the ride, not by distance. A single ride, on either the bus or Métro, costs C$3.25 (reduced fare of C$2.25 for ages 6-17 and 65 and older). Automatic vending machines take credit cards. You can purchase tickets with cash only from a booth attendant at a Métro station. Tickets serve as proof of payment, so hold onto them for the duration of your trip. Transit police make periodic checks at transfer points or upon exiting and the fine for not having a ticket can run as high as C$500.

Single tickets can be purchased as a set of 10 tickets for C$26.50.

One- and 3-day passes are a good deal if you plan to use the Métro more than twice a day. You get unlimited access to the Métro and bus network for 1 day for C$10 or 3 consecutive days for C$18. The front of the card has scratch-off sections like a lottery card—you scratch out the month and day (or 3 consecutive days) on which you're using the card. They're available at select stations; find the list at www.stm.info.

You'll see locals using the OPUS smart card, on which fares can be loaded on automated machines. Blank OPUS cards must first be purchased for C$15 before any value is loaded onto them, so unless you're a frequent traveler to the city, the paper tickets and 1- or 3-day passes are your best bets.

To pay, some tickets simply need to be tapped at the turnstile on the card reader. Others need to be slid through a slot in the turnstile and taken out as it comes out. You can also show your pass to the booth attendant. A single paper ticket acts as its own transfer ticket; you have 2 hours from the time a ticket is first validated to transfer, and you insert the ticket into the machine of the next bus or Métro train.

Note: **Métro accessibility is severely limited for wheelchairs and strollers.** Accessibility is often difficult for people with mobility restrictions or parents with strollers. Only eight Métro stations, all along the orange line, have elevators, and even those are not always operating. Parents with strollers often have to put strollers on escalators (a practice not discouraged here, as it is throughout the U.S., for instance) and are faced an equal number of instances with simply a staircase as an entrance or exit option. Traveling by bus can be the better option, especially if you don't have a two-adult to one-stroller ratio to make the transfers possible—all buses are wheelchair accessible with front-door access ramps.

Smartphone users can download the STM app for daily bus and subway schedules.

By Bus

Bus fares are the same as fares for Métro trains, and Métro tickets are good on buses, too. Exact change is required if you want to pay on the bus. Buses run throughout the city and give tourists the advantage of traveling aboveground, although they don't run as frequently or as swiftly as the Métro (see "Montréal by Métro," above). As noted above, all buses have front-door access ramps for wheelchairs and strollers.

By Bike

Montréal has an exceptionally good system of bike paths, and bicycling is as common for transportation as it is for recreation.

Since 2009, a self-service short-term bicycle rental program called BIXI (www.bixi.com; © **877/820-2453** or 514/789-2494) has become a big presence in the city. A combination of the words *bicyclette* and *taxi,* BIXI is similar to programs in Paris, London, and Toronto, where users pick up bikes from special BIXI stands throughout the city and drop them off at any other stand, for a small fee. Some 5,200 bikes are in operation and available at 460 stations in Montréal's central boroughs from April through November. The program shuts down during the harsh winter months.

Zipping on and off BIXI bikes throughout the day can be both an economical and a fun way to get around. Visitors have three short-term options: a one-time use for C$2.75, a 24-hour access pass for C$5, or a 72-hour access pass for C$12. With the access passes, you can borrow bikes as many times as you want. For each trip, the first 30 minutes are free. Trips longer than 30 minutes incur additional charges. Thirty-day and 1-year subscriptions are also available. No matter which plan you use, note that BIXI will place a security deposit of C$100 per bike on your credit card, which will stay there for 10 days.

If you'll be using a bike for a full day or longer, it will be cheaper to rent from a shop (you'll also get a helmet and lock, which BIXI doesn't provide). One option is **Ça Roule/Montréal on Wheels** (www.caroulemontreal.com; © **877/866-0633** or 514/866-0633), at 27 rue de la Commune est, the waterfront road in Vieux-Port. All-day rentals there are C$30 on weekdays and C$35 on weekends.

A huge network of bicycle paths runs throughout the city, with whole sections of roads turned into bike lanes during the warm months. The nonprofit biking organization **Vélo Québec** (www.velo.qc.ca; © **800/567-8356** or 514/521-8356) has a host of information for cyclists (*vélo* means "bicycle" in French). The organization helps put on a week-long bike festival in late May each year, which includes a daytime Tour de l'Île de Montréal, with 50 km (31 miles) of car-free streets and a 21 km (13 miles) nighttime tour that attracts up to 17,000 cyclists, many in costumes.

Passengers can take bicycles on the Métro from 10am to 3pm and after 7pm on weekdays, and all day weekends and holidays. This rule is suspended on special-event days, when trains are too crowded. Board the first car of the train, which can hold a maximum of six bikes (if there are already six bikes on that car, you have to wait for the next train). Details are online at **www.stm. info/en/info/advice/bicycles**.

Several taxi companies participate in the **Taxi+Vélo** program. You call, tell them you have a bike to transport, and a cab with a bike rack arrives. Up to three bikes can be carried, and the cost is C$3 for each bike (on top of the overall cab fee). Participating companies are listed at www.velo.qc.ca (search for *taxi+vélo*) and include **Taxi Diamond** (© **514/273-6331**).

By Taxi

Cabs come in a variety of colors and styles, so their principal distinguishing feature is the sign on the roof. The sign is illuminated at night when the cab is available. The initial charge is C$3.45. Each additional kilometer (½ mile) adds C$1.70, and each minute of waiting adds C63¢. A short ride from one point to another downtown usually costs about C$8. Tip 10 to 20%.

The staff of hotels and restaurants can call cabs. Look for taxis lined up outside most large hotels or you can hail one on the street.

Montréal taxi drivers range in temperament from unstoppably loquacious to sullen and cranky—just like in any other city. Similarly, some know the city well; others have sketchy geographical knowledge and poor language skills. It's a good idea to have your destination written down—with the cross street—to show your driver. Not all drivers accept credit cards.

Uber, the San Francisco-based company which coordinates drivers with customers, launched in Montréal in 2014. As of mid-2015 it was under siege by the city government, which has called the use of drivers who don't have taxi licenses illegal. Uber's local website, **www.uber.com/cities/montreal**, might have updated news.

By Car

Montréal is an easy city to navigate by car, although traffic during morning and late-afternoon rush hour can be heavy.

If your smartphone is enabled with an international data plan, you can easily use your device's GPS navigation function (keep in mind that this uses a lot of data roaming). Apps such as **NavFree GPS Canada** can be used offline to view pre-loaded maps much as you would a traditional paper map.

Montréal has plenty of metered parking spaces. Traditional meters are set well back from the curb so they won't be buried by plowed snow in winter, but you'll most likely find computerized Pay and Go stations. Look for the black metal kiosks, columns about 1.8m (6 ft.) tall, with a white "P" in a blue circle. Press the "English" button, enter the letter and number from the space where you are parked (such as "A 107"), and then pay with cash or a credit card, following the onscreen instructions. You keep the ticket, which tells you when your time expires (there's no need to put the ticket on your dashboard; payment is electronically monitored). Parking costs C$3 to C$4 per hour depending on the neighborhood, and meters are in effect every day until 9pm. Check for signs noting parking restrictions, usually shown by a red circle with a diagonal slash. Details and FAQs are listed at www.statdemtl.qc.ca.

Most downtown shopping complexes have underground parking lots, as do the big downtown hotels. Some hotels offer in and out privileges, letting you take your car in and out of the garage without a fee—useful if you plan to do some sightseeing by car.

The limited-access expressways in Québec are called autoroutes, with distances given in kilometers (km) and speed limits given in kilometers per hour (kmph). Because French is the province's official language, most highway signs are only in French. Some bridges and autoroutes includes dual-language signs. In Québec, the highway speed limit is 100 kmph (62 mph). Toll roads are rare.

One traffic light function often confuses newcomers: When you see a **green arrow pointing straight ahead** instead of a green light, that means pedestrians have the right of way in the intersection. After a moment, the light will turn from an arrow to a regular green light and you can then turn left or right in addition to going straight.

A **blinking green light** means that oncoming traffic still has a red light, making it safe to make a left turn. Turning **right on a red light is prohibited** on the island of Montréal, except where specifically allowed by an additional green arrow. Off the island, it is legal to turn right after stopping at red lights, except where there's a sign specifically prohibiting that move.

Drivers using cellphones are required to have hands-free devices. Radar detectors are illegal in Québec. Even if it's off, you can be fined for having a detector in sight.

While most visitors arriving by plane or train will want to rely on public transportation and cabs, a **rental car** can come in handy for trips outside of town or if you plan to drive to Québec City. Terms, cars, and prices for car rentals are similar to those in the rest of North America and Europe, and all the major companies operate in the province. Rental-car agencies are required to provide snow tires on car rentals December 15 until March 15, and many charge an extra fee.

[FastFACTS] MONTRÉAL

Below are useful facts and phone numbers while you're traveling in the city. For more information about the province overall, see chapter 18.

ATMs/Banks ATMs (*guichet automatique*) and banks are easy to find in all parts of the city.

Business Hours Most stores in the province are open from 9 or 10am until 5 or 6pm daily, with longer evening hours on Thursday and Friday. That said, Montréal is in the middle of an experiment (running through 2020) that allows stores in much of the city to remain open 24/7, so some store may have extended hours during festival events.

Doctors & Hospitals Hospitals with emergency rooms include **Hôpital Général de Montréal,** 1650 rue Cedar (ⓒ **514/934-1934**), and **Hôpital Royal Victoria,** 687 av. des Pins ouest (ⓒ **514/934-1934**). **Hôpital de Montréal pour Enfants,** 2300 rue Tupper (ⓒ **514/412-4400**), is a children's hospital. All three are associated with McGill University.

Emergencies Dial ⓒ **911** for police, fire, or ambulance assistance.

Internet Access Most public spaces now have free Wi-Fi.

Mail & Postage About one out of four post offices in the city offers English-language services, including at 157 rue St-Antoine ouest in Vieux-Montréal and 800 René-Lévesque ouest in downtown. See p. 273 in chapter 18 for postage rates.

Newspapers & Magazines *The Globe and Mail* (www.theglobeandmail.com) is Canada's national English-language paper, and the *Montréal Gazette* (www.montrealgazette.com) is the city's primary English-language paper.

Pharmacies A pharmacy is called a *pharmacie;* a drugstore is a *droguerie.* A large chain in Montréal is **Pharmaprix** (www.pharmaprix.ca; ⓒ **800/746-7737**).

WHERE TO STAY IN MONTRÉAL

Montréal's boutique hotels are the superstars of the city's accommodations. In Vieux-Montréal, historical buildings have been transformed into chic modern getaways—it's hard to top the ambience of old stone walls while you cozy up in crisp white sheets. Decor ranges from Asian minimalist to country luxury.

On the flip side, familiar hotel chains, many of which were built for Expo 67, may have time against them, but their central location downtown is key, particularly for festival-goers. Recent renovations at several addresses have put some back in the stylish category, often with the added bonus of a pool. For some travelers, they will hold more appeal.

The province tourist authorities have their own rating system (zero to five stars) for establishments that host travelers. A shield bearing the assigned rating is posted near the entrance to most hotels. The Québec system is based on quantitative measures such as the range of services and amenities.

The stars you see in this book are based on our own rating system, developed by Frommer's, which is more subjective than the state's. We take into account price-to-value ratios, quality of service, ambience, and helpfulness of staff.

All rooms have private bathrooms unless otherwise noted. Most Montréal hotels are entirely nonsmoking.

Because the region is so cold for so many months of the year, tourism here is cyclical. That means that prices drop—often steeply—at many properties for much of the September-through-April period. Hotel rates are highest during the region's busiest times, from May to October, reaching a peak during Grand Prix in June, and remaining highest in July and August. Rates also inflate during the winter carnivals in January and February. (Festivals and dates are listed on p. 130.) For those periods, reserve well in advance.

Most goods and services in Canada have a federal tax of 5% (the TPS). On top of that, the province of Québec adds a tax that comes out to 9.975% (the TVQ). An additional accommodations tax of 3.5% is in effect on hotel bills in Montréal. Prices listed in this book do not include taxes.

5

best HOTEL BETS

- **Best Hotels for a Romantic Getaway:** The sunny atrium, cozy lobby, and luxurious amenities at **Hôtel Nelligan**—not to mention the cobblestoned streets and passing horse-drawn carriages outside—make this Vieux-Montréal spot a choice retreat for couples. **Auberge du Vieux-Port,** around the corner and owned by the same hotel group, is smaller and cozier still. See p. 65.

- **Best High-End Design Hotel:** **Hôtel Gault** leaves its raw concrete uncovered and incorporates candy-colored furniture. See p. 64.

- **Best Uniquely Québec B&B–like Hotel:** In a 1723 structure in the heart of Vieux-Montréal near the Old City's top attractions, **Hôtel ÉPIK Montréal** combines the upscale feel of a modern boutique hotel with the friendly, personal service of a B&B. New owners added a small restaurant and cafe in 2014. See p. 66.

- **Best Value Hotels:** The decor at **Auberge Bonaparte** is quintessential Old Montréal, and morning meals are large and served in the elegant Bonaparte restaurant. If you want to be closer to the arts district of Quartier des Spectacles, consider **Hôtel Le Dauphin Montréal-Downtown.** And if you want to be based in the Plateau, **Hôtel de l'Institut,** run by students at the city's premier hospitality school, is always in tip-top shape and has an excellent in-house restaurant. See p. 65, 62, and 70 respectively.

Rooms in the Hôtel Nelligan mix period elements with modern comforts

o **Best Hotels for Families:** Downtown, **Hôtel Bonaventure Montréal** is a former Hilton and has amenities that are especially welcome for families: long halls for energetic toddlers to burn off steam, a year-round outdoor pool, and, in spring, a resident family of ducks. Also downtown, rooms in the converted warehouse **Le Square Phillips Hôtel & Suites** provide ample space and everything needed for a home away from home, including en-suite kitchens, and a pool and rooftop terrace are nice bonuses. In Vieux-Montréal, every unit at **Le Saint-Sulpice Hôtel Montréal** is a suite, and every nearby street has some sort of attraction targeted to kids. (A cupcake cafe also happens to be just across the street.) See p. 61, 63, and 67 respectively.

DOWNTOWN/CENTRE-VILLE

Montréal's central business area is home to big hotel chains, but you can also find a sprinkling of boutique hotels. This area holds a lot of appeal for business travelers or folks attending any of the festivals that take place around the Quartier des Spectacles. Shoppers, too, will appreciate this area since it's in the heart of retail heaven. The downside, however, is that most of the newest bars and restaurants are in Vieux-Montréal or the Plateau, so staying here might require a few taxi rides.

Good global chain outposts are **Sofitel Montréal Golden Mile,** 1155 rue Sherbrooke ouest (www.sofitel.com; ⓒ **800/763-4835** or 514/285-9000); **Le Centre Sheraton Montréal Hôtel,** 1201 boulevard René-Lévesque ouest (www.sheraton.com/lecentre; ⓒ **888/627-7102** or 514/878-2000); and **Hilton Garden Inn,** 380 rue Sherbrooke ouest (www.hiltongardenmontreal.com; ⓒ **877/STAY-HGI** or 514/840-0010). The **Le Westin Montréal,** 270 St. Antoine ouest; westinmontreal.com; ⓒ **514/380-3333)** has a convenient location across from the convention center and near the Old City and a family-friendly glass bottom indoor pool.

You can also find your fill of dependable high-end chain properties too: **Ritz-Carlton Montréal,** 1228 rue Sherbrooke ouest (www.ritzmontreal.

Downtown Montréal Hotels

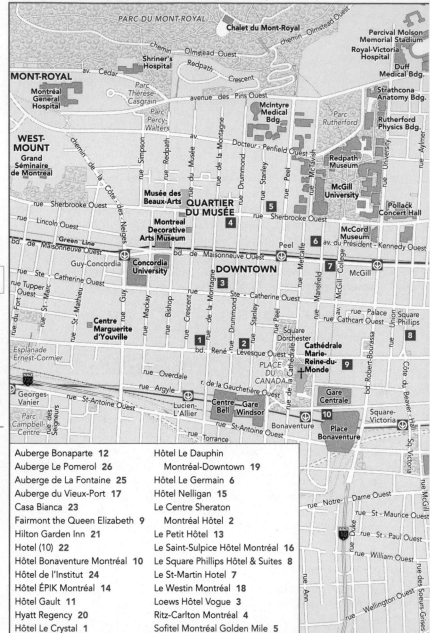

Auberge Bonaparte **12**
Auberge Le Pomerol **26**
Auberge de La Fontaine **25**
Auberge du Vieux-Port **17**
Casa Bianca **23**
Fairmont the Queen Elizabeth **9**
Hilton Garden Inn **21**
Hotel (10) **22**
Hôtel Bonaventure Montréal **10**
Hôtel de l'Institut **24**
Hôtel ÉPIK Montréal **14**
Hôtel Gault **11**
Hyatt Regency **20**
Hôtel Le Crystal **1**

Hôtel Le Dauphin
  Montréal-Downtown **19**
Hôtel Le Germain **6**
Hôtel Nelligan **15**
Le Centre Sheraton
  Montréal Hôtel **2**
Le Petit Hôtel **13**
Le Saint-Sulpice Hôtel Montréal **16**
Le Square Phillips Hôtel & Suites **8**
Le St-Martin Hotel **7**
Le Westin Montréal **18**
Loews Hôtel Vogue **3**
Ritz-Carlton Montréal **4**
Sofitel Montréal Golden Mile **5**

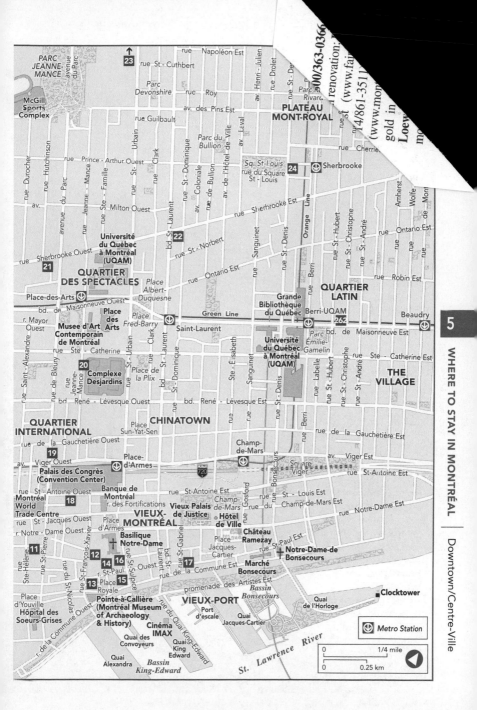

or 514/842-4212), which recently underwent a C$150- **Fairmont the Queen Elizabeth,** 900 boul. René-Lévesque mont.com/queen-elizabeth-montreal; ℂ **866/540-4483** or), with 982 rooms; **Hyatt Regency,** 1255 rue Jeanne-Mance real.hyatt.com; ℂ **800/233-1234** or 514/982-1234), which won the province's tourism awards a few years ago; and the ever-chic s **Hôtel Vogue,** 1425 rue de la Montagne (www.loewshotels.com/ ntreal-hotel; ℂ **800/465-6654** or 514/285-5555).

The hotels listed below offer either exceptional value for budget-minded travelers or an atmosphere that is unique to Montréal.

Expensive

Hôtel Le Crystal ★★ The Crystal was a big deal when it opened in 2008 as a boutique hotel in a neighborhood not known for them (most are in Vieux-Montréal). Today, it's still a most welcome property for the area. Its location close to the Centre Bell arena (home to the beloved Canadiens hockey team and venue for big touring musical events) ensures that the swanky Crystal gets its share of visitors who are taking in (or performing at) these shows. A top-floor pool (indoor, ringed by glass windows) and outdoor all-season Jacuzzi and well-maintained wooden terrace are a big part of the Crystal's appeal. All the rooms are suites and the smallest, called the "Urban

The Fairmont Queen Elizabeth dining room has a decidedly luxurious feel.

Suite," is certainly ample for most guests: 46 sq. m (495 sq. ft.), with separate living and sleeping areas and a kitchenette. Enveloping sheets and luxurious mattresses are part of the mix, of course. The raucousness of rue Crescent and the endless shopping of rue Ste-Catherine are steps away.

1100 rue de la Montagne (at boul. René-Lévesque). www.hotellecrystal.com. © **877/861-5550** or 514/861-5550. 131 units. From C$229 suite. Children 17 and under stay free in parent's room. Packages available. Valet parking C$33. Métro: Lucien L'Allier. Pets accepted (C$75 cleaning fee). **Amenities:** Restaurant; wine bar; concierge; exercise room; Jacuzzi; pool; room service; spa service; free Wi-Fi.

Hôtel Le Crystal near the Centre Bell arena

Hôtel Le Germain ★★ Stylish design, comfortable beds, large bathrooms with quality amenities, and a location on a quiet street just steps from main thoroughfares—those are four big pluses in this trim hotel's favor. As at its sister boutique hotel, the equally desirable **Hôtel Le Germain-Dominion** in Québec City (p. 189), this Germain creates a cozy-chic atmosphere, from the lobby (elegant and cool) to the rooms themselves (white bedding with dark headboards and decor with accents in fuchsia and lime green). The hotel draws a mix of business people, vacationers, and families of students at McGill University, just up the street. The ample "deluxe continental" breakfast buffet, included in the room rate, usually includes egg dishes, cold cuts, cheeses, chocolate croissants, *crêpes*, fruit, yogurt, cappuccinos, and Montréal bagels.

2050 rue Mansfield (at av. du President-Kennedy). www.germainmontreal.com. © **877/333-2050** or 514/849-2050. 101 units. From C$210. Rates include breakfast. Packages available. Valet parking C$30. Métro: Peel. Pets accepted (C$30 per day). **Amenities:** Restaurant; bar; concierge; exercise room; room service; free Wi-Fi.

Moderate

Hôtel Bonaventure Montréal ★★ Housed atop an office building built for Expo 67, the Bonaventure calls itself a "penthouse hotel," and that's accurate: It takes up the top floor of a concrete monster of a building. Don't be put off by the building's brutalist exterior. The hotel is lovely: The 395 rooms and suites are all on the top floor, 9 floors above ground (another 8 are below ground, which accounts for the "17th floor" location) and all have either expansive views of the city or a peek at the rooftop gardens that feature a resident family of ducks (and ducklings in spring), small walking paths, and a corker of a pool—outdoor, heated, and open year round. Until 2015 the hotel was part of the Hilton chain (it's now independently owned), and it so far has retained some of the signature Hilton touches: a competent in-house restaurant and bar, long hallways with large attached conference rooms (and a regular influx of conference attendees), and wild patterns on carpets in the public spaces. Splurge for a package that includes free access to the Executive Lounge, a private dining room where a deluxe continental breakfast buffet is put out each morning, snacks (followed by desserts) are served late afternoon, and drinks are available all day.

900 rue de la Gauchetiere ouest (at rue Mansfield). www.hotelbonaventure.com. ⓒ **888/267-2575** or 514/878-2332. 395 units. C$159–C$349. Packages available. Valet parking C$29 (SUVs C$39). Métro: Bonaventure. Pets accepted (C$50 cleaning fee). **Amenities:** Restaurant; bar; babysitting; concierge; exercise room; year-round outdoor heated pool; room service; free Wi-Fi.

Hôtel Le Dauphin Montréal-Downtown ★★

The little Dauphin tries so hard and succeeds so well. It attracts both business people on a budget—it's right next door to the convention center—and families. The modest breakfast room where the free continental breakfast is served has a kind of genial hostel feeling. All rooms are the same size, but with

The gardens at the Hôtel Bonaventure

different bed configurations. A few have two beds, about a quarter have kings, and the rest have queens. There are also four junior suites. Rooms are simple, but still modern (think Ikea), and kept in tip-top shape. The location is generally quiet except nights when the convention center is hosting big festivals; it's about a 15-minute walk to Vieux-Montréal in one direction and the Quartier des Spectacles in the other. Because so many guests are single travelers, listed prices are for one guest, with a second guest for an additional C$10 per night.

1025 rue de Bleury (near av. Viger). www.hoteldauphin.ca. ✆ **888/784-3888** or 514/788-3889. 72 units. C$130–C$180 single; C$10 for a second person. Rates include breakfast. Packages available. Parking C$20 at convention center. Métro: Place d'Armes. **Amenities:** Exercise room; free Wi-Fi.

Le Square Phillips Hôtel & Suites ★★ This is one of the great downtown hotel options for families, especially on weekends when business travelers have cleared out and the prices are often lower. Rooms here are big with high ceilings, thanks to the building's previous life as a warehouse, and some have dramatic columns and arches, also remnants from its previous incarnation. Even the smallest of rooms are decent-sized studios, with the bed separated from the living area. Amenities include an indoor rooftop pool, a laundry room, and every unit has a full kitchen including a large fridge and stove. The staff has been getting raves from customers for years for their helpfulness, particularly for visiting families. The warehouse walls are also handy for muffling the noise: rooms here are close to a lot of action (both the busy shopping street rue Ste-Catherine and the Quartier des Spectacles arts district are around the corner), but seem to be totally insulated from it. It's exactly what you want on a holiday.

1193 Square Phillips (south of rue Ste-Catherine ouest). www.squarephillips.com. ✆ **866/393-1193** or 514/393-1193. 160 units. Studios from C$140; suites from C$160. Rates include breakfast. Packages available. Valet parking C$22. Métro: McGill. **Amenities:** Babysitting; concierge; exercise room; laundry room; heated indoor pool; free Wi-Fi.

Le St-Martin Hotel ★ Opened in 2010, the St-Martin has a nightclubby feel to it, with its neon pink and cobalt blue accent lighting, chic in-house restaurant, and outdoor lap pool looking out over the city. Some rooms have unique glass corner windows, while others have modern-design standalone bathtubs or electric fireplaces. Given its young age, all the furniture and public areas are especially fresh and updated. Highrises on this block are tall, so rooms don't have much of a view, but that won't matter for most guests. The restaurant (**Bistro L'Aromate**) serves inventive bistro-style cuisine with modern twists on many French classics—try the Wagyu beef tartare or the unique version of the sugar pie, served as bite-sized nuggets coated in nut flour and accompanied by caramel ice cream. The restaurant spills out to a sidewalk terrace for al fresco dining, and has a mezzanine in the lobby, too.

980 boul. de Maisonneuve ouest (at rue Mansfield). www.lestmartinmontreal.com. ✆ **877/843-3003** or 514/843-3000. 123 units. From C$209 double. Packages available. Valet parking C$29. Métro: Peel. **Amenities:** Restaurant; bar; fitness lounge; heated pool; room service; free Wi-Fi.

VIEUX-MONTRÉAL

Abutting the St. Lawrence River, Old Montréal was once the epicenter of activity in the city. As Montréal grew, a "new" downtown emerged slightly to the north, and Vieux-Montréal fell into disrepair. But local business owners began a concerted effort to revitalize the neighborhood, and today Vieux-Montréal is thriving and vibrant. Bars and avant-garde fashion boutiques have followed hoteliers' lead into the area, making it one of the city's hottest spots for both tourists and locals. Couples love it for its romantic appeal and foodies flock here for its great restaurants. Be prepared for lots of tourists, especially in summer.

Expensive

Auberge du Vieux-Port ★★   The stately Auberge du Vieux-Port offers a level of luxury that many try to copy, but few get right. Many rooms have expansive views of Vieux-Port and the St. Lawrence River, and the rooftop terrace provides an unobstructed panorama of both the waterfront and the Old City—the perfect backdrop to enjoy a meal or sip a cocktail. As with many upscale hotels in the Old City, here the owners celebrate the building's centuries-old history by incorporating the original brick, stone, and exposed beams into the architecture, while providing tasteful contemporary touches, as evidenced by the sleek and modern bathrooms in all rooms. Beds are enveloping and sexy. *Two tips:* The rooftop terrace is a perfect spot to enjoy a drink while watching the Montréal Fireworks Competition, which runs from late June through July. The owners also offer a selection of studio, 1-, and 2-bedroom loft style apartments not far from the hotel, ideal for families and long-term stays.

97 rue de la Commune est (near rue St-Gabriel). www.aubergeduvieuxport.com. ⓒ **888/660-7678** or 514/876-0081. 45 units. C$190–C$340 double. Rates include full breakfast. Valet parking C$32. Métro: Place d'Armes or Champs-de-Mars. **Amenities:** Bar; babysitting; concierge; exercise room at sister hotel; room service; free Wi-Fi.

Hôtel Gault ★★   The Gault sets itself apart from its counterparts in many ways. For starters, although it's located in an ornate building from 1871, the interior design is sleek and minimalist. The blond wood and smooth concrete walls and floors of the lobby are counterbalanced by colorful contemporary furniture and

The atmospheric Auberge du Vieux-Port

Some of the more popular areas for hotels, including rue St-Paul in Vieux-Montréal, have bars and nightlife close by—a great location for partying, maybe not so good for sleeping. Bars are open until 3am in Montréal, so light sleepers should request rooms that face the back of the hotel or an inside courtyard.

photography by local artists. At just 30 rooms, attention to detail and style is customized for each of the spacious rooms. Some feature exposed brick walls adorned with several pieces of art; others feel more modern and feature taupe curtains and painted gray walls with gorgeous wood entryways. Colorful area rugs offset the cool feeling of the concrete floors and polished steel lamps. Rooms on the top floor all have balconies, providing a gorgeous view. The spacious lobby has candy-colored modernist seating for guests, and the library behind the check-in desk area features books and design magazines—an obvious nod to the management's eye for detail.

449 rue Ste-Hélène (near rue Notre-Dame). www.hotelgault.com. © **866/904-1616** or 514/904-1616. 30 units. C$179–C$249 double; C$209–C$569 suite. Rates include full breakfast. Packages available. Valet parking $35. Métro: Square Victoria. Pets accepted (C$60 per day). **Amenities:** Cafe; bar; babysitting; concierge; exercise room; room service; spa; free Wi-Fi.

Hôtel Nelligan ★★ Named after local 19th-century poet Émile Nelligan, this is the perfect compromise between the spaciousness of an upscale chain hotel and the chic decor and personalized service of a boutique property. Located in a series of converted 19th-century warehouses, the romantic 105-room Nelligan incorporates vintage style while maintaining the comforts and amenities of the 21st century. Amid all the brick and gray stone walls, dark wood, and leather furnishings, the rooms are comfortable and welcoming. The common spaces create a communal feel that will make you want to stay all day—certainly doable considering the many private corners for reading or enjoying a cocktail from either the atrium bar or rooftop terrace. A breathtaking central atrium adorned with contemporary art provides a glimpse toward the glass ceiling several stories up, and many rooms have a window overlooking it. But be warned: chatter from the downstairs **Verses Bar,** which serves drinks and food into the evening, can create unwanted background noise in some rooms.

106 rue St-Paul ouest (at rue St-Sulpice). www.hotelnelligan.com. © **877/788-2040** or 514/788-2040. 105 units. From C$250 double. Packages available. Valet parking C$32. Métro: Place d'Armes. **Amenities:** 2 restaurants; bar; babysitting; concierge; exercise room; room service; free Wi-Fi.

Moderate

Auberge Bonaparte ★★ Auberge Bonaparte is one of the best deals in the city. The accommodations, quality of service, and amenities are

If you're staying at a hotel that doesn't have a fitness center or whose exercise room is modest, keep **Club Sportif MAA** in mind (www.clubsportifmaa.com; ℂ **514/845-2233**). Located centrally downtown at 2070 rue Peel, between rue Sherbrooke and boulevard de Maisonneuve, the luxury facility has a 743-sq.-m (8,000-sq.-ft.) state-of-the-art gym with cardio and strength-training equipment, a lap pool, and a full schedule of classes—everything from spinning to Pilates to yoga. Day passes are available for C\$30 and include most classes and use of the pool.

comparable to its higher-priced competitors, yet you'll pay significantly less. Rooms at the lowest price point are small but comfortable—a great option for those who plan to be out every day. Square footage increases as you move up in price. Some rooms feature gorgeous exposed brick walls, and all have custom-built furniture. Rooms on the courtyard side have an appealing view of the Basilique Notre-Dame, which can also be seen from a rooftop terrace accessible to all guests. In 2013, the **Bonaparte** restaurant, where the complimentary breakfast is served, got a new bar and more dining space. At night, the restaurant is usually packed, dishing out classic French cuisine (we highly recommend the Dover sole meunière).

447 rue St-François-Xavier (just north of rue St-Paul). www.bonaparte.com. ℂ **514/844-1448**. 30 units (and 1 suite). C\$150–C\$240 double; C\$315–C\$360 suite. Rates include full breakfast. Parking C\$15 per day. Métro: Place d'Armes. **Amenities:** Restaurant; child daycare service; concierge; access to nearby health club; room service; free Wi-Fi.

Hôtel ÉPIK Montréal ★★ Located smack dab in the center of Vieux-Montréal, this 1723 building was formerly the Auberge Les Passants du Sans Soucy, a long-time Frommer's favorite. New owners took over in 2014, and the building has undergone significant renovations for a sleek, modern feel. Gone are the lace curtains and floral bedspreads. Its 9 rooms now have LED lights, new bathrooms with glass shelves and "rainhead" showers, Tempur-Pedic mattresses, and a modern color scheme consisting of chocolate brown, white, and charcoal. The lobby was expanded to make room for a cafe, and the back of the ground floor is now a 30-seat restaurant serving Mediterranean cuisine. Despite the modern upgrades, a concerted effort has been made to retain the building's original charm. This includes many rooms with ceiling beams that still bear the original carpenters marks, and more exposure of the mortar and stone walls. The upper floors, formerly the private residence of the previous owners, have been turned into a luxe 2-bedroom penthouse.

171 rue St-Paul ouest (at rue St-François-Xavier). www.epikmontreal.com. ℂ **877/841-2634**. 10 units. From C\$160 double. Check website for rates of penthouse apartment. Rates include full breakfast. Parking C\$20 per day. Métro: Place d'Armes. **Amenities:** Dry cleaning service; free Wi-Fi.

Le Petit Hôtel ★   Le Petit Hôtel is a chic and trendy standout of Old Montréal's hospitality landscape. Everything—from the funky artwork to the music playing in the lobby—skews toward a younger demographic. The individual rooms have a unique approach to design. Instead of being adorned with art, the stone walls are generally left blank, providing an opportunity for the black furniture, white bedspreads, and neon orange chairs to create an appealing contrast of color. Rooms vary in size from tiny to extra large, so pick what suits your needs. Breakfast is served in the lobby cafe, which also serves bakery items and doubles as a bar.

168 rue St-Paul ouest (at rue St-François-Xavier). www.petithotelmontreal.com. ⓒ **877/530-0360** or 514/940-0360. 28 units. C$209–C$299 double. Rates include continental breakfast. Packages available. Valet parking C$32 per day. Métro: Place d'Armes. **Amenities:** Cafe; concierge; access to exercise rooms at sister hotels Hôtel Nelligan and Place d'Armes; free Wi-Fi.

Le Saint-Sulpice Hôtel Montréal ★★★   The Saint-Sulpice stands out from nearly all other boutique hotels in the city because each of its 108 units is a suite with a fully equipped kitchen. Even the smallest units are spacious and feel like decked-out efficiency apartments. The middle and upper tier rooms feature separate bedrooms and larger floor plans. Rooms have a

Guest room at Le Petit Hôtel in Vieux-Montréal

A suite at Le Saint-Sulpice Hôtel Montréal

modern chic aesthetic—predominantly shades of charcoal, sand, and mahogany, offset by touches of red. The main lobby area continues this color scheme. Suites are well-suited for travelers who need extra space, and are ideal for families. All have a pullout sofa, and several have two bedrooms. In the lobby is a well-stocked bar, and there's an outdoor terrace where you can enjoy a meal at the **Sinclair Restaurant,** which serves contemporary French cuisine in the full dining room on the bottom floor. Customer service is of the highest order here, from the valets who open the doors to the thoughtful cleaning crew who often fold stray articles of clothing you've left lying about.

414 rue St-Sulpice (near rue St-Paul ouest). www.lesaintsulpice.com. © **877/785-7423** or 514/288-1000. 108 units. From C$189 suite. Rates include continental breakfast. Parking C$32 per day. Pets accepted (C$50 per stay). Métro: Place d'Armes. **Amenities:** Restaurant; concierge; access to nearby health clubs and spa; room service; free Wi-Fi.

PLATEAU MONT-ROYAL

Staying in this neighborhood, with its arty bohemian feel, gives you the chance to bypass the tourist-heavy locations and spend time where real Montréalers live, work, and play. Because it's mostly residential, the hotel selection is not huge, and virtually nothing is on par with the design or grandeur of downtown or Vieux-Montréal.

The lower end of the Plateau flows into the **Quartier Latin.** We don't recommend staying in that neighborhood for a first visit—it lacks the charm of other parts of the city—but return visitors who are familiar with all its messiness might find its central location appealing. One option is **Auberge Le Pomerol,** 819 de Maisonneuve est (www.aubergelepomerol.com; ✆ **514/526-5511**). Its 27 rooms run from C$110 in low season to C$215 in high season. Staff is friendly and the shared living room and breakfast room are cozy. Executive rooms offer a little more space.

Expensive

Hotel (10) ★ Here's a hotel with dual personalities: On weekdays it hosts business clients and some families, but on the weekends, clubbers pack the expansive terrace of its bar. It's a good option for tourists who want to stay where they play. The structure began life in 1914 as the first poured-concrete building in North America and was a boutique hotel named for its architect, Joseph-Arthur Godin, until the Opus group purchased it in 2007. A late 2012 transformation softened the all-nighter ambience with improved lighting and more neutral decor, but sound still reverberates through the bedrooms' concrete ceilings. For a quieter room, ask for one facing rue Clark.

10 rue Sherbrooke ouest (near rue St-Laurent). www.hotel10montreal.com. ✆ **855/390-6787** or 514/843-6000. 136 units. C$209–C$429 double; C$349–C$599 suite. Children 12 and under stay free in parent's room. Packages available. Valet parking C$28 per day (indoor garage). Pets accepted (C$50 per stay). Métro: St-Laurent. Car service to downtown (free). **Amenities:** Restaurant; bar; concierge; health club; room service; free Wi-Fi.

Moderate

Auberge de La Fontaine ★★ This easygoing hotel has four big things going for it: the location across the street from a pretty part of Parc de La Fontaine; the fact that it sits along some central bike paths (a feature used by many guests); it's within walking distance to Plateau dining and shops; and it has a friendly, hostel-like atmosphere even though the rooms are private. Guests can raid the kitchen for a free afternoon snack or buy beer or wine from the front desk and head to the third floor terrace, which overlooks the park. Families are warmly accommodated. The breakfast buffet (pastries, cereals, yogurt, fresh fruit, local cheeses, and cold cuts), always included, is one reason guests return to this *auberge* time and time again.

1301 rue Rachel est (at rue Chambord). www.aubergedelafontaine.com. 21 units. ✆ **800/597-0597** or 514/597-0166. C$122–C$157 double; C$159–C$209 suite. Rates include breakfast. Packages available. 3 free parking spots; free street parking. Métro: Mont-Royal. **Amenities:** Concierge; kitchen; free Wi-Fi.

Casa Bianca ★★ As the name suggests, this elegant B&B is a white house, as well as an architectural landmark. It's on the corner of a tree-lined residential street adjacent to Parc Jeanne-Mance and a stone's throw from Parc du Mont-Royal. If the weather is cooperating, the organic breakfast is served on a breezy patio. Yoga instruction can be planned in advance with an in-house yoga instructor. Rooms are spacious with antique touches, and many have claw-foot bathtubs that add to the homey feel. If you're looking to do

The (Green) Keys to the City

The Hotel Association of Canada (HAC) oversees the **Green Key Eco-Rating Program** (in French, *Clé Verte*), which awards a rating of one to five green keys to hotels that minimize waste and reduce their carbon footprint. While HAC does not verify the audits on a national scale, the Corporation de l'industrie touristique du Québec (www.citq.info) does so within the province of Québec. Recipients often display a Green Key/Clé Verte plaque in a prominent location alongside other commendations. To locate Green Key hotels, visit **www.greenkeyglobal. com**.

some shopping, it's close to the boutiques along boulevard St-Laurent and avenue Mont-Royal.

4351 av. de L'Esplanade (at rue Marie-Anne). www.casabianca.ca. (✆) **866/775-4431** or 514/312-3837. 5 units. C$119–C$269 double; from C$199 suite. Rates include breakfast. Packages available. Self-parking C$10 per day. Métro: Mont-Royal. Pets not accepted. **Amenities:** Free Wi-Fi.

Hôtel de l'Institut ★★★   For visitors who've "done" Old Montréal and want access to the Plateau's buzz of everyday Montréal life, there is no better option. Primely located and well-priced, this elegant hotel is expertly run by students who are learning the province's signature style of hospitality. Rooms are up to date, tidy, and spacious. There's a work desk if needed, but better to throw open the curtains and catch a sunset from the 8th floor, ideally on a Mont Royal–facing terrace. Each stay includes breakfast in the student-run **Restaurant de l'Institut** (p. 90), a fine choice for any meal, even amid the plethora of neighborhood spots. During the school year dining is also available at Salle Paul-Émile-Lévesque on the second floor. Parking is conveniently located below the hotel.

3535 rue St-Denis (near rue Sherbrooke). www.ithq.qc.ca/en/hotel. (✆) **855/229-8189** or 514/282-5120. 42 units. From C$129 double, from C$229 suite. Rates include breakfast. Packages available. Children 12 and under stay free in parent's room. Self-parking C$19 per day. Métro: Sherbrooke. **Amenities:** Babysitting; concierge; 2 restaurants (one seasonal); shop; free Wi-Fi.

WHERE TO EAT IN MONTRÉAL

Foie gras, steak *tartare*, and charcuterie plates are just a few of the rich, savory items that highlight Montréal's hedonistic culinary scene. Smoked meat, croissants, and homemade chocolates are also featured highlights at every turn. Add a penchant for local products (known as *terroir*) such as duck, award-winning cheeses, and iconic maple syrup, and you could happily spend your entire visit grazing in all the corners of the city.

While white-linen restaurants were once a classic Québec culinary art, the high end of the restaurant food chain has shrunk considerably in recent years. Instead, it's the bustling come-as-you-are upscale bistros that are now the heart of Montréal's food culture. Foodies may want to consider a trip built around the annual **Montréal en Lumière** culinary festival in February (p. 132) or the **Taste of Montréal** restaurant week (**www.mtlatable.com**), which takes place in November.

Many of the city's best restaurants are in Old Montréal (which we highly recommend), but be forewarned that due to the high rent many restaurants have to pay in this neighborhood, prices have crept up here compared to other parts of the city. For quick and inexpensive meals, take a look at the city's sizable selection of ethnic restaurants—Chinatown has an abundance of options, for instance. More than 200 restaurants are BYOB, where you bring your own beer or wine, with no corkage fee, which results in substantial savings; look for the sign APPORTEZ VOTRE VIN.

Like many big cities, the food-truck craze has hit the streets of Montréal. The city-sanctioned program started in 2013 and has grown to nearly 50 trucks, which rotate in and out of pre-determined spots from May through early October. For a great interactive map showing who, what, when and where, check out **www.montreal.streetfoodquest.com/en**; or see #streetfoodmtl on Twitter. The website **www.cuisinederue.org/en**, run by the Québec Street Food Association, is another good resource for food truck info.

Here's what you can expect to pay for your main course at a Montréal restaurant:

Expensive   C$25 and up
Moderate   C$15–C$25
Inexpensive   Under C$15

BEST EATING BETS

o **Best Classic French Bistro:** Plateau Mont-Royal's most Parisian spot, **L'Express,** is where you come to see what the Francophone part of this city is all about. From the black-and-white-checkered floor to the grand, high ceilings to the classic cuisine, this is where Old France meets New France. Another good bet is **Leméac** in the chichi Outremont neighborhood. See p. 91 and 95 respectively.

o **Best Guilty Treat:** *Poutine* is a plate of French fries *(frites)* drenched with gravy afloat with cheese curds; it's the bedrock of Québec comfort food and the national hangover remedy. **La Banquise,** near Parc La Fontaine's northwest corner, offers upwards of 30 variations and is open 24 hours a day, 7 days a week. See p. 93.

o **Best Smoked Meat:** There are other contenders, but **Chez Schwartz Charcuterie Hébraïque de Montréal,** known simply as Schwartz's, serves up the definitive version of regional brisket. A takeout counter next door is

Toqué!

a practical option when the line for sit-down spots snakes its way down the street. See p. 92.

○ **Best Breakfast:** The city has seven outposts of **Eggspectation,** and they all do brisk business serving funky, creative breakfasts with loads of egg options. The menu is extensive, prices are fair, and portions are huge. For a more elevated experience, **Lawrence,** in Mile End, serves up wonderfully rich British-style brunch. See p. 78 and 94 respectively.

○ **Best Restaurants for a Special Event:** Chef Normand Laprise keeps Vieux-Montréal's **Toqué!** in sparkling shape. This dazzlingly postmodern venue is now a deserving member of the gold-standard organization Relais & Châteaux. Downtown. **Europea** offers a spectacular tasting menu in elegant, old-world surroundings. See p. 83 and 74 respectively.

RESTAURANTS BY CUISINE

BAKERY

Fairmount Bagel ★★★ ($, p. 98)
Nocochi ★ ($, p. 79)
Olive et Gourmando ★★★ ($, p. 86)
St-Viateur Bagel ★★ ($, p. 98)

BISTRO

Le Balmoral ★★ ($$, p. 76)
Leméac ★★ ($$$, p. 95)
Lawrence ★★★ ($$$, p. 94)
L'Express ★ ($$, p. 91)
Marché de la Villette ★ ($, p. 86)
Modavie ★ ($$, p. 85)

BRASSERIE

Brasserie T ★★★ ($$, p. 77)
Holder ★ ($$, p. 84)

BREAKFAST/BRUNCH

Café Cherrier ★ ($$, p. 91)
Eggspectation ★★★ ($, p. 78)
Le Cartet ★★ ($$, p. 85)

CONTEMPORARY FRENCH

Beaver Hall ★★ ($$, p. 76)
Europea ★★★ ($$$, p. 74)
Le Local ★ ($$$, p. 83)
Restaurant de l'Institut ★ ($$$, p.90)
Toqué! ★★★ ($$$, p. 83)

CONTEMPORARY QUÉBÉCOIS

Au Pied de Cochon ★ ($$$, p. 87)
Chez l'Épicier ★ ($$$, p. 80)
Hôtel Herman ★★ ($$, p. 95)
Le Club Chasse et Pêche ★★★
($$$, p. 82)

DELI

Chez Schwartz Charcuterie Hébraïque
de Montréal ★ ($, p. 92)

DESSERT

Bilboquet ★★ ($, p. 97)
Juliette et Chocolat ★ ($, p. 92)

DINER

Beauty's Luncheonette ★★
($, p. 91)
Deville Dinerbar ★ ($$, p. 78)
Wilensky Light Lunch ★★
($, p. 99)

INDIAN

Gandhi ($, p. 84)
Taj ($, p. 84)

ITALIAN

Graziella ★★★ ($$$, p. 82)
Hostaria ★ ($$$, p. 94)

KEY TO ABBREVIATIONS:
$$$** = Expensive   **$$** = Moderate   **$ = Inexpensive

LIGHT FARE

Java U ★ ($, p. 79)

La Banquise ★ ($, p. 93)

Nocochi ★ ($, p. 79)

Olive et Gourmando ★★★ ($, p.86)

St-Viateur Bagel ★★ ($, p. 98)

Titanic ★ ($, p. 87)

PIZZA

Magpie Pizzeria ★ ($, p. 98)

POLISH

Stash Café ★★ ($$, p. 85)

PORTUGUESE

Ferreira Café ★★★ ($$$, p. 74)

SEAFOOD

Ferreira Café ★★★ ($$$, p. 74)

Joe Beef ★★ ($$$, p. 100)

Le Garde Manger ★★ ($$$, p. 82)

SOUTH AMERICAN

Mezcla ★★★ ($$$, p. 99)

STEAKHOUSE

Joe Beef ★★ ($$$, p. 100)

Moishes ★★ ($$$, p. 90)

Vieux-Port Steakhouse ★ ($$, p. 86)

TAPAS

Le Filet ★★ ($$$, p. 87)

VEGETARIAN/VEGAN

Aux Vivres ★★ ($, p. 96)

Gandhi ($, p. 84)

Green Panther ★★ ($, p. 98)

Resto Vego ★ ($, p. 79)

Taj ($, p. 84)

Centre-Ville/Downtown

Two of the restaurants listed here, **Le Balmoral** (p. 76) and **Brasserie T** (p. 77) are in the Quartier des Spectacles, on the far eastern end of downtown. In addition to the restaurants listed below, we recommend the excellent wine bar **Pullman** (p. 137) in downtown.

Expensive

Europea ★★★ CONTEMPORARY FRENCH   Montréal has a handful of celebrity chefs, and Europea's Jérôme Ferrer is justifiably one of them. While many upscale white-tablecloth restaurants have fallen by the wayside, this special spot persists. For the full treatment, order the extravagant *menu dégustation,* which starts with a lobster cream "cappuccino" with truffle puree and goes on to include maple bark stewed foie gras, prawn risotto, cornish hen encapsulated in breakable clay, and *l'arbre à sucreries de Sainte Culpabilité,* translated as "candy tree from Guilty land." There are two (relatively) moderate ways to experience Ferrer's touch: come at lunch, when a three-course meal goes for C$35, or try his more affordable **Beaver Hall** restaurant (p. 76), which is also downtown. Europea is a member of the prestigious Relais & Châteaux.

1227 rue de la Montagne (near rue Ste-Catherine). www.europea.ca. 🕐 **514/398-9229.** Reservations recommended. Main courses C$43–C$58; table d'hôte C$90; 10-course *menu dégustation* C$120. Tues–Fri noon–1:30pm; Sun–Fri 6–9:30pm; Sat 6–10pm. Métro: Peel.

Ferreira Café ★★★ PORTUGUESE/SEAFOOD   Ferreria exudes a warm, festive, Mediterranean grace, and you can't go wrong with its take on

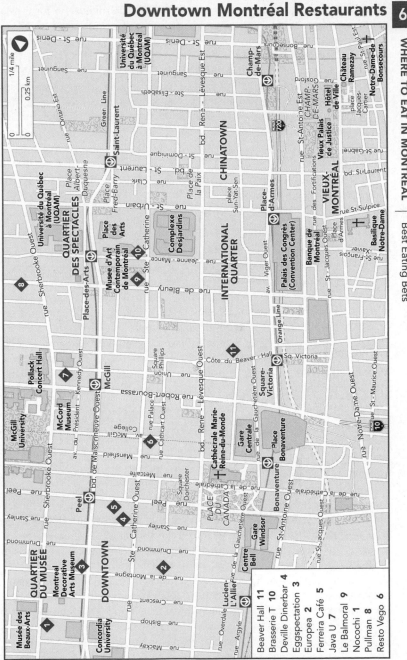

Beaver Hall 11
Brasserie T 10
Deville Dinerbar 4
Eggspectation 3
Europea 2
Ferreira Café 5
Java U 7
Le Balmoral 9
Nocochi 1
Pullman 8
Resto Vego 6

Portuguese classics, including oysters (*huîtres à la portugaise;* 6 for C$21), salted cod (*morue salée rôtie en croûte;* C$35), and bouillabaisse (C$36). A smaller, late-night menu for C$24 is available from 10pm Monday through Saturday. For lighter and less expensive fare, Ferreira's sister venue, **Café Vasco de Gama,** on the same block, at 1472 rue Peel (© **514/286-2688**), offers big breakfasts, a variety of salads, and delectable desserts indoors and at sidewalk tables in warm months. It's open daily into the early evening. The owners also operate **Taverne F** (© **514/289-4558**), a trendy restaurant specializing in *petiscos* (small plates to be shared among friends). The restaurant is in a glass box on the sidewalk of the Quartier des Spectacles, next to **Brasserie T** (see below).

1446 rue Peel (near boul. de Maisonnueve). www.ferreiracafe.com. © **514/848-0988.** Main courses C$28–C$45. Mon–Fri 11:45am–3pm; Sun 5:30–10pm; Mon–Wed 5:30–11; Thurs–Sat 5:30pm–midnight. Confirm Sun hours in winter. Métro: Peel.

Moderate

Le Balmoral ★★ BISTRO   This restaurant serves top-notch bistro fare, with a particular affinity for beef. You'll find a classic rendition of beef tartare, burgers, a grilled strip loin with a perfectly seared and salty outer crust, braised beef cheek, and a French-Japanese fusion of beef tataki with sesame seeds and maple vinaigrette. Sandwiches, salads, and lighter fare are available at lunch. Le Balmoral is a sharp-looking room that overlooks Quartier des Spectacles, and is notably a nonprofit. Proceeds fund the *Maison du Festival Rio Tinto Alcan*, the organizers behind the incomparable **Festival International de Jazz de Montréal** (p. 132). It's housed in the historic Blumenthal Building, a National Heritage site built in 1910 that was donated to the Jazz Festival in the 1990s. Thursday through Saturday evenings, the restaurant becomes a jazz club featuring local and national musical acts. Upstairs one floor is a small but worthwhile jazz museum about the history of the festival and some of the artists who have played there.

305 rue Ste-Catherine ouest (at rue Balmoral). www.bistrobalmoral.ca. © **514/288-5992.** Main courses C$18–C$26. Mon 11:30am–2pm; Tues–Fri 11:30am–2pm and 5–9:30pm; Sat 4:30–9:30pm. Métro: Place-des-Arts.

Beaver Hall ★★ CONTEMPORARY FRENCH   With the same chef as the esteemed **Europea** (p. 74), this "Bistro Gourmand par Europea" offers similarly spectacular food, but with a less over-the-top service experience (and at a more relaxed price). Great mains include braised beef shoulder with homemade cavatelli and a panko-crusted poached egg, fish and chips, and a wonderful spinach ravioli with dill and feta cheese. Picture windows look down the street toward Basilique-Cathédrale Marie-Reine-du-Monde, a cathedral that is a copy of Rome's St. Peter's Basilica (see our downtown walking tour, p. 152). The location north of the Convention Center and Vieux-Montréal and east of downtown is not likely next to anything you'd be

Fish and chips at Beaver Hall

visiting, but it's an easy 15-minute walk from the heart of both downtown and Vieux-Montréal.

1073 Cote du Beaver Hall (at rue Belmont). www.beaverhall.ca. ℭ **514/866-1331.** Main courses C$15–C$39; table d'hôte C$16–C$38. Mon 11:30am–3pm; Tues–Wed 11:30am–10pm; Thurs–Fri 11:30am–10:30pm; Sat 5–10:30pm. Métro: Square-Victoria.

Brasserie T ★★★ BRASSERIE   This newest restaurant from chef Normand Laprise of the city's top restaurant, **Toqué!** (p. 83), opened in 2010. It's fun, flirty, adventurous, and romantic; it wows us at every turn. Its location, in a unique all-glass box perched on a sidewalk in the city's newly renovated fine-arts neighborhood, the Quartier des Spectacles, is right in front of the **Musée d'Art Contemporain de Montréal** (p. 105). The food is spectacular: The hamburger is arguably the best in the city, and we love the garlic sea snails, pan-seared foie gras with candied fennel, strawberries, and popcorn, and the *saucisse de Montréal* (sausage) with quinoa salad. You can make a creative meal out of just the appetizers, charcuteries, and *tartares*. At night in warm months, a pool of water alongside the restaurant and the length of a city block has a "dancing waters" lightshow. The restaurant is extremely popular, so make reservations.

1425 rue Jeanne-Mance (near rue Ste-Catherine). www.brasserie-t.com. ℭ **514/282-0808.** Main courses C$18–C$25. Sun–Wed 11:30am–10:30pm; Thurs–Sat 11:30am–11:30pm. Métro: Place-des-Arts.

The glassy and classy Brasserie T

Deville Dinerbar ★ DINER This splashy downtown restaurant is packed with local businesspeople at lunchtime and a partying crowd at night. It claims to take its cue from American diners, but that goes only as far as its use of booths for some of the seating and its enormous portions; you'd be hard pressed to find an American diner with a marble bar, sparkly chandeliers, and reputation for killer fish tacos. Choices include salads, sandwiches, burgers, pastas, and specialties such as lamb shanks, diver scallops, and chicken schnitzel and spaetzle. If you have the stomach for it, try the so-called "R-rated shakes" such as The Beaux Dimanches: a concoction of Montréal-made Sortilège maple whiskey, coconut cream, and vanilla ice cream.

1425 Stanley St. (at rue Ste-Catherine). www.devilledinerbar.com. ℂ **514/281-6556.** Main courses C$20–C$45. Sun–Thurs 11am–11pm; Fri–Sat 11am–midnight. Métro: Peel.

Inexpensive

Eggspectation ★★★ BREAKFAST/BRUNCH Don't be put off by the goofy name, the 15-page menu, or the fact that this is a small chain (with seven outposts in Montréal alone). This breakfast-centric restaurant delivers. Food is fresh and comes out fast, despite crowds that would slow a lesser place down. The menu has 10 versions of eggs benedict alone ("Montréal Style" comes with smoked meat) as well as non-breakfast foods such as burgers and club sandwiches. Other central outposts include 190 Ste-Catherine ouest at the Quartier des Spectacles and 12 rue Notre-Dame est in Vieux-Montréal.

1313 de Maisonneuve ouest (at rue de la Montagne). www.eggspectation.com. ℂ **514/842-3447.** Most items less than C$12. Daily 6am–5pm. Métro: Peel.

Java U ★ LIGHT FARE This cheery Java U is part of a local cafe chain that got its start in 1996 at Concordia University. College students and families make up most of the clientele at this particular outlet, which is a buttoned-up venue with friendly, laid-back staff. Options include quiches, salads, sandwich wraps, croissants, ice cream from local purveyor Bilboquet, and St-Ambroise beer, brewed at Montréal's own Brasserie McAuslan. Coffee options include espresso "con panna," which is espresso with whipped cream. Other locations are scattered throughout the city, and offer a good budget-friendly option for breakfast or lunch if you plan to splurge come dinner time (that's what we do!).

626 rue Sherbrooke ouest (at av. Union). www.java-u.com. ℂ **514/286-1991.** Most items less than C$9. Mon–Fri 7am–8pm; Sat–Sun 8am–8pm. Métro: McGill.

Nocochi ★ BAKERY/LIGHT FARE For a breakfast *crêpe* or omelet, or an afternoon sweet treat (*macarons* are a specialty) or a glass of wine, try this bright little cafe and pâtisserie just one block west of the Musée des Beaux-Arts. The airy room is a balm after taking in the mountains of art at the museum or browsing the upscale antique shops and boutiques nearby.

2156 rue Mackay (at rue Sherbrooke). www.nocochi.com. ℂ **514/989-7514.** Most plates are under C$15. Mon–Tues 8am–9pm; Wed–Sat 8am–11pm; Sun 9am–10pm. Métro: Guy-Concordia.

Resto Vego ★ VEGETARIAN This bright, open, second floor space with floor-to-ceiling windows overlooks the always bustling rue Ste-Catherine and avenue McGill. Formerly known as Le Commensal, the owners revised the menu and re-branded in 2014 after a disastrous attempt to incorporate chicken and fish into the menu. Now completely vegetarian again, food here is buffet-style, and you pay by the weight of your plate—about C$12 for an ample portion. The expansive buffet tables have a rotating selection of options, including vegetable lasagna, quesadillas, ginger tofu, beet and apple salad, and puff pastry with asparagus and mushrooms. Another outpost is in the Quartier Latin, at 1720 rue St-Denis (ℂ **514/845-2627**). The downtown location is directly above the well regarded meat-centric deli **Reuben's,** 1116 rue Ste-Catherine ouest (www.reubensdeli.com; ℂ **514/866-1029**), if you're traveling with someone tofu-adverse.

1204 av. McGill College (at rue Ste-Catherine). www.restovego.ca. ℂ **514/871-1480.** Pay by weight: C$2.35 per 100 g (approx. ¼ lb.), or about C$12 for a dinner portion. Fixed price C$7.95 for children 10 and under. Sun–Wed 11:30am–9:30pm; Thurs–Sat 11:30am–10pm. Métro: McGill.

TABLE D'HÔTE & MORE RESTAURANT basics

Our number-one tip when eating in Québec: Always look for **table d'hôte meals.** These are fixed-price menus with three or four courses, and they usually cost just a little more than a single main course. You'll find them at restaurants of all price ranges, and they usually present the best dining value. To sample some of the city's top restaurants for a bargain, check if they have table d'hôte menus at lunch, when the menus are even cheaper.

A few **French dining terms** that are important to know: the midday meal is called **dîner** (which is lunch, not dinner) and the evening meal is *souper* (supper). An **entrée** is an appetizer, and a **plat principal** is a main course. **Menu midi** (often abbreviated to "midi") is the lunch menu.

Prices listed here are for supper unless otherwise indicated and do not include the cost of wine, tip, or the 5%

federal tax *and* 9.975% provincial tax that are tacked on the restaurant bill. Lunch prices are usually lower. Montréalers consider 15% of the check (before taxes) to be a fair tip, increased only for exceptional food and service. In all, count on taxes and tip to add another 30% to the bill.

Except in a handful of luxury restaurants, **dress codes** are nonexistent. But Montréalers are a fashionable lot and manage to look smart, even in casual clothes. Save the T-shirts and sneakers for another city.

Insider blogs featuring reviews and observations about the Montréal dining scene include **www.shutupandeat.ca,** the descriptive **www.willtravelforfood. com**, and the Twitter feed of *Montréal Gazette* restaurant critic Lesley Chesterman **@lesleychestrman.**

VIEUX-MONTRÉAL (OLD MONTRÉAL)

In addition to the restaurants listed below, food is also available in cheery indoor/outdoor **Le Jardin Nelson** (p. 138), which has live jazz and a terrace, and is popular with families and kid-free folks alike.

Expensive

Chez l'Épicier ★ CONTEMPORARY QUÉBECOIS   Chef Laurent Godbout's inspiring haute cuisine menu provides a perfect example of modern gastronomy in Montréal. The ever-changing menu features playfully crafted food with a focus on local ingredients and a global feel. Recent standout items include duck charcuterie with cauliflower-miso puree and dashi broth, sea scallops with sea urchin roe and carrot cream, and salsify tagliatelle with lemon whipped ricotta and honey mushrooms. A section of the dining room features shelves of Québec-made and imported products for sale such as fruit preserves, specialty vinegars, and high-quality olive oils (the name of the restaurant translates to "house of the grocer"). The many windows provide a light, airy feeling throughout, with stone and exposed brick walls punctuated by a long, robin's egg blue wall with chalkboards displaying the evening's

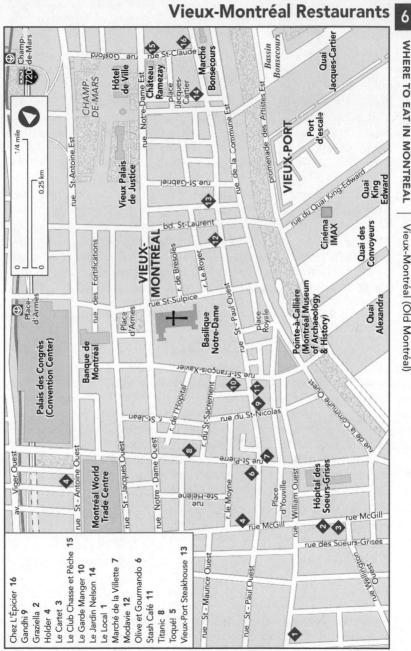

Chez L'Épicier 16
Gandhi 9
Graziella 2
Holder 4
Le Cartet 3
Le Club Chasse et Pêche 15
Le Garde Manger 10
Le Jardin Nelson 14
Le Local 1
Marché de la Villette 7
Modavie 12
Olive et Gourmando 6
Stash Café 11
Titanic 8
Toqué! 5
Vieux-Port Steakhouse 13

specials. You'll feel welcomed and comfortable from the moment you sit down. *Tip:* If you plan to order the chef's tasting menu, leave ample time since the meal will likely last longer than 3 hours.

311 rue St-Paul est (at rue St-Claude). www.chezlepicier.com. ℂ **514/878-2232.** Main courses C$31–C$40; 7-course tasting menu C$85. Daily 5:30–10pm. Métro: Champ-de-Mars.

Graziella ★★★ ITALIAN Graziella's open kitchen plan lets diners watch chef-owner Graziella Battista and her staff prepare modern Italian dishes served in understated yet beautiful presentations, like little works of art. Blonde wood and soft, creamy tones create a calming backdrop, and the high ceilings and votive candles on the tables give it a spa-like atmosphere. Menu items are uniformly excellent, but if we could recommend only one thing, it would be the fall-off-the-bone *osso buco.* On any given night are a variety of homemade pasta dishes—like capon-filled tortelli with speck and a buttery sauce infused with sage. Service can be slow during peak dinner hours, but the quality of the food and excellent wine list make it worth the wait. A lunchtime table d'hôte (dubbed "formule Graziella" on the menu) is a good alternative to the hefty prices of the dinner menu. Reservations are recommended.

116 rue McGill (3 blocks east of rue Notre-Dame ouest). www.restaurantgraziella.ca. ℂ **514/876-0116.** Main courses C$26–C$45; table d'hôte lunch Mon–Fri C$27. Mon–Fri noon–2:30pm; Mon–Sat 6–10pm (check if open Monday in the winter.) Métro: Square-Victoria.

Le Club Chasse et Pêche ★★★ CONTEMPORARY QUÉBE-COIS This is one of the top restaurants in Montréal. In English, the name means Hunting and Fishing Club, paying homage to the sportsmen's club that once occupied the building. The short, but well-executed menu keeps this theme going: grilled octopus or hamachi *tartare* share the menu with renditions of game meat such as bison ravioli and roasted duck. Like many at restaurants in town, chef Claude Pelletier's menu changes frequently. Despite that, certain favorites are always on the menu, including braised piglet risotto with fois gras shavings. The nondescript entrance is easily missed, marked only by a small sign with a crest on it. The stone and brick dining room is dark and masculine, with leather chairs and waterfowl-themed light fixtures. You can almost imagine yourself hunting deep in the forest at dusk. For a more casual experience, check out sister restaurant **Le Filet** (p. 87) in the Plateau neighborhood.

423 rue St-Claude (btw. rue St-Paul and rue Notre-Dame). www.leclubchasseetpeche. com. ℂ **514/861-1112.** Main courses C$34–C$39. Year-round Tues–Sat 6–10:30pm. Métro: Champ-de-Mars.

Le Garde Manger ★★ SEAFOOD At this supper club, everything is a little different. For starters, the staff greet you in English, not French. The exterior has no signage other than a dimly lit neon pink square out front. The interior decor is half hunting lodge, half antique shop. Celebrity chef-owner

Chuck Hughes, star of the Canadian Food Network show *Chuck's Day Off*, features a wildly creative seafood menu. Though Hughes himself is often absent from the kitchen (he's usually off filming one of his multiple TV shows), his chefs pump out top-notch grub that locals continually rave about. Lobster *poutine* is a perennial hit, and on a recent visit, devilled eggs with bacon-wrapped oysters were flying out of the kitchen, as was the pork liver sausage paired with octopus and cheese grits. Meatier choices include braised short ribs (always on the menu) and seared fois gras, always paired with some kind of meat over a maple-soaked waffle (recently: a perfectly seared pork chop). The menu changes seasonally, so be prepared for new surprises with each visit. Expect a packed house, loud music, and a cool crowd in skinny jeans and copious tattoos. Reservations recommended.

408 rue St-François-Xavier (north of rue St-Paul). www.gardemanger.ca. © **514/678-5044.** Main courses C$28–C$50. Tues–Sun 5:30–11:30pm. Bar Tues–Sun 6pm–3am. Métro: Place d'Armes.

Le Local ★ CONTEMPORARY FRENCH   In a brick building that was a foundry many lifetimes ago, the interior at Le Local is industrial-chic: Polished cement floors and exposed beam-and-brick ceilings and walls hint of the building's former life, while contemporary touches such as black leather furniture, colorful throw pillows, and gorgeous chestnut tables provide a clubby feel. It's popular among local trendsetters, and the place is packed even on weeknights. An attractive, fashionably dressed staff provides competent service. The open kitchen cranks out French bistro classics such as beef and salmon *tartare* and duck leg confit, along with inspired pan-European dishes such as seared Arctic char with chorizo roasted cabbage and fennel and tarragon arancini. In the evenings, tapas-style dishes are available during the early part of happy hour, many for only a few dollars each.

740 rue William (at rue Prince). www.lelocal.ca. © **514/397-7737.** Main courses C$25–C$34; table d'hôte C$23. Mon–Wed 11:30am–10pm; Thurs–Fri 11:30am–11pm; Sat 5:30–11pm; Sun 5:30–10pm. Métro: Square-Victoria.

Toqué! ★★★ CONTEMPORARY FRENCH   When chef Normand Laprise opened this gem in 1993, the city's culinary reputation was virtually nonexistent. Toqué! changed all that, and more than 20 years later it's still the local standard-bearer. The decor is both refined and whimsical: it's one of the few white-tablecloth restaurants left in the city, but it's hardly a stuffy affair. A playful sunflower sculpture greets you out front, and inside you'll marvel at the glass-paneled wine cellar that extends from below-ground to create a visual centerpiece with wine bottles suspended in midair. The menu is equally playful and is heavily influenced by local ingredients. Items change regularly, but you're likely to find some perennial favorites such as a version of Magret duck and one or two outstanding pasta dishes, such as squash cavatelli or rabbit-stuffed pasta with ricotta and rabbit *jus*. Adventurous eaters should try the seven-course tasting menu (C$120). It changes nightly and serves up the

veg out IN MEATY MONTRÉAL

Québec cuisine is traditionally very meat-centric, but vegetarian foods have made inroads onto menus as both perfunctory options and centerpiece main events. Whether you are totally vegetarian or simply looking for lighter fare after days of indulgence, here are some places to keep in mind:

o **Resto Vego** (p. 79): With locations both downtown and in Quartier Latin, Resto Vego is a terrific go-to option for both vegetarians and for meat-eaters who need a little detox. Both locations are large and bright, and they feature inviting buffets. You pay by the weight of your plate—about C$12 for a dinner portion, and a fixed price of C$7.95 for children 10 and under. Open daily for lunch and dinner.

o **Aux Vivres** (p. 96): Year after year, this appealing, continually expanding vegan restaurant on the Plateau continues to serve some of the best healthy cuisine in town. Chapati flatbread wraps are made-to-order and stuffed with flavors from every corner of the globe.

o **The Green Panther** (p. 98). Another good bet on the Plateau, with the option for smallish portions (you can order a half pita) and a full menu of power drinks such as a wheatgrass–boosted smoothie.

o **Le Taj,** 2077 rue Stanley (www.restaurantletaj.com; *©* **514/845-9015**):. Choose from 12 vegetarian main courses (C$12–C$16) at this great Indian restaurant in downtown, but if you come at lunch take a look at the C$17 buffet (C$9 for kids 10 and under), which includes samosas, lentil curry, and vegetable dishes. The decor is just fancy enough to feel special without being intimidating. It's open for lunch Sunday through Friday and daily for dinner.

o **Gandhi,** 230 rue St-Paul oust (www.restaurantgandhi.com; *©* **514/845-5866**). Another good Indian option, in Vieux-Montréal right on rue St-Paul. It's bright, airy, and fast. Skip the duck, lamb, and chicken dishes in favor of over a dozen vegetarian options (C$13–C$15), including classics such as the chickpea dish *chana masala* and *matter panir*, a homemade cheese with green peas. It's open for lunch on weekdays and dinner daily.

best the kitchen has to offer. On offer at lunchtime during the week is a more wallet-friendly (but still a bit pricey) table d'hôte. For a more casual meal, visit **Brasserie T** (p. 77), also owned by Laprise. Reservations, not always necessary in this city, are recommended here.

900 Place Jean-Paul-Riopelle (at rue St-Antoine). www.restaurant-toque.com. *©* **514/499-2084.** Main courses C$42–C$52; tasting menu C$120; table d'hôte lunch C$27–C$48. Tues–Fri 11:30am–1:45pm; Tues–Thurs 5:30–10pm; Fri–Sat 5:30–10:30pm. Métro: Square-Victoria.

Moderate

Holder ★ BRASSERIE This large, high-ceilinged space offers a chic atmosphere with copper walls, tall columns, and expansive windows overlooking busy rue McGill. Chalkboards throughout feature the day's specials, along with wine and beer selections. Holder offers good value for what you get: The expansive menu of primarily French classics will satisfy nearly every appetite. Standout items include *fois gras au torchon* and gravlax appetizers, and classic beef *tartare* in both appetizer and main course sizes. Holder's take on steak frites featuring grilled hanger steak is dependably good, as is the lobster ravioli, served with truffle oil and beurre blanc. The weekend brunch offers more modestly priced items that are just as good, but more along the lines of typical breakfast food.

407 rue McGill (corner of rue St. Paul). www.restaurantholder.com. © **514/849-0333.** Main courses C$17–C$26; table d'hôte weekdays C$20. Mon–Fri 11:30am–11pm; Sat–Sun 10am–3pm; Sat 5:30–11pm; Sun 5:30–10pm. Métro: Square-Victoria.

Le Cartet ★★ BREAKFAST/BRUNCH   Catering to the many media and technology professionals who work just west of rue McGill, Le Cartet is a sharp, tall-ceilinged, appealing cafe focused on breakfast and lunch. Plates are expansive, such as the Brunch Santé ("Healthy Brunch"), which comes with *biologique* (organic) granola, yogurt topped with berries, poached eggs on wheat bread, goat cheese with pesto, figs, and fresh fruit (C$14). The front part of the cafe is a small store stocked with prepared salads and meals, baguettes and croissants, and fancy jams and chocolates. Brunch, which runs on Saturday and Sunday from 9am to 3:30pm, is especially popular.

106 rue McGill (at rue Wellington). www.lecartet.com. © **514/871-8887.** Most items under C$15. Mon–Fri 7am–7pm; Sat–Sun 9am–4pm. Métro: Square-Victoria.

Modavie ★ BISTRO   Featuring a unique combination of French bistro classics and Italian-influenced pasta dishes, Modavie hits all the right notes. It's a place where the atmosphere is loud but convivial, and everyone seems to be in a good mood. The service is attentive without being overbearing— you'll leave feeling well taken care of. Live jazz plays every evening in the upstairs lounge (no cover), making this a comfortable place for singles as well as couples and groups. On the menu, steak frites are always excellent, and an entire section of the menu is dedicated to lamb. The lamb *mille-feuilles* features succulent braised lamb shank and mushrooms tucked between layers of flaky puff pastry—so delicious you may just want to order it again for dessert.

1 rue St. Paul ouest (corner of rue St-Laurent). www.modavie.com. © **514/287-9582.** Main courses C$17–C$38; table d'hôte lunch C$15, dinner C$29. Sun–Thurs 11:30am–10:30pm; Fri–Sat 11:30am–11pm. Métro: Place d'Armes.

Stash Café ★★ POLISH   Hidden among the myriad expensive French restaurants and steakhouses of Old Montréal sits this old fashioned gem serving traditional Polish cuisine at extremely affordable prices—main courses are almost all in the C$15 range, a rarity in this part of town. It's the real deal: You'll likely overhear the servers speaking to each other in Polish. We highly recommend the *golabki*, cabbage leaves stuffed with pork and rice in a savory tomato sauce, and the *pierogis*, potato dumplings filled with meat, cheese and potato, or mushrooms and cabbage. There's a variety of classic soups and game meats, including roast boar and duck—a nod to Poland's traditional game hunting culture. Decor features brick and stone walls, colorful hanging lights, and a central seating area of pews from an old church and a number of refectory tables saved from a convent (smaller tables line the periphery). Another unique touch is the pianist who plays each night starting at 6pm.

200 rue St-Paul ouest (corner of rue St-François-Xavier). http://restaurantstashcafe.ca. ⓒ **514/845-6611.** Main courses C$12–C$19; table d'hôte C$23–39. Mon–Thurs 11:30am–10pm; Fri 11:30am–11pm; Sat noon–11pm; Sun noon–10pm. Métro: Place d'Armes.

Vieux-Port Steakhouse ★ STEAKHOUSE   Bring a huge appetite to this massive steakhouse (we're talking over 1,000 seats) and tuck into one of their hearty options that includes T-Bone, filet mignon, and New York–cut sirloin, among others. Other choices include a tangy Santa Fe grilled chicken and herbed rack of lamb. A lunchtime table d'hôte (C$15.50) includes soup or salad plus a wide selection of mains and dessert. In summer you may want to opt for a table on the 300-seat outdoor terrace. The place runs like a well-oiled machine: A veritable army of servers, cooks, runners, and other staff are always on the go. Thanks to its size you probably won't have to wait long for a table.

39 rue St-Paul est (at rue St-Gabriel). www.vieuxportsteakhouse.com. ⓒ **514/866-3175.** Main courses C$17–C$54; table d'hôte lunch C$15.50, dinner C$29–C$32. Mon–Thurs 11:30am–10pm; Fri–Sat 11:30am–11:00pm; Sun 10am–10pm. Métro: Place d'Armes.

Inexpensive

Marché de la Villette ★ BISTRO   This rustic-looking, cheery deli was originally a boucherie (butchery) and charcuterie, evidenced by the old-fashioned lettering on the window. These days, it's known to locals as one of the best spots for a weekday lunch. This is a place for stick-to-your-ribs fare, including homemade pâtés, a variety of quiches, and a delicious, addictive *cassoulet de maison.* Locals swear by their *soupe à l'oignon gratinée* (French onion soup). Lighter options include salads and crêpes. The daily table d'hôte costs C$15, with the option on Friday and Saturday to add fois gras for C$5 more.

324 rue St-Paul ouest (at rue St-Pierre). www.marche-villette.com. ⓒ **514/807-8084.** Most items under C$16; table d'hôte C$15. Mon–Thurs 9:30am–6pm; Fri 9:30am–10pm; Sat 8:30am–10pm; Sun 8:30am–6pm. Métro: Square-Victoria.

Olive et Gourmando ★★★ BAKERY/LIGHT FARE   O+G started as a bakery but soon expanded to include a dining room and quickly became the go-to lunch spot in Vieux-Montréal (it's packed during peak hours). The wide-ranging menu is a hit with everyone from grown-ups to toddlers. You're greeted by a gorgeous display of baked goods, ranging from croissants and muffins to biscotti, and warm, nature-inflected decor. A branch and twig chandelier adds a quirky touch of earthiness to the dark red room. Check the chalkboard menu to see what's available that day. Options always available include the Cuban sandwich and a deliriously good truffle mac 'n' cheese with caramelized onions.

351 rue St-Paul ouest (at rue St-Pierre). www.oliveetgourmando.com. (C) **514/350-1083.** Most items under C$15. Cash only. Tues–Sat 8am–5pm. Métro: Square-Victoria.

Titanic ★ LIGHT FARE The ambience at this breakfast and lunchtime spot could best be described as frayed chic. Feeling a bit like you're entering a 1920s speakeasy, you descend a flight of stairs into a basement with a labyrinth of pipes overhead, chipped exposed brick walls, and worn wooden floors. The bare-bones room is counterbalanced by pops of artistic bric-a-brac and black and white photography that tie it all together. The decor sets the scene nicely: These are arguably the best sandwiches in town. Everything is made from scratch, including the baguettes. Don't miss the pork Milanese sandwich: thin pork cutlets breaded and fried to a crisp and served on a ciabatta bun with coleslaw and veggies. It sells out daily, so come early. You can also choose from a variety of other meat and vegetarian options, plus hot and cold entrees.

445 rue St-Pierre (1 block south of rue Notre-Dame). www.titanicmontreal.com. (C) **514/849-0894.** Most sandwiches C$10. Cash only. Mon–Fri 8am–4pm. Métro: Square-Victoria/Place d'Armes.

PLATEAU MONT-ROYAL

Expensive

Au Pied de Cochon ★ CONTEMPORARY QUÉBECOIS Celebrity chef Martin Picard led Montréal's meat "new wave" by opening Au Pied de Cochon (translation: the Pig's Foot) in 2001, and its patrons and personnel today bank on a seemingly indelible reputation. The foie gras, served at least seven different ways, one as *poutine,* still merits high praise. And sure enough, it's fun to open Duck in a Can right at the table. But in all the bustle and frenzy you may receive your entrée a split second after your salad and be asked if you want dessert a minute after that. Tables of four or more seem to have more time and space to have a few drinks and laughs. An elaborate raw bar is on view near the entrance of this low-key, upscale, always packed restaurant, and includes oysters, lobster, and local catch. Picard's newest enterprises include a seasonal *cabane à sucre* (sugar shack) and an award-winning cookbook with its recipes. Reservations are recommended.

536 rue Duluth est (near rue St-Hubert). www.restaurantaupieddecochon.ca. (C) **514/281-1114.** Main courses C$15–C$51. Wed–Sun 5pm–midnight. Métro: Sherbrooke.

Le Filet ★★ TAPAS Seafood's profile gets bumped up another few notches on Montréal's dining scene with Le Filet, which opened in 2011. Let the menu's categories of First Set, Second Set, and Third Set add an air of

NOSH & shop AT MONTRÉAL'S GLORIOUS PUBLIC MARKETS

If you're planning a picnic or a meal in, or just want to shop for treats and food gifts to take home, make like a local and head to one of city's big year-round farmers markets: **Marché Atwater** (Atwater Market) to the west of Vieux-Montréal in Little Burgundy, or **Marché Jean-Talon** (Jean-Talon Market), north in Mile End.

Both markets make for wonderful excursions. At 138 av. Atwater, at the corner of rue Notre-Dame, Marché Atwater is a few blocks from the Lionel-Groulx Métro stop or an easy bicycle ride along the Lachine Canal, which also has picnic tables. Free outdoor parking is available at the market, if you drive. Stalls stocked with gleaming produce and flowers border a long interior shed. The two-story center section is devoted to vintners, butchers, bakeries, and cheese stores. **La Fromagerie Atwater** (© 514/932-4653) lays out more than 750 local and international cheeses—with hundreds from Québec alone—as well as pâtés and charcuterie. **Première Moisson** (© 514/932-0328) is filled with the tantalizing aromas of breads and pastries—oh, the pastries!—and has a seating area at which to nibble baguettes or sip a bowl of café au lait. **Satay Brothers** (© 514/

933-3507), a Singaporean and Malaysian food stall, is also popular.

Locals in the northern part of the city rely on Marché Jean-Talon as a point of sale for regional farms' seasonal harvests—from strawberries and asparagus in late spring to squash of all shapes and colors in fall. Visiting gourmands will certainly want to make a pilgrimage here. The buzz and energy of the city surround the market on all sides, and it is adjacent to Montréal's Little Italy. Stalls, some permanent and some seasonal, sell smoked seafood, cured meat, fresh flowers, local wine and cheese, and delightful local products such as sprays of fresh lavender and trays of pastel-hued *macarons*. From the counter of **La Boîte aux Huîtres** (www.laboiteauxhuitres.ca; © 514/277-7575), you can watch the master oyster shuckers at work while you wait for your own plate (C$30 per dozen oysters). **Aqua Mare** (© 514/277-7575), just adjacent, sells fish n' chips, fried calamari, shrimp, and *éperlans* (smelt), as well as fresh fish to go. Jean-Talon is at 7070 av. Henri-Julien, just a few blocks from the Jean-Talon Métro stop.

Information on both markets is online at **www.marchespublics-mtl.com**. Both are open daily.

intrigue since you really can't go wrong. All plates are small and meant to be shared (order at least two per person) and there's no delineation between appetizers and main courses. Oysters are creatively garnished with yuzu marmalade or jalapeño and maple cracker. The half lobster comes with a luscious, buttery Hollandaise with the surprising addition of silky-smooth sea urchin in the sauce. Fans of **Le Club Chasse et Pêche** restaurant (p. 82), take note: The same team is in charge here and thus game meat is also on the menu. Seats on the terrace have a view of Parc Jeanne-Mance. Reservations are recommended.

219 av. du Mont-Royal ouest (near av. du Parc). www.lefilet.ca. © **514/360-6060.** Main courses C$13–C$28. Tues–Fri 5:45–10:30pm; Sat 5–10:30pm. Métro: Mont-Royal.

Plateau Mont-Royal & Mile End Restaurants

Au Pied de Cochon **18**
Aux Vivres **12**
Beauty's Luncheonette **11**
Bilboquet **2**
Café Cherrier **20**
Chez Schwartz Charcuterie
  Hébraïque de Montréal **16**
Fairmount Bagel **7**
Green Panther **4**
Hostaria **3**

| 0 | | 1/4 mile |
| 0 | 0.25 km | |

ⓘ Tourist Information
Ⓜ Metro Station

Hôtel Herman **9**
Juliette et Chocolat **19**
L'Express **17**
La Banquise **14**
Lawrence **5**
Le Filet **10**
Leméac **1**
Magpie Pizzeria **6**
Mezcla **22**
Moishes **15**
Restaurant de l'Institut **21**
St-Viateur Bagel & Café **13**
Wilensky Light Lunch **8**

Moishes ★★ STEAKHOUSE   Montréal has a handful of culinary institutions and for steak lovers it's Moishes. Long-time patrons may favor the classic bone-in rib steak while the younger crowd opts for marinated shish kabab or organic salmon. With an ever-evolving menu and cozy, but sophisticated atmosphere, it's common to find three generations at one table celebrating a special occasion (the prices alone make it one). Looking for a way to have your shrimp cocktail and martini, too/ After 9pm from Thursday through Saturday order the C$25 three-course menu. The restaurant's rich history reaches back more than 75 years, when Moishe Lighter worked his way up from busboy to mignon mogul. Moishes' sons, co-owners Lenny and Larry, carry on the tradition and are often on hand to suggest pairings from the restaurant's reputable wine list. Reservations are recommended.

3961 boul. St-Laurent (north of rue Napoléon). www.moishes.ca. ℂ **514/845-3509.** Main courses C$25–C$85. Mon–Tues 5:30–10pm; Wed 5:30–11pm; Thurs–Fri 5:30pm–midnight; Sun 5–10pm. Métro: Sherbrooke.

Restaurant de l'Institut ★ CONTEMPORARY FRENCH   Apart from the name, you'd never know that this restaurant is run largely by students from the Institut de Tourisme et d'Hôtellerie du Québec. The menu reflects of-the-moment experimentation by beginner chefs and is presented by warm and eager wait staff in training. For value, try the C$20 three-course lunch (weekdays) or the C$25 and C$35 three-course dinners (Tues and Wed). Floor-to-ceiling windows and louvered wooden blinds add elegance to the

Moishes steakhouse, a Montréal institution

comfortable dining room. Upstairs is a training hotel at a remarkably good value (p. 70).

3535 rue St-Denis (1 block north of rue Sherbrooke). www.ithq.qc.ca/restaurants. © **514/282-5155.** Main courses C$22–C$29; table d'hôte lunch C$20, dinner Tues–Wed C$25 and C$35. Tues–Wed. Mon–Fri 7–9:30am and noon–1:30pm; Sat–Sun 7:30–10:30am; Tues–Sat 6–9pm. Métro: Sherbrooke.

Moderate

Café Cherrier ★ BREAKFAST/BRUNCH It's not about the food, exactly, at this amiable cafe—though it is quite tasty. Through rain, sleet, or shine, students, older couples, and families gather under the wrap-around awning to sip coffee and people watch. Summer brings bowls of gazpacho and crisp pours of white wine. In winter, it's grilled steak and Cabernet at the indoor counter. A group of actors could be crammed into a corner, talking shop, or it could just as easily be politicians or bankers. Brunch is especially busy though some tables stay full long after dark. For a charming bistro atmosphere, especially in fair weather, it's a keeper.

3635 rue St-Denis (2 blocks north of Sherbrooke). www.cafecherrier.ca. © **514/843-4308.** Main courses C$15–C$26; table d'hôte lunch C$18–C$25, dinner C$18–C$27. Mon–Fri 7:30am–11pm; Sat–Sun 8:30am–11pm. Métro: Sherbrooke.

L'Express ★ BISTRO Beloved by Montréalers and visitors alike for its old-timey Parisian style, L'Express almost always has a wait. Main courses include the usual bistro fare, from pot-au-feu to duck confit, and the maple syrup pie is outstanding. (It's possible that the globe lights, glossy maroon walls, and checkered floor make the food taste even more French.) A 50-person service team runs a smooth ship, though at busier times, like brunch, the kitchen may grind to a halt. Try for a reservation or drop in to see if the bar has an opening. One more thing: It's easy to miss. Look for the name spelled out in tile on the sidewalk out front.

3927 rue St-Denis (just north of rue Roy). www.restaurantlexpress.com. © **514/845-5333.** Main courses C$12–C$27. Mon–Fri 8am–2am; Sat 10am–2am; Sun 10am–1am. Métro: Sherbrooke.

Inexpensive

Beauty's Luncheonette ★★ DINER At this iconic diner, you'd be right to deduce that a long line means good food, as it has since 1942. On Saturdays and Sundays the breakfast line often wraps around the corner and down the street. If you're lucky, Beauty himself (a bowling nickname for the 93-year-old owner, Hymie Sckolnick) will see that you have strong coffee and a banquette seat as quickly as possible. The bagels are local, from **St-Viateur Bagel** (p. 98), and the orange juice is fresh-squeezed. Loyalists debate which of the two signature dishes is more quintessentially Montréal: the Mish-Mash omelet with hot dog, salami, fried onion, and green pepper, or Beauty's Special, a bagel sandwich with lox, cream cheese, sliced tomato, and onion—Beauty calls it their "Big Mac." Service can sometimes be hit-or-miss when the restaurant is at capacity (as it often is) but the food remains as good as ever. If you want a delicious, home-cooked slice of Montréal, get in line!

93 av. du Mont-Royal ouest (corner of rue St-Urbain). www.beautys.ca. *C* **514/849-8883.** Most items less than C$13. Mon–Fri 7am–3pm; Sat–Sun 8am–4pm. Métro: Mont-Royal.

Chez Schwartz Charcuterie Hébraïque de Montréal ★ DELI   Tell friends you've recently visited Montréal and one will inevitably ask if you made it to the famous Schwartz's deli. Smoked meat sandwiches here are hand-sliced and come piled high on fresh rye; the plates have a side of fries, sour pickle, and cole slaw. Choose your degree of "fat"—most folks opt for medium or medium-fat. This is one of many city landmarks created by a Jewish immigrant, in this case by Reuben Schwartz in 1928, making it Canada's oldest deli. Tables are communal and space is at a premium so come prepared to rub elbows with strangers. Takeout is an option, as is a midnight snack; Schwartz's is open 'til 12:30am during the week, later on weekends.

3895 boul. St-Laurent (just north of rue Roy). www.schwartzsdeli.com. *C* **514/842-4813.** Sandwiches and meat plates C$7–C$22. No credit cards. Daily 8–10:30am takeout only; Sun–Thurs 10:30am–12:30am; Fri 10:30am–1:30am; Sat 10:30am–2:30am. Métro: Sherbrooke.

Juliette et Chocolat ★ DESSERT   This chocolate-centric cafe has been steadily expanding its locations over the years, probably because it fills the broad need of coffee house, luncheonette, and purveyor of exceptional chocolate desserts. You can also order wine or beer, and savory options, too, such as buckwheat *crêpes* and a salad with dark chocolate vinaigrette. Chocolate

QUÉBEC'S BEST comfort FOODS

While you're in Montréal, indulge in at least a couple of Québec staples. Though you'll find them dolled up on some menus, these are generally thought of as the region's basic comfort foods:

o **Poutine:** French fries doused with gravy and cheese curds. Poutine's profile has risen outside of the province in recent years, with *The New Yorker* magazine positing that the "national joke" may be becoming the national dish.

o **Tarte au sucre:** Maple-sugar pie, like pecan pie without the pecans.

A French-Canadian classic.

o **Smoked meat:** A maddeningly tasty sandwich component particular to Montréal. Its taste is similar to pastrami and corned beef.

o **Cretons:** A pâté of minced pork, allspice, and parsley.

o **Tourtière:** A meat pie of spiced ground pork, often served with tomato chutney.

o **Queues de Castor:** A deep-fried pastry served with your choice of sweet or savory toppings. The name means "beaver tails" because its size is comparable.

The legendary Schwartz's deli

comes in all forms: as hot and cold beverages, in crêpes, in dense brownies (11 kinds!), as sauce over ice cream, in fondue. Take-home goodies like chocolate shaped into fried-egg or avocado forms add to the fun. There are six locations in all, including in Outremont at 377 rue Laurier ouest (© **514/510-5651**), downtown at 1626 Ste-Catherine ouest (© **514/508-4800**), and in the Latin Quarter at 1615 St-Denis (© **514/287-3555**).

3600 boul. St-Laurent (corner of rue Prince Arthur ouest). www.julietteetchocolat.com. © **438/380-1090.** Reservations available for parties of six or more before 9pm. Most items under C$15. Sun–Thurs 11am–11pm; Fri–Sat 11am–midnight. Métro: Sherbrooke.

La Banquise ★ LIGHT FARE   Open since 1968, the classic French-Canadian *poutine* is served in a dizzying 30-plus ways, all day, every day. Twists on the comfort food include La Dan Dan (with pepperoni, bacon, and onions) and La Kamikaze (merguez sausages, hot peppers, and Tabasco). And yes, vegetarian is now on the menu. Despite *poutine*'s reputation for being a post-2am binge food, La Banquise is incredibly kid-friendly and located on the north end of the Plateau's Parc La Fontaine, where the whole family can stretch their legs after a meal. In addition to *poutine,* breakfast items, salads, burgers, hot dogs, pogos (meat on a stick), and cold beer round out the menu. If you've worked your way through the menu and need a new challenge, step into the hot debate about *poutine's* origin . . . although you may need to argue *en Français.*

994 rue Rachel est (near rue Boyer). www.labanquise.com. © **514/525-2415.** Poutine C$7–C$16: most other items less than C$10. Cash only. Daily 24 hr. Métro: Mont-Royal.

MILE END & BEYOND
Expensive

Hostaria ★ ITALIAN Hostaria garnered attention for its simple, but formidable Italian cuisine, developed from inherited recipes—the bonus is there's not a bad seat in the house. In this intimate restaurant, established in 2009, white tablecloths dress the tables, even at lunch, and most seats overlook a quiet side street in Little Italy. Dishes are arranged as expected—antipasti, primi, secondi, and so on, and portions are modest. That's okay, because flavors plumb rich and earthy depths, especially so in the marinated vegetable antipasti, homemade pasta, and perfectly seasoned Petite-Nation Bison rib eye. Wine is a showpiece here, literally encased in a glass walk-in, and staff will guide you to a bottle that fits your budget. Sitting in a swivel chair along the lengthy marble-top bar is an ideal spot for taste testing. It's out of the way for the average tourist, which may be exactly why you seek it out. The location is three subway stops north of Mile End in the Rosemont-La-Petite-Patrie neighborhood, near the Jean-Talon Market. Reservations are recommended.

236 Rue Saint Zotique est (at rue Alma). www.hostaria.ca. © **514/273-5776.** Antipasti and primi C$9–C$26; main courses C$24–C$34. Wed 6pm–midnight; Thurs–Fri noon–3pm and 6pm–midnight; Sat 6pm–midnight. Métro: Beaubien.

Lawrence ★★★ BISTRO When clotted cream gets top billing, you know a place is serious about their brunch. Emblematic of everything that's exciting

The dining room and menu Lawrence speak to its British roots.

Leméac, a French foodie's delight

about the Mile End dining scene, Lawrence takes modern British cuisine to a new level. Chef Marc Cohen's hugely popular English breakfast and brunch are what most people rave about, but the lunch and dinner menus are equally outstanding. Decor in the 40-seat room hints at its British roots: Think plaid banquettes and dark wood paneling reminiscent of a pub, yet that's offset by a refined gray and white color scheme bordering on monochromatic. Chef Marc Cohen takes masterful turns with pub standards like bubble and squeak and traditional English fare such as kedgeree, suet dumplings (served with succulent braised oxtail), or pickled herring. Breakfast and brunch stay true to British culinary tradition, while lunch and dinner fare seems get a touch of classic French technique, just enough to make old things seem new again.

5201 blvd. St. Laurent (at av. Fairmount est). www.lawrencerestaurant.com. © **514/503-1070.** Brunch main courses C$12–C$16. Dinner main courses C$27–C$30. Tues–Fri 11:30am–3pm and 5:30–11pm; Sat 10am–3pm and 5:30–11pm; Sun 10am–3pm. Métro: Laurier.

Leméac ★★ BISTRO   For dinner or weekend brunch, this classic bistro is competent, elegant, yet refreshingly at ease. Tucked on the western end of the upscale avenue-Laurier, it's a neighborhood go-to as well as a destination for those who want beef *tartare* or *moules frites* and want it done right. Service is gracious and unassuming. The kitchen often prepares as many as 12 different desserts (moist chocolate and banana cake with house-made popcorn ice cream, for example). The colorful split fieldstone floor and cherry wood ceiling add subtle flair to the ambience. With a lovely terrace for al fresco dining and an intense wine list, it's the **Café Cherrier** (p. 91) for the well-heeled foodie. Planning a late night/ After 10pm there's a C$25 appetizer-plus-main menu.

1045 av. Laurier ouest (corner of av. Durocher). www.restaurantlemeac.com. © **514/270-0999.** Main courses C$24–C$48; late-night menu C$25; weekend brunch C$12–C$18. Mon–Fri noon–midnight; Sat–Sun 10am–midnight. Métro: Laurier.

Moderate

Hôtel Herman ★★ CONTEMPORARY QUÉBECOIS   Hôtel Herman re-defines hip, both in atmosphere and food quality. First the interior: pine

Hip dining in Mile End at Hôtel Herman

plank floors, industrial fixtures, and exposed brick could add up to retro-chic blah, yet the U-shaped, beaming white bar anchors the establishment and transforms the place to impeccably cool. And the food: On paper it's spare, *terroir* (meaning locally sourced), and predictably Québécois ("Duck from the Goulu farm, sweet onions, black chanterelles"), but one bite in and, *wow*. Plates range from small to mid-size and you'll want to order at least two per person. The restaurant is intense about cocktails, too, down to the glassware. The one thing this *hôtel* doesn't have is a room for rent. Well, they'll need to get rid of you somehow. Reservations recommended.

5171 blvd. St-Laurent (just south of av. Fairmount). www.hotelherman.com. © **514/278-7000.** Small plates C$9–C$21. Mon, Wed–Sun 5pm–midnight. Métro: Laurier.

Inexpensive

Aux Vivres ★★ VEGAN In a town of meat—smoked meat, pig's feet, meat pie—it shouldn't be such a surprise that the veggie way hasn't taken firmer root. Thankfully, Aux Vivres has been hitting all the right notes since 1997, and with an especially open spirit. It's set up like a diner, with flavors from every continent: gyro with souvlaki-style seitan, baked-to-order chapati with vegelox and tofu cream, a BLT with bacon made from coconut. There are also salads, rice bowls, soups, desserts, and a daily chef's special. The default recipes are vegan made with organic vegetables, local whenever possible. The high-octane juice bar runs all year although the patio out back, even for this crowd, is seasonal. Next door, owners recently opened a vegan market and

THE GREAT bagel DEBATE

Ketchup or pickle potato chips/ Atlantic or Pacific oysters/ Canadians love to debate and defend their homegrown cuisine and Montréal's bagels often top that list. While locals may lock horns over **Fairmount Bagel** (p. 98) versus **St-Viateur Bagel** (p. 98), and tourists pilgrimage to both to determine their favorite, the debate often boils down to just how much better Montréal's bagels are than "all the rest." As one blogger puts it, the Montréal-style bagel has to be made by hand, "while those NY bagels can be (and are) made by soulless, and probably quite aggressive, machines."

This city's thin O-shapes are made crispy and slightly sweet by being proofed in honey water and then baked in wood-fire ovens. Sure, the taste is out of this world, but what makes the Montréal bagel truly special is that they are only of this world, here in Montréal. The baking process is a marvel in itself and on view 24/7; and in the case of Fairmount, it's a process that hasn't changed since 1919. Though the shops are probably open right now while you are reading this (Fairmount, anyway, is open 24 hours), in our humble opinion, the case for the Montréal bagel is closed.

express counter featuring select items from the menu as well as soups, sandwiches, snacks, and packaged meals to go.

4631 boul. St-Laurent (north of av. du Mont-Royal). www.auxvivres.com. Ⓒ **514/842-3479.** Most items under C$15. Cash only. Mon–Fri 11am–11pm; Sat–Sun 10am–11pm. Métro: Mont-Royal.

Bilboquet ★★ DESSERT   Slowly and surely this little ice cream joint has been taking over Montréal. The more artful and fitting term for it is an *artisan glacier,* and it's the real deal of handmade ice cream and sorbet, with no powder flavor additives. This Outrement location is the original and out of the typical tourist's geographic reach, but there are now six additional storefronts, including one on Plateau Mont-Royal at 1600 Laurier east (Ⓒ **514/439-6501**). But let's get to the good part: the flavors. Maple taffy, honey lavender, cassis

Ice cream cake from Le Bilboquet

sorbet (seedless) raspberry, and moka-fouilli (chocolate and coffee ice cream with bits of salty caramel crunch), to name a few. Select restaurants and kiosks in the heart of Vieux-Port also serve Bilboquet ice cream in warm months.

1311 rue Bernard ouest (at av. Outremont). www.bilboquet.ca. Ⓒ **514/276-0414.** Most ice cream under C$8. Cash only. March–mid-May daily 11am–9pm; Summer daily 11am–midnight; Mid-Sept–Dec daily 11am–9pm. Closed Jan–Mar. Métro: Outremont.

Fairmount Bagel ★★★ BAKERY   There's only so much convincing one can do: Visitors must try a bagel while in Montréal! It's a whole different ballgame from bagels elsewhere. Bagels here are thinner and closer to a soft pretzel in appearance, as compared to the fluffy stand-ins you may be used to. Bakers hand-roll each bagel from an enormous slab of dough, then they're dropped in boiling water sweetened with a touch of honey, and baked in big wood-fired ovens on the premises. Poppy seed is the original flavor, though sesame may be the most popular. Founded in 1919, Fairmount offers nearly 20 types, including the Bozo (three bagels twisted to one, which Fairmount calls "a bagel for lovers"). The shop is small, to go only, but absolutely worth popping in to see the bakers in action. No planning needed since it's always open—24 hours a day, 7 days a week—even on Jewish holidays.

74 av. Fairmount ouest (near rue St-Urbain). www.fairmountbagel.com. ✆ **514/272-0667.** Most bagels under C$1. Cash only. Daily 24 hr. Métro: Laurier.

Green Panther ★★ VEGAN   This sunny vegan and vegetarian pita spot has something called "hippie sauce" on the menu. Need we say more? Now in three locations (the others are downtown at 2153 Mackay, ✆ **514/903-4744;** and on the Plateau at 145 Mont-Royal est, ✆ **514/503-4800**), Green Panther does veggies up right with traditional falafel and a variety of other healthy combos, with a choice of healthy-sounding sauces, or tahini, or the aforementioned "hippie." Kombucha and other organic beverages are available as well as vegan baked goods and smoothies. *Note:* The soundtrack may be all Bob Marley.

160 St-Viateur (near rue St-Urbain). www.thegreenpanther.com. ✆ **514/508-5564.** Most items less than C$8. Cash only. Mon–Sat 11am–10pm; Sun 11am–9pm. Métro: Rosemont or Laurier.

Magpie Pizzeria ★ PIZZA   Come to Magpie for wood-fired pizza in a rustically hip atmosphere. Schoolhouse-style chairs surround thick pine tables and industrial pendants light the space. Simplicity rules the menu with Italian-sourced and fresh ingredients. Choose from nine different thin-crust options with mouth-watering toppings like caramelized onions and ricotta, and always a 'Za of the week. It's fine to bring kids (service is friendly, but can be slow) and adults can opt to make a meal of oysters, salad, and charcuterie if they're pizza-ed out. In addition to a beer and wine list, the aperitifs include Chinotto punch and a house Bloody Mary. Unlike most pizza joints, this one is serious about dessert. *Tarte tatin* with lemon *crème anglaise* over almond shortbread/ Yes, please! In 2014 a second location opened in the Village at 1237 rue Amherst, ✆ **514/544-2900.** Reservations recommended.

16 rue Maguire (near boul. St-Laurent). www.pizzeriamagpie.com. ✆ **514/507-2900.** Pizzas C$13–C$19. Tues–Fri 11:30am–3pm and 5:30–11pm; Sat 5:30–11pm; Sun 5:30–10pm. Métro: Laurier.

St-Viateur Bagel & Café ★★ BAKERY/LIGHT FARE   Myer Lewko-wicz brought his bagel recipe from eastern Europe in 1957 and St-Viateur's many outposts still follow it to a T. Like **Fairmount Bagel** (above), the process includes shaping each bagel by hand, dressing with seeds or spices, and baking in a wood-fired oven (a great photo spread of this is on the St-Viateur website). Let's be clear: both bakeries make darn good bagels, though some locals would stake their fortune on one versus the other. In addition to taking bagels to go, at this location you can eat in and enjoy bagel sandwiches, soup, or salad. The original, flagship bakery is still at 263 rue St-Viateur ouest in the Mile End neighborhood. As a sign of the evolving times, St-Viateur has joined the food-truck revolution and is on Twitter @StViateurBagel.

1127 av. du Mont-Royal est (at av. Christophe-Colomb). www.stviateurbagel.com. ✆ **514/528-6361.** Most items under C$13; bagels are C$1 each. Cash only. Daily 6am–10pm. Métro: Mont-Royal.

Wilensky Light Lunch ★★ DINER   The thought that comes to mind when you step through the doors here is "time travel." Every year that Wilensky's adds to its history, the more devoted people become to it's remaining exactly as-is. The interior is spare and so, well, 1952. That's when it moved to this locale, though Harry Wilensky started the business in 1932. Either way, it's not hard to imagine the Jewish immigrants who used to sit at one of nine counter stools and order a Moe, better known as The Special: a grilled, all-beef salami and bologna with mustard. It's a crowd-pleaser to present day, largely because it's one of the few menu items to choose from. (*Insider tip:* Don't ask to hold the mustard and don't ask to have your sandwich cut in two.) The old prices are still on the wall and the new prices remain miraculously low. Another miracle/ Genuine, old-time egg cream or cherry cola sodas made in house.

34 rue Fairmount ouest (1 block west of boul. St-Laurent). www.wilenskys.com. ✆ **514/271-0247.** All items less than C$5. Cash only. Mon–Fri 9am–4pm; Sat 10am–4pm. Métro: Laurier.

GAY VILLAGE

Expensive

Mezcla ★★★ SOUTH AMERICAN   Word spread like wildfire when this *nuevo latino* bistro opened in 2012. It could've been the novelty—to prepare traditional Peruvian recipes with European cooking techniques—but more likely it was the outstanding results. Start with a Pisco Sour, a South American cocktail topped with egg white, a rare treat since this city is still catching on to the cocktail renaissance. If ordering a la carte, the ceviche, served with mix-ins of spicy fried corn, yucca, and carrot (*mezcla* is Spanish for mixture) is a must. But a majority of the mature and smartly dressed patrons order the C$39 five-course tasting menu, which includes two seafood dishes (all from environmentally responsible fisheries) and two meats. Thin slices of veal tongue arrive with truffled peaches and a concoction of lime, maple, black sesame, and aji Amarillo—a pepper unique to Peru and frequently used by this kitchen. Servers astutely describe each course and leave ample time in between. For better or worse, voices carry in this relaxed space, making a weeknight feel like Saturday. Reservations are strongly recommended. Mezcla is tucked away in an unexpected spot for a restaurant, and finding it will require dedication. It's worth it.

1251 rue de Champlain (at rue Sainte-Rose). www.restaurantmezcla.com. © **514/525-9934.** Main courses C$26–C$39; 5- or 7-course tasting menu C$39–C$59. Wed–Fri 11:30am–2:30pm and 5:30–10:45pm; Sat 5:30–10:45pm. Métro: Papineau.

LITTLE BURGUNDY

The restaurant listed here anchors a several-blocks-long strip of new restaurants and bars in this neighborhood west of Vieux-Montréal (you'll want to take a cab or the Métro). Other options within a few blocks are the **Le Vin Papillon,** 2519 rue Notre-Dame ouest (www.vinpapillon.com; no phone), by the same owners behind Joe Beef (see below); the bar **Drinkerie,** 2661 rue Notre-Dames ouest (www.drinkerie.ca; © **514/439-2364**) and British-style pub **Burgundy Lion,** 2496 rue Notre-Dame ouest (www.burgundylion.com; © **514/934-0888**); and the chichi pâtisserie and wine bar **Patrice,** 2360 rue Notre-Dame St ouest (www.patricepatissier.ca; © **514/439-5434**).

Expensive

Joe Beef ★★ SEAFOOD/STEAKHOUSE   Foodies will have heard of the glutton-creating Joe Beef before arriving in Montréal, and it's likely that some of them will have planned their trip around dining here. Co-founder David McMillan and the restaurant—think boisterous diner with adventurous food—have been profiled everywhere since the 2005 opening. Many guests start with oysters or the Foie Gras Double Down: two slabs of deep-fried foie gras sandwiching bacon, cheddar, and maple syrup (no one seems to care that *Food & Wine* magazine quoted McMillan saying that the dish was a joke that took on a life of its own). The menu often includes chicken, grits, and crayfish; cornflake sturgeon nuggets; and *saucisse de lapin* (rabbit and pork sausage). The restaurant describes itself as "an homage to Charles 'Joe-Beef' McKiernan, 19th-century innkeeper and Montréal working class hero" and "a drunken crawl away from the Historic Atwater market."

2491 rue Notre-Dame ouest (near rue Vinet). www.joebeef.ca. © **514/935-6504.** Main courses C$19–C$50. Tues–Sat 6pm–late. Métro: Lionel-Groulx.

EXPLORING MONTRÉAL

Montréal is a feast of choices, able to satisfy the desires of active and culturally curious visitors. Hike up the city's mountain, Mont Royal, in the middle of the city; cycle for miles beside 19th-century warehouses and locks on the Lachine Canal; take in artworks and ephemera at more than 30 museums and as many historic buildings; attend a Canadiens hockey game; party until dawn on rue Crescent, The Main, or in Vieux-Montréal; or soak up the history of 400 years of conquest and immigration. It's all here for the taking.

Getting from hotels to attractions is easy. Montréal has an efficient Métro system, a popular bike-share program, a logical street grid, and wide boulevards that all aid in the largely uncomplicated movement of people from place to place.

If you're planning to check out several museums, consider buying the Montréal Museums Pass (see "Money Savers" on p. 108). *Tip:* Some museums have good restaurants or cafes. Remember, too, that most museums—though not all—are closed on Mondays.

MONTRÉAL'S ICONIC SIGHTS

Montréal Attractions

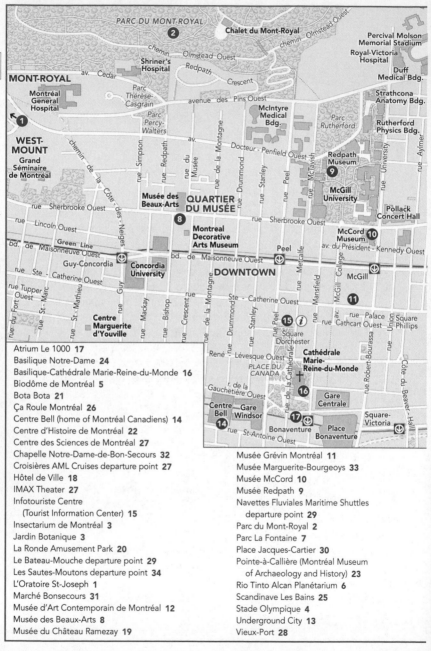

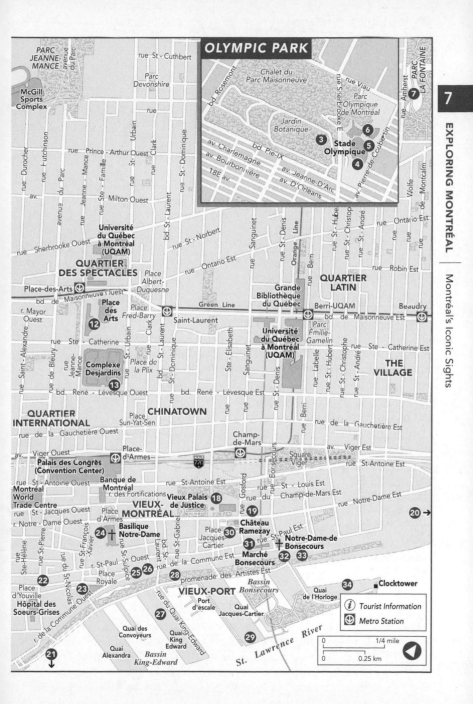

OTHER TOP ATTRACTIONS

DOWNTOWN ATTRACTIONS

If this is your first trip to Montréal, consider starting with the downtown walking tour in chapter 9 and taking in the view from the new observatory atop the **Place Ville-Marie** office building. The observatory is scheduled to open in early 2016 and will include panoramic views of the city, a restaurant, a permanent exhibition about Montréal, and all-season terraces. See p. 155.

Basilique-Cathédrale Marie-Reine-du-Monde Montréal's "Mary Queen of the World" cathedral is a scaled-down homage to St. Peter's Basilica in Rome. Bishop Ignace Bourget oversaw its construction after the first Catholic cathedral here burned to the ground in 1852. Most impressive is the 76m-high (249-ft.) dome, about a third of the size of the Italian original. The statues standing on the roofline represent patron saints of the Québec region, providing a local touch. The interior is less rewarding visually than the exterior, but the ceiling and high altar are worth a look.

1085 rue de la Cathédrale (at rue Mansfield). www.cathedralecatholiquedemontreal.org. ✆ **514/866-1661.** Free admission; donations accepted. Daily 6:30am–7pm. Métro: Bonaventure.

Montréal Canadiens Hockey ★ The city's beloved hockey team plays downtown at the Centre Bell arena. The Canadiens have won 24 Stanley Cups (the most of any team, although the most recent was in 1992–93). The season runs from October to April, with playoff games potentially continuing through May. A Hall of Fame in the arena basement includes a life-size replica of the 1976–77 Canadiens dressing room; entrance fees are C$11 for ages 17 and older, C$8 for seniors and children 5 to 16, and C$6 for all game-day ticket holders.

Centre Bell arena, 1909 av. des Canadiens-de-Montréal (at rue de la Montagne). www.
canadiens.com. ℰ **877/668-8269** or 514/790-2525 (Hall of Fame 514/925-7777). Game
tickets C$22–C$439. Métro: Bonaventure or Lucien-L'Allier.

Musée d'Art Contemporain de Montréal ★★

The Museum of Contemporary Art revels in the eclectic. Two or three exhibitions are usually open (check the website for current offerings), and they most often include not just artwork hanging on the walls but video installations, digital robotic arts, or studio glass creations as well. An outdoor sculpture garden is open from May through October. The museum has a restaurant (lunch Tues–Fri, dinner Thurs–Sat) and an appealing boutique with many items handmade by Québec artisans.

185 rue Ste-Catherine ouest. www.macm.org. ℰ **514/847-6226.** Admission C$14
adults, with discounts for students and seniors; free for children 12 and under; half-
price Wed 5–9pm. Tues 11am–6pm; Wed–Fri 11am–9pm; Sat–Sun 10am–6pm (check
website for frequent changes for holidays). Métro: Place-des-Arts.

Musée des Beaux-Arts ★★★

In recent years, Montréal's glorious Museum of Fine Arts has undergone dramatic new growth, sprouting new buildings and taking over an adjacent church. What was once one building on the north side of rue Sherbrooke is now a sprawling complex on both sides of the city's grand boulevard. A new four-level pavilion devoted to the Old Masters is in the works and is slated to open by 2017, to coincide with Montréal's 375th anniversary celebrations. All this enhances the museum's position as tops in the province. One caveat: The permanent collection used to be free, but that changed in 2014. Still, if you can get to only one museum on your trip, make it this one. Popular recent shows have included the dazzling glassworks of Dale Chihuly, the jewel-like Russian Fabergé eggs, and the art of Morocco.

Be sure to make time for the museum's pavilion of Québécois and Canadian Art. The collection of more than 2,000 pieces includes 500 Inuit works and 180 Amerindian artifacts displayed on six levels. Particularly engaging is the "Age of the Manifesto" gallery, featuring modernist works from the 1940s through 1960s by important Québécois including Alfred Pellan, Paul-Émile Borduas, and Jean-Paul Riopelle.

The museum also inaugurated the Bourgie Concert Hall inside an 1894 church as part of the 2011 renovation. The hall features 20 Tiffany stained-glass windows. The church/concert hall is only open to visitors on tours (infrequent; check the website) or when attending a concert.

A street-level museum store, **M Boutique and Bookstore,** has an impressive selection of exhibition and signature products. Bistro **Café des Beaux-Arts** is an elegant dining option to contrast the more modest cafeteria.

1380 rue Sherbrooke ouest (at rue Crescent). www.mmfa.qc.ca. ℰ **514/285-2000.**
Admission to permanent collection C$12 adults 31 and over, free for ages 30 and
under; free for adults 65 and over on Thurs. Admission to temporary exhibitions
(includes entrance to permanent collection) C$20 adults 31 and over, C$12 ages 13–30,
free for children 12 and under. Wed 5–9pm C$10 ages 13 and up. Tues–Sun 10am–5pm
plus Wed until 9pm. Métro: Guy-Concordia.

Exhibits at the Musée des Beaux Arts range from the Old Masters to rare Québécois artists.

Musée Grévin Montréal ★★   An offshoot of the popular Musée Grévin wax museum in Paris, this Canada-rich version opened in 2013 and has become a top attraction. This is no stodgy dust-laden relic: Instead, you enter through a long dimly lit hallway with thousands of color-changing fiber optic threads hanging from the ceiling and eerie music playing. In an atmospherically fantastical room, a 5-minute 3D movie of psychedelic nature scenes and booming music that rattles the floor sets the stage. The goal is to disorient you from the outside world as you enter an alternate reality. Once inside, sound effects and music play overhead as you visit with lifelike replicas of figures grouped by theme. The focus is heavy on Canadian personalities, such as hockey greats Wayne Gretzky, Mario Lemieux, and Guy Lafleur, and historic New France characters dating back to Québec's beginnings in the 16th century, such as Jacques Cartier and Paul Chomedey de Maisonneuve. In The Ballroom, entertainers including Lady Gaga, Céline Dion, Brad Pitt, and Elvis Presley fill a star-studded room that feels like an Academy Awards gala (albeit a gala with one foot in the afterworld). Other rooms feature John Lennon and Yoko Ono in their 1969 "bed-in" at Montréal's Fairmont hotel, Nelson Mandela, and Canadian astronaut Julie Payette—among 120 others. If you're traveling with kids below age 5, we recommend having a backup plan—we've witnessed several young children get spooked by the unmoving but extremely lifelike statues.

705 rue Ste-Catherine ouest (inside the Montréal Eaton Centre). www.grevin-montreal. com. © **514/788-5211.** Admission C$19.50 adults, with discounts for students and seniors; C$13.50 for children ages 6–12; free for children 5 and under. Mon–Sat 10am–6pm; Sun 11am–5pm. Access to museum closes 1 hour before closing. Métro: McGill.

Musée McCord ★★   This museum is fresh at each visit. Yet it boasts two appealing permanent exhibitions: "Montréal: Points of View," touching on the lives of first inhabitants and the spirit of the city today, and "Wearing Our Identity: The First People's Collection," which presents a respectful look at the relationship of the region's First Nations to their clothing, which often is made of animal pelts. Temporary exhibitions are edgier and recently included the first major retrospective fashion photographer Horst (a frequent contributor to *Vogue* in the 20th century) and a collection of "queer baroque" ceramics works. The museum recently added a collection of online exhibits that gives a taste of its playful voice and point of view. A strong museum shop features locally made bags and jewelry, aboriginal artwork, and children's toys. Each exhibition is small, and won't take most visitors more than 15 minutes each, but at least two temporary shows are usually on in addition to the two permanent displays.

690 rue Sherbrooke ouest (at rue University). www.mccord-museum.qc.ca. © **514/398-7100.** Admission C$15 adults, C$12 seniors, C$9 students, free for children 12 and under; free admission Wed 5–9pm. Tues and Thurs–Fri 10am–6pm; Wed 10am–9pm; Sat–Sun 10am–5pm. Also open occasional Mon 10am–6pm (holidays and summer). Métro: McGill.

Musée Redpath   Run by McGill University, this old-time museum focuses on natural history and is best known for its Egyptian collection—including mummies and a sarcophagus—and a small display of fully constructed dinosaur skeletons. It's the kind of stuff kids love (although note that it doesn't have ramps or elevators and is therefore not accessible to strollers or wheelchairs). There's an impressive collection of minerals from Québec province and a geological garden displaying examples of minerals and fossils from all parts of Canada. The museum is in a nice part of downtown on the McGill campus.

859 rue Sherbrooke ouest (rue University). www.mcgill.ca/redpath. © **514/398-4086.** Free admission (contributions of C$5 adults and C$2 children suggested). Mon–Fri 9am–5pm; Sun 11am–5pm (summer Sun 1–5pm). Closed Saturdays, public holidays, and most long weekends. Métro: McGill.

Shopping in Downtown

Among locals, shopping ranks right up there with dining out as a prime activity. Many Montréalers are of French ancestry, after all, and impeccable taste must bubble up through the Gallic gene pool. The city has produced a thriving fashion industry, from couture to ready-to-wear, with a history that reaches back to the earliest trade in furs and leather.

MONEY savers

○ **Buy the Montréal Museums Pass.** This pass grants entry to over 40 museums and attractions, including many of those mentioned in this chapter. The C$80 pass is good for 3 consecutive days plus unlimited access to public transportation (including the airport shuttle, bus no. 747); the C$75 pass is good for any 3 days within a 3 week period and does not include public transport. Look for the pass at museums or the tourist office at 1255 rue Peel (downtown). Info is online at www.montrealmuseums.org.

○ **Visit La Vitrine for last-minute ticket deals.** Regular priced and same-day discount tickets for a huge variety of cultural events (concerts, theater, comedy) are available online at www.lavitrine. com and at La Vitrine's high-tech ticketing center at 2 Ste-Catherine est (℃ **866/924-5538** or 514/285-4545).

○ **Flash your AAA card.** Members of the American Automobile Association (AAA) get the same discounts as members of its Canadian sister organization, the CAA. That includes reduced rates at many museums, hotels, and restaurants.

○ **Time your trip to coincide with the free Montréal Museums Day.** On a Sunday in late May, over 30 museums welcome visitors for free in a citywide open house. Free shuttle buses help ferry people between the venues. Visit www.montrealmuseums.

THE BEST BUYS

The province's daring **high-fashion designers** produce appealing clothing at prices that are often reasonable. Superbly constructed **furs and leather goods** that recall Montréal's long history as part of the fur trade remain high-ticket items. While not cheap, **Canadian Inuit sculptures** and 19th- to early-20th-century **country furniture** are handsome and authentic. Less expensive crafts are also available, including quilts and drawings by First Nation and other folk artists, and jewelry and craftwork by local artisans.

THE BEST SHOPPING AREAS

In downtown, **rue Sherbrooke** is a major high-end shopping street, with international and domestic designers, luxury shops, art galleries, and the high-end **Holt Renfrew** department store (1300 rue Sherbrooke ouest, at rue de la Montagne). Also downtown, **rue Ste-Catherine** is home to the city's department stores and mid-priced shopping—it's the central, crowded commercial artery. From the cross street rue Aylmer, where the department store **La Baie** is located, Ste-Catherine heading west offers a 12-block stretch of stores that includes super-high-end jeweler **Henry Birks,** the moderately priced **Simons** department store, and the swank **Ogilvy** department store, where a bagpiper still announces the noon hour amid glowing chandeliers and wide aisles. International labels including **Zara, Kiehl's,** and **H&M** are all represented. Streets are crowded, and the atmosphere can be frenetic. *Note:* Ste-Catherine also has a smattering of adult strip clubs and sex shops (usually on the second floor) right alongside the family-friendly fare; the street's mixed use is a Montréal signature.

DOWNTOWN'S UNDERGROUND CITY

A unique shopping opportunity is the **underground city,** also known as the underground pedestrian network and officially called RÉSO (from *réseau,* which means network in French). It's a mish-mash of passageways connecting shopping malls and some 1,700 stores. Most of the malls have floors both at street level and below ground. The network also connects to most subway stations downtown.

Typical of the malls is the **Complexe Desjardins** (www.complexe desjardins.com; ☎ **514/281-1870**), in the heart of downtown. It has entrances at both street level and underground, and is bounded by boulevard René-Lévesque and rues Ste-Catherine, St-Urbain, and Jeanne-Mance. Inside are fountains, trees and hanging vines, lanes of 110 shops that head in every direction, a fast-food court that can accommodate 1,000 people, and a social schedule that includes fairs, exhibits, and concerts.

Navigating the underground city is a challenge: Maps, signage, and even numbering of levels can differ from one section to the next. The main thing to remember is that when you enter a street-level shopping emporium downtown, it's likely that you'll be able to descend to a lower level and connect to the tunnels and shopping hallways that lead to another set of stores.

FAVORITE DOWNTOWN STORES

We love **bookstores** (naturally) and many of our favorites are downtown: **Archambault** specializes in children's books along with CDs and musical instruments. Its largest store and the historic location which opened in 1930 is at 500 rue Ste-Catherine est, at rue Berri (www.archambault.ca; ☎ **514/849-6201**); it's also at Place des Arts at 1501 rue Jeanne-Mance (☎ **514/281-0367**). **Indigo Musique & Café** has a street-level store in Place Montréal Trust, and operates a cafe upstairs, at 1500 av. McGill College (at rue Ste-Catherine; www.chapters.indigo.ca; ☎ **514/281-5549**).

Guilde Canadienne des Métiers d'Art ★   In English, it's called the Canadian Guild of Crafts. The meticulously arranged gallery displays a well-curated collection of items, including blown glass, tapestries, and wooden bowls. The store is particularly strong in avant-garde jewelry and Inuk sculpture. A small carving might be had for C$100 to C$300, while larger, more important pieces go for thousands. 1460 rue Sherbrooke ouest (near rue Mackay), downtown. www.canadianguild.com. ☎ **866/477-6091.**

VIEUX-MONTRÉAL ATTRACTIONS

Vieux-Montréal's central plaza is **Place Jacques-Cartier,** a one-time fruit and vegetable market and the focus of much activity in the warm months. The plaza consists of two repaved streets bracketing a center promenade that slopes down from rue Notre-Dame to Old Port, with venerable stone buildings from the 1700s along both sides. Horse-drawn carriages gather at the plaza's base, and outdoor cafes, street performers, and flower sellers recall a Montréal of a century ago. Locals insist they would never go to a place so overrun by tourists—which makes one wonder why so many of them do, in fact, congregate here. They soak up the sun and sip sangria on the terraces nearly as much as visitors do, enjoying the unfolding pageant.

If this is your first trip to Montréal, consider the **Vieux-Montréal walking tour** in chapter 9. It leads past most of the sites listed here and can help you get your bearings.

Basilique Notre-Dame ★★★ Breathtaking in the richness of its interior furnishings and big enough to hold 4,000 worshipers, this magnificent structure was designed in 1824 by James O'Donnell, an Irish-American Protestant architect from New York—who was so profoundly moved by the experience that he converted to Catholicism after its completion. The impact is understandable. Of Montréal's hundreds of churches, Notre-Dame's interior is the most stunning, with a wealth of exquisite details, most of it carved from rare woods that have been delicately gilded and painted. O'Donnell, clearly a proponent of the Gothic Revival style, is the only person honored by burial in the crypt. The main altar was carved from linden wood, the work of Québécois architect Victor Bourgeau. Behind it is the **Chapelle Sacré-Coeur (Sacred Heart Chapel),** much of which was destroyed by an arsonist in 1978; it was rebuilt and rededicated in 1982. The altar displays 32 bronze panels representing birth, life, and death, cast by Montréal artist Charles Daudelin. A 10-bell carillon resides in the east tower, while the west tower contains a single massive bell, nicknamed **"Le Gros Bourdon,"** which weighs more than 12 tons and emanates a low, resonant rumble that vibrates right up through your feet. Choirs both well known and more modest give concerts here, and legendary tenor Luciano Pavarotti performed his famous Christmas concert here in 1978. French-Canadian songstress Céline Dion had her Cinderella wedding here in 1994.

110 rue Notre-Dame ouest (on Place d'Armes). www.basiliquenddm.org. ⓒ **514/842-2925.** Basilica C$5 adults, C$4 children 7–17, free for children 6 and under; includes optional 20-min. guided tour. Daily at least 7:30am–4pm, with longer summer hours; details online. Métro: Place d'Armes.

Bota Bota ★ Housed in a converted boat docked on the far western end of Vieux-Port, Bota Bota's highly modern, all-season spa offers a luxurious water circuit of dry saunas, steam rooms, and three Jacuzzis, two of which are outside and offer stunning northern views of the Old Port. You can also come for relaxing body treatments in one of the many well-appointed private rooms or enjoy a manicure or pedicure in the boat's bow that also gives lovely views through its panoramic windows. Access to the boat's water circuit starts at C$35 (depending on time of day) for 3 hours in all the water facilities, lounges, and bistro. An extension—onto dry land—opened in 2015 and includes an infinity pool and gardens.

The boat is docked in the water near the corner of rue de la Commune ouest and rue McGill. www.botabota.ca. (C) **855/284-0333** or 514/284-0333. Mon–Thurs 10am–10pm, Fri–Sun 9am–10pm. Métro: Square-Victoria.

Centre d'Histoire de Montréal ★

Formerly a fire station, this 1903 building at Place d'Youville is now a well-run museum chronicling the history of Montréal. Its permanent exhibit covers Montréal's beginnings in the 16th-century all the way through to the modern day. You'll learn about the native people who first inhabited the region, the effect of European settlement, and how the city continues to advance while still looking back to its storied past. A well-curated collection of domestic artifacts spans the 20th-century through today.

335 Place d'Youville (at rue St-Pierre). www.ville.montreal.qc.ca/chm. (C) **514/872-3207.** Admission C$6 adults, with discounts for students, children, and seniors; free for children 5 and under. Wed–Sun 10am–5pm. Métro: Square-Victoria.

Centre des Sciences de Montréal ★★

The Montréal Science Centre is a family-friendly complex that approaches science and technology in a hands-on way. Some of its programming is geared toward children and young teens (a show about sex was extremely straightforward and popular), while other exhibits will tap the inner kid in all visitors, such as the recent show that revisited the history of video games and included 100 games and consoles. The permanent exhibition "Clic!" is really just a play space for younger children; the museum says it's for 4–7 year olds but our 2 year old was so happy running around here that we returned for a second visit soon after. Also onsite is an **IMAX theater** (p. 129) and a small gift shop. An international food court is next door and, in summertime, a mall of boutiques aligns the building.

2 rue de la Commune ouest, on Quai King Edward, Vieux-Port. www.montrealscience centre.com. (C) **877/496-4724** or 514/496-4724. Admission C$21 adults, C$18 ages 13–17 and 60+; C$12 ages 4–12; free for children 3 and under; C$58 family package. Admission to permanent exhibitions only C$4–C$6 less per ticket. Daily at least 10am–4pm; check website for extended hours, which change. Métro: Place d'Armes or Champ-de-Mars.

Chapelle Notre-Dame-de-Bon-Secours/Musée Marguerite-Bourgeoys ★

Just to the east of the indoor market complex Marché Bonsecours is Notre-Dame-de-Bon-Secours Chapel. This petite outpost is called the Sailors' Church because of the special attachment that fishermen and other mariners have to it. Their devotion is manifest in the several ship models hanging from the ceiling inside. Additionally, you get an excellent view of the harbor from the church's tower.

The first building, which no longer stands, was the project of an energetic teacher named Marguerite Bourgeoys (1620–1700) and built in 1675. Bourgeoys had come from France to undertake the education of the children of the colonists and, later, the native peoples. She and other teachers founded the

Congregation of Notre-Dame, Canada's first nuns' order. The pioneering Bourgeoys was canonized in 1982 as the Canadian church's first female saint, and in 2005, for the chapel's 350th birthday, her remains were brought to the church and interred in the left-side altar.

A restored 18th-century crypt under the chapel houses the museum. Part of it is devoted to relating Bourgeoys's life and work, while another section displays artifacts from an archaeological site here, including ruins and materials from the colony's earliest days. An Amerindian campsite on display dates back more than 2,400 years.

400 rue St-Paul est (at the foot of rue Bonsecours). www.marguerite-bourgeoys.com. © 514/282-8670. Free admission to chapel. Museum (includes archaeological site) C$10 adults, C$7 seniors and students, C$5 kids ages 6–12, free for children 5 and under. C$20 families. May to mid-Oct Tues–Sun 10am–5:30pm; mid-Oct to mid-Jan and Mar–April 11am–3:30pm. Closed mid-Jan through Feb. Métro: Champ-de-Mars.

Hôtel de Ville   City Hall, finished in 1878 (and then burned to the ground in a 1922 fire and rebuilt), is relatively young by Vieux-Montréal standards, and it's still in use, with the mayor's office on the main floor. The French Second Empire design makes it look as though it was imported, stone by stone, from the mother country: Balconies, turrets, and mansard roofs decorate the exterior. The details are particularly visible when the exterior is illuminated at night. The Hall of Honour is made of green marble from Campan, France, and houses Art Deco lamps from Paris and a bronze-and-glass chandelier, also from France, that weighs a metric ton. It was from the balcony above the awning that, in 1967, an ill-mannered Charles de Gaulle, then president of France, proclaimed, *"Vive le Québec Libre!"* ("Long live free Québec!")—a gesture that pleased his immediate audience, but strained relations with the Canadian government for years.

275 rue Notre-Dame est (at the corner of rue Gosford). www.ville.montreal.qc.ca. © 514/872-0311. Free admission. Mon–Fri 8:30am–5pm. Closed public holidays. Métro: Champ-de-Mars.

Marché Bonsecours   Bonsecours Market is an imposing neoclassical building with a long façade, a colonnaded portico, and a silvery dome that can be seen from many parts of Vieux-Montréal. It was built in the mid-1800s— the Doric columns of the portico were cast of iron in England—and first used as the Parliament of United Canada, and then as Montréal's City Hall until 1878. The architecture alone makes a brief visit worthwhile. For many years after 1878, it served as the city's central meat market. Essentially abandoned for much of the 20th century, it was restored in 1964 to house city government offices. Today it anchors the eastern end of rue St-Paul and contains restaurants, art galleries, and boutiques of Québécois products. The building also has public restrooms.

350 rue St-Paul est (at the foot of rue St-Claude). www.marchebonsecours.qc.ca. © 514/872-7730. Free admission. Fall–spring daily 10am–6pm; summer daily 10am–9pm. Métro: Champ-de-Mars.

Musée du Château Ramezay ★ Named for Claude de Ramezay, governor of Montréal from 1704 to 1724, this château was built in 1705. It served as home to Ramezay and then the city's other governors until it was sold in the mid-1700s. It became the local headquarters to the American Continental Army in 1775 when revolutionary forces took control of the city from the British. Benjamin Franklin stayed here for a time in 1776 as he tried to convince the Québécois to side with the Americans in revolt against the British—to no avail. The building was subsequently used for a variety of purposes, including home to the English governors of Lower Canada, as a faculty building for Laval University's school of medicine, and as a government office building. In 1895, it was turned into a museum, and today it provides an excellent primer on the history of Montréal. In summertime, costumed interpreters talk about what life was like in early Montréal. Other features include a historically accurate garden of medicinal herbs, vegetables, and ornamental flowers popular around the time the château was built, and a cafe with a garden terrace open for lunch during summer. Several permanent exhibits are worth taking in, including one that outlines what life was like in the city in the 18th century.

280 rue Notre-Dame est. www.chateauramezay.qc.ca. ⓒ **514/861-3708.** Museum admission C$10 adults, with discounts for students, children, and seniors; free for children 4 and under. Free admission to governor's garden. June to mid-Oct daily 9:30am–6pm; mid-Oct to May Tues–Sun 10am–4:30pm. Cafe June to mid-Sept 11am–2:30pm. Métro: Champ-de-Mars.

Pointe-à-Callière (Montréal Museum of Archaeology and History) ★★★

Several Montréal museums provide a thorough history of the city, but none quite match the heft of this one. For starters, Pointe-à-Callière consists of six buildings spread out exactly where the original colonists settled in the 1640s and is a bona fide archaeological site. Permanent exhibits include a multimedia show and self-guided tour through the heart of the building. Underground tunnels wind their way to the Custom House, and along the path are centuries-old foundations of the original buildings that once stood here. Illuminated displays show off artifacts found during the excavations that took place, as well as the city's first Catholic cemetery, dating to 1643. The design of the newest building—the Éperon building—is a perfect example of contrasts, with a contemporary exterior and triangular shape reminiscent of the Victorian-era Royal Insurance building that stood here until 1951. Much of the museum is better for adults than children, but a new "Archaeo-Adventure" space opened in 2012 in the museum's Mariners' House, targeting kids 8 to 14; it simulates an archaeological dig for children and families, including a chance to role-play in the head archaeologist's tent and lab space. The well-regarded top-floor cafe offers great views (lunch and weekend brunch only). To sample the museum's collection online, search for it at www.google.com/artproject.

350 Place Royale (at rue de la Commune). www.pacmusee.qc.ca. ⓒ **514/872-9150.** Admission C$20 adults, with discounts for students, children, and seniors; free for children 5 and under. Tues–Fri 10am–5pm, Sat–Sun 11am–5pm. Métro: Place d'Armes.

Scandinave Les Bains ★ Bath complexes are common throughout Scandinavia, but less so in North America. This center brings Euro-style relaxation-through-water to Montréal. Visitors check in, change into bathing suits, and then have the run of the complex for the visit. There's a warm bath the size of a small swimming pool with jets and a waterfall, a steam room thick with the scent of eucalyptus oil, and a Finnish-style dry sauna. Peppered throughout the hallways are sling-back chairs, and one room is set aside just for relaxing or having a drink from the juice bar. The recommended routine is to heat your body for about 15 minutes, cool down in one of the icy rinse stations, and relax for 15 minutes—and then repeat the circuit a few times. Call to reserve a spot, and inquire about when the spa is emptiest—that's when the routine is most soothing. 71 rue de la Commune ouest. www.scandinave.com. ⓒ **514/288-2009.** Admission C$49 Fri–Sun; C$35 Mon–Thurs. Packages available with massage. Must be 16 or older. Daily 8:30am–9pm. Métro: Champ-de-Mars.

Shopping in Vieux-Montréal

Strolling the cobblestoned **rue St-Paul** in Vieux-Montréal ranks as a highlight for many travelers. The street has the aura of days gone by and is one of the most picturesque corners of Canada. Restaurants, hotels, and some avant-garde fashion and art work line both side of the street. Here are favorite shops in Vieux-Montréal where you can find uniquely Québécois goods:

Galerie Images Boréales Galleries featuring Inuit art are found throughout the city, but few are as accessible as this one, in the heart of Vieux-Montréal. Here, shoppers can find handmade pieces by Inuk artists from Cape Dorset, Lake Harbour, and Baffin Island—carved bears, seals, owls, and tableaus of mothers and children. Pieces range in price from about C$150 to C$25,000 and are certified by the Canadian government. 4 rue St-Paul est (at bd. St-Laurent), Vieux-Montréal. www.imagesboreales.com. ⓒ **514/439-1987.**

Galerie Zone Orange ★ Sleepy-eyed owl pillows, jewelry made from recycled inner tubes, and nifty iPhone cases with original artwork are on display at the small Zone Orange, which also has a teeny espresso bar in its center. Everything sold here is made by independent Québec artists. 410 rue St-Pierre (near rue St-Paul), Vieux-Montréal. http://shop.galeriezoneorange.com. ⓒ **514/510-5809.**

Marché Atwater ★★ Atwater is an important indoor-outdoor daily farmer's market. French in flavor, it has fresh fruits, vegetables, and flowers along with *patisseries, boulangeries, fromageries*, and shops with easy-to-travel-with food. From Vieux-Montréal, it's a 45-minute walk (head west on rue Notre-Dame then turn left at avenue Atwater), a 15-minute bike ride (take rue Notre-Dame or the bike path along the canal), or a Métro trip to Lionel-Groulx. Foodies looking for fresh treats or gifts to take home will want to make a visit here a priority. See p. 88 in chapter 6 for more. 138 av. Atwater (between rue Notre-Dame and the Lachine Canal), west of Vieux-Montréal. www.marche-atwater.com.

CIRQUE DU SOLEIL: MONTRÉAL'S HOMETOWN circus

The whimsical band of artists that became Cirque du Soleil began as street performers in Baie-St-Paul, a river town an hour north of Québec City. These stilt walkers, fire breathers, and musicians had one pure intention: to entertain. The troupe formally founded as Cirque du Soleil (Circus of the Sun) in 1984 has matured into a spectacle like no other. Using human-size gyroscopes, trampoline beds, trapezes suspended from massive chandeliers, and the like, Cirque creates worlds that are spooky, sensual, otherworldly, and beautifully ambiguous. More than 1,300 of the company's acrobats, contortionists, jugglers, clowns, and dancers tour the world, and perform the resident shows in Las Vegas, Orlando, and New York.

The company's offices are in Montréal in the Saint-Michel district, not far beyond the Mile End neighborhood. And they're not just offices. Cirque has been developing a small campus of buildings in this industrial zone since 1997. All new artists come here to train and live in residences onsite. The complex has a dance studio, acrobatic training rooms, workshops where the elaborate costumes and props are made, and a space large enough to erect a circus tent indoors.

The company doesn't have permanent performances in Montréal, although it frequently sets up its signature blue and yellow tents in spring or summer in Vieux-Port for up to 10 weeks. For information about when they're coming to the province (and where else in the world you can find a show), visit **www.cirquedusoleil.com**.

Harricana ★   One designer taking a unique cue from the city's long history with the fur trade is Mariouche Gagné. Her company recycles old fur into funky patchwork garments. A leader in the *ecoluxe* movement, Gagné's workshop-boutique is close to the Marché Atwater (above) and the Lionel-Groulx Métro station. 3000 rue St-Antoine ouest (at av. Atwater), west of Vieux-Montréal. www.harricana.qc.ca.© **877/894-9919** or 514/287 6517.

MONT ROYAL & PLATEAU MONT-ROYAL ATTRACTIONS

The mountain from which the city gets its name, Mont Royal, is a popular public park with woods, paths, and meadows open all four seasons. See p. 158 for a walking tour of the mountain and more details about the park's attractions and history. Wonderful views can be had from the Chalet du Mont-Royal at the mountain's peak, and the front terrace here offers the most popular panoramic view of Montréal and the river. You can also go straight to the top with a taxi ride or bus #11, which runs between Métro stations Mont-Royal and Chemin de la Côte-des-Neiges.

The Plateau Mont-Royal residential neighborhood can be explored on foot or bike. **Fitz & Follwell Co.** (www.fitzandfollwell.co; © **514/840-0739**) offers walking tours and bike tours including a "Hoods & Hidden Gems" (C$95) bike tour around Plateau Mont-Royal and the adjoining neighborhoods Mile End, Little Italy, and Outremont. On the itinerary is a tasting of fresh Montréal bagels, a stop by the Jean-Talon farmer's market (p. 119), and a picnic lunch.

L'Oratoire St-Joseph ★★ This huge Catholic church—dominating Mont Royal's north slope—is seen by some as inspiring, by others as forbidding. It's Montréal's highest point, with an enormous dome 97m (318 ft.) high. Consecrated as a basilica in 2004, it came into being through the efforts of Brother André, a lay brother in the Holy Cross order who earned a reputation as a healer. By the time he had built a small wooden chapel in 1904 on the mountain, he was said to have performed hundreds of cures. His powers attracted supplicants from great distances, and he performed his work until his death in 1937. His dream of building a shrine to honor St. Joseph, patron saint of Canada, became a reality in 1967. In 1982, he was beatified by the pope—a status one step below sainthood—and in 2010 he earned the distinction of sainthood, too. An exhibit was created shortly thereafter to commemorate this honor. There's even a Facebook page in his name maintained by the church, at www.facebook.com/saintfrereandre.

The church is largely Italian Renaissance in style, its giant copper dome recalling the shape of the Duomo in Florence, but of greater size and lesser grace. Inside is a sanctuary and exhibit that displays Brother André's actual heart in a formalin-filled urn. His original wooden chapel, with its tiny bedroom, is on the grounds and open to the public. More than two million pilgrims visit annually, many seeking intercession from St. Joseph and Brother André by climbing the middle set of 99 steps on their knees. The 56-bell carillon plays Wednesday to Friday at noon and 3pm, Saturday at noon at 2:30pm, and Sunday at 12:15 and 2:30pm. Also onsite is an oratory museum featuring over 200 nativity scenes from 111 countries.

Since 2002, the oratory has been implementing a multi-phase renovation project to improve overall accessibility for the ever-increasing number of visitors. Completed projects include a new access road, additional elevators, including one to the basilica, and a full cleaning of the

L'Oratoire St-Joseph attracts pilgrims from around the world.

stained-glass windows. A new visitor's center and an observatory at the top of the basilica's dome are in the works and are expected to be complete by the end of 2017.

3800 chemin Queen Mary (on the north slope of Mont Royal). www.saint-joseph.org. © **877/672-8647** or 514/733-8211. Free admission to most sights, donations requested; oratory museum C$4 adults, C$3 seniors and students, C$2 children 6–17. Oratory museum daily 10am–4:30pm and weekends Jul–Aug till 5:30pm. C$5 for parking. Métro: Côtes-des-Neiges or Snowdon. Bus: 166, 165, or 51.

Shopping in Plateau Mont-Royal (& Mile End)

A trip to the shops in the bohemian Plateau and adjacent Mile End neighborhoods should send you home with a dash of local style. In Plateau Mont-Royal, **rue St-Denis** north of Sherbrooke has blocks of shops filled with fun, funky items. **Boulevard St-Laurent** sells everything from budget practicalities to off-the-wall handmade fashions.

For ritzier offerings, go further north: **Avenue Laurier,** between boulevard St-Laurent and avenue de l'Epée, is home to Parisian boutiques, furniture and accessories shops, and products from the ateliers of young Québécois designers. This is a vibrant, upscale street, with a rich selection of restaurants, too. Pop into **Pâtisserie De Gascogne,** 237 av. Laurier ouest (www.degascogne. com; © **514/490-0235**), for a decadent sweet treat as part of your tour.

Montréal boasts an enviable network of **vintage boutiques**—it's no secret that this is where many of Montréal's artsy style-mavens procure their looks. Many *friperies,* as they're called in French, are scattered in these neighborhoods, especially on boulevard St-Laurent near the cross street avenue Duluth and on **avenue du Mont-Royal** west of rue St-Denis. Also on this street is **Aime Com Moi,** 150 av. du Mont-Royal est (© **514/982-0088**), which offers enticing "créateurs quebécois"—all of its fashionable clothes are from Québec designers.

Other special shops where you can find uniquely Québécois goods:

Arthur Quentin   Doling out household products of quiet taste and discernment since 1975, this St-Denis stalwart sells chic tableware, leather goods, kitchen gadgets, and home decor. That means Le Jacquard Francais French linens and Limoges china, carafes and Le Creuset casseroles, and English tea trays and French barrettes. 3960 rue St-Denis (south of av. Duluth), Plateau Mont-Royal. www.arthurquentin.com. © **514/843-7513.**

Drawn & Quarterly   This Mile End bookstore is a cultural hub, with book launch parties, a graphic novel book club, and food writing workshops. It specializes in graphic novels, including those from its own publishing company, but also has children's books, quirky notecards, and fine arts books. 211 rue Bernard ouest (at rue Jeanne-Mance), Mile End. http://211blog.drawnandquarterly. com. © **514/279-2224.**

Kanuk ★   One of the top Canadian manufacturers of high-end winter jackets makes its clothes right in Montréal and has a warehouse-like factory store in the heart of Plateau Mont-Royal. Like L.L. Bean in the U.S., the first

JEWISH MONTRÉAL: NEIGHBORHOODS, ARTS, & food

At the turn of the 20th century, Montréal was home to more Jewish people than any other Canadian city, attracting a large Yiddish-speaking population from eastern Europe. Today, Toronto has many more Jewish residents, but vestiges of the community's history and ongoing practices remain in Montréal's Plateau, Mile End, and Outremont neighborhoods. Here, places of worship, celebration of Jewish culture through arts, and the so-called bagel-and-smoked-meat wars smolder on, to the delight of local and visiting connoisseurs.

Author Mordecai Richler set most of his books in the working-class Jewish neighborhood of the Plateau of the 1940s and 1950s (his most famous book is *The Apprenticeship of Duddy Kravitz*). The **Bagg Street Shul,** also called Temple Solomon or Congregation Beth Shloime, is the heart of this neighborhood, at 3919 rue Clark (www.baggstreetshul.com; ℭ **514/481-9542**). It began as a two-family residence, was converted to a synagogue in 1920 to 1921, and has been in continuous use ever since. A replica of the old eastern European synagogues of Poland and Ukraine, its interior features robin's-egg-blue walls and paintings of the 12 zodiac signs, labeled in Hebrew—unique for an orthodox shul.

Edibles abound. Start the day with a bagel from either **St-Viateur Bagel &**

Café, at 1127 av. Mont-Royal est, or **Fairmont Bagel,** at 74 av. Fairmont ouest in Mile End. Get a pressed salami and bologna sandwich while traveling back in time at **Wilensky Light Lunch,** 34 rue Fairmount ouest. For dinner, try an unforgettable smoked meat sandwich at **Schwartz's,** 3895 bd. St-Laurent, or opt for a steak at (much) higher end **Moishes,** 3961 bd. St-Laurent. See chapter 7 for details on all the restaurants.

The Snowdon neighborhood in western Montréal is home to the city's contemporary Jewish organizations. The **Jewish Public Library,** 5151 Côte-Ste-Catherine (www.jewishpubliclibrary.org; ℭ **514/345-2627**) has a large circulating collection of Judaica and hosts year-round lectures, readings, and cultural events. Its archive of more than 17,000 photos of Montréal's Jewish history is in the process of being digitized to be put online. The library shares its Cummings House building with the **Montréal Holocaust Memorial Centre** (www.mhmc.ca; ℭ **514/345-2605**) and about a dozen Jewish community-service agencies. Just across the street, at 5170 Côte-Ste-Catherine, is the **Segal Centre for Performing Arts** (www.segalcentre.org; ℭ **514/739-7944**), which presents plays in Yiddish, offers theater workshops, and has film programs.

customers for Kanuk's heavy parkas were outdoor enthusiasts. Today, clientele includes the general public. Heavy-duty winter coats cost nearly C$1,000, but they're extremely popular. More modestly priced winter caps make nice (and cozy) souvenirs. Look, too, for end-of-season sales. 485 rue Rachel est (near rue Berri), Plateau Mont-Royal. www.kanuk.com. ℭ **877/284-4494** or 514/284-4494.

Les Chocolats de Chloé ★ If you approach chocolate the way certain aficionados approach wine or cheese—that is, on the lookout for the best of the best—then the teeny Chocolats de Chloé will bring great delight. Perhaps a cardamom bonbon? Or a pop of "pâte de pistache" enrobed in milk chocolate?

546 rue Duluth est (near rue St-Hubert), Plateau Mont-Royal. www.leschocolatsdechloe.
com. ✆ **514/849-5550.**

Marché Jean-Talon ★★ As with the **Marché Atwater** (earlier in this
chapter), Marché Jean-Talon is a must-visit for food fans looking for a fun
destination. On our most recent visit, we were taken in by the maple butter
chocolate and golden *madeleines*—petite, traditional butter cakes of France—
from **Chocolats Privilège** (✆ **514/276-7070**). The market isn't near any of the
sites or restaurants listed in this guidebook, but it's an easy ride on the
Métro—just head north to the Jean-Talon stop. 7070 av. Henri-Julien (at rue Jean-
Talon est), north of Mile End. www.marche-jean-talon.com.

Raplapla ★ Sweet dolls for infants and young children made from organic
cotton are the specialty of this local company and sold directly from this
studio-boutique. Look for the rectangular-shaped Monsieur Tsé-Tsé doll,
which is soft and adorable and something of an icon for the Montréal hand-
craft movement. 69 rue Villeneuve ouest (at rue St-Urbain), Plateau Mont-Royal. www.
raplapla.com. ✆ **514/563-1209.**

Zone A Québec company with a half dozen locations, this housewares
store features colorful bowls and plates, clocks and frames, furnishings, and
more. Think clean lines of Ikea products, but a step up in style and flair. 4246
rue St-Denis (at rue Rachel est), Plateau Mont-Royal. www.zonemaison.com.
✆ **514/845-3530.**

OLYMPIC PARK ATTRACTIONS

A 20-minute drive east of downtown on rue Sherbrooke or an easy Métro trip
is **Olympic Park,** located in a neighborhood called Hochelaga-Maisonneuve.
It has five attractions: **Stade Olympique** (Olympic Stadium), **Biodôme de
Montréal, Insectarium de Montréal, Jardin Botanique** (Botanical Garden), and the **Rio Tinto Alcan Planétarium.** The latter four attractions are
branded under the name "Espace Pour la Vie," or Space for Life. They share
a website, www.espacepourlavie.ca/en (which is a little more complicated to
navigate than it should be). The venues are all walking distance from each
other. Kids especially love the Biodôme and Insectarium. Combination ticket
packages are available, and entrance to all except the Olympic Stadium are
included in the **Montréal Museum Pass** (see "Money Savers", p. 108). Parking is C$16 (C$20 during stadium events).

Biodôme de Montréal ★★★ A terrifically engaging attraction for
children of nearly any age, the delightful Biodôme houses replicas of four
ecosystems: a tropical rainforest, a Laurentian forest, the St. Lawrence marine
system, and the Labrador Coast and sub-polar regions. Visitors walk through
each and hear the animals, smell the flora, and (except in the polar region,
which is behind glass) feel the changes in temperature. The rainforest area is
the most engrossing (the subsequent rooms increasingly less so), so take your
time there. Animals here include the capybara, which looks like a large guinea

The thick rainforest at the Biodôme de Montréal

pig, and adorable golden lion tamarin monkeys that swing on branches only an arm's length away. Bats, fish, and penguins are behind glass. The facility also has a hands-on activity room called Naturalia, a shop, a bistro, and a cafeteria.

4777 av. Pierre-de-Coubertin (next to Stade Olympique). www.espacepourlavie.ca/en/biodome. © **514/868-3000.** Admission C$19.25 adults, C$17.75 seniors, C$14.25 students, C$9.75 children 5–17. Hours change seasonally; confirm online. Métro: Viau.

Insectarium de Montréal

The Insectarium is part of the Jardin Botanique (below) and admission is included in the (rather steep) joint ticket price for the gardens. If you are already planning a trip to the gardens, this is worth taking in; otherwise, it's pretty small to justify a trip and a ticket on its own. That said, it's the place to be if bugs and spiders make you squirm with delight. Live exhibits show off all sorts of insects from scorpions and tarantulas to ants and hissing cockroaches. Alongside the crawly little creatures are thousands of mounted ones, including butterflies and beetles. An outdoor playground is well designed for children 12 and under.

4581 rue Sherbrooke est. www.espacepourlavie.ca/en/insectarium. © **514/872-1400.** Tickets may only be purchased in a package with the Jardin Botanique (see below). Hours change seasonally; confirm online. Métro: Pie-IX.

Jardin Botanique ★★★

Spread across 75 hectares (185 acres), Montréal's Botanical Garden is a fragrant oasis all year round. The 10 large exhibition greenhouses each have a theme: One houses orchids; another has tropical food and spice plants, including coffee, cinnamon, and ginger; another features rainforest flora. In a special exhibit each spring, live butterflies flutter among the nectar-bearing plants, occasionally landing on visitors. In September, visitors can watch monarch butterflies being tagged and released for their annual migration to Mexico.

Outdoors, spring is when things really kick in: lilacs, tulips, and blooming crabapple trees in May, lilies in June, and roses from mid-June until the first frost. For the last several years, from early September through October, the garden hosted the popular **Gardens of Light** Chinese Lantern Festival, with magical colored lanterns lighting the paths; check the calendar to see if this program is on the current schedule. Otherwise, just take in the **Chinese Garden,** a joint project of Montréal and Shanghai, which evokes the 14th- to 17th-century era of the Ming Dynasty and was built according to the landscape principles of yin and yang. It incorporates pavilions, inner courtyards, ponds, and plants indigenous to China. A serene **Japanese Garden** fills 2.5 hectares (6.25 acres) and has a stone garden, a tea garden used for tea ceremonies, and a stunning bonsai collection with miniature trees as old as 350 years. The wooded **First Nations Garden** highlights native knowledge of plants and the agricultural focus on the "three sisters" of corn, beans, and squash. The grounds are also home to the **Insectarium** (above).

4101 rue Sherbrooke est (opposite Olympic Stadium). www.espacepourlavie.ca/en/ botanical-garden. ✆ **514/872-1400.** Admission C$19.25 adults, C$17.75 seniors, C$14.25 students, C$9.75 children 5–17. includes access to the Insectarium. No bicycles or dogs. Hours change seasonally; confirm online. Métro: Pie-IX.

Crabapple orchard in Jardin Botanique

Rio Tinto Alcan Planétarium ★ The planetarium moved to Olympic Park in 2013 from its long-time location downtown. The planetarium has two theaters: one show is focused on science, and the other is focused on the poetic majesty of the stars. Most shows are in French, but several a day are in English. Architecturally, it's a stunning building, with arcs and curves and a metal exterior that evoke Frank Gehry's Guggenheim Museum Bilbao.

4801 av. Pierre-de Coubertin. www.espacepourlavie.ca/en/planetarium. ⓒ **514/868-3000.** Admission C$19.25 adults, C$17.75 seniors, C$14.25 students, C$9.75 children 5–17. Hours change seasonally; confirm online. Shows begin every half-hour starting from 9:30am; check website for English show times. Métro: Viau.

Stade Olympique Montréal's space-age Olympic Stadium, the centerpiece of the 1976 Olympic Games, continues life as a sporting facility and public stadium. Many tourists come to visit the 165m (541-ft.) inclined tower, a city icon which leans at a 45-degree angle (it looks a bit like a giant stapler) and does duty as an observation deck, with a *funiculaire* that whisks passengers to the top in 2 minutes. On a clear day, the deck bestows an expansive view over Montréal and into the neighboring Laurentian mountains. At C$22.50, though, the admission price is as steep as the tower.

The complex includes a stadium that seats up to 56,000 for sporting events and music concerts (pop supernovas One Direction made a stop in 2015). The Sports Centre was recently renovated after being closed for nearly a year in 2014. It houses swimming pools that are generally open for public swimming and classes. A 20-minute guided "quick tour" describing the 1976 Olympic Games and use of the center today are available daily for C$10. The roof doesn't retract anymore—it never retracted well anyway. That's one reason why "the Big O" was scorned as "the Big Woe" and then "the Big Owe" after cost overruns led to heavy tax increases.

4141 av. Pierre-de-Coubertin. www.parcolympique.qc.ca. ⓒ**877/997-0919** or 514/252-4141. Tower admission C$22.50 adults, C$20.25 seniors, $18 students, C$11.25 children 5–17. Hours change seasonally; confirm online. Métro: Viau.

ORGANIZED TOURS

An introductory guided tour is often the best—or, at least, most efficient—way to begin exploring a new city. It can certainly give you a good lay of the land and overview of Montréal's history.

Most land tours leave from the Square Dorchester, right at the tourist office. Most boat tours depart from Vieux-Port (Old Port), the waterfront bordering Vieux-Montréal. The dock has parking, or take the Métro to the Champ-de-Mars or Square Victoria Station and then walk toward the river.

Walking & Cycling Tours

Guidatour (www.guidatour.qc.ca; ⓒ **800/363-4021** or 514/844-4021) offers a variety of tours for large and small groups that range from 90 minutes to 3½ hours. The 90 minute tours of Vieux-Montréal east (including Notre-Dame

Basilica), and Vieux-Montréal west (also including Notre-Dame) cost C$23 for adults, with discounts for children and seniors. Separate culinary tours of Vieux-Montréal and Little Italy that include food and beverage stops costs C$59. Guidatour also offers bus tours that cover a larger footprint of the city, and bicycle tours in conjunction with **Ça Roule Montréal.** The bicycle tours last 3 to 6 hours, so although they're described as "easy" tours, be sure you're willing and able. The classic tour is C$79, which includes rental of a bike, helmet, and lock for the day. Tours start at the bike shop at 27 rue de la Commune est in Vieux-Port (also see "Bicycling & In-Line Skating," below). Reservations are required.

Fitz & Follwell Co. (www.fitzandfollwell.co; ✆ **514/840-0739**) also offers walking tours and bike tours, and throws in snowshoeing tours as well. The company's "Hoods & Hidden Gems" bike tour zips around Plateau Mont-Royal, Mile End, Little Italy, and Outremont, and includes stops for espresso and bagels. That 4-hour tour costs C$95 and includes a picnic lunch.

Boat Tours

Among numerous opportunities for experiencing Montréal and its environs by water, here are a few of the most popular:

Croisières AML Cruises (www.croisieresaml.com; ✆ **866/856-6668**): One of the more popular cruise operators includes a weekend brunch cruise (C$53 for adults and 17 and older, C$31 children 6–16). Guided history trips run throughout the day, and a fireworks cruise and gourmet dinner cruises run at night. Tours are offered year round. Most boats depart from the Convoyeurs Pier (next to King Edward Pier), in Vieux-Port.

Le Bateau-Mouche (www.bateaumouche.ca; ✆ **800/361-9952** or 514/849-9952): An air-conditioned, glass-enclosed vessel reminiscent of those on the Seine in Paris, Le Bateau-Mouche plies the St. Lawrence River from mid-May to mid-October. The shallow-draft boat takes passengers on a route inaccessible by traditional vessels, passing under several bridges and providing sweeping views of the city, Mont-Royal, and the St. Lawrence and its islands. Cruises run for 60 and 90 minutes, and there's both a breakfast and an evening dinner cruise. The 60-minute tours cost C$25 for adults, with each adult ticket including two children's tickets. The tours depart from the Jacques-Cartier Pier, opposite Place Jacques-Cartier.

Les Sautes-Moutons (also known as **Lachine Rapids Tours;** www. jetboatingmontreal.com; ✆ **514/284-9607**): These tours provide an exciting—and wet—experience. Operating from May through October, wave-jumper powerboats take on the St. Lawrence River's roiling Lachine Rapids. The streamlined jet boat makes the trip in about an hour. It takes a half-hour to get to and from the rapids, which leaves 30 minutes for storming along the 2.4m to 3.7m (8–12-ft.) waves. Reservations are required. Plan to arrive 45 minutes early to obtain and don rain gear and a life jacket. Bring a towel and change of clothes, as you almost certainly will get splashed or even soaked. Fares are C$67 adults, with discounts for children. Smaller speed boat rides are also an option (and at a cheaper price) although they don't go into the rapids. Jet boats depart from the Clock Tower Pier (Quai de l'Horloge).

Navettes Fluviales Maritime Shuttles (www.navettesmaritimes.com; ℰ **514/281-8000**): From Jacques-Cartier Pier in Vieux-Montréal to either Île Ste-Hélène or Longueuil, these are much milder water voyages, but still offer great views. It's one way to begin or end a picnic outing or extend a bike ride beyond Old Montréal. Both ferries operate from mid-May to mid-October, with daily departures every hour in the high season, and cost C$7.50 per person (free for children 5 and under).

Land Tours

Gray Line (www.grayline.com/things-to-do/canada/montreal; ℰ **800/472-9546**) offers commercial guided tours in air-conditioned motorcoach buses daily year round. The basic city tour takes 3 1/2 hours and costs C$44 for adults and children 12 and over, C$28 for children 5 to 11. Tours depart from 1001 Dorchester Square in downtown. The motorcoach tours offer an option to pick you up at selected hotels. The shorter 2-hour "Hop-on-Hop-Off" tour is on a London-style double-decker bus.

Amphi-Bus (www.montreal-amphibus-tour.com; ℰ **514/849-5181**) is something a little different: It tours Vieux-Montréal much like any other bus—until it waddles into the waters of the harbor for a dramatic finish. Departures are hourly late June through August with four departures daily from May to June and September to October. Check website for schedules. Fares are C$35 adults, with discounts for children and seniors. Reservations are required. The bus departs from the intersection of rue de la Commune and boul. St-Laurent.

Montréal's *calèches* are horse-drawn open carriages whose drivers serve as guides. They operate year round, and in winter, the horse puffs steam clouds in the cold air as the passengers bundle up in lap rugs. Carriages wait at Place Jacques-Cartier and rue de la Commune, and at Place d'Armes opposite Basilique Notre-Dame. A 30-minute ride costs C$48 and an hour costs C$80. All of the guides speak French and English.

Food & Wine Tours

VDM Global (www.montrealfoodtours.com; ℰ **514/933-6674**) offers three food-centered walking tours, all of which cost C$59: "Flavours and Aromas of Old Montréal," which focuses on the city's French heritage; "A Foodie's Tour of Little Italy," which includes several restaurants as well as the **Jean-Talon Market** (p. 119); and "Excursion into the Belly of Montréal," offered in winter only, which takes you on a culinary expedition of the underground city. All tours are bilingual and the fees include food tastings.

If you have a car, the **Route des Vins (Wine Route)** is a pleasant driving tour of the vineyards of Québec. It's in the Cantons-de-l'Est region, a pretty, rural region 103km (64 miles) southeast of Montréal. See the Day Trip on p. 170.

OUTDOOR ACTIVITIES

After such long winters, locals pour outdoors to get sun and warm air at every possible opportunity (though there's also lots to do when there's snow on the ground). **Parc du Mont-Royal** and **Parc La Fontaine** (both listed below) are the city's biggest parks. The **Jardin Botanique** (p. 120) is also a beautiful oasis to spend a day strolling.

This is a walking city, and in the warm months, Montréal closes off large sections of main streets for pedestrian-only traffic, including rue Ste-Catherine both in the Village and adjacent to Quartier des Spectacles. For special events, rue St-Paul in Vieux-Montréal and rue St-Laurent in the Plateau shuts down as well.

Parc du Mont-Royal ★★ Montréal is named for this 232m (761-ft.) small mountain that rises at its heart—Mont Royal, or the "Royal Mountain." Walkers, joggers, cyclists, parents with strollers, dog owners, and in-line skaters all use this largest of the city's green spaces throughout the year. In summer, sunbathers and picnickers surround **Lac des Castors (Beaver Lake),** though no swimming is allowed. In winter, the lake becomes a skating rink, while cross-country skiers and snowshoers follow miles of paths and trails laid out for their use through the park's 200 hectares (494 acres). Ice-skates, skis, poles, and snowshoes can all be rented for adults and children at the Beaver Lake Pavilion, the glass-windowed building with a rippled roof. **Chalet du Mont-Royal** near the crest of the hill is a popular destination, providing a sweeping view of the city from its terrace. **Maison Smith,** which houses the information center at the middle the park, includes a cafe serving light fare. Up the hill behind the chalet is the spot where, legend says, Paul de Chomedey, Sieur de Maisonneuve, erected a wooden cross after the colony sidestepped the threat of a flood in 1643. The present incarnation of the steel **Croix du Mont-Royal** was installed in 1924 and is lit at night.

On the eastern edge of the park, near the corner of avenue du Parc and rue Rachel, hundreds of drummers convene on Sundays from early May to late September for **Les Tam-Tams du Mont-Royal.** Anyone can join into the groove with a drum or just a picnic lunch to take it in.

See chapter 9 for a suggested park walking tour.

Downtown (entrances include one at rue Peel and av. des Pins). www.lemontroyal. qc.ca. ⟨ **514/843-8240** (the Maison Smith information center in the park's center). Métro: Mont-Royal. Bus: 11.

Parc La Fontaine ★ The European-style park in Plateau Mont-Royal is one of the city's oldest and most popular. Illustrating the traditional dual identities of the city's populace, half the park is landscapes in the formal French manner, the other in the more casual English style. You can ice skate on the central lake in winter, when snowshoe and cross-country trails wind through trees. In summer, these trails become bike paths, and tennis courts become active. An open amphitheater, the **Théâtre de Verdure,** offered free outdoor theater, music, and tango dancing in the past, but closed in the 2014 and 2015 seasons after falling into disrepair. Hope springs eternal that the much beloved facility will reopen in the future. **Espace La Fontaine** is picking up some of the slack with a bistro offering light meals, local beers, an outdoor patio, and an exhibition and entertainment space. The northern end of the park is more pleasant than the southern end (along rue Sherbrooke), which attracts a seedier crowd.

Bounded by rue Sherbrooke, rue Rachel, av. Parc LaFontaine, and av. Papineau. www. espacelafontaine.com. Métro: Sherbrooke.

Vieux-Port ★★★ Montréal's Old Port at the base of Vieux-Montréal was transformed in 1992 from a dreary commercial wharf area into a 2km-long (1¼-mile), 53-hectare (131-acre) promenade and public park with bicycle paths, benches, and lawns. The wharves house exhibition halls, summertime cafes, a wintertime ice-skating rink, and a variety of other family activities, including the **Centre des Sciences de Montréal** (p. 111). It stretches along the waterfront, parallel to rue de la Commune, from rue McGill to rue Berri.

The area is open year round and most active from mid-May through October, when harbor cruises take to the waters and bicycles, in-line skates, and family-friendly quadricycle carts are available to rent. The summertime-only **Scena Bistro-Terrace** (www.scena.ca) is an appealing terrace/bar at the Jacques-Cartier Pier. In winter, things are quieter, but an outdoor ice-skating rink is a big attraction. At the port's far eastern end, in the last of the old warehouses, is a 1922 clock tower, **La Tour de l'Horloge,** with 192 steps leading past the exposed clockworks to observation decks overlooking the St. Lawrence River (free admission).

Quai King Edward (King Edward Pier). www.oldportofmontreal.com. ⟨⟩ **800/971-7678** or 514/496-7678. Métro: Champ-de-Mars, Place d'Armes, or Square Victoria.

Warm-Weather Activities
BICYCLING & IN-LINE SKATING

Bicycling and rollerblading are hugely popular in Montréal, and the city helps people indulge these passions with an expanding network of more than 600km (373 miles) of cycling paths and bike lanes (60km/37 miles, are maintained year round, even in the snow). In warm months, car lanes in heavily biked areas are blocked off with concrete barriers, creating protected bike-only lanes.

The city's self-service bicycle rental program, BIXI, lets users pick up bikes from designated bike stands in the city and drop them off at other stands for a small fee. To rent a bike for a few hours or more, you are better off going to a bike shop. See p. 51 in chapter 4 for details on both BIXI and rentals.

While street biking is fairly safe, the peaceful **Lachine Canal** is an appealing nearly flat 11km (6¾-mile) bicycle path, open year round and maintained by Parks Canada from mid-April through October. It travels alongside locks and over small bridges.

Also for rent at Vieux-Port are **quadricycles** (www.oldportofmontreal.com/ activity/quadricycle-rental; ⟨⟩ **514/465-0594**), or "Q-cycles"—four-wheeled bike-buggies that hold up to six people. You can ride them only along Vieux-Port; the rental booth is in the heart of the waterfront area, next to the Pavillon

Jacques-Cartier. Half-hour rentals cost C$22 for a three-seater with additional spots for two small children, and C$44 for a six-seater.

If you're serious about cycling, get in touch with the nonprofit biking organization **Vélo Québec** (p. 52). Vélo helped spur the development of a 5,000-km (3,107-mile) bike network called **Route Verte (Green Route)** that stretches from one end of the province of Québec to the other. Many inns and restaurants along the route accommodate the nutritional, safety, and equipment needs of cyclists. The Day Trip "Biking the Route Verte (Green Route)" in chapter 10 has one suggested destination. The Vélo website has up-to-date information on the annual Montréal Bike Fest, new bike lanes, and more. It also offers **guided tours** throughout the province.

GRAND PRIX AUTO RACING

The **Grand Prix** (www.grandprixmontreal.com) international auto race attracts more than 100,000 people to the city's track. Those visitors also pour into downtown hotels and restaurants, bringing in more than C$100 million in tourism dollars and making it the biggest tourism event of the year. It's usually held during the first full weekend in June. Tickets range from C$43 to C$120 for general admission, and C$66 to C$543 for grandstand seats.

HIKING

The most popular hike is to the top of **Mont Royal.** A web of trekking options weave their way up the small mountain, such as the broad and handsome pedestrian-only **chemin Olmsted** (a bridle path named for Frederick Law Olmsted, the park's nominal landscape architect), or the smaller paths and sets of stairs. The park is well marked and small enough that you can wander without getting too lost, but the walking tour on p. 158 suggests one place to start and a number of options once you're inside.

JOGGING

In addition to the areas described above for biking and hiking, consider heading to **Parc La Fontaine** in the Plateau Mont-Royal neighborhood (p. 125), which is formally landscaped and well used for recreation and relaxation. To try some recent routes run by locals, go to www.mapmyrun.com/ca/montreal-quebec.

KAYAKING & ELECTRIC BOATING

It's fun to rent kayaks, pedal boats, or small eco-friendly electric boats on the quiet **Lachine Canal,** just to the west of Vieux-Port. **H₂O Adventures** (www. h2oadventures.com; ✆ **514/842-1306**) has rentals that start as low as C$10 per half hour for a two-person pedal boat. They also offer 2-hour introductory kayak lessons. The season runs from about May 1 to the end of September. The company is based at the Lachine Canal Nautical Center. It's on the opposite side of the canal from the Marché Atwater (p. 114), just over a footbridge. Pick up lunch or snacks from the inside *boulangerie* or *fromagerie,* adjacent to the canal.

SWIMMING

On Parc Jean-Drapeau (www.parcjeandrapeau.com; ✆ **514/872-6120**), the man-made island park just across the harbor of Vieux-Port, is an outdoor **swimming** pool complex (in French, *complexe aquatique*) and a **lakeside beach** (*plage*). The beach is small, but very popular, and open mid-June through August. Admission to the beach is C$9 for adults and children 14 and older, C$4.50 for children 3 to 13, and free for kids 2 and under. Métro: Jean-Drapeau.

Although you can't swim there, **Plage de l'Horloge** (Clock Tower Beach) is a new "urban beach" at Quai de l'Horloge in Vieux-Port that debuted in the summer of 2012. It has sand, sun umbrellas, lounge chairs, and a terrace with drinks, and is open June through August. See www.vieuxportdemontreal.com for details.

Cold-Weather Activities

CROSS-COUNTRY SKIING

Parc du Mont-Royal has an extensive cross-country course, as do many of the other city parks, though skiers have to supply their own equipment. Just an hour from the city, north in the Laurentides and east in the Cantons de l'Est, are numerous options for skiing and rentals.

DOWNHILL SKIING

The city itself does not have options for downhill skiing, but mountains in the Laurentians and Cantons are just a couple hours drive away. See chapter 10 and the Day Trip "Skiing at Mont-Tremblant."

ICE SKATING

In the winter, outdoor skating rinks are set up in Vieux-Port, Lac des Castors (Beaver Lake), and other spots around the city; check tourist offices for your best options. One of the most agreeable venues for skating any time of the year is **Atrium Le 1000** (p. 129) in the downtown skyscraper at 1000 rue de la Gauchetière ouest. It's indoors and warm, and surrounded by cafes for relaxing after twirling around the big rink. And yes, it's even open in the summer.

ESPECIALLY FOR KIDS

For families, few cities assure children will have as good a time as this one. In the warm months there are riverboat rides (p. 129), summer fireworks at **La Ronde Amusement Park** (below), and magical circus performances by the many troupes that come through this circus-centric city.

If you've traveling with toddlers who simply want to run around on a playground on a warm day, head to the less-touristy neighborhoods. You'll find most parks are well-maintained and safe for children, and many include playgrounds. Look in Plateau Mont-Royal, Mile End, and Outremont, the neighborhood west of Mile End. One option we recommend: Take the Métro orange line to Laurier, a nice residential neighborhood where the Plateau meets Mile End. Walk south on rue Berri one block to **Parc Albert-Saint-Martin.** This compact urban playground includes a play area for 18 months to 5 year olds and another for 5 to 12 year olds. (The park is also a 10-minute walk from our favorite doll store, **Raplapla,** p. 119, and a favorite kid-friendly restaurant,

Aux Vivres, p. 96). Also recommended is a visit to the large **Parc La Fontaine** (p. 125), a much grander full-service green space.

When in doubt, head to the multi-venue **Olympic Park** (p. 119) and start at the **Biodôme** (p. 119). It's good all four seasons. Another go-to is the **Centre des Sciences de Montréal** (p. 111), which has a play space for toddlers and interactive exhibits for tweens.

Note: Some hotels, if booked through **Tourisme Montréal**'s website, include a "Family Pass" which provides two free tickets for children 12 and under with the purchase of one adult ticket. Search for "Family Pass" at **www. tourisme-montreal.org** for current offers.

Plenty of attractions earlier in this chapter will appeal to the under-15 crowd, but the venues and programs below cater to them primarily.

Atrium Le 1000 ★   This medium-size indoor ice-skating rink in the heart of downtown offers skating year round under a glass ceiling. Skate rentals are available, and a food court surrounds the rink. It attracts a full mix of patrons: groups of giggling teenage girls, middle-aged friends chatting and skating side by side, and young children teetering in helmets. Tiny Tots Time, typically Saturday and Sunday from 11:00am to 12:30pm, is reserved for children 12 and younger and their parents.

1000 rue de la Gauchetière ouest. www.le1000.com. ✆ **514/395-0555.** Admission C$7.50 adults, with discounts for children and seniors. Skate rental C$7. Open daily; check website for schedules. Métro: Bonaventure.

IMAX Theater ★   Images and special effects are way larger than life and visually dazzling on this screen in the **Centre des Sciences de Montréal** (p. 111). Recent films have highlighted underwater expeditions and pandas (both in 3-D). Running time is usually less than an hour. One screening per day is in English, and you can order tickets and check the schedule online.

Quai King Edward, Vieux-Port. www.montrealsciencecentre.com. ✆ **877/496-4724** or 514/496-4724. Movie tickets C$11.50 adults, with discounts for children and seniors, and free for children 3 and under. Shows daily. Métro: Place d'Armes or Champ-de-Mars.

La Ronde Amusement Park ★   Part of the American-owned Six Flags theme-park empire, this park has roller coasters galore, family-friendly rides, and kid rides (including a carousel and a small train for tots), so there's ample selection for all. Other attractions include a Ferris wheel, acrobatic shows, and front-row seats in an open-air theater to the huge fireworks competition that takes place over nine evenings in summer (see **L'International des Feux Loto-Québec;** p. 133). La Ronde is located on Parc Jean-Drapeau, which sits in the St. Lawrence River near Vieux-Port's waterfront. The park is mostly car-free and accessible by Métro, car, and bike.

22 chemin. Macdonald, Parc Jean-Drapeau on Île Ste-Hélène. www.laronde.com. ✆ **514/397-2000.** Admission C$62 adults, C$45 children 1.37m (54 in.) or shorter and seniors, free for children 2 and under. Parking C$20–C$27. Summer daily 11am–9pm (until 11:00pm most Saturdays); spring and fall Sat–Sun only (confirm hours). Métro: Papineau, then bus no. 769; Parc Jean-Drapeau, then bus no. 767

FESTIVALS & NIGHTLIFE IN MONTRÉAL

8

From the esteemed annual summer jazz fest to the winter *Fête des Neiges*, Montréal's festivals and nightlife pull locals and visitors out of their private spaces and into the streets, public squares, concert halls, nightclubs, and restaurant terraces of the city. Snow is no deterrent, with arctic temperatures merely a barometer for how many layers to wear. It's a city where people come together to celebrate life and the seasons with gusto. The city boasts an outstanding symphony, dozens of French- and English-language theater companies, an events calendar with over 100 festivals, and the incomparable Cirque du Soleil.

Montréal is planning big celebrations in 2017 for its 375th birthday, so in addition to what's listed in this chapter, visit **www.375mtl. com** for up-to-date information about one-time-events.

Montréal's reputation for effervescent nightlife reaches back to the Roaring Twenties—specifically, to the 13-year period of Prohibition in the U.S. from 1920 to 1933. Americans streamed into Montréal for relief from alcohol deprivation (while Canadian distillers and brewers made fortunes). Montréal already enjoyed a sophisticated and slightly naughty reputation as the Paris of North America, which added to the allure.

Nearly a century later, packs of Americans still travel across the border to go to the city's bars and strip clubs (as do Canadians from other provinces) for bachelor and bachelorette weekends. Clubbing and barhopping are hugely popular activities, and nightspots stay open until 3am—much later than in many U.S. and Canadian cities, which still heed Calvinist notions of propriety and early bedtimes. The legal drinking age is also only 18.

That said, the city's nocturnal pursuits are often as sophisticated and edgy as anywhere else. Montréal is on the standard concert circuit, so internationally known entertainers, music groups, and dance companies pass through. A French enthusiasm for film, as well as the city's reputation as a movie-production center, ensures support for film festivals and screenings of offbeat and independent movies.

Maison symphonique de Montréal, home to the Orchestre Symphonique de Montréal

WHERE TO PLAY, NIGHT & DAY

Here's a quick look at the neighborhoods best known for nightlife, the performing arts, and Montréal's many festivals:

Vieux-Montréal, especially along rue St-Paul, has a universal quality, with many of its bars and clubs showcasing live jazz, blues, and folk music. The **Little Burgundy** hub, west of Vieux-Montréal, has a small but sophisticated mix of bars and restaurants.

Quartier des Spectacles is where many of the performing arts venues are located. It's also where many of the outdoor festivals take place.

In **Plateau Mont-Royal,** boulevard St-Laurent, known locally as "The Main," is a miles-long haven of hip and hipster restaurants and clubs. It starts roughly from rue Sherbrooke and goes all the way north into **Mile End** to rue Laurier. It's a good place to wind up in the wee hours, as someplace always has the welcome mat out, even after the official 3am closings. If you've still got steam after that, the **Gay Village** has after-hours dance clubs. Rue Ste-Catherine est in the Village closes in summer to cars and becomes flush with people as the cafes and bars that line the street build temporary terraces.

Downtown's parallel blocks of rue Crescent, rue Bishop, and rue de la Montagne north of rue Ste-Catherine are where much of the city's hardcore partying takes place, with rows of bars with outdoor terraces. Especially on summer weekend nights, the streets swarm with people careening from bar to restaurant to club. It's young and noisy—and also considered to be a tourist

Last-Minute Tickets for Less

A ticket office for Montréal cultural events is centrally located at the Place des Arts, in the Quartier des Spectacles district. **La Vitrine** is at 2 rue Ste-Catherine est (www. lavitrine.com; 𝄐 **866/924-5538** or 514/285-4545) and sells last-minute deals, as well as full-price tickets.

trap to locals, although many still end up there. This area has a pronounced Anglophone (English-speaking) character.

Francophones dominate the area known as the **Quartier Latin,** with college-age patrons most evident along the lower reaches of rue St-Denis, and their elders gravitating to the nightspots on the slightly more uptown blocks of the same street.

Most bars and clubs don't charge a cover, and when they do, it's rarely more than C$10. Happy hour is locally known as *cinq-à-sept* (5-to-7), although many venues offer specials that start earlier than 5pm and go later than 7pm. On Thursdays, many bars and restaurants offer some sort of food and drink special.

Festivals: Montréal's Big, Welcoming Personality

Once known as the city of 100 churches, Montréal is now the city of 100+ festivals. The biggest is the annual summer jazz fest, or **Festival International de Jazz de Montréal,** an internationally celebrated heavyweight offering not only lots of ticketed performances but also hundreds of free shows at outdoor spots in the city's streets and plazas, too. See p. 134 for more.

Year-round, it's nearly impossible to miss a celebration of some sort. For an exhaustive list of festivals beyond those listed here, check the "What to Do" section of Tourisme Montréal's website, at **www.tourisme-montreal.org/what-to-do/events**. At last check, it had nearly 150 festival entries. Below is a selection of some of the most popular annual events.

JANUARY

La Fête des Neiges (The Snow Festival). Montréal's answer to Québec City's February winter Carnaval (p. 235) features dog-sled runs, a human foosball court, and tobogganing. It's held on weekends from 10am to 8pm on Saturday and 10am to 6pm on Sunday in January and the beginning of February. Visit www.parcjeandrapeau.com and search for "Fête des Neiges" or call 𝄐 **514/872-6120.** Check the website for current dates.

Igloofest. An electronic dance festival. Outdoors. In the arctic cold of winter. (The heartiness of the Québécois truly knows no bounds.) The dancing takes place at night, at a stage along the river, in Vieux Port. Igloofest runs Thursdays through Saturdays for four weekends, and features local and international DJs. Visit **igloofest.ca/en**. Beginning mid-January.

FEBRUARY

Festival Montréal en Lumière (Montréal High Lights Festival). At the heart of this winter celebration are culinary competitions and wine tastings. There are also multimedia light shows, classical and pop concerts, outdoor activities for children at the Quartier des Spectacles, and the "Nuit blanche" all-night party where everyone dresses in white and heads to a free breakfast at dawn. Did we mention that the average monthly temperature in February is –4°C (24°F) and –12°C (10°F)/ Visit www.montrealhighlights. com or call 𝄐 **855/864-3737** or 514/288-9955, for details. Beginning mid-February.

Nuit Blanche (White Night). The annual one-night event, part of Festival Montréal en Lumière (above), is especially emblematic of Montréal's ability to put on a city-wide party: it's an all-night affair, with over 200 activities in clubs, bars, concert halls, galleries, theaters, spas, and cafes around town. Shuttle buses and the Métro run all night for free. Events in previous years have included an open house at the gorgeous outdoor rooftop pool of the Hotel Montréal Bonaventure (p. 61); yoga by candlelight; wall climbing; skating in Atrium Le 1000 (p. 129); and open soccer at Olympic Stadium (p. 119). Visit www.montrealhighlights.com or call ✆ **855/ 864-3737** or 514/288-9955, for details. Last Saturday night of February.

APRIL

Bal en Blanc Party Week. Drawing crowds of an estimated 15,000 people, this 5-day "White Ball" rave/dance party is one of the biggest such events in the world. Everyone wears white and grooves to house and trance DJ events at Palais des Congrès and the W Hotel. Visit **www.balenblanc.com**.

MAY

Montréal Museums Day. This event is an open house for most of the city's museums, with free admission and free shuttle buses. Visit www.museesmontreal.org or call the tourism office (✆ **877/266-5687**) for details. Late Sunday in May.

Montréal Bike Fest. For 8 days, tens of thousands of enthusiasts converge on Montréal to participate in cycling competitions that include a nocturnal bike ride (Tour la Nuit) and the grueling Tour de l'Île, a 52-km (32-mile) race around the island's rim. It draws some 30,000 cyclists, shuts down roads, and attracts more than 100,000 spectators. The nonprofit biking organization Vélo Québec (✆ **800/567-8356** or 514/521-8356) lists details at www.velo.qc.ca. Begins in late May.

JUNE

Les FrancoFolies de Montréal. Since 1988, this music fest has featured French-language pop, hip hop, electronic, world beat, and *chanson*. It's based at the Quartier des Spectacles downtown, with shows both outdoors on the plaza and inside the many theater

halls in and around the area. Check www.francofolies.com or call ✆ **855/372-6267** or 514/876-8989. Begins in mid-June.

Mondial de la Bière. Yes, beer fans, this is a 5-day festival devoted to your favorite beverage. Admission at the Palais des congrès (Convention Center) is free, and tasting coupons are C$1 each, with most tastings costing two to six coupons for 3- or 4-ounce samples. Showcased are world brands and boutique microbreweries. For all the sudsy details, check www.festivalmondialbiere.qc.ca or call ✆ **514/722-9640.** Begins in mid-June.

Jean-Baptiste Day. Honoring St. John the Baptist, the patron saint of French-Canadians, this day is marked by far more festivities and enthusiasm throughout Québec than Canada Day on July 1 (see below). It's Québec's own *fête nationale* with fireworks, bonfires, music in the parks, and parades. Visit www.fetenationale.qc.ca or call ✆ **514/527-9891** for details. June 24.

L'International des Feux Loto-Québec (International Fireworks Competition). Great fun, starting at 10pm on 9 summer evenings. These fireworks are presented in an Olympics-style competition, with countries vying for best in show. You can either enjoy the pyrotechnics for free from almost anywhere overlooking the river, or buy tickets to watch from the open-air theater in La Ronde amusement park on Île Ste-Hélène (tickets have the added benefit of admission to the amusement park operated by Six Flags). Kids, needless to say, love the whole explosive business. *Tip:* The Jacques Cartier bridge closes to traffic during the fireworks and offers an unblocked, up-close view. Go to www.internationaldesfeuxloto-quebec.com or call ✆ **514/397-2000** for details. In recent years, shows have been held on selected Wednesdays, Fridays, and Saturdays from late June to early August.

JULY

Canada Day. On July 1, 1867, three British colonies joined together to form the federation of Canada, with further independence from Britain coming in stages in the 1880s. Celebrations of Canada's birthday are biggest in Ottawa, though Montréal and

Québec City have their share of concerts, flag raisings, and family festivities too. July 1.

Montréal Complètement Cirque. Founded in 2010 in part by the Cirque du Soleil, this international festival of circus arts is a particularly zesty event. It features indoor and outdoor shows, and special family performances. It takes place at TOHU (below) and spills over into Quartier des Spectacles and rue St-Denis. In addition to local troupes, performers from as far away as Spain and Australia have appeared in recent editions. Visit montrealcirquefest.com or call ☎ **855/770-3434** or 514/285-9175. Begins in early July.

Festival International de Jazz de Montréal. Since Montréal has a long tradition in jazz, this is one of the monster events on the city's calendar, celebrating America's art form since 1979. Although jazz is the focus, many genres are represented, including rock, folk, R&B, and soul music. Recent editions have featured performances by Michael Bublé, the Glenn Miller Orchestra, Esperanza Spalding, Beck, and hundreds more. It costs serious money to hear the big stars, and tickets often sell out months in advance, but hundreds of free or nearly free performances also take place during the party, many right on downtown plazas. Visit www.montrealjazzfest.com or call ☎ **855/299-3378** or 514/871-1881. Late June through early July.

Festival Juste pour Rire (Just for Laughs Festival). Held throughout July, the largest comedy festival in the world has been going strong for nearly 35 years. In 2015, Dave Chappelle did six performances, and comedy galas were hosted by Wanda Sykes, Neil Patrick Harris, and Jane Lynch. Other recently featured comedians include Kevin Hart, Lewis Black, Kate McKinnon, Don Rickles, and Aziz Ansari. Visit www.hahaha.com or call ☎ **888/244-3155** or 514/845-2322.

AUGUST

Festival des Films du Monde. This long-running international film festival is a must for any movie buff. Each year, nearly half a million attendees come to see hundreds of films from across the globe. Visit www.ffm-montreal.org or call ☎ **514/848-3883.** Begins in late August.

THE PERFORMING ARTS

Circus

The extraordinary circus company **Cirque du Soleil** is based in Montréal. Each show is a celebration of pure skill and is nothing less than magical, with acrobats, clowns, trapeze artists, and performers costumed to look like creatures not of this world—iguanas crossed with goblins, or peacocks born of trolls. Although Montréal does not have a permanent show, the troupe usually comes through the city at least once a year. Check **www.cirquedusoleil.com** for the current schedule.

Other circus companies fill in the gap, though. **Les 7 Doigts de la Main** (www.7doigts.com; ☎ **514/521-4477**), founded in Montréal in 2002, is especially well regarded. The troupe tours the world and has frequent performances in its home city. In July, **Montréal Complètement Cirque**, an annual circus festival, takes place at TOHU (below) and on the streets of the city.

La Pavillon de la TOHU ★ Adjacent to Cirque du Soleil's training complex and company offices, TOHU is a performance space devoted to the circus arts. TOHU features an intimate in-the-round hall done up like an old-fashioned circus tent, and an exhibit space displays more than 100 circus

For details about performances or special events when you're in town, the website **"Cult MTL"** (www.cultmontreal.com) offers timely previews. A fun blog is **Me, Myself, and Montreal** (www.en.memyselfandmontreal.com) written by a team who cover everything from food to fashion. The city's tourism office hosts an informative blog (www.tourisme-montreal.org/blog) that includes lots of activities and places to visit, including many overlooked hidden gems.

artifacts. The annual May to June shows by students of the National Circus School present many of the top rising stars, and in July TOHU hosts a 12-day circus festival. The entire venue was built with recycled pieces of an amusement park bumper-car ride and wood from a dismantled railroad. The facility is in the lower-income Saint-Michel district well north of downtown, but is accessible by Métro and bus, as well as taxi. Most of its programming information is in French. 2345 rue Jarry est (corner of rue d'Iberville, at Autoroute 40). www.tohu.ca. © **888/376-8648** or 514/376-8648. Free to view facility and exhibits. Performances from C$25 adults, from C$15 children 15 and under. 8km (5 miles) from downtown, up rue St-Denis and east on rue Jarry to where it meets Autoroute 40. Métro: Jarry or Iberville. Bus: 94 nord.

Classical Music & Ballet

Many churches have exemplary classical music programs. At **Cathédrale Christ Church,** 635 rue Ste-Catherine ouest (www.montrealcathedral.ca; © **514/843-6577**), a top-notch choir sings Sundays at 10am and 4pm with programs that often include modernists such as Benjamin Britten.

Les Grands Ballets Canadiens ★★ Founded in 1957, this prestigious touring company performs both a classical and a modern repertoire and has developed a following far beyond national borders. In the process, it has brought prominence to many gifted Canadian choreographers and composers. The troupe's production of *The Nutcracker* is always a big event each winter. Performances are held October through May. Place des Arts, 175 rue Ste-Catherine ouest (main entrance), downtown. www.grandsballets.com. © **866/842-2112** or 514/842-2112. Tickets from C$53. Métro: Place-des-Arts.

Opéra de Montréal ★ Founded in 1980, this outstanding opera company mounts five productions per year in Montréal, with artists from Québec and abroad participating in such shows as Gershwin's *Porgy and Bess* and Puccini's *Madama Butterfly*. Video translations are provided from the original languages into French and English. Performances are held from September through May. 260 boul Maisonneuve ouest (Box office at Place des Arts, 175 rue Ste-Catherine ouest,) downtown. www.operademontreal.com. © **877/385-2222** or 514/985-2222. Tickets from C$21. Métro: Place-des-Arts.

8

FESTIVALS & NIGHTLIFE IN MONTRÉAL

The Performing Arts

Orchestre Symphonique de Montréal (OSM) ★★ The orchestra got a gorgeous new home in 2011, **Maison symphonique de Montréal,** which is designed "shoebox" style, with seats on multiple balcony levels surrounding the performers. Music director Kent Nagano focuses the symphony's repertoire on works by Beethoven, Bach, Brahms, and Mahler. It has programs for children 5 to 12 and special prices for people 34 and under, 25 and under, and 17 and under. Place des Arts, 1600 rue St-Urbain, downtown. www. osm.ca. © **888/842-9951** or 514/842-9951. Tickets from C$42; discounts available for various age groups. Métro: Place-des-Arts.

Concert Halls & Auditoriums

Centre Bell Seating 21,273 for most events, Centre Bell is the home of the Montréal Canadiens hockey team and host to the biggest international rock and pop stars traveling through the city, including Québec native Céline Dion. The venue has guided tours and a Montréal Canadiens Hall of Fame (**www.hall.canadiens.com**). Centre Bell's street was renamed in 2009 for the 100th anniversary of the Canadiens; the former address was 1260 rue de la Gauchetière ouest. 1909 avenue des Canadiens-de-Montréal, downtown. www. centrebell.ca. © **877/668-8269** or 514/790-2525. Métro: Bonaventure.

Métropolis After starting life as a skating rink in 1884, the 2,300-capacity Métropolis is now a prime showplace for both traveling rock groups—it has recently hosted Soundgarden and Panic! at the Disco—and annual events such as the summer jazz festival. 59 rue Ste-Catherine est, downtown. www.montreal metropolis.ca/metropolis. © **855/790-1245.** Métro: St-Laurent or Berri-UQAM.

Place des Arts ★★★ Since 1992, Place des Arts has been the city's central entertainment complex, presenting performances of musical concerts, opera, dance, and theater in seven halls, including **Salle Wilfrid-Pelletier** (2,996 seats, where the Opéra de Montréal and Les Grands Ballets Canadiens both perform), and the new **Maison symphonique de Montréal** (2,100 seats), where the Orchestre Métropolitain du Grand Montréal performs. The concert halls and outdoor plaza provide the stages for many of the city's arts festivals, as well as traveling productions of Broadway shows. Place des Arts is at the center of the larger cultural hub known as the Quartier des Spectacles. Place des Arts, 175 rue Ste-Catherine ouest (main entrance and ticket office), downtown. www.placedesarts.com. © **866/842-2112** or 514/842-2112. Métro: Place-des-Arts.

BARS & NIGHTCLUBS

Some nightclubs, restaurants, and bars position themselves as **supper clubs:** all-in-one venues where you go for drinks, stay for dinner, and then hang around drinking and possibly dancing until closing. Nightclubs can be exclusive—waiting in line is an unfortunate reality—and while there aren't dress codes for women (except for the unwritten rule that the shorter the dress, the more likely you are to be let in), some clubs have rules for men prohibiting baseball caps, sneakers, T-shirts, and messy jeans. Regular bars stay open until 3am.

Downtown

Bar Furco ★ Industrial-chic Berlin meets an old Montréal fur warehouse. That's the inspiration for this downtown hotspot for cocktails and wine (the food menu kicks in after 5pm). Attractive 20- and 30-somethings gather after work and will even wait in line to soak up Furco's vintage-mod vibe. 425 rue Mayor (near Quartier des Spectacles). www.barfurco.com. ℂ **514/764-3588.** Métro: Place-des-Arts or McGill.

Brutopia ★ This pub pulls endless pints of its own microbrews, which might include maple cream or java stout on a given day. With three levels, a terrace in back, and a street-side balcony, it draws a mixed crowd, students with laptops, and old friends just hanging out. Unlike other spots on rue Crescent, where the sound levels can be deafening, here you can actually have a conversation. Bands perform most evenings starting at 10pm. 1219 rue Crescent (north of boul. René-Lévesque). www.brutopia.net. ℂ **514/393-9277.** Métro: Lucien L'Allier.

Hurley's Irish Pub In front is a street-level terrace, and in back are several semi-subterranean rooms. Celtic instrumentalists perform nightly, usually starting around 9:30pm. Choose from 19 beers on tap and more than 50 single-malt whiskeys. 1225 rue Crescent (at rue Ste-Catherine). www.hurleysirishpub.com. ℂ **514/861-4111.** Métro: Guy-Concordia.

Maison du Jazz This New Orleans–style jazz venue has been on the scene for decades. Lovers of barbecued ribs and jazz arrive early to fill the room, which is decorated in mock–Art Nouveau style with tiered levels. Live music starts around 8pm most evenings. The ribs are okay, and the jazz is of the swinging mainstream variety, with occasional digressions into more esoteric forms. Popular bands can sell out the venue, so we recommend making reservations just to be safe. 2060 rue Aylmer (south of rue Sherbrooke). www. houseofjazz.ca. ℂ **514/842-8656.** Cover C$10. Métro: McGill.

Pullman ★★ This sleek wine bar has dozens of wines as well as aperitifs and ports by the glass and offers both 2- and 4-oz. pours, so you can sample a number of vintages. In summer, try a Coimbra, a sangria-like drink with *porto blanco,* tonic, and lime. A competent tapas menu with standards like charcuterie and fun oddballs like grilled cheese bedazzled with port are prepared with the precision of a sushi chef. Pullman is a smartly designed multi-level space with pockets of ambience, from cozy corners to tables drenched in natural light. It's open daily from 4:30pm to 1am. 3424 av. du Parc (north of Sherbrooke). www.pullman-mtl.com. ℂ **514/288-7779.** Métro: Place-des-Arts.

Sir Winston Churchill Pub ★ This complex consists of three levels of bars and cafes that are rue Crescent landmarks, and the New Orleans–style sidewalk and first-floor terraces (open in warm months) make perfect vantage points from which to check out the pedestrian traffic. With English ales on tap, the pub imitates a British public house and gets a mixed crowd of young professionals. 1459 rue Crescent (near rue Ste-Catherine). www.swcpc.com. © **514/288-3814.** Métro: Guy-Concordia.

Upstairs Jazz Bar & Grill ★   The Upstairs Jazz Bar, actually *down* a few steps from the street, has been hosting live jazz music nightly since 1995. Big names are infrequent, but the groups are more than competent. Sets begin at 8:30pm, usually with three each night, 7 nights a week. Food ranges from bar snacks to more substantial meals. It's more of a middle-aged crowd, but a younger jazz-curious crew has been settling in, too. The cover charge varies but is usually C$5 to C$20. 1254 rue Mackay (south of rue Ste-Catherine). www.upstairsjazz.com. © **514/931-6808.** Métro: Guy-Concordia.

Vieux-Montréal

Le Deux Pierrots   This has traditionally been one of the best known of Montréal's *boîtes-à-chansons* (song clubs), but its more visible persona these days is sports bar. The sports posters are what you'll mostly see when you walk by, but look for the smaller posters of musicians. On Friday and Saturday nights, a French-style cabaret still brings in singers who interact animatedly, and often bilingually, with the crowd. Arrive by 9pm or make a reservation because tables can fill up. 104 rue St-Paul est (west of Place Jacques-Cartier). www.2pierrots.com. © **514/861-1270.** Métro: Place d'Armes.

Le Jardin Nelson ★★   In the summer, the outdoor dining options that line Place Jacques-Cartier are tempting but touristy. Le Jardin Nelson has a people-watching porch adjacent to the plaza, but you're better off tucking into its large tree-shaded garden court, which sits behind a stone building dating from 1812. It's still touristy, but a pleasant hour or two can be spent listening to live jazz, played every afternoon and evening. Food takes second place, but the kitchen does well with its pizzas and sweet or savory *crêpes*. Outdoor heaters cut the chill, though you can sit at the indoor tables too. When the weather's nice, it's open as late as 1am; it's closed November through mid-April. 407 Place Jacques-Cartier (at rue St-Paul est). www.jardinnelson.com. © **514/861-5731.** Métro: Place d'Armes or Champ-de-Mars.

Méchant Boeuf ★   A young, stylish crowd piles into the bar of this brasserie during happy hour and doesn't seem to leave (a DJ keeps revelers moving with nonstop techno-pop). The menu has a large selection of shareable appetizers such as fried calamari and chicken wings, but the real focus is on beef. The array of well-crafted burgers and AAA-grade cuts of such as New York strip and bone-in filet mignon will delight any carnivore. The well-stocked raw bar is popular, and a late night bar menu is available after 11pm. Reservations recommended on weekends. 124 rue St-Paul ouest (near rue St-Sulpice). www.mechantboeuf.com. © **514/788-4020.** Métro: Champs-de-Mars.

Philémon ★   The look here is chalet-chic, while the crowd is urban single professional. As one blogger put it, "you can always count on its strong quick 'n' dirty drinks, relaxed vibe, fashionable and good-looking 20 to 40 year old crowd . . . Oh, and being hit on." The oysters are good and as well as the great charcuterie platter. 111 rue St-Paul ouest (at rue St-Urbain). www.philemonbar.com. © **514/289-3777**. Métro: Place d'Armes.

Suite 701 When **Place d'Armes Hôtel** converted its lobby and wine bar into this spiffy lounge, young professionals got the word. It's a beautiful hotel bar in a central location (right on Place d'Armes), and it makes a point of catering to the *cinq-à-sept* (5-to-7pm happy hour) after-work crowd, especially on Thursdays. 701 Côte de la Place d'Armes (at rue St-Jacques). www.suite701. com. © **514/904-1201**. Métro: Place d'Armes.

Velvet ★ This cavernous nightclub cultivates the feel of an underground speakeasy, courtesy of its virtually nonexistent signage and its tunnel entrance through the bar of Auberge St-Gabriel. Even the website is hard to decipher. Some of the bartenders here are models and many of the patrons have deep pockets, so, yes, come dressed to impress. Music ranges from house, hip hop to electro. 426 rue St-Gabriel (near rue St. Paul est). Enter through the hotel bar. www. velvetspeakeasy.ca. © **514/995-8754**. Métro: Place d'Armes.

Plateau Mont-Royal & Mile End

Baldwin Barmacie ★ The split-level space of this all-white bar attracts more of a young professional than starving-artist crowd. Sometimes a DJ spins, sometimes it's just owner Alex Baldwin's iTunes library, consisting of classic rock and old-school hip hop. Bottles line the walls as they would in an old-time pharmacy. This is a place to give a very fancy cocktail a try. 115 av. Laurier ouest (at rue St. Urbain). www.baldwinbarmacie.com. © **514/276-4282**. Métro: Laurier.

Bílý Kun ★★ Pronounced "Billy Coon," this popular bar is a bit of Prague right in Montréal, from the avant-garde decor (mounted ostrich heads ring the room) to the full line of Czech beers, local microbrews, and dozen-plus scotches. Martini specials include the Absinthe Aux Pommes. Students and professionals jam in for the relaxed candle-lit atmosphere, which includes twirling ceiling fans and picture windows that open to the street. Most nights include live jazz or DJs spinning upbeat pop. Get here early to do a little shopping in the hipster boutiques along the street. 354 av. du Mont-Royal est (near rue St-Denis). www.bilykun.com. © **514/845-5392**. Métro: Mont-Royal.

Brasserie Harricana ★ This massive brewpub opened at the very end of 2014 right near **Marché Jean-Talon** (p. 119) and the Mile-Ex and Little Italy neighborhoods. It boasts some 40 beers on tap, with about 10 house labels and the rest from throughout Québec. Rums, bourbons, and ciders are also on tap and the lunch and dinner menu includes a *"poutine bun"*: fries, cheese curds, and gravy in a hot dog bun. Reservations are available for groups of 15 or more. 95 rue Jean-Talon ouest (at boul. St. Joseph ouest). www.brasserieharricana.com. © **514/667-0006**. Métro: Jean-Talon.

Buvette Chez Simone ★ Simone is one of a group of friends who own this popular bar. The terrace (framed by greenery in summer) is a coveted spot in sunny weather. Stripped-down industrial chic in the interior envelops a central, oval-shaped bar. The menu has a satisfying selection of small eats, including *charcuterie* and cheeses, as well as a strong selection of wines by the glass. 4869 av. du Parc (at boul. St. Joseph ouest). www.buvettechezsimone.com. ℓ **514/750-6577**. Métro: Mont-Royal or Laurier.

Casa del Popolo Set in a scruffy storefront, Casa del Popolo serves vegetarian food, operates a laid-back bar, and has a small first-floor stage. Across the street is a larger, sister performance space, **La Sala Rossa** (below). The two venues constitute the heart of the Montréal indie music scene. 4873 boul. St-Laurent (near boul. St-Joseph). www.casadelpopolo.com. ℓ **514/284-3804**. Cover C$5–C$15. Métro: Laurier.

Champs You like sports/ Looking for a particular soccer/hockey/baseball/ football game/ Chances are good that it will be on here, in this three-story sports emporium. Games from around the world are fed to walls of TVs, and more than a dozen athletic events might be showing at any given time. The food is what you'd expect—burgers, steaks, and such. 3956 boul. St-Laurent (near av. Duluth). ℓ **514/987-6444**. Métro: Sherbrooke.

Dieu du Ciel ★★★ This is our favorite of the 20 or so microbreweries in Montréal. Tucked into a corner building on rue Laurier, this neighborhood artisanal brewpub offers an alternating selection of some dozen beers, including house brews and exotic imports. The place buzzes, even midweek. With good conversation and some friends to sample the array, what more do you need/ If it's guidance on where to begin, how about starting with the Première Communion (First Communion), a Scottish ale; moving on to the Rosée d'Hibiscus, which is less sweet than feared; and finishing with the Rigor Mortis ABT. Dieu du Ciel beers are also bottled and sold throughout the province. 29 av. Laurier ouest (near boul. St. Laurent). www.dieuduciel.com. ℓ **514/490-9555**. Métro: Laurier.

La Sala Rossa ★ A bigger venue than its sister performance space **Casa del Popolo** (see above), La Sala Rossa has a calendar of interesting rock, experimental, and jazz music. The attached **Sala Rosa restaurant** serves up hearty Spanish food with a big menu of tapas and paella—and, every Thursday, live flamenco music with dancing and singing. Reserve your spot a week or more in advance. 4848 boul. St-Laurent (near boul. St-Joseph). www.casadelpopolo.com. ℓ **514/844-4227**. Cover C$5–C$30. Métro: Laurier.

Vices & Versa ★ Since 2004, this *bistro au terroir* has featured microbrews on draft and in cask as well as regional eats. It's a low-key, local joint with occasional musical acts and a lovely backyard beer garden. 6631 bd. St-Laurent (near rue St-Zotique). www.vicesetversa.com. ℓ **514/272-2498**. Métro: Beaubien.

Gay Village & Quartier Latin

Cabaret Mado ★ The glint of the sequins can be blinding! Inspired by 1920s cabaret, this drag theater has a dance floor, performances most nights, and is considered a premiere venue. We're still kicking ourselves for missing the "Spice Girls Drag World Tour" show. Look for the pink-haired drag queen on the retro marquee. 1115 rue Ste-Catherine est (near rue Amherst). www.mado. qc.ca. ℂ **514/525-7566.** Cover: varies, usually around C$10. Métro: Beaudry.

Club Soda The long-established rock club in the old Red Light District of the Latin Quarter (and on the edge of the hotter Quartier des Spectacles) hosts national and international acts, cover bands, fashion shows, and parts of the city's music and comedy festivals. Occasionally they'll show pay-per-view sporting events too. 1225 boul. St-Laurent (at rue Ste-Catherine). www.clubsoda.ca. ℂ **514/286-1010.** Tickets from C$17. Métro: St-Laurent.

Sky Club & Pub A complex that includes drag performances in the cabaret room, a pub serving dinner daily, a hip hop room, a spacious dance floor often set to house music, and a popular roof terrace, Sky is thought by many to be the city's hottest spot for the gay, young, and fabulous. It's got spiffy decor and pounding music. Did we mention the terrace also has a pool and a hot tub/ 1474 rue Ste-Catherine est (near rue Plessis). www.complexesky.com. ℂ **514/529-6969.** Métro: Beaudry.

Outer Districts

Piknic Electronik ★★ From late May to late September on Sunday afternoons and into the evenings, it's a dance party at Parc Jean-Drapeau. Hipster kids, families with young children, and dancing queens who just didn't get enough on Saturday night gather and shake it outdoors under the Alexander Calder sculpture, *Man and His World,* located on the Belvedere on the north shore of Île Sainte-Hélène, facing the river. They are all grooving to a DJ and, sometimes, live acts. Music starts early afternoon and runs until about 9:30pm. To find the outdoor locale, the website suggests taking the Métro and just following the rhythms when you exit. Belvedere in Parc Jean-Drapeau (Ile Ste-Hélène). www.piknicelectronik.com. ℂ **514/904-1247.** Admission C$15 adults, free for children 12 and under. From late May through September. Sun 2–9:30pm. Métro: Jean-Drapeau.

MONTRÉAL WALKING TOURS

9

Cities best reveal themselves on foot, and Montréal is one of North America's most pedestrian-friendly locales. The concentrated neighborhoods have much to see—cobblestoned Vieux-Montréal, downtown and its luxurious "Golden Square Mile," and Mont Royal itself—and this chapter describes strolls that will take you through the highlights of all of them.

The city's layout is mostly straightforward and simple to navigate, and the extensive Métro system gets you to and from neighborhoods with ease. These strolls will give you a taste of what's best about old and new Montréal, and send you off to discover highlights of your own.

WALKING TOUR 1: VIEUX-MONTRÉAL

GETTING THERE:	**If you're coming from outside Vieux-Montréal, take the Métro to the Place d'Armes station, which lets off next to the Palais des Congrès, the convention center. Follow the signs up the short hill 2 blocks toward Vieux-Montréal (Old Montréal). You'll find yourself in a central outdoor plaza.**
START:	**Place d' Armes, opposite the Notre-Dame Basilica**
FINISH:	**Vieux-Port**
TIME:	**2 hours**
BEST TIMES:	**Almost any day the weather is decent. Vieux-Montréal is lively and safe, day or night. Note: Most museums are closed on Monday. Montréalers and visitors turn out in full force, enjoying the plazas, the 18th- and 19th-century architecture, and the ambience of the most picturesque part of their city on warm weekends and holidays.**
WORST TIMES:	**Evenings, days that are too cold, and times when museums and historic buildings are closed. Sunny days in winter are known to be particularly cold (as opposed to those when it is snowing and temperatures are notably warmer), but you can take advantage of the bright light. Do as the locals do and wear a warm coat, hat, gloves, and good boots.**

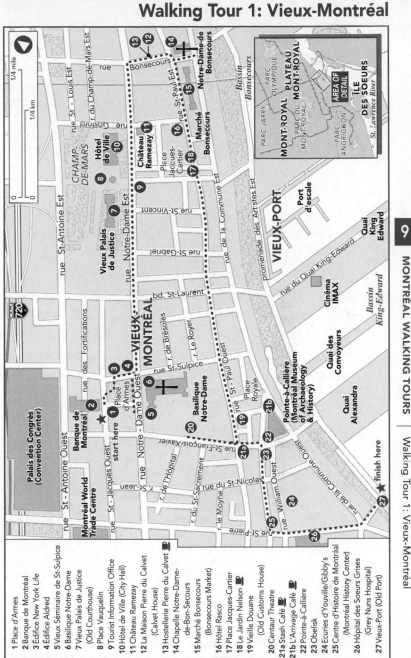

1 Place d'Armes
2 Banque de Montréal
3 Édifice New York Life
4 Édifice Aldred
5 Vieux Séminaire de St-Sulpice
6 Basilique Notre-Dame
7 Vieux Palais de Justice (Old Courthouse)
8 Place Vauquelin
9 Tourist Information Office
10 Hôtel de Ville (City Hall)
11 Château Ramezay
12 La Maison Pierre du Calvet (Calvet House)
13 Hostellerie Pierre du Calvet
14 Chapelle Notre-Dame-de-Bon-Secours
15 Marché Bonsecours (Bonsecours Market)
16 Hôtel Rasco
17 Place Jacques-Cartier
18 Le Jardin Nelson
19 Vieille Douane (Old Customs House)
20 Centaur Theatre
21a Stash Café
21b L'Arrivage Café
22 Pointe-à-Callière
23 Obélisk
24 Écuries d'Youville/Gibby's
25 Centre d'Histoire de Montréal (Montréal History Center)
26 Hôpital des Soeurs Grises (Grey Nuns Hospital)
27 Vieux-Port (Old Port)

Vieux-Montréal is where the city was born. Its architectural heritage has been substantially preserved, and restored 18th- and 19th-century structures now house shops, boutique hotels, galleries, cafes, bars, and apartments. This tour gives you a lay of the land, passing many of the neighborhood's highlights and some of its best and most atmospheric dining spots. We mention lots of great eating stops along the way. We know you couldn't possibly take us up on all our recommendations, but perhaps one or two of them will suit you when hunger strikes!

Start at:

1 Place d'Armes

The architecture of the buildings that surround this plaza is representative of Montréal's growth: the Sulpician residence of the 17th century (see no. 5, below); the Banque de Montréal (see no. 2) and Basilique Notre-Dame (see no. 6) of the 19th century; and the Art Deco Édifice Aldred (see no. 4) of the 20th century.

The centerpiece of the square is a monument to city founder Paul de Chomedey, Sieur de Maisonneuve (1612–1676). The five statues mark the spot where settlers defeated Iroquois warriors in bloody hand-to-hand fighting, with de Maisonneuve himself locked in combat with the Iroquois chief. De Maisonneuve won and lived here another 23 years. The inscription on the monument reads (in French): YOU ARE THE BUCKWHEAT SEED WHICH WILL GROW AND MULTIPLY AND SPREAD THROUGHOUT THE COUNTRY.

The sculptures at the base of the monument represent other prominent citizens of early Montréal: Charles Lemoyne (1626–1685), a farmer; Jeanne Mance (1606–1673), a woman who founded the city's first hospital; Raphael-Lambert Closse (1618–1662), a soldier and the mayor of Ville-Marie; and an unnamed Iroquois brave. Closse is depicted with his dog, Pilote, whose bark once warned the early settlers of an impending Iroquois attack.

On the north side of the plaza, at 119 St-Jacques, is the domed, colonnaded:

2 Banque de Montréal

Montréal's oldest bank building dates from 1847. From 1901 to

The Aldred and New York Life buildings on Place d'Armes

1905, American architect Stanford White (1853–1906) extended the original building and in this enlarged space he created a vast chamber with green-marble columns topped with golden capitals. The public is welcome to stop in for a look. Besides being lavishly appointed inside and out, the bank also houses a small and quirky **banking museum,** which illustrates early operations. It's just off the main lobby to the left; admission is free.

Facing the Notre-Dame Basilica from the square, look over to the left. At the corner of St-Jacques is the:

3 Édifice New York Life

This red-stone Richardson Romanesque building, with a striking wrought-iron door and clock tower, is at 511 Place d'Armes. It's also known as the Québec Bank Building. At all of eight stories, this became Montréal's first skyscraper in 1888; furthermore, it was equipped with a technological marvel—an elevator.

Next to it, on the right, stands the 23-story Art Deco:

4 Édifice Aldred

If this building looks somehow familiar, there's a reason: Built in 1931, it clearly resembles New York's Empire State Building, also completed that year. The building's original tenant was Aldred and Co. Ltd., a New York–based finance company with other offices in New York, London, and Paris.

Facing the Notre-Dame Basilica again, just to its right is the:

5 Vieux Séminaire de St-Sulpice

The city's oldest building, surrounded by equally ancient stone walls, this seminary was erected by Sulpician priests who arrived in Ville-Marie in 1657, 15 years after the colony was founded (the Sulpicians are part of an order founded in Paris in 1641). The clock on the façade dates from 1701, and its gears are made almost entirely of wood. Unfortunately, the seminary is not open to the public.

After a look through the seminary's iron gate, head to the magnificent Gothic Revival–style church itself:

6 Basilique Notre-Dame

James O'Donnell, an Irish Protestant living in New York, designed this brilliantly crafted church in 1824. Transformed by his experience, he converted to Roman Catholicism and is the only person interred here. The main altar is made from a hand-carved linden tree. Behind it is the Chapel of the Sacred Heart (1982), a perennially popular choice for weddings (Québec-born singer Céline Dion married René Angélil here in 1994). The chapel's altar, 32 bronze panels by Montréal artist Charles Daudelin, represents birth, life, and death. Some 4,000 people can attend mass at a time, and the bell, one of North America's largest, weighs 12 tons. Next to the chapel is a small museum. Come back at night for a romantic take on the city, when more than a score of buildings in the area, including this one, are illuminated. During the Christmas season, three white angels suspended at the entrance are lit with ethereal blue lighting. See p. 148 for more about the church.

Exiting the basilica, turn right (east) on rue Notre-Dame. Cross rue St-Sulpice. Walk 4 blocks, passing chintzy souvenir shops, until you reach, on the left side, the grand:

7 Vieux Palais de Justice (Old Courthouse)

Most of this structure was built in 1856. The third floor and dome were added in 1891, and the difference between the original structure and the addition can be easily discerned with a close look. A second city courthouse, designed by Ernest-Cormier, was built in 1925 with a long colonnade and is across the street. Since 1971, all legal business has been conducted in a third courthouse, the glass-encased building 1 block back, at 1 rue Notre-Dame est. The statue beside the Old Courthouse, called *Homage to Marguerite Bourgeoys,* depicts a teacher and nun and is the work of sculptor Jules LaSalle.

Also on your left, just past the courthouse, is:

8 Place Vauquelin

This small public square, with a splashing fountain and view of the Champ-de-Mars park, was created in 1858. The statue is of Jean Vauquelin (1728–1772), commander of the French fleet in New France. Vauquelin stares across rue Notre-Dame at his counterpart, the English admiral Horatio Nelson (1758–1805). The two statues are symbols of Montréal's French and British duality.

On the opposite corner is a small but helpful:

9 Tourist Information Office

A bilingual staff stands ready to answer questions and hand out useful brochures and maps. It's open daily from May through early November and closed in winter. The famed Silver Dollar Saloon once stood on this site. It got its name from the 350 silver dollars that were embedded in its floor.

Around the corner, on the right, is the Place Jacques-Cartier, a magnet for locals and visitors year-round, which we will visit later in the stroll. Rising on the other side of rue Notre-Dame, opposite the top of the square, is the impressive, green-capped:

10 Hôtel de Ville (City Hall)

Built between 1872 and 1878 in the florid French Second Empire style, the edifice is seen with particular advantage when it is illuminated at night. In 1922, it barely survived a disastrous fire. Only the exterior walls remained, and after substantial rebuilding and the addition of another floor, it reopened in 1926. Take a minute to look inside at the generous use of French marble, the Art Deco lamps, and the bronze-and-glass chandelier. The sculptures at the entry are "Woman with a Pail" and "The

MONTRÉAL WALKING TOURS | Walking Tour 1: Vieux-Montréal

The Hôtel de Ville, Montréal's City Hall

Sower," both by Québec sculptor Alfred Laliberté. See p. 112 for more details.

Exiting City Hall, across rue Notre-Dame, you'll see a small, terraced park with orderly ranks of trees. The statue inside the park honors Montréal's controversial longtime mayor, Jean Drapeau (1916–1999). Next to the park is:

11 Château Ramezay

Beginning in 1705, this was the home of the city's French governors for 4 decades, starting with Claude de Ramezay, before being taken over and used for the same purpose by the British. In 1775, an army of American rebels invaded and held Montréal, using the house as their headquarters. Benjamin Franklin was sent to try to persuade Montréalers to join the American revolt against British rule, and he stayed in this château. He failed to sway Québec's leaders to join the radical cause. Today, the house shows off furnishings, oil paintings, costumes, and other objects related to the economic and social activities of the 18th century and the first half of the 19th century. See p. 113 for more about the museum.

Continue in the same direction (east) along rue Notre-Dame. In the far distance, you'll see the Molson beer factory. At rue Bonsecours, turn right. Near the bottom of the street, on the left, is a house with a low maroon roof and an attached stone building on the corner. This is:

12 La Maison Pierre du Calvet (Calvet House)

Built in the 18th century, this house was sumptuously restored between 1964 and 1966. A fairly well-to-do family inhabited it in the early years.

Pierre du Calvet, believed to be the original owner, was a French Huguenot who supported the American Revolution. Calvet met with Benjamin Franklin here in 1775 and was imprisoned from 1780 to 1783 for supplying money to the Americans. The building of Montréal gray stone has a characteristic sloped roof meant to discourage snow buildup and raised end walls that serve as firebreaks. It is now a restaurant and *hostellerie* with an entrance at no. 405.

13 Hostellerie Pierre du Calvet 🍴
A voluptuously appointed dining room is inside the Hostellerie Pierre du Calvet, 405 rue Bonsecours, called **Les Filles du Roy** (*📞* **866/544-1725** or 514/282-1725), and it's a real splurge (we're talking C$28–C$42 mains). In the warm months, lunches, dinners, and Sunday brunches are served in an outdoor courtyard. Take a peek to see the greenhouse and parrots that lead to the stone-walled terrace.

The next street, rue St-Paul, is Montréal's oldest thoroughfare, dating from 1672. The church at this intersection is the small:

14 Chapelle Notre-Dame-de-Bon-Secours
Called the Sailors' Church because so many made pilgrimages here to give thanks for being saved at sea, this chapel was founded by Marguerite Bourgeoys, a nun and teacher canonized in 1982. Excavations have unearthed foundations of her original 1675 church—although the building has been much altered, and the present façade was built in the late 18th century. A **museum** (p. 111) tells the story of Bourgeoys's life and incorporates the archaeological site. Climb up to the tower for a view of the port and Old Town.

Head west on rue St-Paul. Just beyond the Sailors' Church is an imposing building with a colonnaded façade and silvery dome, the limestone:

15 Marché Bonsecours (Bonsecours Market)
Completed in 1847, this building was used first as the Parliament of United Canada and then as the City Hall, the central market, a music hall, and then the home of the municipality's housing and planning offices. It was restored in 1992 for the city's 350th birthday celebration to house temporary exhibitions and musical performances. It continues to be used for exhibitions, but it's more of a retail center now, with an eclectic selection of local art shops, clothing boutiques, and sidewalk cafes. When Bonsecours Market was first built, the dome could be seen from everywhere in the city and served as a landmark for seafarers sailing into the harbor. Today, it is lit at night.

Continue down rue St-Paul. At no. 281 is the former:

16 Hôtel Rasco
The Italian Francisco Rasco came to Canada to manage a hotel for the Molson family (of beer-brewing fame) and later became successful with his own hotel on this spot. The 150-room Rasco was the Ritz-Carlton of

MONTRÉAL WALKING TOURS | Walking Tour 1: Vieux-Montréal

its day, hosting Charles Dickens and his wife in 1842, when the author was directing his plays at a theater that stood across the street. The hotel lives on in legend, if not in fact, as it's devoid of much of its original architectural detail and no longer hosts overnight guests. Between 1960 and 1981, the space stood empty, but the city took it over and restored it in 1982. It has contained a succession of eateries on the ground floor. The current occupant is **L'Autre Version** restaurant, whose inner courtyard and al fresco dining space is a hidden gem (www.restoversion.com).

Continue heading west on rue St-Paul, turning right when you reach:

17 Place Jacques-Cartier

Opened as a marketplace in 1804, this is the most appealing of Vieux-Montréal's squares, even with its obviously touristy aspects. The square's cobbled cross streets, gentle downhill slope, and ancient buildings set the mood, while outdoor cafes, street entertainers, itinerant artists, and assorted vendors invite lingering in warm weather. The Ben & Jerry's ice cream shop doesn't hurt either. *Calèches* (horse-drawn carriages) depart from both the lower and the upper ends of the square for tours of Vieux-Montréal.

Walk slowly uphill, taking in the old buildings that bracket the plaza (plaques describe some of them in French and English). All these houses were well suited to the rigors of life in the raw young settlement. Their steeply pitched roofs shed the heavy winter snows, rather than collapsing under the burden, and small windows with double casements let in light while keeping out wintry breezes. When shuttered, the windows were almost as effective as the heavy stonewalls in deflecting hostile arrows or the antics of trappers fresh from nearby taverns. At the plaza's northern end stands a monument to Horatio Nelson, hero of Trafalgar, erected in 1809. This monument preceded London's much larger version by several years. After years of vandalism, presumably by Québec separatists, the statue had to be temporarily removed for restoration. The original Nelson is now back in place at the crown of the column.

18 Le Jardin Nelson 🍴

Most of the old buildings in and around the inclined plaza house restaurants and cafes. For a drink or snack during the warm months, try to find a seat in **Le Jardin Nelson** (no. 407), near the bottom of the hill. It's extremely popular with tourists, and for good reason. The tiered courtyard in back often has live jazz, while tables on the terrace overlook the square's activity. See p. 138 for details.

Return to rue St-Paul and continue west. Take time to window-shop the many art galleries that have sprung up alongside the loud souvenir shops on the street. If time permits, enjoy a drink at one of the bars along the way. The street numbers will descend as you approach boulevard St-Laurent, the north-south thoroughfare that divides Montréal into its east and west halves. Numbers will start to rise again as you move onto St-Paul ouest (west). At 150 rue St-Paul ouest is the neoclassical:

19 Vieille Douane (Old Customs House)

Built from 1836 to 1838, this building doubled in size when an extension to the south side was added in 1882; walk around to the building's other side to see how the addition is different. That end of the building faces Place Royale, the first public square in the 17th-century settlement of Ville-Marie. It's where Europeans and Amerindians used to come to trade.

Continue on rue St-Paul to rue St-François-Xavier. Turn right for a short detour; up rue St-François-Xavier, on the right, is the stately:

20 Centaur Theatre

The home of Montréal's principal English-language theater is a former stock exchange building. The Beaux Arts architecture is interesting in that the two entrances are on either side, rather than in the center, of the façade. American architect George Post, who was also responsible for designing the New York Stock Exchange, designed this building, erected in 1903. It served its original function until 1965, when it was redesigned as a theater with two stages.

Return back down rue St-François-Xavier to rue St-Paul.

21 Stash Café & L'Arrivage 🍴

One possibility for lunch or a pick-me-up is the moderately priced **Stash Café** at 200 rue St-Paul ouest (at the corner of rue St-François-Xavier; p. 85). It specializes in Polish fare and opens daily at noon. Another option is the glass-walled, second-floor **L'Arrivage** at the Pointe-à-Callière museum, your next stop. Its lunchtime "express menu" starts at C$12.

Continue on rue St-François-Xavier past St-Paul. At the next corner, the gray wedge-shaped building to the left is the:

22 Pointe-à-Callière

Known in English as the **Museum of Archaeology and History,** Pointe-à-Callière (p. 113) is a top-notch museum, packed with artifacts unearthed during more than a decade of excavation of the spot where the settlement of Ville-Marie was founded in 1642. An underground connection also incorporates the **Old Customs House** you just passed.

A fort stood here in 1645. Thirty years later, a château rose up on the site for Louis-Hector de Callière. He was the governor of New France, and now the namesake of the museum and its triangular square. At that time, the St. Pierre River separated this piece of land from the mainland. It was made a canal in the 19th century and later filled in. The museum's gift shop is in the **Mariner's House building** at 165 Place d'Youville.

Proceeding west from Pointe-à-Callière, near rue St-François-Xavier, stands an:

23 Obelisk

Commemorating the founding of Ville-Marie on May 18, 1642, the obelisk was erected here in 1893 by the Montréal Historical Society. It bears the names of some of the city's early pioneers: French officer Paul Cho-medey de Maisonneuve, who landed in Montréal in 1642; and fellow settler Jeanne Mance, who founded North America's first hospital, l'Hôtel-Dieu de Montréal.

Continuing west from the obelisk 2 blocks to 296–316 Place d'Youville, you'll find, on the left, the:

24 Ecuries d'Youville (Youville Stables)

Despite the name, the rooms in the iron-gated compound, built in 1825 on land owned by the Grey Nuns, were used mainly as warehouses, rather than as horse stables (the actual stables, next door, were made of wood and disappeared long ago). Like much of the waterfront area, the horse shoe-shaped Youville building was run-down and forgotten until the 1960s, when a group of enterprising businesspeople bought and reno-vated it. Today, the compound contains offices and a steakhouse, **Gib-by's,** 298 Place d'Youville (© **514/282-1837**), which is an institution, although not as hip with locals as **Moishes** (p. 90). If the gates are open, go through the passage toward the restaurant door to see the inner courtyard.

Continue another block west to the front door of the brick building on your right, 335 Place d'Youville and the:

25 Centre d'Histoire de Montréal (Montréal History Center)

Built in 1903 as Montréal's central fire station, this building now houses exhibits about life in Montréal, past and present. Visitors learn about traditions of the Amerindians, early exploration, and the evolution of industry, architecture, and professions in the city from 1535 to current day. See p. 111 for details.

Head down rue St-Pierre toward the water. Midway down the block, on the right at no. 138, is the former:

26 Hôpital des Soeurs Grises (Grey Nuns Hospital)

The Charon Brothers founded this hospital in 1693 to serve the city's poor and homeless. After it went bankrupt in 1747, Marguerite d'Youville, founder in 1737 of the Sisters of Charity of Montréal, commonly known as the Grey Nuns, took it over. It was expanded several times, but by 1871, the nuns had moved away and portions were demolished to extend rue St-Pierre and make room for commercial buildings. A century later, the Grey Nuns returned to live in their original home. From the sidewalk, visitors can see a very cool contemporary sculpture of inscribed bronze strips that cover the surviving chapel walls. The text on the sculpture comes from a letter signed by Louis XIV in 1694, incorporating the hos-pital. Three exhibition rooms are open to the public, but by appointment only (© **514/842-9411**).

Continue down rue St-Pierre and cross the main street, rue de la Commune, and then the railroad tracks to this tour's final stop:

27 Vieux-Port (Old Port)

Montréal's historic commercial wharves have been reborn as a waterfront park, which, in good weather, is frequented by cyclists, in-line skaters, joggers, walkers, strollers, and couples. Across the water is the distinctive 158-unit modular housing project **Habitat 67,** built by famed architect Moshe Safdie for the 1967 World's Fair, which Montréal called Expo 67. Safdie's vision was to show what affordable community housing could be. Today, it's a higher-end apartment complex and not open to the public (aerial photos are at Safdie's website, www.msafdie.com). River surfers are known to "hit the waves" in a not-so-publicized spot just in back of this building.

Walk to your right. The triangular building you see is the entrance to **Jardin des Ecluses (Locks Garden),** a canal-side path where the St. Lawrence River's first locks are located. From here, you have several options: If the weather's nice, consider entering the Jardin des Ecluses to stroll the path along **Lachine Canal.** In under an hour, you'll arrive at Montréal's colorful **Marché Atwater** (p. 114), which is 3.8km (2.25 miles) down the path. If you walk the other direction, you'll take in the busiest section of the waterfront park and end at Place Jacques-Cartier.

To get to the subway, walk north along rue McGill to the Square-Victoria Métro station. An authentic Art Nouveau portal, designed by Hector Guimard for the Paris subway system, marks the Métro staircase.

Or return to the small streets parallel to rue St-Paul, where you'll find more boutiques and one of the highest concentrations of art galleries in Canada.

WALKING TOUR 2: **DOWNTOWN MONTRÉAL**

START:	**Bonaventure Métro station**
FINISH:	**Musée des Beaux-Arts and the lively rue Crescent**
TIME:	**2 hours**
BEST TIMES:	**Weekday mornings or after 2pm, when the streets hum with big-city vibrancy but aren't *too* busy.**
WORST TIMES:	**Weekdays from noon to 2pm, when the streets are crowded with businesspeople on lunchtime errands; Monday, when museums are closed; and Sunday, when many stores are closed and much of downtown is nearly deserted.**

After a tour of Vieux-Montréal, a look around the commercial heart of the 21st-century city will highlight the ample contrast between these two areas. To see the city at its contemporary best, take the Métro to the Bonaventure stop to start this tour.

Walking Tour 2: Downtown Montréal

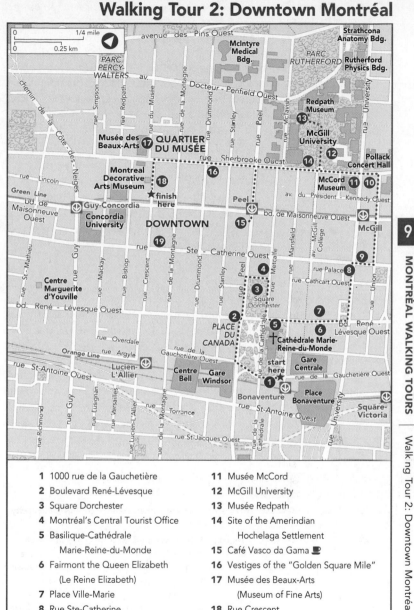

1. 1000 rue de la Gauchetière
2. Boulevard René-Lévesque
3. Square Dorchester
4. Montréal's Central Tourist Office
5. Basilique-Cathédrale
   Marie-Reine-du-Monde
6. Fairmont the Queen Elizabeth
   (Le Reine Elizabeth)
7. Place Ville-Marie
8. Rue Ste-Catherine
9. Cathédrale Christ Church
10. Java U 🍺

11. Musée McCord
12. McGill University
13. Musée Redpath
14. Site of the Amerindian
    Hochelaga Settlement
15. Café Vasco da Gama 🍺
16. Vestiges of the "Golden Square Mile"
17. Musée des Beaux-Arts
    (Museum of Fine Arts)
18. Rue Crescent
19. Sir Winston Churchill Pub 🍺

After you've emerged from the Métro station, the dramatic skyscraper immediately to the west (or directly above you, depending on which exit you take) is:

1 1000 rue de la Gauchetière

Also called "Le 1000," this contribution to downtown Montréal is easily identified along the skyline by its copper-and-blue pyramidal top, which rises to the maximum height permitted by the municipal building code. Although it's mostly offices inside, it also has a year-round indoor skating rink (p. 129) under a glass dome.

Walk west on rue de la Gauchetière. Ahead is Le Marriott Château Champlain, whose distinctive façade of half-moon windows inspired its nickname "the Cheese Grater." Turn right on rue de la Cathédrale, heading north. At the next corner, you reach:

2 Boulevard René-Lévesque

Formerly Dorchester Boulevard, this street was renamed in 1988 following the death of René Lévesque, the Parti Québécois leader who led the movement for Québec independence and the province's use of the French language. Boulevard René-Lévesque is the city's broadest downtown thoroughfare.

Across bd. René-Lévesque is:

3 Square Dorchester

This is one of downtown's central locations. It's a gathering point for tour buses and horse-drawn *calèches*, and the square's shade trees and benches invite lunchtime brown-baggers. This used to be called Dominion Square, but it was renamed for Baron Dorchester, an early English governor, when the adjacent street, once named for Dorchester, was changed to boulevard René-Lévesque. The square was built over an old cemetery for victims of the 1832 cholera epidemic. Along the square's east side is the **Sun Life Insurance building,** built in three stages between 1914 and 1931, and the tallest building in Québec from 1931 until the skyscraper boom of the post–World War II era.

At the north end of the square is:

4 Montréal's Central Tourist Office

The Infotouriste Centre at 1255 rue Peel has maps and brochures and bilingual attendants, who are eager to answer questions, point you in the right direction, or give advice about hotels or tours. It's open daily (p. 43).

On bd. René-Lévesque at the corner of Square Dorchester is the:

5 Basilique-Cathédrale Marie-Reine-du-Monde

Suddenly get the feeling you're in Rome? This cathedral is a copy of St. Peter's Basilica, albeit a fraction of the size. It was built as the headquarters for Montréal's Roman Catholic bishop. The statue in front is of Bishop Ignace Bourget, the force behind the project. Construction lasted from 1875 to 1894, its start delayed by the bishop's desire to place it not in Francophone east Montréal, but in the heart of the Protestant Anglophone west. Read more on p. 104.

Continue on bd. René-Lévesque past the cathedral. In the next block, on the right, is:

6 Fairmont the Queen Elizabeth (Le Reine Elizabeth)

Montréal's largest hotel is right above **Gare Centrale,** the main railroad station. The Fairmont (www.fairmont.com/queen-elizabeth-montreal; ✆ **866/540-4483** or 514/861-3511) is a beautifully appointed hotel. It's also where John Lennon and Yoko Ono held their famous weeklong "Bed-in for Peace" in 1969 (memorialized at the city's new wax museum, **Musée Grévin Montréal,** p. 106).

On the other side of bd. René-Lévesque, directly across from the hotel, is:

7 Place Ville-Marie

One thing to keep in mind is that the French word *place,* or plaza, sometimes means an outdoor square, such as Place Jacques-Cartier in Vieux-Montréal. Other times, it refers to a building or complex that includes stores and offices. Place Ville-Marie is in this category. Known as PVM, the glass building was considered a gem of the 1960s urban redevelopment efforts. Its architect was I.M. Pei, who also designed the glass pyramid at the Louvre in Paris. Pei gave the skyscraper a cross-shaped footprint, recalling the cross atop Mont Royal. The underground houses a large shopping mall. A new **observatory** at the very top of PVM is scheduled to open in early 2016 and will offer panoramic views of the city, a permanent exhibition about historical and contemporary Montréal, and all-season terraces (**www.placevillemarie.com**).

Continue on bd. René-Lévesque to the end of the block and turn left on bd. Robert-Bourassa (formerly rue University). As you walk, look to the top of the skyscraper a few blocks down; this pink, postmodern glass office building is Tour KPMG, completed in 1987. The two-peaked top is meant to resemble a bishop's miter, or cap, but many see the ears and mask of a certain DC Comics superhero. In 2 blocks, you'll reach:

8 Rue Ste-Catherine

This is one of the city's prime shopping streets, with name brands, local businesses, and department stores. Among them, to the right, is **La Baie**—or the Bay—successor to the famous fur-trapping firm Hudson's Bay Co., founded in the 17th century. Also here is **Henry Birks et Fils,** a preeminent jeweler since 1879 (the company is now known as Maison Birks, but the original name remains on the building.) The Birks Café is a decidedly posh spot to enjoy lunch, high tea, or buy super-premium chocolates or *macarons.*

If you're in the mood to shop, stroll west on this main shopping drag. (Be aware that there are adult shops here, too, most of which are above street level.) If you were to turn right and walk 5 short blocks to the east, you would reach Quartier des Spectacles, the city's central arts district. To continue the tour, return to this corner and the:

9 Cathédrale Christ Church

Built from 1856 to 1859, this neo-Gothic building stands in glorious contrast to the city's downtown skyscrapers and is the seat of the

Anglican bishop of Montréal. The church garden is modeled on a medieval European cloister. It offers a Sunday 10am Sung Eucharist and 4pm Choral Evensong, and weekday services at 8:15am, 12:15pm, and 5:15pm. **www.montrealcathedral.ca**.

Walk east on rue Ste-Catherine to avenue Union, where the La Baie department store is. Turn left on av. Union and go north 3 blocks, to rue Sherbrooke. As you cross boulevard de Maisonneuve, note the prominent bike lanes the city has installed, part of its massive biking network. At rue Sherbrooke, you'll be in front of McGill University's Schulich School of Music.

10 Java U ☕

This casual eatery at 626 rue Sherbrooke ouest offers fresh and healthy options: sandwiches, quiche, fresh fruit, ice cream, and pastries. The atmosphere is collegiate and slightly upscale (p. 79).

Head left (west) on rue Sherbrooke. This is the city's grand boulevard, and the rest of the tour will take you past the former mansions, ritzy hotels, high-end boutiques, and special museums that give it its personality today. One block down on the left is:

11 Musée McCord

This museum of Canadian history opened in 1921 but has a contemporary, playful zest. Named for its founder, David Ross McCord, the museum maintains an eclectic collection of photographs, paintings, and First Nations folk art, and its edgy special exhibits make it especially worth a visit. Hours and other details are on p. 107.

Continue west. On your right is:

12 McGill University

The gate is usually open to Canada's most prestigious university, founded in 1821 after a bequest from a Scottish-born fur trader, James McGill. The central campus mixes modern concrete and glass structures alongside older stone buildings and is the focal point for the school's 39,000 students.

On campus is the:

13 Musée Redpath

This quirky natural history museum is in an 1882 building with a grandly proportioned and richly appointed interior. Its main draws—worth a half-hour visit—are the mummies and coffin that are part of Canada's second-largest collection of Egyptian antiquities, and skeletons of whales and prehistoric beasts. Admission is free. See p. 107.

Continue on rue Sherbrooke. About 9m (30 ft.) past McGill's front gate, note the large stone on the lawn. This marks the:

14 Site of the Amerindian Hochelaga Settlement

Near this spot was the village of Hochelaga, a community of Iroquois who lived and farmed here before the first Europeans arrived. When French explorer Jacques Cartier stepped from his ship onto the land and visited Hochelaga in 1535, he noted that the village had 50 large homes, each housing several families. When the French returned in 1603, the village was empty. Read more about this history on p. 31 in chapter 3.

15 Café Vasco da Gama ☕

Downtown is full of restaurants both fancy and casual. Right in between is **Café Vasco Da Gama**, 1472 rue Peel (1 block south of rue Sherbrooke; ℭ **514/286-2688**), a sleek, high-ceilinged eatery with a Portuguese feel—the owners also run the esteemed **Ferreira Café** (p. 74) on the same block. It features big breakfasts, pastries, sandwiches, and tapas.

Two blocks farther down on rue Sherbrooke, at no. 1188, just past rue Stanley, is:

16 Vestiges of the "Golden Square Mile"

Rue Sherbrooke is the heart of what's historically been known as the "Golden Square Mile." This is where the city's most luxurious residences of the 19th and early 20th centuries were, and where the vast majority of the country's wealthiest citizens lived. (For a period of time, 79 families living in this neighborhood controlled 80% of Canada's wealth.) Many of the neighborhood's stately homes were torn down when skyscrapers began to rise here after World War II, but some remain. They include Maison Alcan, at no. 1188, now a modern office building that has nicely incorporated one of those 19th-century mansions into its late-20th-century façade; and, on the opposite side of the street, Maison Louis-Joseph Forget at no. 1195 and Maison Reid Wilson at no 1201. Both of those buildings are designated historic monuments.

Continue on rue Sherbrooke, passing on your left the newly renovated Ritz-Carlton and the high-end Holt Renfrew department store. At the corner of rue Crescent is:

17 Musée des Beaux-Arts (Museum of Fine Arts)

This is Canada's oldest museum and Montréal's most prominent. Enter through the modern annex added in 1991 on the left side of rue Sherbrooke. It connects to the original stately Beaux Arts building (1912) on the right side via an underground tunnel that doubles as a gallery. The adjacent church, with its Tiffany windows, was converted in 2011 into an addition to the museum, although it can only be visited on guided tours or when attending a classical concert there. See p. 105 for details.

You have several options at this point. If you have time to explore the museum, take the opportunity—a visit to the Musée des Beaux-Arts should be part of any trip to Montréal. For high-end boutique shopping, continue on rue Sherbrooke. For drinking or eating, turn left onto:

18 Rue Crescent

Welcome to party central. Rue Crescent and nearby streets are the focal point of the downtown social and dining district. The area is largely yuppie-Anglo in character, if not necessarily in strict demographics. Crescent's first block has small boutiques and jewelers, but the next 2 blocks are a jumble of terraced bars and dance clubs, inexpensive pizza joints, and upscale restaurants, all drawing enthusiastic consumers looking to party the afternoon and evening away. It's hard to imagine that this was once a run-down slum slated for demolition. Luckily, buyers saw potential in these late-19th-century row houses and brought them back to life.

19 Sir Winston Churchill 🍺
Lively spots for food and drink are abundant along rue Crescent. **Sir Winston Churchill Pub** (no. 1459) is one. If you can, find a seat on the balcony. See p. 137.

WALKING TOUR 3: **PARC DU MONT-ROYAL**

START:	**At the corner of rue Peel and avenue des Pins**
FINISH:	**At the cross on top of the mountain (la Croix du Mont-Royal)**
TIME:	**1 hour to ascend to the Chalet du Mont-Royal and its lookout over the city and come back down if you go by the fastest route; 3 hours if you take the more leisurely chemin Olmsted route and see all the sites listed. It's easy to leave out some sites to shorten the walk. City bus no. 11 travels along chemin de la Remembrance (Remembrance Rd.) on the mountaintop.**
BEST TIMES:	**Spring, summer, and autumn mornings**
WORST TIMES:	**During the high heat of midday in summer, or on winter days when more ice than snow is on the ground**

Join the locals: With a reasonable measure of physical fitness, the best way to explore the jewel that is Parc du Mont-Royal is simply to walk up it from downtown. It's called a mountain, but it is a very small one. A broad pedestrian-only road and smaller footpaths form a web of options for strollers, joggers, cyclists, and in-line skaters of all ages. Anyone in search of a little greenery and space heads here in warm weather, while in winter, cross-country skiers follow miles of paths and snowshoers tramp along trails laid out especially for them.

The 200-hectare (494-acre) urban park was created in 1876 by American landscape architect Frederick Law Olmsted, who also designed Central Park in New York City and parks in Philadelphia, Boston, and Chicago. In the end, though, relatively little of Olmsted's full design for Mont Royal actually came into being. You can pull up a terrific interactive map on your smartphone at **www.lemontroyal.qc.ca/carte/en/index.sn**. You can also download podcasts for guided audio-video walks at the same website.

Start at the corner of rue Peel and av. des Pins, at the:

1 Downtown Park Entrance
After years of construction, this entrance is finally a thing of beauty, with broad steps and beautiful plantings. (***Note:*** If you're heading up with a stroller or wheelchair, an accessible entrance is about 30m/98 ft. to the left.) From either entrance, it's possible to reach the top of this small

Walking Tour 3: Parc du Mont-Royal

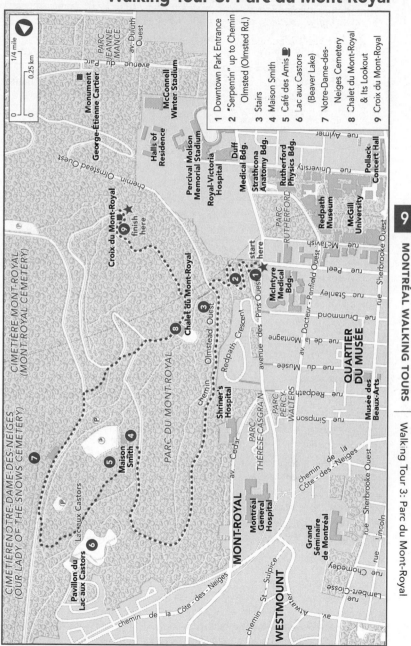

1 Downtown Park Entrance
2 "Serpentin" up to Chemin Olmsted (Olmsted Rd.)
3 Stairs
4 Maison Smith
5 Café des Amis
6 Lac aux Castors (Beaver Lake)
7 Notre-Dame-des-Neiges Cemetery
8 Chalet du Mont-Royal & Its Lookout
9 Croix du Mont-Royal

mountain by a variety of routes. Hearty souls can choose the quickest and most strenuous approach—taking the steepest sets of stairs at every opportunity, which go directly to the Chalet du Mont-Royal and its lookout at the top (see no. 9). Those who prefer to take their time and gain altitude slowly can use the switchback bridle path. Or mix and match the options as you go along. Don't be too worried about getting lost; the park is small enough that it's easy to regain your sense of direction no matter which way you head.

Head up the footpath at this entrance. You'll soon reach the broad bridle path:

2 Serpentin & Chemin Olmsted (Olmsted Rd.)

The road zigzags here, giving this short stretch the name "Serpentin." It passes some beautiful stone houses to the left. If you want to bypass some of the switchbacks, use any of a number of paths for a shortcut—but stay only on established trails to prevent erosion. After about the fourth switchback, you'll reach an intersection with the option to go left or right. Turn left. This is chemin Olmsted (Olmsted Rd.), designed by Frederick Law Olmsted. It was built at a gradual grade for horse-drawn carriages, so that horses could pull their loads up the hill at a steady pace and not be pushed from behind by the weight of the carriage on the way down. Thankfully, this road remains closed to automobiles even today. Following this shaded, pleasant road in the woods will lead you to Maison Smith (see no. 4, below) in about 45 minutes.

Another option is to take the:

3 Stairs

Numerous sets of stairs through the woods let you bypass the Serpentin's broad switchbacks. These steps get walkers to the Chalet du Mont-Royal and its lookout (see no. 9) more quickly. *Fair warning:* The last 100 or so steps go almost straight up. On the plus side, you'll get to share sympathetic smiles with strangers you pass. Taking the steps bypasses sites no. 4, 5, and 6.

If you're taking chemin Olmsted, you eventually arrive at:

4 Maison Smith

Built in 1858, this structure has been used over the years as a park rangers' station and park police headquarters. Today, it's a year-round information center (© **514/843-8240**) with a small exhibit about the park, a cafe, and a gift shop.

5 Café des Amis 🔲

Café des Amis (© **514/843-8240**), inside Maison Smith and spilling out onto a lovely terrace from mid-May through mid-October, offers sandwiches, homemade soups, sweets (try the pineapple-carrot cake if they have it), and beverages including beer, wine, and fair trade Camino hot chocolate.

From Maison Smith, walk through the field of sculptures, away from the radio tower, until you reach:

6 Lac des Castors (Beaver Lake)

This lake's name refers to the once-profitable fur industry, not to the actual presence of the long-gone animals. In summer, sunbathers and picnickers surround the lake and paddleboats are for rent. In the winter, it becomes an ice skater's paradise and, after the snow, a cross-country ski retreat and tobogganing wonder.

Walk to the main road, chemin de la Remembrance (Remembrance Rd.), to enter:

7 Notre-Dame-des-Neiges Cemetery

This is the city's predominantly Catholic cemetery, and from here, you can visit the adjacent Protestant Mount Royal graveyard. Behind it (to the north), if you're up for a longer walk, is the small adjoining Jewish and Spanish-Portuguese cemetery. Notre-Dame-des-Neiges Cemetery reveals much about Montréal's ethnic mix: engraved on headstones, some with likenesses in photos or tiles, are surnames as diverse as Zagorska, Skwyrska, De Ciccio, Sen, Lavoie, O'Neill, Hammerschmid, Fernandez, Müller, Haddad, and Boudreault.

This is another spot where you have the option of picking up the no. 11 bus on chemin de la Remembrance to head east toward the Guy Métro station. To continue the tour, head back toward Maison Smith and follow the signs on the main path for:

8 Chalet du Mont-Royal & Its Lookout

The front terrace here offers the most popular panoramic view of the city and river. The chalet itself was constructed from 1931 to 1932 and has been used over the years for receptions, concerts, and various other events. Inside the chalet, take a look at the 17 paintings hanging just below the ceiling. They relate the region's history and the story of the French explorations of North America.

Facing the chalet from the terrace, locate the path running off to the right, marked by a sign that says CROIX, which means "cross." Follow it for about 10 minutes to the giant:

9 Croix du Mont-Royal

Legend has it that Paul de Chomedey, Sieur de Maisonneuve, erected a wooden cross here in 1643 after the young colony survived a flood threat. The present incarnation, installed in 1924, is steel and 31.4m (103 ft.) tall. It is lit at night and visible from all over the city. Beside the cross is a plaque marking where a time capsule was interred in August 1992, during Montréal's 350th-birthday celebration. Some 12,000 children ages 6 to 12 filled the capsule with messages and drawings depicting their visions for the city in the year 2142, when Montréal will be 500 years old and the capsule will be opened.

To return to downtown Montréal, you can go back along the path to the chalet terrace. On the left, just before the terrace, is another path. It leads to the staircase described in no. 3 and descends to where the tour began. The walk down by this route takes about 15 minutes. The no. 11 bus going east runs from the summit to the Mont Royal Métro. Bus stops are at Beaver Lake and along chemin de la Remembrance.

DAY TRIPS FROM MONTRÉAL

You don't have to travel far from Montréal to reach mountains, bike trails, or vineyards. In fact, great touring regions are a mere 30-minute drive from the city. Both the **Laurentian Mountains** (to the north) and **Cantons-de-l'Est** (also known by its British name, the Eastern Townships, to the southeast) have year-round vacation retreats, with skiing in winter, biking and boating in summer, maple sugaring in spring, and vineyard touring and leaf peeping in fall.

The pearl of the Laurentians (also called les Laurentides) is **Mont-Tremblant,** eastern Canada's highest peak and a winter mecca for skiers and snowboarders from all over North America. The bucolic Cantons-de-l'Est were known as the Eastern Townships when they were a haven for English Loyalists and their descendants.

Because both regions rely heavily on tourism for their livelihoods, knowledge of at least rudimentary English is widespread, even outside hotels and restaurants. Still, having at least a few phrases of French at your disposal will help immensely as you tour these Francophone-centric regions.

SKIING AT MONT-TREMBLANT ★★★

145km (90 miles) N of Montréal

Don't expect spiked peaks or high, ragged ridges. The Laurentian Shield's rolling hills and rounded mountains average between 300m and 520m (984 ft.–1,706 ft.) in height, with the highest being Mont-Tremblant, at 875m (2,871 ft.). These are not the Alps or the Rockies, but they're welcoming and embracing to skiers of most levels. Within a 64-km (40-mile) radius are 12 ski centers, with Mont-Tremblant itself being the most popular, with a vibrant pedestrian village at its base that is a kind of Aspen-meets-Disneyland. Skiers can usually expect reliable snow from early December to late March. The busiest times are February and March.

10

Mont Tremblant, a Ski Magazine top-rated ski resort

Essentials
GETTING THERE

BY CAR   The fast and scenic **Autoroute des Laurentides,** also known as **Autoroute 15,** goes straight from Montréal to the Laurentians. About 15km (9 miles) before Mont-Tremblant, 15 ends and merges with the older **Route 117,** which also runs parallel with Autoroute 15. (If you have the time to meander, you can exit 15 at St-Jérôme and pick up the smaller Route 117, which passes through many appealing small towns.) Montréalers fill the highways when they "go up north" on weekends, particularly during the top skiing months, so try to avoid driving on Friday afternoons.

Driving in this area can be confusing (see "Getting Around," below). Route 117 has four exits to the Mont-Tremblant ski area. The first is exit 113, which takes visitors through Centre-Ville Mont-Tremblant (formerly the village of St-Jovite), a pleasant small town with a main street, rue de St-Jovite, lined with cafes and shops. From the center of town, Route 327 heads to the mountain.

The fourth exit, exit 119, bypasses Centre-Ville and goes directly to the mountain. Watch for signs with the resort's logo, which use the "A" in "Tremblant" to represent a ski mountain.

BY BUS   **Galland** buses (www.galland-bus.com; ✆ **877/806-8666** or 450/ 687-8666) depart from **Gare d'autocars de Montréal,** 1717 rue Berri, and stop in the larger Laurentian towns, including Mont-Tremblant. The ride to Mont-Tremblant takes just under 3 hours.

VISITOR INFORMATION

Tourist offices are plentiful throughout the Laurentians—just look for the blue "?" signs. A major information center is at exit 51 off Autoroute 15. It shares a building with a McDonald's. Called **Tourisme Laurentides** (www. laurentides.com; (C) **800/561-6673** or 450/224-7007), it has racks of brochures and a helpful staff. In the summer high season, it's open daily 8:30am to 7pm. Though open the remainder of the year, typically 9am to 5pm, hours can vary, so call ahead. Closer to the ski mountain is an office at 5080 Montée Ryan ((C) **877/425-2434** or 819/425-2434), open year-round daily 9am to 5pm. You can also check **www.tourismemonttremblant.com**, an official tourism site, and **www.tremblant.ca**, the Mont-Tremblant ski resort's website.

GETTING AROUND

You can certainly settle in for a day of skiing, eating, and shopping at the Mont-Tremblant ski center and resort village and get around by foot. If you want to visit Scandinave Spa (below), you'll need a car.

If you drive through the area, keep this in mind: The abundant use of the name "Tremblant" can be very confusing. Foremost is Mont-Tremblant, the mountain itself. Then there's the resort village that is sometimes called the pedestrian village, sometimes called Tremblant, and sometimes called Mont-Tremblant Station. Then there's the old village of Mont-Tremblant about 5km (3 miles) northwest of the resort, which long ago was the region's center. There's Centre-Ville Mont-Tremblant, the cute commercial district about 12km (7½ miles) south of the mountain that used to be known as St-Jovite. Feeding the confusion is the fact that, in 2005, the villages of St-Jovite and Mont-Tremblant and the pedestrian village combined to become a single entity named Ville de Mont-Tremblant—but many maps and residents still refer to the areas by their old names. You'll also see signs for a lake, Lac Tremblant, next to the pedestrian village, and the large national park, Parc National du Mont-Tremblant. Clear as mud, right?

PARKING

Parking lots are right in the pedestrian village, and, if those are full, you'll find others close by (and well marked) that are served by shuttles to the village.

Hitting the Slopes (& the Spa)

The **Mont-Tremblant ski resort** (www.tremblant.ca; (C) **888/738-1777** or 514/764-7546) draws the biggest downhill crowds in the Laurentians and for 15 years running was ranked as the top ski resort in eastern North America by *Ski Magazine*. Founded in 1939, it's one of the oldest in North America. Mont-Tremblant was considered a pioneer for creating trails on both sides of a mountain and was the second mountain in the world to install a chairlift. The vertical drop is 645m (2,116 ft.). When the snow is deep, skiers here like to follow the sun around the mountain, making the run down the eastern slopes in the morning and down the western-facing ones in the afternoon. Certainly there are higher mountains with longer runs and steeper pitches, but

Skiing at Mont-Tremblant

DAY TRIPS FROM MONTRÉAL

something about Mont-Tremblant compels people to return time and again. The resort has snowmaking capability to cover almost three-quarters of its 268 hectares (662 acres) of skiable terrain. Of its 96 downhill runs and trails, half are expert terrain, about a third are intermediate, and the rest beginner. The longest trail, Nansen, is 6km (3¾ miles).

For *après-ski* (or instead of skiing), an appealing European-style Nordic spa is nearby, built adjacent to a river and featuring both outdoor and indoor spaces. You can easily spend at least 3 hours at **Scandinave Spa,** 4280 Montée Ryan, Mont-Tremblant (www.scandinave.com; ℂ **888/537-2263**), open year-round. It's a rustic-chic complex of small buildings among evergreen trees on the Diable River shore. Few activities are more magical than being in a warm outdoor pool as snow falls, the sun sets, and the temperature plummets. For C$48, visitors (18 and older only) have run of the facility. Options include outdoor hot tubs designed to look like natural pools (one is set under a man-made waterfall); an indoor Norwegian steam bath thick with eucalyptus; indoor relaxation areas with super-comfortable, low-slung chairs; and the river itself, which the heartiest of folk dip into even on frigid days. (A heat lamp keeps a small square of river open, even through the iciest part of winter.) The idea is to move from hot to cold to hot, which supposedly purges toxins and invigorates your skin. Bathing suits are required, and men and women share all spaces except the changing rooms. Massages are available for extra fees.

If you visit in warm weather, a downhill dry-land alpine **Skyline Luge** (www.skylineluge.com; ℂ **819/681-3000**) is set up right on the ski mountain at the pedestrian village. The gravity-propelled, engineless sleds reach speeds of up to 48kmph (30 mph), if you so choose (it's easy to go down as a slow-poke, too). Rides are priced by number of descents, starting at C$13 for one ride (C$3 for kids 6 and under). The village has other games and attractions, such as outdoor climbing walls and forest zip lines.

Where to Eat & Shop

The pedestrian-only resort village on Mont-Tremblant's slope is the social hub of the region. The village has the prefabricated look of a theme park, but at least planners used the Québécois architectural style of pitched or mansard roofs in bright colors, not ersatz Tyrolean or Bavarian Alpine flourishes. For a sweeping view of the entire complex, take the **panoramic gondola** from the bottom of the village to the top; it zips over the walkways, candy-colored hotels, and outdoor swimming pools. It costs C$17 for adults, C$13 for ages 6 to 12 and C$4.20 for children 5 and under. Many pedestrian village hotels include a free ride. The **casino gondola,** which travels across the mountainside, is always free.

Otherwise, you can stroll the village easily. Small lanes lead up past 35 shops that sell clothing, sporting goods, sweets, and gifts. The village also has 36 restaurants and bars. In the pedestrian village, restaurants open as early as 5:30am and bars stay open until 3am. In the surrounding area, opening hours can be shorter. Expect restaurants to serve dinner until 8 or 9pm during the week and until 10 or 11pm on the weekends.

Bistro Au Grain de Café (www.augraindecafe.com; ✆ **819/681-4567**), tucked into a corner of the upper village just off the main plaza called Place St-Bernard, is a reliable choice for coffee and sandwiches (daily 7:30am–11pm during ski season).

Like at most ski mountains, beer, burgers, and roast chicken are abundant. Slope-side drink palaces **Le Shack** (www.leshack.com; ✆ **819/681-4700**) and **La Forge** (www.laforgetremblant.com; ✆ **819/681-4900**) are full of TVs and music and feature perfectly agreeable family-friendly cuisine. For something a little different, the New Orleans' inspired **Fat Mardi's** (www.fatmardis.com; ✆ **819/681-2439**) just across the square (Place St-Bernard) is another fine choice. The smaller microbrewery **Microbrasserie La Diable** (www.microladiable.com; ✆ **819/681-4546**), housed in a free-standing chalet at 117 chemin Kandahar, is more laid back and offers seven home brews and a menu that includes veggie and salmon burgers along with the expected burgers, salads, chili, and good sausage with homemade sauerkraut. Be warned that it's a bit of a walk down chemin Kandahar from the base of the ski mountain, especially in those clunky boots, but the location makes it easier to get a table.

After 20 years on-mountain, one of our favorite spots for sweet and savory *crêpes,* **Crêperie Catherine** (www.creperiecatherine.ca; ✆ **819/681-4888**), moved to 977 rue Labelle, Centre-Ville Mont-Tremblant. If you go, be sure to try the house specialty, *sucre a la crème* (a concoction of brown sugar and butter). You can order from any part of the menu any time of day.

BIKING THE ROUTE VERTE (GREEN ROUTE) ★

Start at Val-David, 80km (50 miles) N of Montréal

Québec is bike crazy, and it's got the goods to justify it. In 2007, the province inaugurated the Route Verte (Green Route), a now-5,000km (3,107-mile) bike network that stretches from one end of the province to the other, linking all regions and cities. It's modeled on the Rails-to-Trails program in the U.S. and famed cycling routes in Denmark, Great Britain, and along the Danube and Rhine rivers in Central Europe. The nonprofit biking organization Vélo Québec initiated the project with support from the Québec Ministry of Transportation. Route Verte won the prestigious Prix Ulysse, one of the grand prizes given annually by the Québec tourist office, right out of the gate. The National Geographic Society went on to declare it one of the 10 best bicycle routes in the world.

Route Verte has a lot of sections, including paths all through the city of Montréal. But if you want to enjoy some countryside, head north out of the city to bike the popular **P'tit Train du Nord bike trail.** It goes through the Laurentians to Mont-Tremblant and beyond. Built on a former railway track, it passes through the scenic villages of Ste-Adèle, Val-David, and Ste-Agathe-des-Monts. Cyclists can easily hop on and off for a day trip or can plan a multi-day trip with transportation assistance for luggage. Food and bike repairs are offered at renovated railway stations along the path.

This day trip begins at a mid-point on the trail, in Val-David—one of the prettiest villages in the region. The town conjures up images of cabin hide-aways set among hills rearing above ponds and lakes, and of creeks tumbling through fragrant forests. Plus, a prominent entrance to the bike path is located here.

Essentials

GETTING THERE

BY CAR Follow the directions above for "Skiing at Mont-Tremblant." At exit 76 of Autoroute 15 (and also along Rte. 117) is the village of Val-David, the region's faintly bohemian enclave.

VISITOR INFORMATION

The **Route Verte website** (www.routeverte.com) provides maps of all the paths by region (look for the "Laurentides" map). Advance planners might want to get the English-language guidebook *Cycling in Québec: Official Guide*, published by Vélo Québec and can be ordered from the site.

Specific details about the P'tit Train du Nord trail are at the **Tourisme Laurentides** website, at www.laurentides.com/en/linearpark. The tourism office also publishes a **P'tit Train du Nord Official Service Guide.** You can find it online at www.myvirtualpaper.com/doc/tourisme-laurentides.

Val-David's **tourist office** is on the main street in the Petite Gare, or old train station, at 2525 rue de l'Église (www.valdavid.com; ✆ **888/322-7030**, ext. 4235, or 819/324-5678, ext. 4235). The building is adjacent to the bike path. It's open daily from 9am to 5pm from mid-May to mid-October, with variable opening hours the rest of the year (call first).

PARKING

A parking lot is next to the tourist office on rue de l'Église, adjacent to the bike path. A second parking lot is on the opposite side of the bike path.

Hopping onto the Bike Path

The P'tit Train du Nord bike trail is 232km (145 miles) long and passes through forests and some lovely villages (Val-David among them), and offers breathtaking mountain vistas. Since it was built on a former railway line, it is relatively flat. Former train stations have been repurposed into cafes, bistros, and covered refuges all along the way. Most have people who can help with bike repairs. Cyclists share the trail with walkers and skaters, bicycles are limited to a speed of 22kmh (14 mph)—fast for casual bikers, though medium speed for road warriors. The trail is free to ride on.

So, which direction to head? You can't go wrong either way. Again, take a look through Tourisme Laurentides' Official Service Guide specifically about the trail (see "Visitor Information," above). You'll see that Val-David is at kilometer 42. Ste-Adèle (pop. 12,137), which has a popular lake, Lac Rond, is just 9km (5³/₅ miles) south. Cafes, galleries, and bakeries line rue Valiquette, the main drag in Ste-Adèle. Heading the other direction on the trail, Mont-Tremblant's splashy pedestrian village (see "Where to Eat & Shop," below) is at kilometer 91, 49km (30 miles) north. The guide lists services along each kilometer of the trail, from bars to bike repairs to banks to supermarkets. The folks at the tourist office in Val-David and at the region's central tourist office at exit 51 off Autoroute 15 can offer suggested itineraries depending on whether you want a leisurely or more challenging ride and on how much time you have.

If you didn't bring your own bike, **bike rentals** (or skis, snow shoes, and ice skates in the winter) are available in Val-David at the tourist office and at **Roc & Ride Sports de Montagne,** 2444 rue de l'Église (www.rocnride.com; ℰ **819/322-7978**).

Where to Eat & Shop

Finding a place to dine out year round in this region will not be a problem. The Route Verte's high season for biking runs from late June through Labour Day and during winter when there's enough snow for cross-country skiing. At those times restaurants are open daily, though some only for dinner. In the quieter season, some restaurants may be closed Monday and Tuesday.

For a relaxing picnic, get fixings in Val-David at the **Metro Supermarket** across from the tourist office on the main street or soups, salads, sandwiches, and pastries at the artisanal bakery **Boulangerie La Vagabonde,** tucked into a house on a wooded side street at 1262 chemin de la Rivière (www.boulangerie lavagabonde.com; ℰ **819/322-3953**). If you're in town on a Saturday morning from late June to late September, look for the organic **farmer's market** on rue de l'Académie (opposite the church).

The village has a lovely picnic spot: From the tourist office, turn left onto the bike path and walk 5 minutes to the North River and the teeny **Parc des Amoureux.** Look for the sign that appropriately says SITE PITTORESQUE.

For a more substantial meal, **Au Petit Poucet,** on Route 117 just south of Val-David (1030 Rte. 117; www.aupetitpoucet.com; ℰ **888/334-2246** or 819/322-2246), evokes a Québec of hunting cabins and hearty sugar-shack cuisine. A floor-to-ceiling fireplace anchors the interior, and the menu features *tourtière* (meat pie), pea soup, baked beans, and sugar pie. A shop here sells food to go.

Though Val-David is small, it has many artist studios. You're in luck if you're visiting in mid-summer: the village hosts a huge **ceramic art festival** (www.1001pots.com; ℰ **819/322-6868**) daily from mid-July to mid-August (July 10–Aug 16 in 2015). Sculptors and ceramicists, along with painters, jewelers, and pewter smiths display their work, and concerts and art demonstrations round out the offerings.

TOURING VINEYARDS IN CANTONS-DE-L'EST ★

Start at Dunham, 95km (59 miles) SE of Montréal, toward Sherbrooke

The rolling countryside of Cantons-de-l'Est to the southeast of Montréal has long served as the province's breadbasket, and that includes grape and apple orchards for wine and cider. Still referred to by many English-speakers as the **Eastern Townships,** the region is largely pastoral, marked by billowing hills and small villages. Except for a few disheartening signs for fast-food stops, the region is largely advertisement-free.

Canada is known more for its beers and ales than its wines, but that hasn't stopped agriculturists from planting vines and transforming fruit into drinkable clarets, chardonnays, and Sauternes. The most successful efforts have blossomed along southern Ontario's Niagara Frontier and in British Columbia's relatively warmer precincts, but in the Cantons-de-l'Est, which enjoys the mildest microclimates in the province, apples and grapes grow. Most vintners and fruit growers are concentrated around Dunham, about 103km (64 miles) southeast of Montréal, with several vineyards along Route 202. The region also produces a special variety of wine known as ice cider *(cidre de glace),* an aperitif made from apples that have frosted over.

Though the region offers plenty of enticing reasons to visit any time of year (beautiful inland lakes in summer, snowy trails and traditional sugar shacks in winter and early spring), autumn presents particular attractions. In addition to the glorious fall foliage (usually best from early September to early October), the orchards around here sag under the weight of apples of every variety, and cider mills hum day and night. Visitors are invited to help with the harvest and can pay a low price to pick their own baskets of fruit. Cider mills open their doors for tours and tastings.

Essentials
GETTING THERE
BY CAR   Leave Montréal by Pont Champlain, the bridge which funnels into arrow-straight Autoroute 10. Go east toward Sherbrooke. Within 20 minutes, you'll be passing fields, clusters of cows, and in summer, meadows strewn with wildflowers. The exit numbers represent the distance in kilometers from Montréal. To get to Dunham, take exit 48 and pick up QC-233 south. Take that 9.5km (6 miles) to Rte. 104 E. Take that 25km (15½ miles) to Rte. 202 West and signs for Dunham.

VISITOR INFORMATION
Tourisme Cantons-de-l'Est (www.easterntownships.org; ✆ **800/355-5755**) provides a slew of information. Driving from Montréal, the first regional **tourist information office** (www.granby-bromont.com; ✆ **866/472-6292** or 450/375-8774) is at exit 68 off Autoroute 10. It's open daily year-round and has free Wi-Fi.

Vineyard Les Pervenches in the Eastern Townships

Touring the Vineyards

A drive through this area and a vineyard tour makes for a pleasant afternoon, but if you're really gung-ho, you can follow the established **Route des Vins,** which passes 21 wineries. A map and travel information is at **www.laroute desvins.ca**.

You can start anywhere, but a popular option is **Vignoble de l'Orpailleur,** at 1086 Rte. 202 in Dunham (www.orpailleur.ca; ✆ **450/295-2763**). It has three types of guided tours daily from late June through October for C$9 to C$19. Its white wines, such as the straw-colored L'Orpailleur, are regulars on Montréal restaurant menus.

Ice cider and ice wine are two regional products that may be new to visitors: They're made from apples and grapes, respectively, left on the trees and vines past the first frost, and served ice-cold with cheese or dessert. One top producer is **Domaine Pinnacle,** at 150 Richford Rd. in Frelighsburg (www. domainepinnacle.com; ✆ **450/298-1226**), about 13km (8 miles) south of Dunham. Its *cidre de glace* is a regular gold medalist in international competitions (it avoids the risk of being cloyingly sweet, which is hard to do for ice cider). The farm's tasting room and boutique are open daily May through December and Saturday and Sunday January through April.

Where to Eat & Shop

Many of the vineyards, including the two listed above, have either restaurants or gourmet food boutiques onsite. Local restaurants serve dinner until 8pm or

SETTLING INTO QUÉBEC CITY

Québec City seduces from first view. Situated along the majestic Fleuve Saint-Laurent (St-Lawrence River), much of the oldest part of the city—Vieux-Québec (Old Québec)—sits atop a rock bluff that once provided military defense. Fortress walls still encase the upper city, and the soaring Château Frontenac, a hotel with castlelike turrets, dominates the landscape. Hauntingly evocative of a coastal town in the motherland of France, the tableau is as romantic as any in Europe.

This was Canada's first European settlement, christened La Nouvelle France in the 16th century. Today, Québec City clings to its French-speaking heritage and Gallic traditions: As it becomes increasingly chic and current, it keeps one foot rooted proudly in the past. It also keeps one foot tapping year round: No matter the season, it seems the city always has a party or festival going on somewhere. From the outdoor-activity-filled Winter Carnaval to the rich calendar of music and theater offerings in summer, the city's *joie de vivre* is ever in the air. While most theater is in French, even non-Francophones can enjoy the artistry of Québécois productions.

ESSENTIALS

Arriving

Served by highways, transcontinental trains and buses, and several airports, Québec City is easily accessible from within Canada, the U.S., or overseas.

BY PLANE

In Québec City, a number of major airlines serve the teeny **Jean Lesage International Airport** (airport code YQB; www.aeroport dequebec.com; © **877/769-2700**). Most air traffic comes by way of Montréal, although some direct flights do connect from Canadian and U.S. cities, including Toronto, Ottawa, Chicago, New York (Newark and JFK airports), and Philadelphia. *Note:* Some direct flights are seasonal only.

9pm during the week and until 10 or 11pm on weekends. Summer and autumn are this region's high season. For a wider variety of food and shopping, we like the village of **Knowlton.** It's at the southern tip of Lac Brome, on Rte 104 East (about 40km/25 miles, from Frelighsburg, above). At no. 39 on historic Victoria Street, **Barne's General Store** (© **450/243-6480**), has been in business since 1890 and is a spot for organic food, tube socks, colored poster board, penny candy, and a spicy Middle Eastern dip made with pomegranate and walnuts called *muhammara.* Mmm! Also here is the **Boutique Gourmet de Canards du Lac Brome,** producer of Lac Brome's famous (in this area, anyway) Pekin duck meat. Though no live ducks are in view, more duck products are on display here than the average non-Québécois can fathom. Located at 40 chemin du Centre (www.canardsdulacbrome.com; © **450/242-3825 ext. 221**), the store is open daily year-round.

If you're touring in the spring, you'll be in the region at the time when every sugar-maple tree is being tapped and "sugared off." The result? **Maple festivals** and farms hosting sugaring parties, with guests wolfing down prodigious country repasts capped by traditional maple-syrup desserts. Montréal newspapers and the regional tourist offices keep up-to-date lists of what's happening and where during the sugaring; many of the festivals and "sugar shacks" are right in this area.

From the airport, a taxi to downtown is a fixed-rate C$34.25. (Likewise, a taxi from downtown to the airport is also C$34.25.) The public bus no. 78 runs only to the Les Saules bus terminal, at the corner of boulevard Massona and rue Michelet, which is well outside the tourist area. You'll need to transfer from there. The bus runs Monday through Friday, though typically adds weekends during the summer, and costs C$3.25, exact change only. Ask at the airport for the best route; you can also visit www.rtcquebec.ca or call © **418/627-2511.**

BY BUS

Québec City's bus terminal, at 320 rue Abraham-Martin (© **418/525-3000**), is just beside the Gare du Palais train station. As from the train station, it's an uphill climb or short cab ride to Upper Town or other parts of Lower Town.

BY CAR

See p. 42 for general driving directions into the province via Montréal.

You have two options when driving between Montréal and Québec City: Autoroute 40, which runs along the St. Lawrence's north shore, and Autoroute 20, on the south side (although not hugging the water at all). Either way, the trip takes about 3 hours.

Québec City is 867km (539 miles) from New York City and 644km (400 miles) from Boston. From New York, follow the directions to Montréal (p. 42), and then pick up Autoroute 20 to Québec City. From Boston, follow the directions to Montréal, but at Autoroute 10, go east instead of west to stay on Autoroute 55. Get on Autoroute 20 to Québec City and follow signs for the Pont Pierre-Laporte, the major bridge into the city. Turn right onto Boulevard Wilfrid-Laurier (Rte. 175) shortly after crossing the bridge. It changes names first to Boulevard Laurier and then to Grande-Allée, a main boulevard that leads directly into the central Parliament Hill area and the Old City. Once the street passes through the ancient walls that ring the Old City, it becomes rue St-Louis, which leads straight to the famed Château Frontenac on the cliff above the St. Lawrence River.

Another appealing option when you're approaching Québec City from the south is to follow Route 132 along the river's southern side to the town of Lévis. A car ferry there, **Traverse Québec-Lévis** (www.traversiers.gouv. qc.ca; © **877/787-7483**), provides a 10-minute ride across the river and a dramatic way to see the city, especially for the first time. The schedule varies substantially through the year and only stops completely in weather emergencies, but the ferry leaves at least every hour from 6am to 2am. One-way costs C$8.25 for a car and driver, C$3.50 for each additional adult, and C$16 for a car with up to six passengers.

BY TRAIN

Québec City's train station, Gare du Palais, is in Lower Town at 450 rue de la Gare-du-Palais. Many of the hotels listed in this book are up an incline from the station, so a short cab ride might be necessary.

The **VIA Rail Canada** (www.via rail.ca; ℃ **888/VIA-RAIL** [888/842-7245]) train ride between Montréal and Québec City takes about 3 hours.

BY BOAT

Québec City is a stop for cruise ships that travel along the St. Lawrence River. Ships dock in a neighborhood called Vieux-Port. As in Montréal, an abundance of restaurants and shops is within walking distance.

Visitor Information

High season in Québec City is from June 24 (Jean-Baptiste Day, a provincial holiday) through Labour Day (the first Monday in September, as in the U.S., a national holiday). For those 11 weeks, the city is in highest gear. Tourist offices, museums, and restaurants all expand their operating hours, and hotels charge top dollar. This book notes the changes in hours and prices throughout the year for many venues, but it's best to call and confirm open hours before making a special trip to an attraction or restaurant outside of the high season.

Rue du Petit-Champlain with the funiculaire above

The most central tourist information center is in Upper Town, across from the Château Frontenac and directly on Place d'Armes. **Centre Infotouriste de Québec,** 12 rue Ste-Anne (www.bonjourquebec.com; ℃ **877/266-5687**), is run by the province of Québec's tourism department and is open daily 9am to 6pm from mid-June through mid-October and daily till 5pm the rest of the year (closed Christmas and New Year's Day). It has brochures, a lodging reservation service, a currency-exchange office, and information about tours by foot, bus, or boat. Also in front of the Château on Dufferin Terrace, is **Kiosk Frontenac,** operated by **Parks Canada** (www.pc.gc.ca; ℃ **888/773-8888** or 418/648-7016). Guided tours of the Fortifications of Québec start here. It's open late May to mid-October from 10am to 4:30pm, with extended hours during high season.

From mid-June to early September, service agents for **Québec City Tourism** (www.quebecregion.com; ℃ **877/783-1608** or 418/641-6290) ride throughout the tourist district on motor scooters to answer any questions you have. In French, they're called the *service mobile,* and their blue mopeds bear flags with a large question mark. Just hail them as they approach—they're bilingual.

City Layout

BASIC LAYOUT Because of its beauty, history, and unique stature as a walled city, Québec City's historic district was named a UNESCO World Heritage Site in 1985. Almost all of a visit to Québec City can be spent on foot in the old Lower Town, which hugs the river below the bluff, and in the old Upper Town, atop Cap Diamant (Cape Diamond). Many accommodations, restaurants, and tourist-oriented services are based in these places.

The colonial city was first built right down by the St. Lawrence River. It was here that the earliest merchants, traders, and boatmen earned their livelihoods. Unfriendly fire from the British and Amerindians in the 1700s moved residents to safer houses atop the cliffs that form the rim of the Cap. The tone and atmosphere of the 17th and 18th centuries still suffuse these areas today.

Basse-Ville (Lower Town) became primarily a district of wharves and warehouses. That trend has been reversed, with small hotels and many attractive bistros and shops bringing life to the area. It maintains the architectural feel of its origins, however, reusing old buildings and maintaining the narrow cobbled streets.

Haute-Ville (Upper Town) turned out to not be immune to cannon fire, as the British General James Wolfe proved in 1759 when he took the city from the French. Nevertheless, the division into Upper and Lower towns persisted for obvious topographical reasons. Upper Town remains enclosed by fortification walls, with a cliff-side elevator (*funiculaire*) and several steep streets connecting it to Lower Town.

MAIN AVENUES & STREETS In Basse-Ville (Lower Town), major streets are **St-Pierre, Dalhousie, St-Paul,** and (parallel to St-Paul) **St-André.** Within the walls of Haute-Ville (Upper Town), the principal streets are **St-Louis** (which becomes **Grande-Allée** outside the city walls), **Ste-Anne,** and **St-Jean.** Detailed maps of Upper and Lower towns and the metropolitan area are available at the tourist offices.

FINDING AN ADDRESS If it were larger, the historic district's winding and plunging streets might be confusing to negotiate. However, the area is very compact. Most streets are only a few blocks long, making navigation and finding a specific address fairly easy.

Neighborhoods in Brief

HAUTE-VILLE

Old Québec's Upper Town, surrounded by thick ramparts, occupies the crest of Cap Diamant and overlooks the Fleuve St-Laurent (St. Lawrence River). It includes many of the sites for which the city is famous, among them the **Château Frontenac** and the **Basilique Cathédrale Notre-Dame.** At a still-higher elevation, to the south of the Château and along the river, is **La Citadelle,** a partially star-shaped fortress built by the French in the 18th century and augmented often by the English (after their 1759 capture of the city) well into the 19th century and is still an active military base.

With most buildings at least 100 years old and made of granite in similar styles, Haute-Ville is visually harmonious, with few jarring modern intrusions. When they added a new wing to the Château Frontenac, for instance, they modeled it after the original—standing policy here.

Terrasse Dufferin is a pedestrian promenade atop the cliffs that attracts crowds in all seasons for its magnificent views of the river and its water traffic, which includes ferries gliding back and forth, cruise ships, and Great Lakes freighters putting in at the harbor below.

BASSE-VILLE & VIEUX-PORT

Old Québec's Lower Town encompasses **Vieux-Port,** the old port district; the impressive **Musée de la Civilisation,** a highlight of any visit; **Place-Royale,** perhaps the most attractive of the city's many small squares; and the pedestrian-only **rue du Petit-Champlain,** which is undeniably touristy, but not unpleasantly so, and has many agreeable cafes and shops. Visitors travel between Lower and Upper towns by the cliff-side elevator *(funiculaire)* at the north end of rue du Petit-Champlain, or by the adjacent stairway.

PARLIAMENT HILL, INCLUDING MONTCALM

Once you pass through the Upper Town walls at St-Louis Gate, you're still in Haute-Ville, but no longer in Vieux-Québec. Rue St-Louis becomes **Grande-Allée,** a wide boulevard that passes the stately Parliament building and runs parallel to the broad expanse of the Plains of Abraham, where one of the most important battles in the history of North America took place between the French and the British for control of the city. This is also where the lively Carnaval de Québec is held each winter. Two blocks after

Parliament, both sides of Grande-Allée are lined with terraced restaurants and cafes. The city's large modern hotels are in this area, and the **Musée National des Beaux-Arts** is a pleasant 20-minute walk up the Allée from the Parliament. Here, the neighborhood becomes more residential and flows into the Montcalm district.

ST-ROCH

Northwest of Parliament Hill and enough of a distance from Vieux-Québec to warrant a cab ride, this newly revitalized neighborhood has some of the city's trendiest restaurants and bars. Along the main strolling street, **rue St-Joseph est,** sidewalks have been widened, new benches added, and artists hired to renovate the interiors and exteriors of industrial buildings. It has all brought a youthful pop and an influx of new technology and media companies to the neighborhood.

Much of St-Roch, including what's referred to as Québec's "downtown" shopping district, remains nondescript and a little grubby. But rue St-Joseph, radiating both directions from rue du Parvis (a nice little street for nightlife), is home to an ever-growing number of top-notch restaurants and cute boutiques. **Note:** On older maps, rue du Parvis was called rue de l'Église.

FAUBOURG ST-JEAN

This area is the continuation of Upper Town's rue St-Jean after you exit the walled city and go through the central square called Place d'Youville. It is definitely a route less traveled by tourists, but it is a vibrant area, packed with shops, bars, and restaurants where many locals work, live, and play.

GETTING AROUND

By Foot

Once you're within or near the walls of Québec City's Old Town, virtually no restaurant, hotel, or place of interest is beyond walking distance. In bad weather, when you're traversing between opposite ends of Lower and Upper towns, a taxi might be necessary. But, in general, walking is the best way to explore.

The oldest streets in Québec City have a distinct European feel.

Travelers in wheelchairs or using strollers will find the city generally accommodating although challenging in the winding, steep, and often cobblestoned Upper and Lower towns. All streets have sidewalks, though, and curb cuts for easy passage onto the streets. Visit www.keroul.qc.ca or see p. 276 in chapter 18 for more information about navigating the city by wheelchair or with a stroller.

By Funiculaire

To get between Upper and Lower towns, you can take streets, staircases, or a cliff-side elevator known as the *funiculaire,* which has long operated along an inclined 64m (210-ft) track. The upper station is near the front of the city's visual center—Château Frontenac and Place d'Armes—while the lower station is at the northern end of the teeny rue du Petit-Champlain, a pedestrian-only shopping street. The elevator offers excellent aerial views of the historic Lower Town on the short trip and runs daily from 7:30am until 11pm all year and until midnight in high season. Wheelchairs and strollers are accommodated. The one-way fare is C$2.25. Read about its history at **www.funiculaire-quebec.com**.

By Taxi

Taxis are everywhere: cruising, parked in front of the big hotels, and in some of Upper Town's larger squares. In theory, they can be hailed, but they are best obtained by locating one of their stands, as in the Place d'Armes or in front of Hôtel-de-Ville (City Hall). Restaurant managers and hotel bell captains will also summon them upon request. The starting rate is C$3.45, each kilometer costs C$1.70, and each minute of waiting adds up to C63¢. Tip 10% to 15%. **Taxi Coop** (www.taxicoop-quebec.com) can be reached at ✆ **418/525-5191.**

By Bus

For travel within the most touristed areas, take the C$2 Route 21 Écolobus (www.rtcquebec.ca). It makes a loop through the city, including stops at Musée de la Civilisation in Lower Town and the Château Frontenac, Hôtel-de-Ville (City Hall), Place D'Youville, and Centre des congrès in Upper Town. Get on and off at any stop. The buses run on electricity, so they're quiet and eco-friendly.

By Car

Québec City is compact, but driving can be tricky because so few roads go between Upper and Lower Town and because many streets are one-way.

On-street parking is very difficult in Québec City's old, cramped quarters. When you find a rare space on the street, be sure to check the signs for hours when parking is permissible. Meters cost C25¢ per 6½ minutes (or C$2.25 per hour), and some meters accept payment for up to 5 hours. Meters are generally in effect Monday through Saturday from 9am to 9pm and Sunday 10am to 9pm. But double-check: Spots along Parc des Champs-des-Batailles (Battlefields Park) require fees 24 hours a day. Disabled parking permit holders may park their vehicle in front of a parking meter free of charge for 3 hours. Handicapped permits from outside Canada are accepted. A free mobile application (**Copilote**, created by the City of Québec) can assist in finding open parking spots in real time and can be found at **www.quebecregion.com**.

Many of the smaller hotels and B&Bs that don't have their own parking lots maintain special arrangements with local garages, with discounts for guests of a few dollars off the usual C$16 or more per day. Check with your hotel.

If a particular hotel or *auberge* (French word for "inn") doesn't have access to a garage or lot, plenty of public ones are available and clearly marked on the foldout city map available at tourist offices and local businesses. Two common choices for visitors are, in Upper Town, the underground lot beneath Hôtel-de-Ville (City Hall), with entrances on rue Ste-Anne and côte de la Fabrique; and, in Lower Town, the lot across the street from Musée de la Civilisation on rue Dalhousie.

Prepare for snow to affect driving, and possibly parking conditions from November to April. Cars that impede snow removal can be fined and towed so underground parking is optimal. Provincial law requires snow tires for

Québec plated vehicles between December 15 and March 15; vehicles plated from the U.S. or other provinces are exempt.

In addition to renting cars at the Jean Lesage International Airport, **Hertz** has an office in Upper Town at 44 Côte du Palais at rue St-Jean. **Avis** has a desk in the Hilton Québec lobby, 1100 René-Lévesque est, and **Budget** is in the same complex; and **Enterprise** has multiple locations, including in the Delta Hotel at 690 René-Lévesque est.

Unlike in Montréal, drivers in Québec City are permitted to turn right at red traffic lights after coming to a full stop and yielding to pedestrians in the crosswalk. Look out for the occasional sign at busy intersections prohibiting right turns on red. Also note that use of cell phones is only permitted with the "hands-free" function while driving. See p. 271 in chapter 18 for additional driving rules in the province.

By Bike

Given Vieux-Québec's hilly topography and tight quarters, cycling isn't the most obvious choice to get from sight to sight either within the walls or in Lower Town. But beyond the walls, bike touring for the fun of it is another story. Québec has a great network of cycling paths—nearly 400km (249 miles) in the Greater Québec Area alone. Downloadable maps are available at **www.quebecregion.com**; search for "bike map." For longer treks, look into the province's **Route Verte** (Green Route)—see "Biking the Route Verte (Green Route)" on p. 166. Downloadable maps, trip calculators, suggested day trips and longer tours are available at www.routeverte.com.

Bicycle rentals are available in Lower Town, near the Gare du Palais train station, at **Cyclo Services,** 289 rue St-Paul (www.cycloservices.net; ✆ **877/692-4050** or 418/692-4052), for C$25 for 4 hours, with daily and weekly rental also available. Choices include cruisers, road bikes, tandem, and kids' bikes. They also rent accessories and do repairs. The shop is open daily from 8am to 8pm. **Vélo Passe-Sport Plein Air,** 35 rue Dalhousie (www.velopasse-sport.com; ✆ **418/692-3643**) rents an assortment of bikes for periods of 2, 4, and 8 hours for C$20 to C$35 (no longer-term rentals). It is open daily in season (May–Oct) from 9am to 6pm. Both bike shops lead guided bike tours within Vieux-Québec or at locations outside the city, such as Île d'Orléans.

The use of motorcycles is prohibited within the walls of Old Québec.

[FastFACTS] QUÉBEC CITY

Below are useful facts and phone numbers while you're traveling in the city. For more information about the province overall, see chapter 18.

ATMs/Banks Desjardins has a handy ATM near Hôtel-de-Ville (City Hall) at 19 rue des Jardins (www.

desjardins.com; ✆ **800/ 224-7737**) and RBC Royal Bank has a location at 700 Place D'Youville (www.rbc.

com; ✆ **418/692-6800**). CIBC, TD Bank, and other Canadian banks also have ATMs in the greater area.

Business Hours Most businesses are open Monday through Saturday from around 9 or 10am and close between 5 and 6pm; some stay open until 9pm on Thursday and Friday. On Sunday, businesses typically open between 10am and noon and close at 5pm. **Bank hours** in Québec City are Monday through Friday from 10am to 3pm; occasionally hours are extended on Thursday and Friday, and Saturday morning. Most **restaurants** serve until 9:30 or 10pm. **Bars** stay open until 3am with some "after hours" options. A list of holidays on which most businesses are closed can be found at www.quebecregion.com. In general, hours are longer in high season (May–Sept) and during Carnaval.

Dentists Tourisme Québec advises calling ⒸＴ **418/666-4363** Monday through Friday or in case of emergency on weekends.

Doctors & Hospitals In Québec City the five-hospital network called CHUQ, is affiliated with the University of Laval's medical school. The L'Hôtel-Dieu de Québec (www.chuq.qc.ca; Ⓒ **418/525-4444**) is in Upper Town at 11 côte du Palais. It's a teaching hospital (and a national historic site of Canada) and has an emergency room.

Emergencies Dial Ⓒ **911** for police, fire, or ambulance assistance.

Internet Access Many public spaces such as cafes have free Wi-Fi; hotel lobbies are often Wi-Fi hotspots but many charge a daily access rate. **Zap Québec** tracks free Wi-Fi hotspots at www.zap quebec.org.

Mail & Postage Québec City's most centrally located post office in the tourist area is at 5 rue du Fort, near Château Frontenac in Upper Town. See p. 273 in chapter 18 for postage rates.

Newspapers & Magazines Québec's source for English-language news is the **Québec Chronicle-Telegraph**, printed every Wednesday and online at www.qctonline.com. As the descendant of several newspapers published for more than 3 centuries, it claims to be North America's oldest newspaper.

Pets In public areas, owners must clean up after pets, and dogs must be on a leash no longer than 2m (6 ft.). In case of veterinary emergency, call Ⓒ **418/872-5355**. If traveling into Canada with a dog, be advised to have a rabies certificate on hand and to consult the Canadian Food Inspection Agency (www.inspection.

gc.ca) for other restrictions on visiting pets.

Pharmacies Brunet, 605 rue St-Joseph est, St-Roch (www.brunet.ca; Ⓒ **418/529-5741**), Pharmaprix, 698 rue St-Jean, Upper Town (www1.pharmaprix.ca; Ⓒ **418/529-2171**), and Uniprix, 369 rue de la Couronne, St-Roch (www.uniprix.com; Ⓒ **418/529-2121**) are three chain pharmacies with multiple outlets in Québec City. **Note:** When searching for a location online, the pharmacy may be listed under the pharmacist's name, but is still a storefront.

Safety The tourist sections of Québec City are well-lit and pedestrian friendly. Generally, it's safe to walk after dark, particularly during one of the city's many festivals when people are out and about. A 2012 Canadian Centre for Justice Statistics study on police-reported crime reported that Canada's crime rate had dipped to its lowest level in 40 years with Québec City reporting the second lowest crime rate of the major cities. Still, always take the usual precautions.

Tipping Québécois are known to add up GST and QST taxes on their restaurant bills to get a quick tip amount of approximately 15%. See p. 276 in chapter 18 for more.

WHERE TO STAY IN QUÉBEC CITY

S taying in one of the small luxurious boutique properties within or below the walls of Vieux-Québec or at the iconic Château Frontenac can be one of your trip's most memorable experiences. On the other end of the size spectrum, the string of skyscrapers just outside Upper Town lack some of the city's historical charm, but offer high-end facilities and some of the best city views.

In addition to the descriptions that follow, *The Official Tourist Guide* published annually by Québec City Tourism is a useful resource for planning your stay, as is its accompanying website www.quebecregion.com. Both list everything from campgrounds to homes for rent as well as B&Bs and the city's most upscale hotels. Free copies of the print guide are available at tourist offices (p. 184). When choosing your destination, keep in mind that standards of amenities fluctuate wildly from one hotel to another, even from room to room within a single establishment. It's reasonable to ask to see two or three options before settling on one.

Most goods and services in Canada have a federal tax of 5% (the TPS). On top of that, the province of Québec adds a tax that comes out to 9.975% (the TVQ). Prices listed in this book do not include taxes.

best HOTEL BETS

o **Best Splurge: Fairmont Le Château Frontenac** and its unforgettable spires soar above this gorgeous city. Nothing can beat it for proximity to all the sights. In fact, "the Château" *is* one of the sights. Even if you don't stay here, stroll by for the view, a meal, or a drink. See p. 186.

o **Best Service:** The staff at **Auberge St-Antoine** is professional without being stuffy. They've been known to call all over town to help find "the big game" on TV and then ask later if your team won. The ancient walls and archeological displays from lobby to bedside make for an exceptionally unique stay. See p. 188.

Toboggan rides in front of the Fairmont Le Château Frontenac

o **Best Romantic Hotel:** The sleek **Le Germain Hotel Québec** is a favorite, infusing a pre–World War I building with the comforts of modern day. The bedding is hands-down gold star luxury. See p. 189.

o **Best Eclectic Auberge:** At **Auberge Place d'Armes,** every room is individually themed. Visitors can stroll the boardwalk in front of Frontenac, squeeze down the narrow, artwork lined rue du Trésor, and call it a night in a wholly original room. See p. 183.

o **Best Cultural Immersion:** The **Hôtel-Musée Premières Nations** in Wendake is modeled after a Huron longhouse. A stay here can include a Huron-Wendat museum visit, First Nations–inspired cuisine, spa massotherapy, and a balcony view of the Akiawenrahk River. See p. 192.

o **Best Location for Peace & Quiet:** The **Parc des Gouverneurs,** next to the Château, offers a tranquil respite that's still close to Upper Town's restaurants and shops. Many B&Bs and small hotels are on the park or nearby, including **Maison du Fort** and **Manoir Sur-le-Cap.** See p. 247, 187, and 187. respectively

o **Best Value: Auberge du Quartier** offers high-end accommodations for budget travelers. It's within walking distance of the Plains of Abraham and the shops on avenue Cartier. See p. 191.

Following is an explanation of the hotel rates as we define them in this book:

Expensive   C$200 and up
Moderate   C$100–C$200
Inexpensive   Under C$100

As with Montréal's hotels, the prices listed here are by no means written in stone, and should be used more as a guideline for comparing properties. Rates provided are typical of Québec City's high seasons in summer (typically June–Aug) and winter (around Christmastime to Carnaval). They can be significantly lower when tourism is slow.

o **Best Eco Hotel: Hôtel du Vieux-Québec** is carbon neutral and solar-powered, it recaptures energy from hot water, and its adjacent restaurant cooks with fresh veggies grown on the roof. See p. 186.

o **Best Adventure Hotel:** Friends may call you crazy, or just plain cold. The **Hôtel de Glace (Ice Hotel),** just 10 minutes from downtown Québec City, is built from scratch each year and open from January to late March. Sleep on a bed of ice or chillax as a day-tripper. See p. 193.

o **Best for Families: Hôtel Château Laurier Québec** has an indoor saltwater pool (and 2 outdoor Jacuzzis), plus it's steps from the main events of Carnaval in winter and Festival d'Été in the summer. See p. 191.

VIEUX-QUÉBEC: HAUTE-VILLE (UPPER TOWN)

Nestled under the wing of the magnificent Château Frontenac, boutique hotels in this lovely area can offer warm personal service and historical charm. That said, this coveted area near the "castle" is in high demand, so prices at some properties can be steep for what they offer.

Expensive

Auberge Place d'Armes ★★   This high-end (yet well-priced) *auberge* has a long history and has taken great care preserving the structural elements from the buildings that now comprise the hotel. One section housed a former provincial prime minister and later became a wax museum; the other was the home of the co-founder of Holt Renfrew, still one of Canada's leading luxury stores. Now carefully renovated guest rooms—each one unique—feature everything from exposed stone walls dating back to 1640 to flatscreen TVs, craft furniture, and rain showers with jets. You can see each room online. This section of rue Ste-Anne is pedestrian-only (though you can drive up to drop off your bags) and lined with outdoor dining, great for people-watching. Breakfast is included and is served at the very good in-house

Québec City Hotels

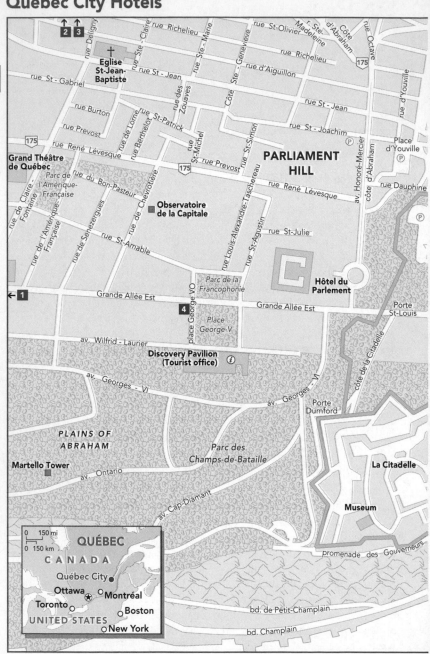

† Église St-Jean-Baptiste

rue Deligny
rue Ste - Claire
rue Richelieu
rue Ste - Marie
rue St-Olivier
r. Ste Madeleine
Côte d'Abraham
av. Octave

rue Richelieu
rue St - Jean
Côte Ste - Geneviève
rue d'Aiguillon
175

rue St - Gabriel
rue des Zouaves
rue St - Jean
rue d'Youville

rue Burton
rue St-Patrick
rue St - Joachim
Place d'Youville

rue Prevost
rue de Lorne
rue Berthelot
rue St-Michel
rue Prevost
rue St-Simon
P

175
rue René Lévesque
rue St-Simon
PARLIAMENT HILL
av. Honoré-Mercier
côte d'Abraham

Grand Théâtre de Québec
rue du Bon-Pasteur
175
rue René Lévesque
rue Dauphine

Parc de l'Amérique-Française
rue de Chevrotière

rue de Claire-Fontaine
Observatoire de la Capitale
rue Louis-Alexandre-Taschereau
rue St-Agustin
P

rue de l'Amérique-Française
rue de Senezergues
rue St-Amable
rue St-Julie

Grande Allée Est
Parc de la Francophonie
Hôtel du Parlement
Porte St-Louis

4
Place George-V
Grande Allée Est
côte de la Citadelle

av. Wilfrid - Laurier
place George VO

Discovery Pavilion (Tourist office) ⓘ

av. Georges - VI
av. Georges - VI
Porte Durnford

PLAINS OF ABRAHAM
Parc des Champs-de-Bataille
La Citadelle

Martello Tower
av. Ontario
Museum

av. Cap-Diamant
promenade des Gouverneurs

0 150 mi
0 150 km

QUÉBEC
CANADA
Québec City ●
Ottawa ⊛ ○ Montréal
Toronto ○ Boston
UNITED STATES ○ New York

bd. de Petit-Champlain
bd. Champlain

184

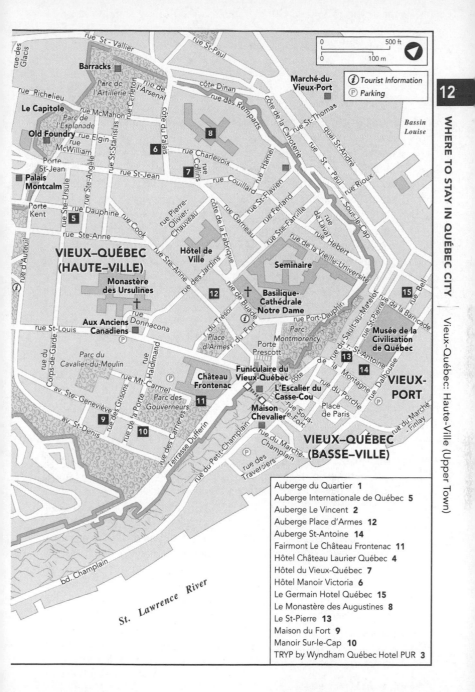

Auberge du Quartier **1**
Auberge Internationale de Québec **5**
Auberge Le Vincent **2**
Auberge Place d'Armes **12**
Auberge St-Antoine **14**
Fairmont Le Château Frontenac **11**
Hôtel Château Laurier Québec **4**
Hôtel du Vieux-Québec **7**
Hôtel Manoir Victoria **6**
Le Germain Hotel Québec **15**
Le Monastère des Augustines **8**
Le St-Pierre **13**
Maison du Fort **9**
Manoir Sur-le-Cap **10**
TRYP by Wyndham Québec Hotel PUR **3**

restaurant **Le Pain Béni** (p. 200). *Note:* You need to use stairs to reach all guest rooms.

24 rue Ste-Anne (at Place d'Armes). www.aubergeplacedarmes.com. (C)**866/333-9485** or 418/694-9485. 21 units. Summer C$229–C$269 double; fall–spring from C$149 double. Rates include continental breakfast. Packages available. Valet parking C$23 (high season only); C$22 self parking. Pets accepted (C$25 per day). **Amenities:** Restaurant; babysitting; room service; free Wi-Fi.

Fairmont Le Château Frontenac ★★★ You will not and should not miss this incredible Québec landmark, fondly called the "castle" or *le château*. Its majestic spires and gabled rooftops have been visible along the cliff overlooking the St. Lawrence River since 1893. The interior is similarly grand, made more so with a recent refurbishment of all 611 guest rooms, the expansion of the pricier Fairmont Gold floor and services (dedicated concierge, bar, and breakfast area), the addition of a luxury spa, and a re-tooling of all onsite dining and entertainment. The classy **Le Champlain Restaurant** underwent a major facelift, and now both atmosphere and menu boast nouveau flair while retaining stately distinction. The similarly glamorous jazz bar and bistro **Le Sam,** embellished with metallic decor, or the airy, circular bar at **1608 Wine & Cheese Bar** (p. 241) are perfect spots to rev up or wind down a celebration. Free-valet parking encourages non-guests to dine at any of these establishments. Although in-person tours are no longer offered, a free mobile app serves as a virtual tour guide, available at www.fairmont.com/frontenac-quebec.

1 rue des Carrières (at Place d'Armes). www.fairmont.com/frontenac-quebec. (C)**866/540-4460** or 418/692-3861. 611 units. From C$399 double; from C$699 suite. Packages available. Valet parking C$34 per day; hybrid vehicles free. Pets accepted (C$35 per day per pet). **Amenities:** 3 restaurants; bar; babysitting; concierge; executive-level rooms; gift shops; health club; 1 indoor and 1 kiddie pool w/outdoor terrace; room service; spa; Starbucks cafe; Wi-Fi (C$14 per day).

Hôtel du Vieux-Québec ★★ Many hotels claim to be in the heart of Old Québec, but this one really is: on a prime corner in the rue St-Jean dining and shopping area (though admittedly all of Upper and Lower Town is very walkable). Either way, it provides consistent accommodations and serves as a role model in sustainability—with a rooftop garden, solar power, and water capture and re-use. The hotel devised an eco-friendly method to provide filtered water to guests. Rooms feature custom furnishings made with carefully harvested local mahogany or maple and are equipped with mini fridges and coffeemakers. In high season, the hotel may require 2- or 3-day minimum stays. An organic bistro, **Tournebroche** (www.tournebroche.com), specializing in rotisserie chicken and pork, opened on the ground level in 2014.

1190 rue St-Jean (at rue de l'Hôtel Dieu). www.hvq.com. (C)**800/361-7787** or 418/692-1850. 45 units. May to late Oct C$208–C$228 double; late Oct to Apr from C$128 double. Rates include continental breakfast for rooms booked directly with hotel. Packages available. Self parking C$17.50. Pets accepted during low season (C$50 per day). **Amenities:** Restaurant; free Wi-Fi.

Hôtel Manoir Victoria ★★   The once antique lobby of this elegant, old-world hotel now greets guests with a more modern air. Updated "contemporary" guest rooms are fashionably sleek and slightly more expensive than their "traditional" counterparts (which are trim and functional, without the pizzazz). In addition, the street-level restaurant **Chez Boulay bistro boréal** (p. 197) has become a magnet for local and visiting foodies. This is one of the more luxurious hotel choices within walking distance of rue St-Jean bar and shopping scene. Another feature that sets this hotel apart: the small indoor pool and full-service spa that even caters to kids and teens. Package options abound, and rebates are available when reserving 2 or more nights. A steep staircase connects the front door to the lobby, although elevators make the trip to most guest rooms.

44 Côte du Palais (at rue St-Jean). www.manoir-victoria.com. ℂ **800/463-6283** or 418/692-1030. 156 units. High season C$189–C$279 "traditional" double; low season C$139–C$229 "traditional" double. High season C$450–C$550 "contemporary" suite; low season C$350–C$450 "contemporary" suite. Packages available. Valet parking C$25. **Amenities:** 2 restaurants; babysitting; exercise room; indoor pool; sauna; room service; spa; free Wi-Fi.

Moderate

Maison du Fort ★   This B&B's home was built in the Georgian style in 1851 by architect Charles Baillargé, and the high ceilings and older woodwork add a bit of romance. Guests here are usually won over by Maison du Fort's friendly owner and purring house cat. The breakfast starts your day nicely with muffins, tea, and coffee. With a nod to the posh Château Frontenac nearby, each room has a goose down duvet. *Note:* You'll need to climb a few stairs to get into the B&B and rooms are located up one, two, or three full flights of stairs.

21 av. Ste-Geneviève (at rue des Grisons). www.hotelmaisondufort.com. ℂ **888/203-4375** or 418/692-4375. 9 units. C$149–C$179 double. Rates include breakfast. Self parking C$22. **Amenities:** Free Wi-Fi.

Manoir Sur-le-Cap ★   Inns on the charming Parc des Gouverneurs, opposite the Château Frontenac, are close to the action, but are quieter and more affordable. This inn distinguishes itself with friendly service and 14 comfy rooms, all unique. Many feature exposed stone or brick walls and some have balconies that overlook the river. Work desks are standard and some rooms feature a clawfoot tub. If stairs are an issue, request a room on the main floor, though you'll have to climb a few steps to the main floor, too.

9 av. Ste-Geneviève (near rue de la Porte). www.manoir-sur-le-cap.com. ℂ **866/694-1987** or 418/694-1987. 14 units. High season C$125–C$185 double; low season C$95–C$145 double. Self parking C$23. **Amenities:** Free Wi-Fi.

Inexpensive

Auberge Internationale de Québec ★   The city's hostel is a comfortable and affordable option. In addition to dorm housing—one room with

OPENING THE MONASTERY for all to heal

In an entirely unique turn of events, the Augustinian Sisters of Québec decided to transform their heritage into a wellness experience, open to persons of any faith. Their home, and home of the first hospital north of Mexico, **Le Monastère des Augustines,** 77 rue des Remparts, Upper Town (www.monastere.ca; ℂ **844/694-1639** or 418/694-1639) is now, at once, a world heritage site, monastery (12 Augustines still reside here), "experiential" hotel, museum, archive, and retreat center. With a grand opening in late 2015, the monastery's historic buildings have been converted anew and the doors flung open to those seeking solace of body and soul. Guests can opt for a spare room "restored in the spirit of monasticism" or a contemporary room with a private bathroom and high-end bedding. A night's stay starts at C$72 and includes breakfast. But that's not the focus. The idea is to have a resting place while on break from daily life and to enjoy such relaxing activities as meditation, yoga, and workshops that cultivate healthy mind, body, and spirit. A museum, with a collection of more than 40,000 artifacts collected by the sisters since their arrival in New France, as well as a holistic restaurant is part of this ambitious, non-profit project.

several bunks—you can also book into modest rooms with either shared or private bathrooms. Interns coordinate group activities such as pub crawls, museum visits, and tours to Montmorency Waterfalls or across the St. Lawrence River. Pillows, sheets, and blankets are provided. Lockers and laundry are available for a fee and you can prep a meal in the modest kitchen. Reservations are strongly recommended in summer.

19 rue. Ste-Ursule (near rue Ste-Anne). www.aubergeinternationaledequebec.com. ℂ **866/694-0950** or 418/694-0755. 25 private rooms, 277 beds. C$86–C$137 private room for 2 with bathroom; C$25–C$35 per person for shared dorm room. Discount available for HI members. Rates for private rooms include breakfast. **Amenities:** Restaurant; self-service kitchen; free Wi-Fi.

VIEUX-QUÉBEC: BASSE-VILLE (LOWER TOWN)/VIEUX-PORT

A photogenic bluff divides Upper Town from Lower Town. A *funiculaire* conveniently connects the two areas, or you can take the adjacent *L'éscalier casse-cou* (Breakneck Stairs)—both of which are not quite as scary or steep as they sound. In this area, travelers can count small hotels that are big on luxury. While the waterfront is lovely and teems with activity in warm months, it (along with some adjacent streets) can seem empty and lonely once winter arrives.

Expensive

Auberge St-Antoine ★★★ This is one of the most memorable and splurge-worthy hotels in Québec City. Ancient walls, beams, and stone floors from the original buildings—used as a wharf, a cannon battery, and by British merchants—were incorporated into the current, cleanly modern design. Artifacts unearthed during a large-scale archeological dig are displayed throughout the hotel with curatorial care. Rooms are luxurious and spacious. Fine linens, cozy bathrobes, and heated bathroom floors are standard; deep tubs, balconies, fireplaces, or kitchenettes are optional. Staff extends a warm welcome and will go out of their way to meet your needs, especially during the off-season. The **Café-Bar Artéfact,** tucked between cathedral-like windows near the lobby, serves snacks, cocktails, table d'hôte dinner, and features live jazz Thursday through Saturday. **Panache** (p. 205), where breakfast is served, offers some of the city's finest dining. This hotel picks up annual national and international awards and is a member of the prestigious Relais & Châteaux luxury group. Free tours are available to guests upon request.

8 rue St-Antoine (next to the Musée de la Civilisation). www.saint-antoine.com. ℭ **888/692-2211** or 418/692-2211. 95 units. C$189–C$439 double; C$600 and up suite. Packages available. Valet parking C$25. Pets accepted (C$35 per night). **Amenities:** 2 restaurants; bar; babysitting; children's programs; cinema; concierge; exercise room; room service; spa treatments; free Wi-Fi.

Le Germain Hotel Québec ★★★   Urban elegance is the ruling principle in one of the city's most refined boutique hotels. Built in 1912, the building formerly housed Dominion Fish & Fruit Limited and became a hotel in 1997. Part of a small chain with locations in Montréal, Toronto, and Calgary, the rooms here are furnished with exceptionally comfortable beds and sheets that are downright heavenly. About two-thirds of the rooms have both tubs and

The refined lobby at Le Germain Hôtel

CONSIDERING A b&b

Vieux-Québec has about 10 B&Bs and that number quadruples if the larger region is an option for you. With rates mostly in the C$80 to C$140 range, they don't necessarily offer substantial savings over the small hotels, but do give you the opportunity to get to know some of the city dwellers. If you discover one while exploring, a property is full if the sign says COMPLET and VACANT if rooms are available. *The Official Tourist Guide* put out by Québec City Tourism lists every member of the Greater Québec Area Tourism and Convention Bureau, including B&Bs, with details about the number of rooms, the price range, and the facilities. It's available at tourist offices (p. 184). There's also a handy search feature for B&Bs at **www. quebecregion.com**.

showers, and bathrooms are well lit and stylish. The continental breakfast (which includes delicious espresso) can be taken on the leafy outdoor terrace in the summer or near the lobby fireplace in colder months.

126 rue St-Pierre (at rue St-Paul). www.legermainhotels.com/en/quebec. © **888/833-5253** or 418/692-2224. 60 units. C$235–C$335 double. Rates include continental breakfast. Valet parking C$25. Pets accepted (C$30 per stay). **Amenities:** Espresso bar; babysitting; concierge; exercise room; room service; free Wi-Fi.

Moderate

Le St-Pierre ★   This is one of the homier options in Old Québec. Owned by the same people as the adjacent, upscale and more contemporary **Hôtel 71** (© **888/692-1171**), which we also recommend, the two properties share **Il Matto** (p. 202), a mod Italian restaurant on the first floor. Rooms at Auberge Le St-Pierre have a living room feel, with creamy walls, light brown wood floors, and an occasional exposed stone wall. It's a good choice for longer stays or families, as units offer room to spread out and some have modest kitchens. Jetted baths and bathrobes are standard. The breakfast here is a plus: always included and cooked to order.

79 rue St-Pierre (behind the Musée de la Civilisation). www.le-saint-pierre.ca. © **888/268-1017** or 418/694-7981. 41 units. C$185–C$225 double; C$225–C$260 suite. Rates include full breakfast. Packages available. Valet parking C$22. **Amenities:** Restaurant, bar; babysitting; concierge; exercise room; free Wi-Fi.

PARLIAMENT HILL (ON OR NEAR GRANDE-ALLÉE)

A flat land that extends away from Vieux-Québec, the area includes green spaces Parc des Champs-de-Bataille and the Plains of Abraham, as well as the Musée National des Beaux-Arts du Québec near the posh Montcalm residential neighborhood. This area is a good choice if touring by car or attending events in the area. Accommodations here have a more generic feel than the options in Vieux-Québec, but if you prefer a familiar chain hotel you'll have more choices in this part of town.

Moderate

Auberge du Quartier ★★ New interiors, affordable, and a stone's throw from any activity on the Plains of Abraham, including **summer festival** (p. 237). Sounds perfect. So what gives? Well, the nearby clubs and sometimes high-decibel hubbub along Grande-Allée are not every visitor's cup of tea. But for those not scared off by the locale, this boutique *auberge* has updated guest rooms with down comforters, high-end sheets, and splashes of mod decor. The **Musée National des Beaux-Arts du Québec** (p. 223) is just down the street and avenue Cartier, right around the corner, has shopping and dining worthy of an afternoon. The friendly staff are willing to go out of their way to help.

170 Grande-Allée ouest (near av. Cartier). www.aubergeduquartier.com. © **800/782-9441** or 418/525-9726. 24 units. High season from C$129 double; low season from C$89 double; high season from C$179 double; low season from C$139 suite. Packages available. Self parking C$15. **Amenities:** Free Wi-Fi.

Hôtel Château Laurier Québec ★★ Sandwiched between the scenic oasis of the Plains of Abraham and the frenetic, club-lined Grande-Allée,

The comfortably mod guest rooms at Auberge du Quartier

A unique **RESORT OUTSIDE THE CITY**

Travelers with agendas other than the century-old sights in Québec City's historic center or those covering a lot of ground by car may want to stay outside the city for a night or two. Note that this resort is a bit of a trek if your interests lie in Québec City.

Every room in the relaxing, earthy **Hôtel-Musée Premières Nations,** 5 Place de la Rencontre, Wendake (www.hotelpremieresnations.ca; © **866/551-9222** or 418/847-2222) features a private balcony that overlooks the Akiawenrahk River. The hotel is situated on a forested section of the First Nations reservation called Wendake, just 15 minutes from Québec City by car. Once here, you'll find everything you need to decompress. The "multisensory" Nation-Santé Spa has a waterfall, heated walkways, a fire pit, and a time-out yurt for quiet relaxation (C$35 per person; nonguests can come for the day). The high-end La Traite restaurant specializes in First Nations–inspired cuisine such as red deer, dried seal, and smoked mackerel. A three-course table d'hôte is priced at C$42 per person; more elaborate and costlier tasting menus are also available. The hotel features paintings and sculpture by First Nations artists throughout and an onsite museum celebrates Huron-Wendat culture. An afternoon could be spent poking around the handful of shops and galleries in Wendake, hiking the adjacent trails, or admiring the nearby Kabir Kouba waterfall. Rates for the 55 units range from C$159 to C$209 for a double. Packages are available. Amenities include free parking, a restaurant, bar, bike rental, room service, and free Wi-Fi. From Rte. 175 north, take exit 154 for rue de la Faune, enter Wendake reservation and follow signs.

Château Laurier is many different hotels in one. For example, it has six categories that vary in age, style, and price. The most affordable are in the "La Classique" category; the "La Luxueuse" rooms are the most up-to-date. An abundance of wheelchair-accessible rooms are available, too. Château Laurier distinguishes itself as a "Franco-responsible" hotel by playing French music and featuring photographs and paintings by French and Québécois artists in the hallways. Self-service wine vending machines are available on select floors and in the lobby. The hotel is also eco-responsible—the pool is saltwater, surplus food is delivered to food banks, recycling is *de rigeur,* and an electric car recharging station is onsite.

1220 Place Georges-V ouest (at Grande-Allée). www.hotelchateaulaurier.com. © **877/522-8108** or 418/522-8108. 282 units. From C$129 low season and from C$174 high season double; from C$234 low season and from C$279 high season La Luxueuse. Packages available. Self parking C$24. **Amenities:** Restaurant; electronic wine bars; concierge; executive-level floors; exercise room; Jacuzzis (1 indoor, 2 outdoor); indoor saltwater pool; room service; Finnish sauna; spa; free Wi-Fi.

ST-ROCH

Young restaurateurs, artists, media techies, and fashionistas have settled into Québec's St-Roch neighborhood, dubbing the area "Le Nouvo St-Roch"

THE coldest RECEPTION IN TOWN

How many chances do you get to sleep in a hotel built from 500 tons of ice? On a bed of ice, near a chandelier made of ice, after dancing in a disco made of ice, ice, ice? Not many, I'm guessing. Québec's **Hôtel de Glace (Ice Hotel),** 9530 rue de la Faune (www.hoteldeglace-canada.com; (✆) **877/505-0423** or 418/623-2888), is built every winter on a site just 10 minutes from downtown. For C$18 you can visit (prices go up with guided tours and other perks), but for C$269 per person (and way up), you can have a cocktail and spend the night. Tempted?

Nearly everything at the Hôtel de Glace is made of ice, from the ice chandelier in the vaulted main hall, to the thick-ice shot glasses in which vodka is served, to the pillars and arches and furniture. That includes the frozen slabs that serve as beds. High-tech sleeping bags provide insulation, and a how-to class explains how to zip yourself up correctly.

Nighttime guests get their rooms at 9pm after the last tour ends, and have to clear out by 9am, before the next day's arrivals. Some rooms are vaguely grand and have specific themes. There could be, for instance, a *Frozen* suite inspired by the Disney film or a hockey suite featuring larger-than-life players with elaborately carved sticks. After all, this is a hotel with an artistic director! Other rooms bring the words "monastic" or "cell block" to mind.

Bear in mind that, except for in the hot tub, temperatures everywhere hover between -5° and -3°C (23° and 27°F). Refrigerators are used not to keep drinks cold, but to *keep them from freezing.*

The hotel has 44 rooms and suites, a wedding chapel, and a nightclub with DJ for guests to shake the chill from their booties. Open each January, it houses guests until late March—after that, it's destroyed.

(pronounce it "Saint-Rock"). Each visit finds new boutiques and restaurants, so don't be surprised if people are talking about venues that aren't mentioned in this book. St-Roch is, however, slightly removed from the main attractions listed in this book.

Expensive

Auberge Le Vincent ★ For years this Vincent Van Gogh–inspired *auberge* was on its own on a desolate corner. Now this stretch of rue Saint-Vallier hosts a handful of worthy spots for food and drink, making Auberge Le Vincent an even more appealing accommodation choice. The friendly owners, Sonia Tremblay and Antonio Soares, pull out all the stops for their guests with goose down duvets, 400-thread-count sheets, in-room espresso, and a fridge for your goodies. There's always a homemade breakfast. Rooms are up either one or two flights of stairs, and the din from the streets below can be heard subtly in the background. Van Gogh-esque murals liven up the common spaces along with work by local artists.

295 rue St-Vallier est (corner of rue Dorchester). www.aubergelevincent.com. (✆) **418/523-5000.** 10 units. High season C$199–C$279 double; low season C$149–C$199 double. Rates include full breakfast. Packages available. Valet parking C$15. **Amenities:** Free Wi-Fi.

Moderate

TRYP by Wyndham Québec Hotel PUR ★ What PUR offers is ultramod accommodations in the hip St-Roch neighborhood, just outside the hub of the main tourist draws but certainly not out of reach by car (or the very ambitious walker). Rooms on the top floors of this high-rise have incredible views and the large indoor pool is an attraction. Furnishings are super spare—white with a shock of orange—but comfy. Because of the large number of rooms, last-minute deals can be had. The ground-floor restaurant, **Table** (www.tablequebec.com), serves bistro cuisine and breakfast for hotel guests.

395 rue de la Couronne (at rue St-Joseph). www.hotelpur.com. ⓒ **800/267-2002** or 418/647-2611. 242 units. C$159–C$269 double. Packages available. Self parking C$21. **Amenities:** Restaurant; fitness center; indoor heated pool; sauna; free Wi-Fi.

WHERE TO EAT IN QUÉBEC CITY

With a little research, it's possible to eat extraordinarily well in Québec City. It used to be that this gloriously scenic town had no *temples de cuisine* comparable to those of Montréal. That's all changed. Québec City now has restaurants equal in every way to the most honored establishments of any North American city, with surprising numbers of creative, ambitious young chefs and restaurateurs bidding to achieve similar status.

best EATING BETS

- **Best Restaurants for a Special Evening: Le Saint-Amour** may be the most romantic restaurant in the city. **Initiale** is hushed and elegant. Both stellar establishments woo you at the door. See p. 201 and p. 203 respectively.
- **Best Bistro:** In a city that specializes in the informal bistro tradition, **Le Clocher Penché Bistrot** offers a cozy atmosphere and a reason to explore the trendy St-Roch neighborhood. See p. 209.
- **Best Bargains:** A main course at **Aux Anciens Canadiens** can set you back C$64 or more (yikes), but every day until 5:45pm this purveyor of classic Québécois fare offers three-course meals with wine or beer for less than C$26. The ritzy **Laurie Raphaël** also has a lunchtime deal of three courses for about C$29. See p. 197 and p. 203 respectively.
- **Best Idyllic Terrace:** The crimson-red main room *is* sexy, but try to have a dinner on the leafy enclosed back terrace of Lower Town's **Toast!** The terrace at the terrific **Panache** is also worth seeking out. See p. 205.
- **Best Boréal Cuisine: Restaurant Légende** and **Chez Boulay** practice high-end "boréal" cooking, which relies on indigenous, in-season ingredients and draws on First Nations culinary traditions. See p. 205 and p. 197 respectively.
- **Best Hipster Night Out:** Let **Le Moine Échanson, L'Affaire est Ketchup,** and **Patente et Machin** duke it out for the cool-kid badge while you relax and enjoy their with-it, home-style cooking. See p. 207, p. 208, and p. 209 respectively.

Aux Anciens Canadiens offers uniquely Québécois cuisine in a 1675 house.

○ **Best for Families:** Large (it seats 180) and jovial, **Le Café du Monde** manages the nearly impossible: classic French food *and* fast service without a compromise in quality, even on crowded holiday weekends. **Phil Smoked Meat** has beer for parents, beer for kids (made from spruce trees), and smoked meat served on spaghetti, pizza, or the old-fashioned way. See p. 206 and p. 209 respectively.

○ **Best Breakfast with Locals:** In the residential neighborhood of Montcalm, not far from the Musée des Beaux-Arts du Québec, **Café Krieghoff** gets a mix of families, singles, and artsy folks of all ages. See p. 207.

RESTAURANTS BY CUISINE

BISTRO

Bistro B ★ ($$$, p. 207)
Chez Boulay ★★ ($$$, p. 197)
L'Affaire est Ketchup ★★ ($$$, p. 208)
L'Échaudé ★ ($$$, p. 204)
Le Clocher Penché Bistrot ★★★ ($$$, p. 209)
Patente et Machin ★ ($$, p. 209)

CONTEMPORARY QUÉBÉCOIS

Initiale ★★★ ($$$, p. 203)
Laurie Raphaël ★★ ($$$, p. 203)
Le Moine Échanson ★★ ($$, p. 207)
Le Pain Béni ★ ($$$, p. 200)
Le Saint-Amour ★★★ ($$$, p. 201)
Panache ★★ ($$$, p. 205)

KEY TO ABBREVIATIONS:
$$$** = Expensive **$$** = Moderate **$ = Inexpensive

VIEUX-QUÉBEC: HAUTE-VILLE (UPPER TOWN)

In addition to the options listed below, food is also available in Upper Town at **Le Jazz Bar** (p. 240) in the Hotel Clarendon, **Pub St-Alexandre** (p. 241), and **1608 Wine & Cheese Bar** (p. 241).

Expensive

Aux Anciens Canadiens ★★ TRADITIONAL QUÉBÉCOIS   Situated within one of Upper Town's oldest homes (circa 1675), under a hard-to-miss, quaintly red roof, is the city's favorite destination for traditional Québécois cuisine. A dinner of pea soup, *tourtiere* (meat pie), baked beans, and maple syrup pie may sound basic, but these and the more contemporary adaptations of game (vacuum-cooked wild caribou filet mignon, for example) are prepared exceptionally well here. Small windows, low ceilings, checked tablecloths, and servers who dress in period costume add warmth and a smidge of whimsy to what is otherwise a fine dining (and expensive) night out. For a bargain, three-course early bird specials (daily until 5:45pm) run less than C$26 and include wine or beer. On the other hand, if you want the filet of wild Inuit caribou, you're looking at C$85.

34 rue St-Louis (at rue des Jardins). www.auxancienscanadiens.qc.ca. ✆ **418/692-1627**. Reservations recommended. Table d'hôte lunch and early bird dinner C$20–C$26; main courses dinner C$36–C$64; table d'hôte dinner starts at C$49. Daily noon–9pm. Check for changes to winter hours.

The Price You'll Pay	
Here's what you can expect to pay for your main course at a restaurant in Québec City:	
Expensive	C$25 and up
Moderate	C$15–C$25
Inexpensive	Under C$15

Chez Boulay Bistro à Boréal ★★ BISTRO It's almost as if chefs Jean-Luc Boulay and Arnaud Marchand anticipated the reviews when naming their restaurant: "Chez Boulay Bistro à Boréal is more than a mouthful . . ." It's much more, actually (and it goes by Chez Boulay for short). The airy, modern

Québec City Restaurants

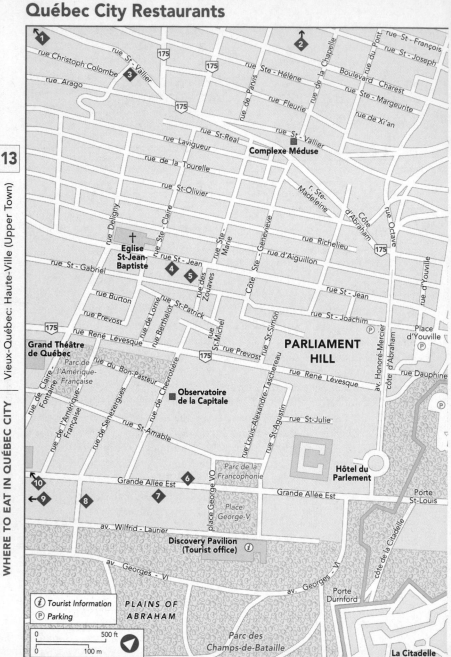

rue St-François
rue St-Joseph
rue du Font
rue Christoph Colombe
rue Arago
rue St-Vallier
175
175
rue Ste-Hélène
rue de la Chapelle
Boulevard Charest
rue Ste-Margeurite
rue de Parvis
rue Fleurie
175
rue de Xi'an
rue St-Real
rue St-Vallier
rue Lavigueur
Complexe Méduse
rue de la Tourelle
rue St-Olivier
r. Ste-Madeleine
Côte d'Abraham
rue Octave
rue de Dél(gny
Eglise
St-Jean-Baptiste
rue Ste-Claire
rue St-Jean
rue Ste-Marie
Côte Ste-Geneviève
rue Richelieu
175
rue d'Youville
rue St-Gabriel
rue d'Aiguillon
rue Burton
rue des Zouaves
rue St-Jean
rue Prevost
rue de Lorne
rue St-Patrick
St-Michel
rue St-Joachim
Place d'Youville
rue René Lévesque
rue Berthelot
rue St-Simon
rue Prevost
PARLIAMENT HILL
Grand Théâtre de Québec
175
rue René Lévesque
av. Honoré-Mercier
côte d'Abraham
rue Dauphine
Parc de l'Amérique-Française
rue du Bon-Pasteur
rue de la Chevrotière
Observatoire de la Capitale
rue Louis-Alexandre-Taschereau
rue St-Agustin
rue St-Julie
rue de Claire Fontaine
rue de l'Amérique Française
rue de Sénézergles
rue St-Amable
place George VO
Parc de la Francophonie
Hôtel du Parlement
Grande Allée Est
Porte St-Louis
Grande Allée Est
Place George-V
côte de la Citadelle
av. Wilfrid-Laurier
Discovery Pavilion (Tourist office)
av. Georges-VI
Porte Durnford
PLAINS OF ABRAHAM
Tourist Information
Parking
0 500 ft
0 100 m
Parc des Champs-de-Bataille
La Citadelle

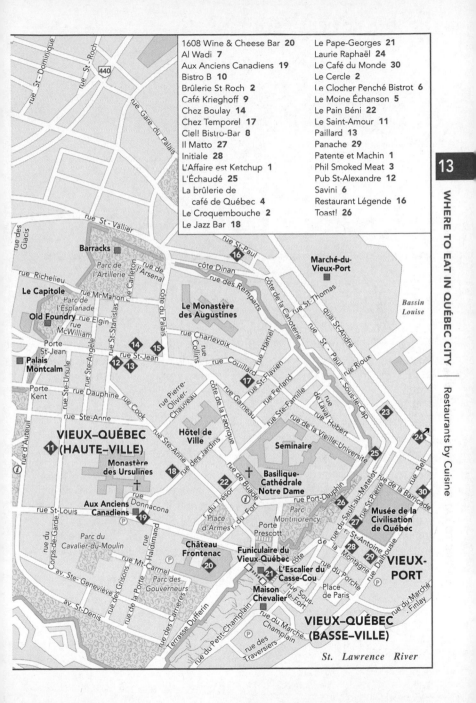

1608 Wine & Cheese Bar **20**
Al Wadi **7**
Aux Anciens Canadiens **19**
Bistro B **10**
Brûlerie St Roch **2**
Café Krieghoff **9**
Chez Boulay **14**
Chez Temporel **17**
Ciel! Bistro-Bar **8**
Il Matto **27**
Initiale **28**
L'Affaire est Ketchup **1**
L'Échaudé **25**
La brûlerie de
    café de Québec **4**
Le Croquembouche **2**
Le Jazz Bar **18**

Le Pape-Georges **21**
Laurie Raphaël **24**
Le Café du Monde **30**
Le Cercle **2**
Le Clocher Penché Bistrot **6**
Le Moine Échanson **5**
Le Pain Béni **22**
Le Saint-Amour **11**
Paillard **13**
Panache **29**
Patente et Machin **1**
Phil Smoked Meat **3**
Pub St-Alexandre **12**
Savini **6**
Restaurant Légende **16**
Toast! **26**

Barracks

Parc de
l'Artillerie

côte Dinan

**Marché-du-
Vieux-Port**

*Bassin
Louise*

Le Capitole

Parc de
l'Esplanade

Old Foundry

rue Elgin

rue
McWilliam

**Le Monastère
des Augustines**

Porte
St-Jean

**Palais
Montcalm**

rue St-Jean

Porte
Kent

rue Dauphine

**VIEUX–QUÉBEC
(HAUTE–VILLE)**

**Hôtel de
Ville**

Seminaire

**Monastère
des Ursulines**

**Basilique-
Cathédrale
Notre Dame**

**Aux Anciens
Canadiens**

rue St-Louis

Donnacona

Parc
Montmorency

**Musée de la
Civilisation
de Québec**

Parc du
Cavalier-du-Moulin

Porte
Prescott

**Château
Frontenac**

**Funiculaire du
Vieux-Québec**

**L'Escalier du
Casse-Cou**

**VIEUX–
PORT**

Parc des
Gouverneurs

**Maison
Chevalier**

Place
de Paris

**VIEUX–QUÉBEC
(BASSE–VILLE)**

Terrasse Dufferin

St. Lawrence River

THE REAL DEAL ABOUT meals

Blatantly touristy restaurants are all along rue St-Louis in Upper Town and around the Place d'Armes, many of them with hawkers outside. They can produce decent meals and are entirely satisfactory for lunch.

At the better places, though, reservations are essential during holidays and festivals. Other times, it's necessary to book ahead only for weekend evenings. Dress codes are rarely stipulated, but "dressy casual" works almost everywhere.

The evening meal tends to be served earlier in Québec City than in Montréal, at 7pm rather than 8pm. In the winter months, when tourist traffic slows, restaurants can close early or reduce the number of days they're open, so confirm before heading out.

The best dining deals in Québec City are table d'hôte, fixed-priced meals. Nearly all full-service restaurants offer them. Generally, these meals include at least soup or salad, a main course, and a dessert. Some places add an extra appetizer and/or a beverage. The total price ends up being approximately what you'd pay for the main course alone. At lunchtime, table d'hôte meals are even cheaper.

bistro was part of a renovation of **Hôtel Manoir Victoria** (p. 187), and it fills a need in this part of Upper Town for an all-around reliably good meal in an upscale, but not over-the-top ambience. Boulay, who has been perfecting his craft for more than 35 years at **Le Saint-Amour** (see below), wouldn't stand for much less than perfection. The "Boréal" menu is inspired by northern game and season cycles. Deer, duck, mackerel, Labrador tea spice, wintergreen, and birch syrup are among the traditional ingredients. Portions are generous, especially at brunch (Sat & Sun 10am–2pm). The clientele is made up of locals with discriminating palettes and visitors looking for a much nicer alternative to the pub fare that seems ubiquitous on this street.

1100 rue St-Jean (near rue St-Stanislas). www.chezboulay.com. ℰ **418/380-8166.** Main courses brunch C$17–C$20; lunch C$16–C$20; dinner C$22–C$35. Mon–Fri 11:30am–10pm; Sat–Sun 10am–10pm.

Le Pain Béni ★ CONTEMPORARY QUÉBÉCOIS If you want to sit outdoors on the touristy, pedestrian-only part of rue Ste-Anne (it can be abuzz with action), find an open table at Le Pain Béni. It pegs its menu as "bistronomique," a mix of high and low, with traditional French fare punctuated by avant-garde experimentation. Here's an example: Smoked duck breast with apple vinegar, mascarpone espuma (foam), and pickled figs. If that's too adventurous for you, Québec cheese fondue may hit the spot. Indoor seating is also a fine choice, with exposed stone and brick walls from the 1600s. The restaurant is in the **Auberge Place d'Armes** (p. 183), right next to the narrow art-lined walkway, **rue du Trésor** (p. 248).

24 rue Ste-Anne (at rue du Trésor). www.painbeni.com. ℰ **866/333-9485** or 418/694-9485. Table d'hôte lunch C$18–C$20; main courses dinner C$24–C$35; table d'hôte dinner cost of main plus C$10, or C$20 for a more elaborate version. Daily 7:30am–10am; May–Oct daily 11:30am–10pm; Nov–Apr Tues–Fri 11:30am–2:30pm and 5:30–10pm and Sat 5:30–10pm.

The modern styling of Chez Boulay

Le Saint-Amour ★★★ CONTEMPORARY QUÉBÉCOIS   The owners of this quirkily exquisite endeavor, Jacques Fortier and head chef Jean-Luc Boulay, wouldn't want a neon arrow pointing to their restaurant. Since they opened Le Saint-Amour in 1978 they've hardly needed a shingle out front. It's tucked away on a quiet Upper Town side street—a sole black awning over an arched doorway—exactly where you'd want to step out of a horse-drawn carriage for a romantic dinner for two. Make reservations. The interior speaks more to the 1970s than to present day, but the service is relentlessly adept and the dishes remain subtly complex. Foie gras is a specialty (seared, in terrine) and though the chef has long embraced the meats, his kitchen turns out incredible meatless options, especially when requested in advance. The now-infamous 2008 visit by Sir Paul McCartney (a vegetarian) to this establishment clearly had an impact. Desserts here may be the best in town.

48 Rue Sainte-Ursule (near rue St-Louis). www.saint-amour.com. ✆ **418/694-0667.** Reservations recommended. Table d'hôte lunch C$18–C$33; main courses C$40–C$52; discovery dinner C$115. Mon–Fri 11:30am–2pm; daily 6–10pm (opens at 5:30pm Saturday).

Inexpensive

In addition to **Paillard,** below, children may like **Casse-Crêpe Breton,** 1136 rue St-Jean (www.cassecrepebreton.com; ✆ **418/692-0438**), for its savory and sweet crepes (C$7–C$10). Centrally located in the heart of Upper Town, it's usually packed at lunch. Go a little early or a little late to avoid the wait.

Chez Temporel ★ LIGHT FARE   Québec's visitors often write up Chez Temporel as a "discovery," or as "authentically Québec" experience. That's what we like about it, too, especially in relation to this part of Upper Town near rue St-Jean, where non-touristy restaurants can be hard to find. This modest, nine-table cafe covers the basics like coffee, quiche, and salad very well. For some reason tourists are unlikely to take a turn off the main drag (but not you!) so you may find yourself among local college students and neighborhood regulars. If you send the cafe a postcard that describes why you liked dining there, they may post it on the wall. In business since 1974, they're clearly doing something right.

25 rue Couillard (near rue Christie). ✆ **418/694-1813.** Most items under C$11. Daily 9am–9pm.

Paillard ★★★ LIGHT FARE   Paillard has a high-end fast food feel, but it's one of a kind, and thoroughly Québec. Frankly, it's what one wishes all fast food could be. The bread is crusty and sometimes piping hot for sandwiches or served with soups that are (and taste) homemade. It's perfect for an affordable lunch or dinner that doesn't take hours, or for a coffee break with a formidable *macaron.* There are also salads and gelati. Combos of the day, which include sandwich, drink, and desert, cost C$5 for kids and C$10 for adults.

1097 rue St-Jean (near rue St-Stanislas). www.paillard.ca. ✆ **418/692-1221.** Most items under C$10. Sun–Thurs 7am–9pm; Fri–Sat 7am–10pm.

VIEUX-QUÉBEC: BASSE-VILLE (LOWER TOWN)/VIEUX-PORT

This part of Lower Town is thick with hotels, and thus tourists, which means you'll encounter numerous dining options beyond what's listed below. Taken as a group, the establishments on or surrounding rue St-Paul and rue Sault-au-Matelot are expensive, but quite good, one to the next. You might have better luck happening upon a decent meal here than the restaurants clustered near Frontenac, or Lower Town near Petit-Champlain or Place Royale. In addition to the options listed below, food is also available in Lower Town at the bar **SSS** (p. 241), and the wine bar/music room **Le Pape-Georges** (p. 241).

Expensive

Il Matto ★ ITALIAN   You might choose Il Matto because you're simply craving Italian or perhaps you want a change-up from Québécois bistro fare. Or maybe you want to sip cocktails among the fresh-faced after work crowd. The menu features Italian comfort food (Caesar salad, minestrone soup, pizza, or agnelotti, the house specialty) in a high-energy, trendy atmosphere. (On a recent visit the house was jammed, midweek, early evening.) The young owner, Rocco Cortina, is gaining a following, with the resultant TV appearances and now, a second location in Sainte-Foy (west of Vieux-Québec).

71 rue St-Pierre (near rue St-Antoine in the hotel Le St-Pierre). www.ilmatto.ca. ✆ **418/266-9444.** Reservations strongly recommended on weekends. Main courses lunch C$13–C$15; dinner C$19–C$30. Mon–Fri 11:30am–2pm and 5:30–11pm; Sat–Sun 5:30–11pm or later.

Contemporary and refined Initiale in Québec's Lower Town

Initiale ★★★ CONTEMPORARY QUÉBÉCOIS Initiale sets the gold standard for dining in Québec City and in the province. Set on a charming corner amidst Lower Town's finest hotels, the entrance radiates an aura of serious decorum—the interior does as well. Ceilings are grandly high and the tables have enough distance between them to allow you to privately gush as each course is expertly presented. That's why both young and mature couples alike celebrate milestone anniversaries here. The menu is designed to hit complex notes in a minimum of four courses with the chef's strong preference that you take the eight-course grand menu (C$139), which might start with locally caught turbot or mackerel with currant lemon sauce and move into carrots with wild rose vinegar or braised pork cheek and black pudding. Duckling breast figures into the heartier dishes (still tiny by most standards), as does leg of lamb. Expect perfection with wine selections; you won't be disappointed. On that note, expect it of desserts, too, such as raspberries in clover sauce with milk *confiture* (a kind of thick, sweet caramel jam).

54 rue St-Pierre (corner of Côte de la Montagne). www.restaurantinitiale.com. *(*) **418/694-1818.** Reservations recommended on weekends. Table d'hôte lunch C$22–C$29; tasting menu lunch C$59; main courses dinner C$46–C$53; grand tasting menu C$139. Tues–Fri 11:30am–2pm; Tues–Sat 5:30–9pm.

Laurie Raphaël ★★ CONTEMPORARY QUÉBÉCOIS Dining in this part of town can be very expensive, especially at accomplished restaurants like Laurie Raphaël. However, here this restaurant has an exceptional three-course "chef, chef!" lunch for C$29 per person. On sunny days, it's ideal to reserve a table on the corner terrace. Ask your server questions (Why "chef, chef!"?), savor starters like pork confit donuts or mains like mackerel with sea herb chimichirri sauce, and ruminate about new combos to try at home. While the food is ultra-gourmet, the service is generous and easygoing. On a recent visit, we were sent home with a cocktail recipe and one of its hard-to-find ingredients. Hands-on learning may be an option because chef and owner Daniel Vézina frequently leads cooking classes onsite. Dinner here can be an extraordinary culinary experience to add to a Québec City vacation.

117 rue Dalhousie (at rue St-André). www.laurieraphael.com. ☏ **418/692-4555.** Reservations recommended. 3-course chef, chef! lunch C$29, main courses dinner C$45–C$50; chef-chef dinner C$65; 10-course dinner C$120. Tues–Fri 11:30am–2pm; Tues–Sat 6–10pm. Note January closures.

L'Échaudé ★ BISTRO This venue has numerous menu combinations, such as table d'hôte and *carte d'hôte* (menu of the day) or additions to entrees or wine flights, which can make dining here a good value. The setting is confidently chic, as if the white linens and silver set themselves. The servers know bistro cuisine and the lengthy wine list like the backs of their hands. That's reassuring and why lots of locals frequent the place. The menu is classic—*tartares*, duck confit, steak frites, crème brûlée for dessert. Some diners may yearn for more excitement or innovation. A late-night discount kicks in after 9pm (21h) when a la carte menu items are 21% off.

73 rue Sault-au-Matelot (near rue St-Paul). www.echaude.com. ☏ **418/692-1299.** Reservations suggested on weekends. Table d'hôte lunch C$25; main courses dinner C$19–C$38; add C$12 for *carte d'hôte* or C$18 for table d'hôte. Mon–Fri 11:30am–2:30pm; Sat–Sun 10am–2:30pm; daily 5:30–10pm.

Foie gras at L'Échaudé

Restaurant Légende ★★ CONTEMPORARY QUÉBÉCOIS   Located across from the train station, in the less touristy part of Lower Town, Légende started drawing praise the moment it opened in 2014. The team behind it has run the mythical La Tanière since 1977, known for its heritage gastronomony (10–20 course meals) and in a rural locale beyond most tourists' reach. The idea was to create a user-friendly "boréal" bistro (that is, use only local, in-season ingredients) and the approach is to offer all dishes as either small or main courses. Don't let your wallet be fooled, this will be an expensive night out. Still, the wine pairings are spot on, the starter cocktail one of the best in the city, and the desert? Phenomenal. We haven't even mentioned the mouth-watering lamb fries with wild peas, shrimp, and fiddleheads or bison tataki with marinated chanterelles and sea buckthorn. While friendly, the service could take a few pointers from the chef's more formal outpost.

255 rue St-Paul (in L'Hôtel des Coutellier). www.restaurantlegende.com. ℭ **418/614-2555.** Reservations recommended. Half portions C$14–C$20, full portions C$28–C$32. Sun–Tues 5–10pm; Wed 11:30am–10pm; Thurs–Fri 11:30am–11pm; Sat 5–11pm. (In fall and winter, closed Mon and Tues for lunch.)

Panache ★★ CONTEMPORARY QUÉBÉCOIS   Panache is a superior restaurant housed in the repurposed buildings that make up the likewise superior hotel, **Auberge St-Antoine** (p. 188). Historic preservationists will appreciate that the massive wood beams and stone walls of a 19th-century wharf have been incorporated into a rough-hewn, cleverly designed dining space (in summer, it has quite a terrace). Oenophiles can choose from an extensive wine list (700+ labels from 14 countries). And locavores should know that the kitchen has an organic garden on the nearby Île d'Orléans. But let's talk meat: Locally sourced beef, veal, and duck are served with the likes of chanterelles and garlic flower or blueberry reduction sauce. Panache has also taken its food on the road with two mobile food trucks and the casual **Café de la Promenade,** on La Promenade Samuel-De Champlain (p. 228).

10 rue St-Antoine (in Auberge St-Antoine). www.saint-antoine.com. ℭ **418/692-1022.** Reservations recommended. Main courses breakfast C$19–C$24, lunch C$20–C$25, dinner C$42–C$56; 6-course signature menu C$119. Mon–Fri 6:30–10:30am and noon–2pm; Sat–Sun 7–11am and 11:30am–2pm; daily 6–10pm.

Toast! ★ CONTEMPORARY QUÉBÉCOIS   Chef and co-owner Christian Lemelin started cooking at age 17 and his menu, agile and daring, still seems young (in a good way). Barbeque octopus and veal sweetbreads are served with sautéed spaetzle, alongside peppers and corn in Madagascar pepper sauce, and a celeriac salad with xérès vinaigrette. And so it goes. Prices are high (add seared foie gras to any entrée for C$20), but the atmosphere is lively and laid-back, especially during summer nights on the patio.

17 rue Sault-au-Matelot (at rue St-Antoine). www.restauranttoast.com. ℭ **418/692-1334.** Reservations recommended on weekends. Main courses C$25–C$45. Sun–Thurs 6–10:30pm; Fri–Sat 6–11pm.

Snag a seat on the patio at Café du Monde near the riverfront.

Moderate

Le Café du Monde ★ TRADITIONAL FRENCH   This spacious waterfront restaurant simultaneously channels T.G.I. Friday's and traditional French cooking, with a long menu that truly has something for everyone. Count on the baby spinach salad, fries cooked in duck fat, or three-cheese fondue for starters and the black pudding as a main course. There's also supertender rotisserie chicken and many options from the sea. Kids love the deep-fried ice cream with caramel sauce for dessert. It's one of few spots with outdoor seating that overlooks the St. Lawrence.

84 rue Dalhousie (next to the cruise terminal). www.lecafedumonde.com. *②* **418/692-4455.** Reservations recommended. Table d'hôte lunch C$15–C$19; main courses dinner C$17–C$39; table d'hôte dinner C$34–C$39. Mon–Fri 11:30am–11pm; Sat–Sun and holidays 9am–11pm.

PARLIAMENT HILL (ON OR NEAR GRANDE-ALLÉE)

If you're a serious (or even a beginning) foodie, you might want to stroll rue St-Jean heading away from Old Town's gates. Along this stretch are artisan bread makers, baristas, tea purveyors, and more (see also p. 221 in chapter 14). **La brûlerie de café de Québec,** 575 rue St-Jean (www.bruleriedecafe. com; *②* **418/529-4769**), roasts its own beans and supplies area restaurants. In addition to the restaurant options listed below, food is also available on Grande-Allée at the bar/restaurant **Savini,** on p. 242 and 28 stories up, at **Ciel! Bistro-Bar,** on p. 241.

Expensive

Bistro B ★ BISTRO This open air, open kitchen bistro is a solid addition to city dining at large and to the Montcalm neighborhood just adjacent to Parliament Hill in particular. For one, it has cocktails that can be enjoyed out front in warm months and indoors at a cozy bar. And the list is neither mediocre nor predictable. Think daily specials with fresh local ingredients like basil gel or peach elixir. The food menu follows suit. A recent visit started with a crisp yellow beet salad with apples and hazelnuts followed by a main course of red deer with a faint (perhaps too much so) truffle sauce. Risotto with morels and asparagus was another appealing option. Photos of the menu handwritten in chalk on the slate above the counter are regularly posted to Facebook.

1144 av. Cartier (at rue Aberdeen). www.bistrob.ca. © **418/614-5444.** Reservations recommended. Main courses C$22–C$32. Mon–Fri 11:30am–2pm; Sun 10am–2pm; daily 6–11pm.

Moderate

Café Krieghoff ★★★ LIGHT FARE Café Krieghoff can be habit-forming, especially if you visit Québec City often enough. It may not wow or woo those seeking haute cuisine, but it can make you feel like you're taking an afternoon off from tourists and settling in to a low-profile Québécois way of life. Partly it's the Montcalm neighborhood, just 10 minutes' walk from the Parliament building down Grande-Allée, a right turn on avenue Cartier. And partly it's the great coffee (included with most breakfasts), reliable cooking, friendly service, and chance to sit outside.

1089 av. Cartier (north of Grande-Allée). www.cafekrieghoff.qc.ca. © **418/522-3711.** Most items under C$19. Mon–Fri 7am–10pm; Sat–Sun 8am–10pm.

Le Moine Échanson ★★ CONTEMPORARY QUÉBÉCOIS This earthy, adventurous restaurant started as a hole-in-the-wall kitchen, with a few

---

EATING vegetarian IN A LAND THAT IS NOT

Vegetarians may be concerned about eating in Québec City, a destination with a rich regional cuisine, where calf brains are a delicacy and pies are made of meat.

Fortunately, many restaurants offer a rotating veggie option, such as the gougère stuffed with Gruyere and cipollini confit and served with Jerusalem artichoke puree, at **Toast!** (p. 205). Others will tweak an entrée if you call ahead and ask.

If you eat dairy products, a cheese plate traditionally served as a last course could become your main dish, although you'll have to ignore the raised

eyebrows. For an extensive cheese selection, visit **La Fromagère du Marché** ((© **418/692-2517,** ext. 238), in the **Marché du Vieux-Port.** The market also has a generous selection of seasonally fresh fruits and vegetables, and freshly baked baguettes.

Tip: If the French language isn't your strong suit, assume that most dishes (even a grilled cheese sandwich) could have meat and learn to recognize a few terms. Sorry to say, saucisse is sausage, not sauce, and fruits de mer do not grow on trees—rather, it's a mix of shellfish.

oak barrels out front and lots of hanging plants. It served funky wines and food in jars and became the go-to for artsy, engaged eaters. Word spread (in part, by us) and it doubled in size and refined its overall look and feel. It still leads the pack for dishes cooked with butter, bacon, and intense cheeses and develops seasonal recipes to complement privately imported batches of wine. Allow yourself to experiment with their offbeat inventory: Glasses run C$7 to C$11 and bottles start at C$36. Appetizers and cheese plates are served on house whim, between the hours of 4pm and 6pm or 10pm and 1am.

585 rue St-Jean (at rue Ste-Marie). www.lemoineechanson.com. (*) **418/524-7832.** Reservations recommended. Main courses C$18–C$24. Daily 6–11pm (variably opens earlier and closes later).

Inexpensive

For a quick snack, **Al Wadi,** 615 Grande-Allée est ((*) **418/649-8345**), in the heart of the Grande-Allée party district, is open 10:30am till 4am Wednesday through Sunday (Mon–Tues till 11:30pm). Gyros, *shawarma,* falafel, and other veggie options are on the menu.

ST-ROCH

St-Roch's still-up-and-coming restaurant scene runs along a street with excellent bakeries, coffee shops, and ethnic food options. Two favorites include **Le Croquembouche,** 225 rue St-Joseph est (www.lecroquembouche.com; (*) **418/523-9009**), for baked goods, and the coffee shop **Brûlerie St-Roch,** 375 rue St-Joseph est (www.brulerie-st-roch.com; (*) **418/529-1559**).

Expensive

L'Affaire est Ketchup ★★ BISTRO   The expression, "*l'affaire est ketchup*," is unique to the province (or so claim the locals) and means "it's all good" or "everything's cool." Rightly so at this boho slip of a restaurant (we are talking small and seriously homespun). You could walk past the half rundown exterior a few times, mistaking it for a soup kitchen. That's just part of the charm. Inside, the chef whips up magic like duck *magret* or sturgeon with celeriac purée from a kitchen that makes an Easy Bake Oven look like a six-burner Viking. It was the city's best-kept secret until American chef and TV host Anthony Bourdain brought the cameras around (but that doesn't mean you shouldn't try it). Reservations recommended because of the restaurant's size and approach: Typically there are only two seatings per night.

46 rue St-Joseph est (near boul. Langelier). www.facebook.com/laffaireest.ketchup. (*)**418/529-9020.** Main courses C$20–C$28. Daily 6–11pm. Winter hours may vary.

Le Cercle ★★★ FUSION   Here's a perfect spot to gather with friends, order *grignotines* (snacks) and choose a bottle or two from a carefully selected wine list. Some small plates are built around homemade sausage, local fish smoked in-house, or incorporate wine into flavorful sauces. Many come with a side of pickled vegetables or other creative condiments. If you plan ahead a week or more (and recruit a small army to join you), you can order a pig roasted "from snout to tail." Le Cercle is a reliable pick for weekend brunch, too. The bar is open late and a plethora of films and other live entertainment is on offer in the adjacent space.

228 rue St-Joseph est (near rue Caron). www.le-cercle.ca. ⓒ **418/948-8648.** Reservations recommended on weekends. Main courses lunch C$13–C$16; small plates C$5–C$14; main courses dinner C$21–C$27. Mon–Wed 11:30am–1:30am; Thurs–Fri 11:30am–3am; Sat 10am–3am; Sun 10am–1:30am.

Le Clocher Penché Bistrot ★★★ BISTRO   Clocher Penché has laid-back European sophistication down pat. Its early presence in the bohemian St-Roch neighborhood paved the way for other experimental, down-home restaurants to take form and it has a loyal local following. Plus, they likely serve the best brunch in town. The shifting menu relies on regional *terroir*—from homemade *cavatelli* with lobster cream to blood sausage over grilled hearts of romaine. Service is efficient and friendly. Definitely save room for dessert.

203 rue St-Joseph est (at rue Caron). www.clocherpenche.ca. ⓒ **418/640-0597.** Reservations recommended. Table d'hôte lunch and weekend brunch C$17; main courses dinner C$21–C$27. Tues–Fri 11:30am–2pm; Sat–Sun 9am–2pm; Tues–Sat 5–10pm.

Moderate

Patente et Machin ★ BISTRO   Not surprisingly, this way casual under-taking has ties to **L'Affaire est Ketchup** (see above, same owners). In this instance the name's rough translation is "thingies and gadgets" or maybe, food-wise, "nibbles and bites." That's how the menu is divided: *Machins* are smallish: oysters, bisques, and such, while *Patentes* are main courses like red deer with juniper berries or giant roasted scallops. *Grosses patentes* are main courses built for two. Dining in this cramped, boisterous spot feels as close to going to a friend's house for dinner as we could imagine—that is, if the friend is into high-quality food and goes the extra mile, but keeps it simple. Service is slow and inattentive but, then again, so it is at a lot of friends'.

82 rue St-Joseph ouest (near rue St-Valier). www.facebook.com/Patente.et.Machin. ⓒ **581/981-3999.** Main courses C$14–C$22. Daily 5–11pm. Winter hours may be shorter.

Phil Smoked Meat ★★ LIGHT FARE   Smoked meat purists may scoff at Phil's "spaghetti smoked meat" or "pizza smoked meat" (while others swear by it); either way, this bright restaurant on the border between St-Roch and Upper Town is a fine choice for a delicious and affordable meal. Vegetarians take note: An order for grilled cheese unexpectedly arrived with meat. Phil returned with an out-this-world sandwich, grilled to perfection, with smoked cheese and caramelized onions. (We've suggested adding it to the menu and considered returning for another a few days later.) Decent beer and a delightful local soft drink, *bière d'épinette* (spruce beer, like a root beer), round off the menu.

275 rue St-Vallier est (at rue Narcisse Belleau). www.philsmokedmeat.com. ⓒ **418/523-4545.** Most items under C$15. Mon–Wed 11am–8.30pm; Thurs–Sat 11am–9pm.

EXPLORING QUÉBEC CITY

14

Wandering the streets of Vieux-Québec is a singular pleasure, comparable to exploring a provincial capital in Europe. You might happen upon an ancient convent, gabled houses with steeply pitched roofs, a battery of 18th-century cannons in a leafy park, or a bistro with a blazing fireplace on a wintry day.

Vieux-Québec (or the Old City) is so compact that it's hardly necessary to plan precise sightseeing itineraries. Most of the historic sights are within the city walls of Haute-Ville (Upper Town) and Basse-Ville (Lower Town). Start at Terrasse Dufferin alongside the Château Frontenac and go off on a whim, down L'Escalier du Casse-Cou (Breakneck Stairs) to the Quartier du Petit-Champlain and Place-Royale, or out of the walls to the military fortress of the Citadelle that overlooks the mighty St. Lawrence River and onto the Plains of Abraham, where generals James Wolfe of Britain and Louis-Joseph, marquis de Montcalm of France, fought to their mutual deaths in a 20-minute battle that changed the continent's destiny.

A few winding, somewhat steep roads (or the Breakneck Stairs or *funiculaire*) connect Upper and Lower Town. Upper Town can also be hilly, with sloping streets, but only people with physical limitations are likely to experience difficulty. Other sights are outside Upper Town's walls, along or just off the boulevard called Grande-Allée. If rain or ice discourages exploration on foot, tour buses and horse-drawn *calèches* are options as well as an electric city bus that loops by most major sights.

QUÉBEC CITY'S ICONIC SIGHTS

- Basilique Cathédrale Notre-Dame de Québec ★★★ p. 217
- Château Frontenac ★★★, p. 218
- Fortifications-de-Québec ★, p. 228
- Hôtel du Parlement ★, p. 222
- La Citadelle ★★, p. 219
- L'Escalier du Casse-Cou ★, p. 211
- Musée de la Civilisation ★★★, p. 211
- Musée National des Beaux-Arts ★★★, p. 223
- Parc des Champs-de-Bataille ★★★, p. 228
- Place-Royale ★★★, p. 214
- Quartier de Petit-Champlain, p. 215

OTHER TOP ATTRACTIONS

- La Promenade Samuel-De Champlain ★★, p. 228
- Marché du Vieux-Port ★★, p. 216
- Musée de l'Amérique Francophone ★★, p. 220
- Observatoire de la Capitale, p. 224
- Rue du Trésor "Outdoor Gallery," p. 220

VIEUX-QUÉBEC: BASSE-VILLE (LOWER TOWN) ATTRACTIONS

If this is your first trip to Québec City, consider starting with the walking tour of this area in chapter 16.

L'Escalier du Casse-Cou ★ These stairs connect Terrasse Dufferin at the top of the cliff (in Upper Town) with rue Sous-le-Fort at the base (Lower Town). The name translates to "Breakneck Stairs," and they are, indeed, very steep, although hardly neck-break-inducing by modern standards. A stairway has existed here since the settlement began. In 1698, the town council had to explicitly forbid citizens from taking their animals up or down the stairway, and those who didn't comply were punished with a fine. Nestled along the northern side of the steps (to the right after you've come down) are good quality bistros, small shops, and even a chocolate store.

Maison Historique Chevalier ★ As part of Les Musées de la Civilisation (see below), this and the adjacent two homes evidence the urban architecture of New France. Built in 1752 and rebuilt 10 years later, Maison Chevalier's asymetrical design followed what used to be a shoreline. Walls, as well as window and door openings, are made of regional sandstone and limestone. The revamped tour, "400 Centuries of History," focuses on how the furnishings, gathered from the museums' collections, represent Québec's different political regimes, especially during the 18th and 19th centuries.

50 rue du Marché-Champlain (at rue Notre-Dame). www.mcq.org. ℂ **866/710-8031** or 418/643-2158. Free admission. Late June to early Sept daily 9:30am–5pm; May to late June Tues–Sun 10am–5pm; Sept–Dec and Jan–May Sat–Sun 10am–5pm. Due to a recent renovation, double-check open hours and admission fees.

Musée de la Civilisation ★★★ This engaging museum can be both a geographic and cultural touchstone for a visit to Québec City. It sits prominently in the center of Lower Town, between rue St-Paul and Dalhousie (entrance side) and promises info-packed, interactive permanent and touring exhibitions. Open since 1988, this is the lead of four related museums whose objectives include ethnographic collecting, preservation, and stimulation of an evolving cultural conversation about the history of Québec and its peoples. (The others are Musée de l'Amérique Francophone, Musée de la place Royale, and Maison Historique Chevalier; you can get a discount for purchasing a three-museum pass.) The permanent exhibit, "People of Québec . . . Then and

Québec City Attractions

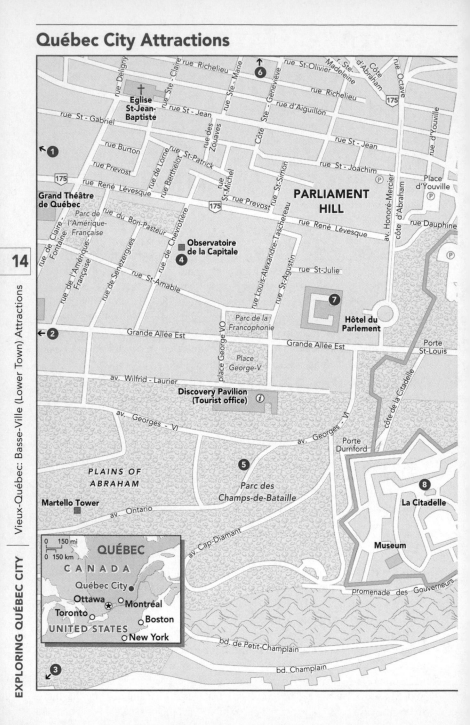

Église St-Jean-Baptiste

Grand Théâtre de Québec

Parc de l'Amérique-Française

Observatoire de la Capitale

PARLIAMENT HILL

Place d'Youville

rue Dauphine

Parc de la Francophonie

Hôtel du Parlement

Porte St-Louis

Place George-V

Discovery Pavilion (Tourist office)

Porte Durnford

PLAINS OF ABRAHAM

Martello Tower

Parc des Champs-de-Bataille

La Citadelle

Museum

promenade des Gouverneurs

QUÉBEC

CANADA

Québec City

Ottawa

Montréal

Toronto

Boston

UNITED STATES

New York

0 150 mi
0 150 km

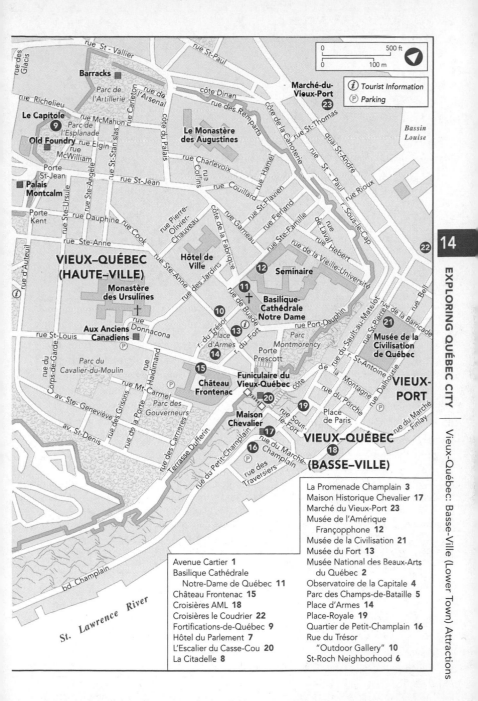

rue St-Vallier

rue St-Paul

rue des Glacis

Barracks

côte Dinan

rue Richelieu

Parc de l'Artillerie

rue de l'Arsenal

rue des Remparts

Marché-du-Vieux-Port
23

côte de la Canoterie

rue St-Thomas

quai St-André

Le Capitole
9

Parc de l'Esplanade

rue McMahon

rue de Carleton

côte du Palais

rue St. - Paul

F. Sous-le-Cap

Bassin Louise

Old Foundry

rue Elgin

rue St-Stanislas

rue McWilliam

Le Monastère des Augustines

rue Charlevoix

rue Hamel

rue St - Paul

rue Rioux

Porte St-Jean

rue St-Angèle

rue St-Jean

rue des Colins

rue Couillard

rue St-Flavien

rue Ferland

Palais Montcalm

Porte Kent

rue Dauphine

rue Cook

rue Pierre-Olivier-Chauveau

rue Garneau

rue Ste-Famille

de Laval Hébert

F. Sous-le-Cap

22

rue Ste-Ursule

rue Ste-Anne

côte de la Fabrique

rue de la Vieille-Université

rue d'Auteuil

VIEUX–QUÉBEC (HAUTE–VILLE)

rue Ste-Anne

Hôtel de Ville

rue des Jardins

12

Séminaire

de la Barricade

rue Bell

14

EXPLORING QUÉBEC CITY | Vieux-Québec: Basse-Ville (Lower Town) Attractions

Monastère des Ursulines

11

10

r. du Trésor

r. de Buade

Basilique-Cathédrale Notre Dame

rue de la Barricade

Aux Anciens Canadiens

rue Donnacona

13

r. du Place d'Armes

r. du Fort

Parc Montmorency

rue Port-Dauphin

rue St-Pierre-de-la-Barricade

21

Musée de la Civilisation de Québec

rue St-Louis

14

Porte Prescott

de la Montagne

rue du Sault-au-Matelot

rue Dalhousie

Parc du Cavalier-du-Moulin

rue du Corps-de-Garde

rue Haldimand

rue Mt-Carmel

rue St-Antoine

VIEUX-PORT

15

Château Frontenac

Funiculaire du Vieux-Québec

côte de la Montagne

rue du Porche

av. Ste-Geneviève

Parc des Gouverneurs

rue de la Porte

20

19

Place de Paris

rue du Marché-Finlay

av. St-Denis

rue des Grisons

Maison Chevalier

rue Sous-le-Fort

VIEUX–QUÉBEC

des Carrières

17

rue du Marché-Champlain

18

16

Terrasse Dufferin

rue du Petit-Champlain

rue des Traversiers

(BASSE–VILLE)

bd. Champlain

St. Lawrence River

0   500 ft
0   100 m

The garden in the Musée de la Civilisation

Now," winds the clock back more than 400 years with audio recordings based on accounts from actual historic figures. Archival documents, flags, clothing, furniture, musical instruments, and toys are also on view with interpretation in French and English. Another permanent exhibit, "Our Story: First Nations and Inuit in the 21st Century," introduces Québec's 11 Aboriginal nations through five themes that evolve chronologically from paleohistory through present day. Plan a few hours to a half day for this museum as it usually has about five concurrent exhibits. The pleasant, onsite, Café 47 overlooks the St. Lawrence and serves wine and beer.

85 rue Dalhousie (at rue St-Antoine). www.mcq.org. (◈ **866/710-8031** or 418/643-2158. Admission C$16 adults, C$15 seniors, C$10 students, C$5 children 12–16, free for children 11 and under; free to all Nov–Mar Tues and Jan–Feb Sat 10am–noon. Three-museum discount (Musée de la Civilisation, Musée de l'Amérique Francophone, and Musée de la place Royale), good for 2 weeks after purchase: C$24 adults, C$22 seniors, C$16 students, C$7 kids 12–16, free under 12. Late June to early Sept daily 9am–6pm; mid-Sept to late June Tues–Sun 10am–5pm. Open some Monday holidays.

Place-Royale ★★★ This small, but picturesque plaza is considered by the Québécois to be the literal and spiritual heart of Basse-Ville—in grander terms, the birthplace of French America. A **bust of Louis XIV** is at the center. In the 17th and 18th centuries, Place-Royal, or "Royal Square," was the town marketplace, and the center of business and industry. **Église Notre-Dame-des-Victoires** (see "350+ Years of Catholic Faith," below) dominates the plaza. It's Québec's oldest stone church, built in 1688 after a massive fire in Lower Town destroyed 55 homes in 1682. The church was restored in 1763 and again in 1969. Its paintings, altar, and large model boat suspended from

must see CIRCUS, QUÉBEC STYLE

The now world-famous **Cirque du Soleil** got its start just north of Québec City. For five summers the innovative troupe put on free—yes, free—outdoor summer shows to help celebrate Québec City's 400th anniversary. Then the troupe relocated its nearest performances more than an hour's drive away. But all is not lost. In 2015, the troupe **Flip FabriQue** (www.flipfabrique.com), also with local roots, picked up the torch to offer free, first-come first-serve shows at the Agora amphitheater at Pointe-à-Carcy. Flip FabriQue is part of a groundswell of circuses that take cues from Cirque du Soleil and then go a step further. Their intense acrobatics incorporate juggling, trampoline, Cyr wheel, diabolos, and hula-hoops. Arrive early and bring the whole family. For performance details visit **www.quebecregion.com**.

the ceiling were votive offerings brought by early settlers to ensure safe voyages. The church is open daily to visitors May through September, and admission is free. Sunday masses are held at 10:30am and noon. During one recent visit a wedding had just ended, and the whole square was there to greet the new couple as they exited their church.

Commercial activity here began to stagnate around 1860, and by 1950, this was a poor, rundown district. Rehabilitation began in 1960, and all the buildings on the square have now been restored, though now only some of the walls are original. One building houses the **Musée de la place Royale,** an affiliate of Les Musées de la Civilisation. Here, "Facing Champlain," a 3-D movie about Samuel Champlain and a hands-on room with costumes enliven the city's 400-year history. When you exit, turn left and, at the end of the block, turn around to view a *trompe l'oeil* mural depicting citizens of the early city.

Musée de la place Royale, 27 rue Notre-Dame. www.mcq.org. ✆ **866/710-8031** or 418/646-3167. Centre admission C$7 adults, C$6 seniors, C$5 students, C$2 children 12–16, free for children 11 and under; free to all Nov–Mar Tues and Jan–Feb Sat 10am–noon. Three-museum discount (Musée de la Civilisation, Musée de l'Amérique Francophone, and Musée de la place Royale), good for 2 weeks after purchase: C$24 adults, C$22 seniors, C$16 students, C$7 kids 12–16, free under 12. Late June to early Sept daily 9:30am–5pm; mid-Sept to late June Tues–Sun 10am–5pm.

Shopping in Lower Town

At the bottom of the Breakneck Stairs and the *funiculaire* is the quaint **Quartier de Petit-Champlain** (www.quartierpetitchamplain.com), an area of *petit* (small) winding cobblestone streets. The curved rue du Petit-Champlain is pedestrian-only and the main point of interest. Restored houses in the *quartier* have been turned into clothing boutiques, specialty shops, and galleries, some of which feature locally made products—but you'll find a substantial number of trinkets and T-shirts sold here, too. Petit-Champlain attracts more visiting shoppers than locals, tilting the products toward Québec-branded items.

About a half-dozen antiques shops line **rue St-Paul** near the waterfront on the opposite end of Lower Town. They're filled with knickknacks, Québec

Place-Royale

country furniture, candlesticks, old clocks, Victoriana, Art Deco and Art Moderne objects, and the increasingly sought-after kitsch and housewares of the early post–World War II period. **La Nouvelle France Antiquités,** 225 rue St-Paul (✆ **418/694-1807**), sells mid-century home goods as well as license plates, beverage signs and boxes, wooden trunks, and more. At **Les Antiquités Bolduc,** 89 rue St-Paul (www.lesantiquitesbolduc.com; ✆ **418/694-9558**), brother-and-sister duo Stéphanie and Frédéric Bolduc sell vintage knick-knacks, such as antique sconces and grandfather clocks.

These are other special shops where you can find uniquely Québécois goods:

Boutique des Métiers d'Art   In a stone building at the corner of Place-Royale, this carefully arranged store displays works by scores of Québécois craftspeople. Among these objects are wooden boxes, jewelry, graphics, and a variety of gifts. When departing, be sure to turn left, walk past the end of the building, and turn around—it's a surprise! 29 rue Notre-Dame. www.metiers-d-art. qc.ca. ✆ **418/694-0267.**

Les Fourrures du Vieux-Port   The fur trade underwrote the development and exploration of Québec and the vast lands west, and continues to be important to the region to this day. This Lower Town merchant, family-owned and in this site for more than 30 years, has as good a selection as any, including knit furs, shearlings, and designer coats. 55 rue St-Pierre (at Côte de la Montagne). ✆ 418/692-6686.

Marché du Vieux-Port ★★   Long a fixture in Lower Town, the location of this indoor farmer's market has been up for debate with a plan to relocate it to the ExpoCité (p. 240) in 2017. Until then (or unless a groundswell of support stops the move), it remains firmly in Old Town and offers local produce, seafood, cheeses, baked goods, and other regional products such as maple syrup, *vin de cidre* (cider wine), and cassis. A handy online guide specifies exactly what's in season when: *betteraves* (sugar beets) from July to November, for example, and *pétoncles* (scallops) every month of the year. Perfect for a stroll and snack. They open at 9am every day and close at 6pm on weekdays, 5pm on weekends. 160 Quai St-André. www.marchevieuxport.com. © **418/692-2517.**

VIEUX-QUÉBEC: HAUTE-VILLE (UPPER TOWN) ATTRACTIONS

One way to think of Upper Town's layout is to imagine what kind of structures you would build on higher ground, especially 400 years ago. Perhaps a glorious castle to welcome visitors as they enter the city? (Château Frontenac has that covered.) Some kind of military protection? (That would be La Citadelle.) How about the mother of all Catholic churches (Notre Dame Basilica, *merci*.)

And what would surround these historic landmarks in modern day? On the streets Côte de la Fabrique and rue St-Jean are shops, bars, and restaurants with a feel that is slightly more everyday than Lower Town's Petit-Champlain. In part, this means McDonald's. It also means that some of Canada's major clothing stores (Simon's, Roots, Bedo) have a presence in this area, which can be its own point of exploration.

A walking tour of the Old City's Upper Town is on p. 243.

Basilique Cathédrale Notre-Dame de Québec ★★★ Notre-Dame Basilica, representing the oldest Christian parish north of Mexico, has weathered a tumultuous history of bombardment, reconstruction, and restoration. In 2014 it celebrated 350 years as home to the mother parish to all of North America. Parts of the existing basilica date from the original 1647 structure, including the bell tower and portions of the walls, but most of today's exterior is from the reconstruction completed in 1771. The interior, a re-creation undertaken after a fire in 1922, is flamboyantly neo-baroque, with glinting yellow gold leaf and shadows wavering by

Basilique Cathédrale Notre-Dame de Québec, the oldest Christian parish north of Mexico

350+ YEARS OF CATHOLIC faith

In 1664, Bishop François de Laval founded what is now considered the "mother-parish" of all North American Catholic parishes on the shores of the mighty St. Lawrence—**Notre-Dame de Québec.** Through those many generations, the parish's many works have included establishing a convent of the Ursuline community (with permission from Louis XIII, King of France) and a seminary to instruct the First Nations. It also established and oversees the **Basilica Cathedral of Notre-Dame de Québec** and the **Notre-Dame-des-Victoires** church, two active faith communities.

The parish celebrated its 350th anniversary in 2014 with feasts, blessings, conferences, special exhibits at local museums, musical performances, self-guided pilgrimages for persons of all faith, as well as the opening and closing of the basilica's Holy Door. As one of the world's seven Holy Doors, it will be re-opened from December 8, 2015 through November 20, 2016 in observance of the Holy Year of Mercy. The Corporation du patrimoine et du tourisme religieux de Québec is responsible for the interpretation of cultural heritage for the area's 26 churches, 3 chapels, and 11 religious institutions. Descriptions of an array of guided tours can be found by visiting **www.patrimoine-religieux.com** or calling ⓒ **418/694-0665.** Advance reservations recommended.

the fluttering light of votive candles. It's beautifully maintained, with pews buffed to a shine. Paintings and ecclesiastical treasures still remain from the time of the French regime, including a chancel lamp given by Louis XIV. More than 900 people are buried in the crypt, including four governors of New France. Groups should reserve the 1-hour guided visits to the cathedral and the crypt in advance by phone.

20 rue Buade (at Côte de la Fabrique). www.patrimoine-religieux.com. ⓒ **418/694-0665.** Free admission; donations encouraged. Crypt C$5. Cathedral Mon–Sat 7am–close (4, 5, or 8:30pm depending on season); Mass Mon–Fri 8am and 12:05pm; Sat 8am and 5pm; Sun 9:30 and 11:30am (and 5pm May–Oct).

Château Frontenac ★★★   It used to be that visitors curious about the interior of Québec City's most iconic building could take guided tours of the hotel. Now, with a recent (and thoroughly modern) update, tours are self-guided and require a mobile app. With or without the app (free on the hotel's website), you can take in the lobby's spectacular fixtures or dine at the freshly made-over restaurant, **Le Champlain,** which has one of the only dedicated cheese rooms in North America. If you're yearning for an aperitif or digestif with a view, look no further than the hotel's two sparkling new additions, the bistro **Le Sam** or the wine and cheese bar, **1608** (p. 241). Designed as a version of a Loire Valley palace, the hotel opened in 1893 to house railroad passengers and encourage tourism. Commanding its majestic position atop Cap Diamant, the rock bluff that once provided military defense, Château Frontenac is visible from almost every quarter of the city.

1 rue des Carrières, at Place d'Armes. www.fairmont.com/frontenac-quebec. ⓒ **866/540-4460** or 418/692-3861.

La Citadelle ★★ Dug into the Plains of Abraham high above Cap Diamant (Cape Diamond), the rock bluff adjacent to the St. Lawrence River, the fort has a low profile that keeps it all but invisible until walkers are actually upon it. The Duke of Wellington had this partially star-shaped fortress built at the south end of the city walls in anticipation of renewed American attacks after the War of 1812. Some remnants of earlier French military structures were incorporated into the Citadelle, including a 1750 magazine. The facility has never actually exchanged fire with an invader, but still continues its vigil for the state. It's now a national historic site and, since 1920, has been home to Québec's **Royal 22e Régiment,** the only fully Francophone unit in Canada's armed forces. That makes it North America's largest fortified group of buildings still occupied by troops. Admission includes a guided tour to the Citadelle and its 25 buildings, as well as entrance to **Le Musée Royal 22e Régiment,** which features the exhibit, "Je me souviens," in honor of the regiment's more than 100 years of service. The hour-long tour of the grounds could test the patience of younger visitors and the legs of many older people, though. (As an active military base, visitors must have an escort and cannot end the tour at whim.) For them, it might be better simply to attend the 35-minute choreographed ceremony of the **Changing of the Guard,** which runs daily at 10am from June 24 until the first Monday of September. It's an elaborate ritual inspired by the Changing of the Royal Guard in London and is included in the regular admission fee. *Note:* It can be cancelled if the weather's bad.

1 Côte de la Citadelle (at rue St-Louis). www.lacitadelle.qc.ca. ℭ **418/694-2815.** Admission C$16 adults, C$13 seniors and students, C$6 children 7–17, free for children 7 and under; families C$32. May–Oct daily 9am–5pm; Nov–April 10am–4pm.

An aerial view of La Citadelle

The Musée de l'Amérique Francophone carefully outlines the history of French-speaking people in the New World

Musée de l'Amérique Francophone ★★

The focal point of this museum is a permanent exhibit that traces the odyssey of French speaking populations to Québec and beyond, including American cities such as St. Louis, Detroit, and New Orleans. "Revelations: Understanding the World Through Art" is an exhibit of paintings, sculpture, gold and silver pieces culled from the Séminaire de Québec's priests' collections. The museum is on the site of the seminary and visitors can tour the now-secularized chapel, which still displays a few saints' relics. The seminary's stunning inner courtyard is one of the most photographed nooks in the city.

2 Côte de la Fabrique (next to Basilique Cathédrale Notre-Dame de Québec). www. mcq.org. ℂ **866/710-8031** or 418/692-2843. Admission C$8 adults, C$7 seniors, C$5.50 students, C$2 children 12–16, free to all Nov–May Tues and Jan–Feb Sat 10am– noon. Three-museum discount (Musée de la Civilisation, Musée de l'Amérique Francophone, and Musée de la place Royale), good for 2 weeks after purchase: C$24 adults, C$22 seniors, C$16 students, C$7 kids 12–16, free under 12. Late June to early Sept daily 9:30am–5pm; mid-Sept to late June Tues–Sun 10am–5pm.

Rue du Trésor "Outdoor Gallery"

Sooner or later, everyone meanders down this small outdoor alley near the Place d'Armes. Artists have been gathering here to exhibit and sell their work since the 1960s. Most of the prints on view are of Québec scenes and can make attractive souvenirs. The artists, many of whom are on hand even on the snowiest days, seem to enjoy chatting with interested passersby.

Rue du Trésor (between rue Ste-Anne & rue Buade). www.ruedutresor.qc.ca.

Shopping in Upper Town

Upper Town shops cater to all ends of the spectrum, from high-end collectors of Inuit art to packs of teenagers on school vacations looking for T-shirts with crude jokes. As with Lower Town, Upper Town is small enough that you can wander at leisure without the risk of getting lost.

Crocs The recipe behind Crocs originated in Québec and this two-story store is chock full of the latest styles made in multicolored, marshmallow rubber. 1071 rue St-Jean (at rue St-Stanislas). www.crocs.com. ℭ **418/266-0262.**

Galerie Brousseau et Brousseau Here, you can buy Native Canadian carvings selected by the Brousseau family, the most prominent of the city's art dealers. Prices are high, but competitive for merchandise of similar quality and often come with certificates of authenticity. The shop is set up like a gallery, so feel free just to browse. 35 rue St-Louis (at rue des Jardins). www.sculpture. artinuit.ca. ℭ **418/694-1828.**

Les Délices de l'Érable It turns out this little shop has a tiny museum (as does its Montréal location) and admission is free. It describes the traditional maple sap harvest methods and the many different products made from the sweet stuff. Many are, of course, available to purchase and sample firsthand. Whether you stop here or some place else selling maple-infused goodies, you shouldn't leave town without some kind of maple experience. 1044 rue St-Jean (near rue Ste-Angele). www.mapledelights.com. ℭ **418/692-3245.**

LOGO Sport A fun stop for the sports-crazed. You can buy brand new Nordique gear here (though Québec's beloved hockey team moved in 1995) and classic Canadian match-ups play on an overhead TV. 1028 rue St-Jean (at rue Ste-Ursule). www.logosport.ca. ℭ **418/692-1351.**

Sachem Fur hats, baby moccasins, carvings, music, and jewelry are all packed into this compact boutique, which specializes in *"art amérindien."* Included are a variety of miniature Inukshuk human figurines, which look like they've been made of stacked rocks. A companion shop, **La Chasse-Galerie,** can be found near Place-Royale. 17 rue des Jardins (near Hôtel-de-Ville). www. nativespiritart.com. ℭ **418/692-3056.**

Simons Vieux-Québec's only department store opened here in 1840. Small by modern standards, a 175-year anniversary expansion upped the ante at this trendy and generally inexpensive clothing retailer for women, men, and teens. 20 Côte de la Fabrique (near the Hôtel-de-Ville). www.simons.ca. ℭ **418/692-3630.**

PARLIAMENT HILL ATTRACTIONS

The imposingly grand Parliament building lies just outside the city walls on Grande-Allée. Where the politics end the party begins: The few blocks west of Parliament pulses with nightlife. Compared to Vieux-Québec the buildings on Parliament Hill are taller and more modern, with open space to spare

RUE ST-JEAN: A feast FOR FOODIES

Take a walk along rue St-Jean and head several blocks past the city walls (and, technically, out of the Old City's Upper Town) and your taste buds will quickly thank you. This section, called Faubourg St-Jean, has a reputation for its grocers, butchers, and gourmet foods. **Épicerie J.A. Moisan,** 699 rue St-Jean, 4 blocks outside Upper Town walls (www.jamoisan.com; © **418/522-0685**) is a can't-miss food emporium. It must stock close to 30 types of olives, for instance, and the case is full of delicious prepared goodies and cooking supplies like duck fat. It claims to be the oldest grocery store in North America (it dates back to 1871). **Choco-Musée Érico,** 634 rue St-Jean (www.chocomusee.com; © **418/524-2122**), about 5 blocks outside Upper Town walls is an adorable chocolate shop that includes a small room with historical information about how chocolate is made. Wondering where to find a bottle of wine to take back to your room? Liquor and other spirits can be sold only in stores operated by **Société des Alcools du Québec,** the provincial agency known as SAQ. One is at 853 rue St-Jean (near aut Dufferin Montmorency; www.saq.com; © **418/643-4337**) and another at 1059 avenue Cartier.

especially since the expansive Plains of Abraham park runs the length of this district.

Hôtel du Parlement ★ Since 1968, what the Québécois call their "National Assembly," has occupied this imposing Second Empire château constructed in 1886. Twenty-two bronze statues of some of the most prominent figures in the province's tumultuous history grace the façade. Inside, highlights include the Assembly Chamber and the Legislative Council Chamber, where parliamentary committees meet. Throughout the building, representations of the fleur-de-lis and the initials VR (for Victoria Regina) remind visitors of Québec's dual heritage. Free 45-minute guided tours are available weekdays year-round, plus weekends in summer. Tours start at the Parliament building visitor center; enter at door no. 3. *Note:* During summer hours, garden tours are also available.

The grand Beaux Arts–style restaurant **Le Parlementaire** (© **418/643-6640**) is open to the public, as well as parliamentarians and visiting dignitaries. Featuring Québec products and cuisine, it serves breakfast and lunch Monday through Friday most of the year, but you should check the schedule for closures (it is closed starting the second week of Dec until the second week of Jan). The much lower-key **Café du Parlement** (© **418/643-5529;** Mon–Fri 7:30am–2pm most of the year) is also an option for coffee, sandwiches, and eco-friendly takeaway. The massive fountain in front of the building, **La Fontaine de Tourny,** was commissioned by the mayor of Bordeaux, France, in 1857. It was installed in 2007 as a gift from the Simons department store to the city for its 400th anniversary. Also outdoors, to the right of the main entrance as you're facing it, is a large **Inukshuk** statue.

Hôtel du Parlement, the "National Assembly" of the Québécois

Entrance at corner of Grande-Allée est and av. Honoré-Mercier. www.assnat.qc.ca. (C) **866/337-8837** or 418/643-7239. Free admission. Guided tours late June to Labour Day Mon–Fri 9am–4:15pm, Sat–Sun and holidays 10am–4:15pm; rest of the year Mon–Fri 9am–4:30pm. Reservations recommended; required for groups 10 or more.

Musée National des Beaux-Arts du Québec ★★★ For almost 40 years, Québec's major art museum sat 100m (328 ft.) from a prison. Designed by Charles Baillairgé in 1867, the prison was almost immediately overpopulated, but did not completely end service until the 1970s. By 1991 the museum had annexed the cell blocks and watchtower into gallery space to grow its presence as the world's leading collector of Québécois art. Another expansion slated to finish in 2016 will only further the museum's ability to showcase local art. Among the permanent collection is "L'Hommage à Rosa Luxemburg," an enormous triptych by Québec abstract expressionist and surrealist Jean-Paul Riopelle (1923–2002). His gallery is one of several stops on a circuit that could start with the dynamic Inuit collection and move through colonial, modernist, figurative, and abstract art, all created by artists from the province.

The museum is on the Parc des Champs-de-Bataille (Battlefields Park), at the fringe of the tourist orbit, and is about a half-hour walk from Upper Town.

Parc des Champs-de-Bataille (near where av. Wolfe-Montcalm meets Grande-Allée). www.mnba.qc.ca. (C) **866/220-2150** or 418/643-2150. Admission C$18 adults, C$16 seniors, C$10 ages 18–30, C$5 ages 13–17, free for children 12 and under, half-price admission Wed 5–9pm. June to Labour Day Thurs–Tues 10am–6pm, Wed 10am–9pm; day after Labour Day to May Tues and Thurs–Sun 10am–5pm, Wed 10am–9pm.

Musée national des Beaux-arts du Québec, the city's major art institution

Observatoire de la Capitale Here's where a rough translation of French may be misleading: The views from here are gorgeous, but they're not of the stars. At 132m (433 ft.) high and 221m (725 ft.) above sea level, this *observatoire* offers a 360-degree view of the Québec City skyline, from the city's highest vantage point. Each year about 70,000 visitors take the 28-second ride up the elevator up to the 31st floor of the Marie-Guyart building. Views can stretch beyond the Laurentian Mountains in one direction and the bridge to Île d'Orléans in another. For kids (and adults), an interactive, touch-screen exhibit provides information about the history of the capital city.

Edifice Marie-Guyart 1037, rue De La Chevrotière, Parliament Hill. www.observatoire-capitale.com. ✆ **888/497-4322** or 418/644-9841. Admission C$10.45 adults, C$8.40 students and seniors, free for children 12 and under. Feb to mid-Oct daily 10am–5pm; Mid-Oct to Jan Tues–Sun 10am–5pm.

ST-ROCH: SHOPPING

Want to know where the cool kids live? Or at least where smart Québécois buy croissants? Nouvo Saint-Roch is a long walk from the tourist zone, but well worth checking out. Most of the appeal is along rue St-Joseph. Grab a cup of coffee from **Brûlerie St-Roch,** 375 rue St-Joseph est (www.lesbruleries.com; ✆ **418/704-4420**) the original location of a growing local chain, or a pain au chocolat from **Le Croquembouche,** 225 rue St-Joseph est (www.le croquembouche.com; ✆ **418/523-9009**) and dodge in and out of the high-end fashion retailers on rue St-Joseph's eastern end to the pawn shops and consignment stores on the western end. If you ask for directions, it's pronounced "Saint Rock."

Benjo ★★★   This toy store is worth a special trip. A bronze frog welcomes kids into this floor-to-ceiling wonderland of toys. Think trains, race cars, and dolls as far as the eye can see. Kids could meet the life-sized robot Monsieur Bidule or catch a children's choir singing traditional Christmas songs in French. There's a great selection of books *en francais* and an ice cream parlor tops it off April through September. Small visitors enter and exit through a tiny VIP door. 550 boul. Charest est (near rue du Parvis). www.benjo.ca. © **418/640-0001.**

Signatures Québécoises ★   Some 557 sq. m (6,000 sq. ft.), 25 cutting-edge clothing designers from Québec, all in an old church. Heavenly, yes, but it's pretty much St-Roch in a nutshell. Harricana fashions (www.harricana. qc.ca) created from recycled fur, silk, and old wedding dresses by Mariouche Gagné, who was born on Île d'Orléans, is just one example. Église Saint-Roch, 560 rue St-Joseph est. www.signaturesquebecoises.com. © **418/648-9976.**

SHOPPING COMPLEXES

Shopping malls on a grand scale aren't found anywhere near Old Town. For that, you need to visit the neighboring municipality of **Sainte-Foy.** Malls here differ little from their cousins throughout North America in terms of layout and available products. With 350 shops, **Laurier Québec,** 2700 boul. Laurier, in Sainte-Foy (www.laurierquebec.com; © **800/322-1828**), is the biggest, and it claims some 12 million shoppers each year. The bookstore **La Maison Anglaise et Internationale** (www.lamaisonanglaise.com; © **418/654-9523**) has been one of the region's leading sources of English and Spanish language books for more than 2 decades. It's in **Place de la Cité** (www.placedelacite. com; © **418/657-7015**), which is within walking distance of Laurier. From mid-May through mid-October, buses shuttle shoppers between Laurier and several hotel stops in Québec City for C$5; call © **418/664-0460** for schedules. If you've got your own wheels, it's a 10-minute drive northwest of Vieux-Québec to **Galeries de la Capitale** (www.galeriesdelacapitale.com; © **418/627-5800**), at 5401 boul. des Galeries. It has an indoor amusement park, ice rink, and IMAX movie theater alongside its 280 shops.

ORGANIZED TOURS

Québec City is small enough that you can get around with a good map and a guidebook, but a tour is tremendously helpful for getting background information about the city's history and culture, grasping the lay of the land, and in the case of bus tours, seeing those attractions that require wheels to reach.

Below are some agencies and organizations that have proved to be reliable. Arrange tours by calling the companies directly or by stopping by the large tourist center at the Place d'Armes in Upper Town.

When you exit the Old City on Grande-Allée est, you'll find hotels, restaurants, and clubs, but shopping doesn't kick in until Grande-Allée meets av. Cartier, a street with gourmet foods, boutique clothing, and few tourists—part of a neighborhood called Montcalm, just beyond Parliament Hill. There's nothing like a lazy afternoon here. You can feel as much like a city-dweller as possible by ordering a latte bowl at **Café Krieghoff** (p. 207), then popping in and out of shops like **Zone,** 999 av. Cartier at the corner of boul. René-Lévesque (www.zonemaison.com; ✆ **418/522-7373**) for mod housewares or **Boutique Ketto,** 951 av. Cartier at Crémazie (www.kettodesign.com; ✆ **418/522-3337**)

for impish pottery, ceramic jewelry, and stationery made in Québec. This street has a fantastic bakery (or two—or is it three?) and unique clothing stores for women young and less young. If you're exploring by car, take Grande-Allée further west (away from the Old City) until it turns into Boulevard Laurier. Turn left on the even less touristy **Avenue Maguire.** There you'll find ethnic restaurants, the city's only wood-oven baked bagels at **Bagel Maguire,** 1332 av. Maguire (www.bagelmaguirecafe.com; ✆ **418/527-2303**), and **Le Canard Goulu,** 1281 av. Maguire (www.canardgoulu.com; ✆ **418/687-5116**), a boutique with artisanal foie gras products.

Bus Tours

Buses are convenient if extensive walking is difficult, especially in hilly Upper Town. Among the established tour operators, **Old Québec Tours,** which also goes by the name **Dupont** (www.toursvieuxquebec.com; ✆ **800/267-8687** or 418/664-0460), operates the city's only open-air double-decker bus. Passes allow for on-off access to 11 stops. The one-day rate for adults is C$36; children over 6 years C$22; free for children 5 and under. The family pass (C$114) includes 2 children's tickets. The company also leads multiple day tours that differ by the season. Summer tours head north into the Charlevoix region for **whale-watching excursion,** a 10-hour day that includes a 3-hour cruise among the belugas (adults C$120; children over 6 C$64; children 5 and under free; family pass C$368). Winter tours head to Montmorency Falls and Île d'Orléans (p. 227; adults C$50; children over 6 C$29; children 5 and under free; family pass C$139).

Horse-Drawn Carriage Tours

A romantic, if expensive, way to see the city at a genial pace is in a horse-drawn carriage, called a *calèche.* Carriages will pick you up or can be hired from locations throughout the city, including at Place d'Armes. A 40-minute ride costs C$90, plus tip, for four people maximum. Carriages operate year-round, rain or shine. Companies include **Calèches du Vieux-Québec** (www.calecheduvieux quebec.com; ✆ **418/683-9222**) and **Calèches Québec** (www.calechesquebec. com; ✆ **418/692-0068**), which also has horse-drawn trams.

River Cruises

Croisières AML (www.croisieresaml.com; ✆ **800/563-4643** or 418/692-1159 in late-spring to mid-fall season) offers a variety of cruises. Its *Louis Jolliet* is a three-decked, 1930s ferry boat–turned–excursion vessel, which carries 1,000 passengers and is stocked with bilingual guides, full dining facilities, and a bar. Three newly-acquired vessels have a signature look—like a glass capsule—designed for panoramic views. The company offers brunch and dinner cruises (starting at C$53 for adults and C$31 for ages 6–16; free for children 5 and under), as well as jaunts that take in the fireworks (starting at C$67 for all ages). The most popular, the "guided sightseeing tour," includes a view of Montmorency Falls (adults C$35; children under 16 free). The boats dock at quai Chouinard, at 10 rue Dalhousie, in Vieux-Port.

The more adventurous may opt for 15-person Zodiac boat rides offered by **Croisières le Coudrier** (www.excursionsmaritimesquebec.com; ✆ **418/845-4564**). Travel from the city's coastline to Montmorency Falls for a 90-minute cruise (starting at C$55 for adults and C$27.50 for children); the guided tour of Île-d'Orléans will take 4½ hours. A longer stopover, with on-island touring, can be added or customized (starting at C$75 per person). There are four cruise departure points, including the Marina Port de Québec near Pointe a Carcy in Lower Town.

Walking Tours

Times and points of departure for walking tours change, so get up-to-date information at any tourist office (p. 174). Many tours leave from the Place d'Armes in Upper Town, just in front of the **Château Frontenac.**

A good complement to the Upper Town and Lower Town walking tours in this book (see p. 243 and p. 253), **Tours Voir Québec** (www.toursvoirquebec.com; ✆ **866/694-2001** or 418/694-2001) specializes in English-only guided tours of the Old City. "The Grand Tour," available year-round, is a 2-hour stroll that covers the architecture, events, and cultural history of the city. Tours are limited to 15 people. Cost is C$23 adults, C$20 students (ISIC, or International Student Identify Card, required), C$11 children 6 to 12, and free for children 5 and under. Foodies will want to note the "Food Tour," which stops at about seven different places, sampling local goodies such as cheese, ice cider, pâté, and chocolate. Cost is C$44 per adult. Private tours may also be arranged.

One way to split the difference between being out on your own and being on a guided tour is to use **Map Old Québec** (www.oldquebecmap.com), a website that offers a beautifully designed map and MP3 files. The audio files are free and a map is available online for C$5 or for C$3 at a few dozen stores around town. Used together you can listen and learn at your own pace.

Tourisme Québec's *The Official Tourist Guide* lists additional tour companies that use limousines, bikes, helicopters, and hot air balloons as forms of transit and offer tours with themes ranging from maple leaf peeping to ghosts and phantoms from the region's past.

OUTDOOR ACTIVITIES

Inside the city, **Parc des Champs-de-Bataille (Battlefields Park;** below) is the most popular park for bicycling and strolling.

Just outside the city, lakes and hills provide countless opportunities for outdoor recreation, including swimming, boating, fishing, skiing, snowmobiling, and sleigh riding. Keep these three centers in particular in mind, all within a 45-minute drive from the capital: the plateaus and glacial valleys of **Parc national de la Jacques-Cartier** (www.sepaq.com/pq/jac/en; ✆ **800/665-6527**) off Route 175 north; **Station touristique Duchesnay** (www.sepaq.com/duchesnay; ✆ **877/511-5885**), a state park resort on the shores of Lac Saint-Joseph, northwest of the city; and **Parc du Mont Ste-Anne** (www.mont-sainte-anne.com; ✆ **888/827-4579**), northeast of the city. All three centers are mentioned in the listings below. From mid-November through March, the **Taxi Coop Québec** shuttle service (www.taxicoop-quebec.com; ✆ **418/525-5191**) picks up passengers at Québec City hotels in the morning to take them to alpine and cross-country ski runs, and to snowmobile trails, with return trips in the late afternoon.

La Promenade Samuel-De Champlain ★★ When Québec City celebrated its 300th anniversary, the government of Québec gave the people **Parc des Champs-de-Bataille** (see above). For the 400th anniversary (in 2008) it created La Promenade Samuel-De Champlain, a scenic path approximately 2.5km long (1½ miles) hugging the St. Lawrence River between Quai des Cageux and Côte de Sillery. (Plans are underway to extend the path to the Parc de la Plages-Jacques-Cartier.) The space required shifting the road inland so that the public could bike, rollerblade, or walk along the water's edge all year long. With Pont de Québec and Pont Pierre Laporte framing the picturesque setting in the Ste-Foy-Sillery-Cap-Rouge *arrondissement,* Québec City has a beautiful new space, which involved planting 1,500 trees and displaying outdoor contemporary art. There is a sports zone for activities such as soccer, quaint picnic nooks, lights at night for evening strolls, and, at the Quai des Cageux, a modular 25m-high (82-ft.) observation tower next to a small cafe, run by **Panache** restaurant (p. 205) where you can enjoy over-the-counter foods like paninis, wraps, hot dogs, ice cream, and beverages.

2795 boul. Champlain. www.quebecregion.com. ✆ **877/783-1608.** Free admission and parking. Observation tower daily 7am–11pm (closed in winter); Cafe daily June–Aug 11am–8pm, depending on weather.

Fortifications-de-Québec ★ The walls and ramparts that once protected Vieux-Québec from its enemies are now under the protection of the national government as part of the **Fortifications of Québec National Historic Site.** The locations that make up this site include the Governors' Garden and Montmorency Park as well as other places of note such as the Québec Garrison Club, Maillou House, Terrasse Dufferin, and the **Promenade des Gouverneurs.** Visitors can tour the series of defensive buildings erected by the French in the 17th and 18th centuries that make up **Parc de l'Artillerie** (Artillery Park) in Upper Town. They include an ammunition factory that was functional until 1964. An iron foundry, officers' mess and quarters, and a scale model of the city created in 1806 are on view. It may be a blow to romantics and history buffs to learn that St-Jean Gate in the city wall was built in 1940, the fourth in a series that began with the original 1693 entrance, which was replaced in 1747, and then replaced again in 1867. Tickets can be purchased at two informational kiosks: in front of Frontenac on Dufferin Terrace and at 2 rue d'Autueil, near the St-Jean Gate.

2 rue d'Autcuil (near Porte St-Jean). www.pc.gc.ca/artillerie. © **888/773-8888** or 418/648-7016. Admission C$3.90 adults, C$3.40 seniors, C$1.90 children 6–16, free for children 5 and under, C$9.80 for groups and families. Additional fees for audio guide, tea ceremony, and special activities. Early May to early June and early Sept to early Oct daily 10am–5pm; late June to early Sept daily 10am–6pm; April to mid-May by reservation.

Parc des Champs-des-Batailles ★★★

Known in English as Battlefields Park, this green gathering place of winding paths and the occasional fountain or monument was Canada's first national urban park. It covers 108 hectares (267 acres) and officials compare it to New York's Central Park or London's Hyde Park. A section called the **Plains of Abraham** is where Britain's General James Wolfe and France's Louis-Joseph, marquis de Montcalm, engaged in their short, but crucial battle in 1759, which resulted in the British defeat of the French troops. It's also where the national anthem, *O Canada*, was first performed. From spring through fall, visit the **Jardin Jeanne d'Arc**

The Fortifications-de-Québec have been rebuilt several times since their inception in the 17th century.

(**Joan of Arc Garden**), just off avenue Wilfrid-Laurier. This spectacular garden combines French classical design with British-style flower beds. In the rest of the park, nearly 6,000 trees of more than 80 species blanket the fields and include the sugar maple, Norway maple, American elm, and American ash. Also in the park are two Martello towers, cylindrical stone defensive structures built between 1808 and 1812 when Québec feared an American invasion.

The **Discovery Pavilion of the Plains of Abraham,** 835 av. Wilfred-Laurier (© **855/649-6157** or 418/649-6157) is the starting point for tours, hosts a multimedia show called "Battles 1759–1760," and houses a scale model of the park. Entrance fees during high season also provide access to activities such as the Martello Tower 1 and a tour on Abraham's Bus. Yet there's much to be said for simply taking in the landscape for exercise or to glimpse the exquisite vantage points of the St. Lawrence. In the winter, the snow can pile higher than parking meters and last through March, and yet the park still has groomed cross-country ski trails. In warmer weather, look for evidence of carpet-bedding, also called mosaiculture—an ornamental garden technique that creates lettering out of plants. This park's horticulturalists are experts and take great pride in creating stunning designs each growing season. The whole park is truly an emblem of the pride this city takes in its vivid history and vibrant present day.

Parc des Champs-des-Batailles. www.ccbn-nbc.gc.ca. © **888/497-4322** or 418/644-9841. Discovery Pavilion admission C$15 adults, C$11 ages 13–17 and seniors, C$5 ages 5–12, free for children 4 and under. July to early Sept daily 9:30am–5:30pm; early Sept to June daily 9:30am–5pm (admissions rates lower in this period).

Warm-Weather Activities

BIKING

The city has lots of good biking, either along the river or up in Parliament Hill in Parc des Champs-de-Bataille. A marked and well-maintained waterfront path for cyclists (and in-line skaters) extends both directions alongside the river and heading out of the city. Tourist information centers provide bicycle-trail maps and can point out a variety of routes. To rent bikes or join a guided tour, see the "Québec City By Bike" section on p. 261. Mountain bikers, meanwhile, head to **Mont Ste-Anne,** which has the most well-known mountain bike network in eastern Canada. It was host to the 2010 Mountain Bike and Trial World Championships, and every year to **Vélirium** (www.velirium. com), the International Mountain Bike Festival and World Cup. It's 42km (26 miles) northeast of Québec City. See the intro above for contact information.

CAMPING

The greater Québec City area has 17 campgrounds, most of which have toilets and showers. For a list of sites and their specs, go to **www.quebecregion.com** and search for "campground." They are also listed in *The Official Tourist Guide* published by Québec City Tourism.

The distinctive, cylindrical Martello towers in Parc des Champs-des-Bataille

GOLF

An 18-hole course, **Golf de la Faune** (www.golfdelafaune.com; ✆ **866/627-8008** or 418/627-1576) is 10 minutes from downtown, at the **Four Points by Sheraton Québec** (www.fourpoints.com/quebec; ✆ **418/627-8008**). The course has eight water hazards and 45 sand traps. Summer season green fees start at C$40 and go up to C$75.

About 40 minutes north of the city at Mont Ste-Anne, **Le Grand Vallon** (www.legrandvallon.com; ✆ **888/827-4579** or 418/827-4653) is an 18-hole, par-72 course with tree-lined stretches, 4 lakes, and 40 sand traps. Summer season rates after 3:30pm start at C$30 and increase with a golf cart or earlier start. Also a short drive west of Québec City, **Golf Le Grand Portneuf** (www.legrandportneuf.com; ✆ **866/329-3662** or 418/873-2000) offers 36 challenging holes in a peaceful, scenic environment, starting at C$24. Other courses are located near Jacques-Cartier national park and on Île d'Orléans.

SWIMMING

Those who want to splash around during their visit have several hotel options with (mostly indoor) pools. Fairmont Le Château Frontenac has one, as do Hôtel Manoir Victoria, Hôtel Château Laurier, and TRYP by Wyndham Québec Hotel Pur. They're all listed in chapter 12. Outside the city, the waterpark at **Village Vacances Valcartier** (p. 234) has more than 35 water slides, a wave pool, and themed rivers, such as the Tropical River or the Crazy Cascades.

For swimming in natural bodies of water less than 30 minutes drive from the city, two nearby lake options are **Lac Saint-Joseph** (www.la-plage.ca; © 877/522-3224) and **Lac Saint-Charles** (www.laccesnature.qc.ca; © 418/849-6163).

Cold-Weather Activities

CROSS-COUNTRY SKIING

With 52 ski centers and at least 2,500km (1,553 miles) of trails, the options to cross-country ski in the Québec City Area are plentiful. Within the city, the **Parc des Champs-de-Bataille,** where Carnaval de Québec establishes its winter playground during February, has a network of free, groomed cross-country trails in winter. You can rent equipment at the **Discovery Pavilion of the Plains of Abraham** (p. 230), near the Citadelle. Thirty minutes outside the city, **Station touristique Duchesnay** (p. 228) offers extensive trails and ski rentals. The **Association of Cross-Country Ski Centers of Québec Area's** website (www.skidefondraquette.com) has venue listings and maps.

DOG SLEDDING

The surrounding area has half a dozen options for dog sledding. **Aventure Inukshuk** (www.aventureinukshuk.qc.ca; © 418/875-0770) is located in Station touristique Duchesnay, in the town of Ste-Catherine-de-la-Jacques-Cartier. Guides show you how to lead a sled pulled by six dogs. A 1-hour "Ballad" ride takes you deep into a hushed world of snow and thick woods, past rows of Christmas trees, and over a beaver pond. The dogs live in a field of individual pens and houses under evergreen trees. Guides train and care for their teams themselves. Overnight camping trips are available. The 1-hour trip, which includes an additional half-hour of training, costs C$90. Children 6 to 12 are half price, and children 2 to 5 go free (children 1 and younger aren't allowed). Expensive, especially for families, but the memory stays with you.

DOWNHILL SKIING

The coastal-hugging mountain **Le Massif** is famous for its "I'm about to drop into the St. Lawrence!" feeling as you shush downhill. Over the years, Le Massif has steadily increased services on-mountain and well as transportation to the mountain. See p. 264 for day trip information. Also: **Mont Ste-Anne** offers eastern Canada's largest total skiing surface, with 69 trails (19 are lit for night skiing). See p. 228 for more information. Another option is **Stoneham Mountain Resort** (www.ski-stoneham.com; © 800/463-6888 or 418/848-2415), about 30 minutes north of the city.

ICE SKATING

From the end of October to mid-March, a mini outdoor rink is set up in Place d'Youville just outside the Upper Town walls. Admission is free and skates are available for rent. A rink on the Plains of Abraham has skate rental, a warming hut, and snacks onsite. If you want to feel like a true northerner and skate through trees to the sound of music, take a quick jaunt west of town to

Centre de plein air de Beauport (www.centrepleinairbeauport.ca; ℂ **877/641-6113** or 418/641-6112), where admission is free on (the less crowded) weekdays and C$4 for adults and C$3 for children and seniors on the weekends.

SNOWMOBILES

Snowmobiles, known here as "ski-doos," are hugely popular. It's said, in fact, that there are more trails for snowmobiling than there is asphalt in Québec City. In addition to options for day trips, many restaurants and hotels outside the city accommodate snowmobile touring, making it possible to travel from locale to locale. **La Fédération des clubs de motoneigistes du Québec** (F.C.M.Q.; www.fcmq.qc.ca) has extensive information about snowmobiling in the province, including maps and trail permits. Also, check the tourist office for current options.

TOBOGGANING

An old-fashioned toboggan run called **Les Glissades de la Terrasse** (www.au1884.ca; ℂ **418/528-1884**) is set up right in the city on the steep wooden staircase at Terrasse Dufferin's south end in winter. The slide extends almost to the Château Frontenac. Next to the ticket booth, a little sugar shack sells hot chocolate and traditional maple taffy. Rides cost is C$3 per person.

ESPECIALLY FOR KIDS

Children who love Harry Potter's adventures or Arthurian tales of fortresses and castles will delight in walking around this storybook city and the **Château Frontenac** (p. 175). On **Terrasse Dufferin** in Upper Town, are coin-operated telescopes, street entertainers, and ice cream stands. In winter, kids can toboggan down a century-old slide (see above). Halfway down **Breakneck Stairs** (**L'Escalier du Casse-Cou;** p. 253) are giant **cannons** ranged along the battlements. The gun carriages are impervious to the assaults of small humans, so kids can scramble all over them at will.

If military sites might be appealing, take them to see the colorful **Changing of the Guard** ceremony at **La Citadelle** (p. 219). Or just head for the **Parc des Champs-de-Bataille (Battlefields Park,** which features the **Plains of Abraham;** p. 229) adjacent to the La Citadelle if young ones need to run off excess energy. Acres of grassy lawn provide room to roam and are perfect for a family picnic. In Lower Town, the **Musée de la Civilisation** (p. 211) presents exhibits for families and, given that it's free for children 11 and younger, it's great value. **The Musée du Fort,** 10 rue Sainte-Anne (www.museedufort. com; ℂ **418/692-2175;** C$8), contains a floor-sized diorama that depicts the French, British, and U.S. battles for control of Québec. It was built by a high school teacher in the 1960s and has had a few updates since, including an accompanying, effective 30-minute presentation of the six sieges.

When in doubt, head to the water. **Montmorency Falls** (p. 227) makes a terrific day trip for children of all ages during any season (in summer, you can picnic; in winter it's an icy wonderland). It's just 10 minutes north of the city by car, and there are bus tours to the site, as well. It costs to park, but walking around near the water is free. On Wednesdays and Saturdays in August, the falls are host to the city's grand fireworks competition, **Les Grand Feux Loto-Québec** (p. 237). It pits international pyrotechnical teams against each other in a contest for who can make the biggest and brightest presentation.

Village Vacances Valcartier (www.valcartier.com; *©* **888/384-5524;** free for children under 3, otherwise rates depend on height, age, and arrival time, with discounts after 3pm, and range from C$24.35–C$34.79; park access without slide access is C$7.40) in St-Gabriel-de-Valcartier, about a half-hour northwest of the city, is a major manmade water park. In summer, it has 35 slides, a gigantic wave pool, a huge pirate ship, and a faux Amazon River for tubing. In winter, the same facilities are put to use for "snow rafting" on inner tubes and skating. Instead of carrying cash or credit cards, visitors can register their credit cards and then pay for food and other services by pressing a finger to a screen. If the weather is terrible, head to **Galeries de la Capitale** (listed in this chapter under Shopping Complexes). It has the province's largest indoor amusement park.

If sea life is of interest, block off time to see the more than 10,000 marine animals at **Aquarium du Québec** (www.sepaq.com/ct/paq; *©* **866/659-5264** or 418/659-5264; adults C$18, kids 3–17 C$9, free admission for children under 3), about 15 minutes west from the city near the bridges. It covers 16 hectares (about 39 acres) with outdoor and indoor activities such as a walrus show, seal training, a touch basin—plus, polar bears! In the winter it's the site of the Festi Lumière (p. 239). Families can bring a picnic or grab a treat onsite.

Québec City is day-trip distance to where whales come out to play each summer. See p. 226 for details about **whale watching.**

If you're going to the wintertime **Carnaval** (p. 235), kids won't want to miss the dog sled race through the Old City streets or the canoe races, where teams push, pull, or paddle (depending on the state of the river) from one side to another. The best place to view the water competition is from the Terrasse Dufferin or from the lookout on the opposite bank in Lévis.

FESTIVALS & NIGHTLIFE IN QUÉBEC CITY

Though Québec City has fewer nighttime diversions than exuberant Montréal, it does offer more than enough to occupy visitors' evenings. Apart from theatrical productions, which are usually in French, knowledge of the language is rarely needed to enjoy the entertainment.

If you want to stroll around and take in the nightlife options, you have three principal streets to choose from in Upper Town: rue St-Jean inside and outside the walls, Grande-Allée outside the walls (where a beery collegiate atmosphere can sometimes rule as the evening wears on), and avenue Cartier in the Montcalm neighborhood. In St-Roch, the hot spots are on or near rue St-Paul.

Happy hour is locally known as *cinq-à-sept* (meaning 5–7pm) and specials are often written on a chalkboard out front as *"5 à 7."* Many venues offer specials that start earlier or go later; some start after 10pm and include discounted late-night food menus.

Festivals: Québec City Celebrates Every Season

The two major festivals to plan around in Québec City are in summer (**Festival d'Eté**) and winter (**Carnaval**). Both include non-stop entertainment for all ages and a chance to swirl among the tens of thousands who gather to celebrate this city's seasonal extremes—sun and snow (the latter being abundant and long-lasting).

But in every season, the city celebrates some kind of festival, anniversary, remembrance, or special event. For an exhaustive list beyond those listed here, check the Events tab of Québec City Tourisme's website, at **www.quebec region.com**. There, you can search for free and tickets events and events by categories of interest.

JANUARY & FEBRUARY

Carnaval de Québec. This wintertime extravaganza takes over the city for more than 2 weeks each February and includes an insanely icy canoe race, dogsled competitions, parades, snow sculptures, and more. Purchase a C$15 badge to gain entrance to two stage areas and more than 300 activities for the duration of the festival. There are also free events and surprise appearances by an enormous, cheery, high-kicking snowman, called Bonhomme. Montréal celebrates its "Fête des Neiges" the previous 2 weeks (p. 132). Visit www.carnaval.qc.ca or call ✆ **866/422-7628** or 418/626-3716. Late January to mid-February.

Parade float in Carnaval de Québec

Pentathlon des Neiges. Skate, ski, snowshoe, run, bike long or short distances on the Plains of Abraham. This annual snowsport competition has something for everyone. Visit www.pentathlondesneiges.com or call ✆ **418/907-5734**. Nine days in late February.

MARCH

FIS Snowboard World Cup. Held at Stoneham Resort, about a 30-minute drive from Québec City, as part of Snowboard Jamboree (with big air, half pipe, slopestyle, and more), spectators can watch this global competition for free. Visit **www.snowjamboree.com** for details. Four days in March (check website to confirm).

MAY

Carrefour International de Théâtre de Québec. Multilingual plays and performances from Canada and abroad have come to venues throughout Québec City each spring for 17 years running. Visit www.carrefourtheatre.qc.ca or call ✆ **888/529-1996** or 418/529-1996. Late May to early June.

JUNE

Festival Grand Rire. New and seasoned comedy talent descends on the city for the 17th year. More than 100 events are held at venues in Place D'Youville and its surrounds. Check www.grandrire.com or call ✆ **877/441-7473** or 418/640-2277. Runs for 10 days in mid-June.

Québec City Staircase Challenge. Some people see the Breakneck Stairs as a challenge, not an obstacle. Those folks race each other to "défi des escaliers de Québec" each June in either the 19k Super Challenge or 13.5k Oasis Challenge up and down the flights that connect Upper and Lower Town. For this and other Québec running races visit www.couriraquebec.com or call ✆ **418/694-4442**. Mid-June.

Gran Fondo Mont-Ste-Anne. This road biking event is open to all riders over 14 who are physically fit. All routes start and finish in the Mont Ste-Anne ski area parking lot, 42km (26 miles) north of Québec City. Participants can choose from three different challenge levels. This is one of six Gran Fondo races held throughout the region. For details, visit **www.granfondoeco.com**. Mid- to late-June.

JULY

Canada Day. Canadian cities, including Québec, celebrate the formation of the federation of Canada with free music, flag raisings, and other activities. July 1.

Massive stage in the Festival d'Été, the city's summer festival

Fête de la Ville de Québec (Québec City Day). Celebrations of the city's founding fill the streets. **www.ville.quebec.qc.ca/ 3juillet**. July 3.

Festival d'Été (Summer Festival). For 11 days, this city forgets all about winter—heck, it hardly remembers to sleep. This is one of the colossal musical events on the yearly calendar and hotels and entertainment venues fill up fast. Purchase wristbands to gain entrance to hear the likes of The Rolling Stones, Foo Fighters, Iggy Izalea, or Megadeth (who performed in 2015). Street acts and DJs perform for free all around town. Billed as world music, the festival also gives Canadian and Québécois performers a decent share of the 10 stages. Visit www. infofestival.com or call ✆ **888/992-5200** or 418/529-5200. Eleven days in early- to mid-July.

Transatlantic Tall Ship Regatta. To mark the 150th anniversary of the Canadian Confederation, Canada will race a fleet of Tall Ships across the North Atlantic. One of the six stops (Portugal and France among them) is Québec City. Confirm details at **www. rendezvous2017.com**. This is a one-time event in 2017 only. July 18–23, 2017.

Velirium and UCI Mountain Bike World Cup. This is the penultimate competition for professional cross-country and downhill mountain bikers, and spectators are invited. This multi-day mountain biking competition on Mont Ste-Anne 42km (26 miles) north of the city features male and female professionals and juniors racing on courses that would give beginners nightmares. Meanwhile, City8 brings dirt biking and free styling right into Québec City at its central Place d'Youville. Also on the calendar are clinics, parties, and competitions for amateur bikers of all ages and bike preferences. Visit www. velirium.com or call ✆ **418/827-1122.** Late July to early August.

AUGUST

Les Grand Feux Loto-Québec. On Wednesday and Saturday nights, crowds gather on the banks of the St. Lawrence for an international fireworks competition. Free for all. Check **www.lesgrandsfeux.com** for details. Early to late August.

Les Fêtes de la Nouvelle-France SAQ (New France Festival). The 17th and 18th centuries come to life during this annual celebration of the birth of New France. Events are held at more than a dozen points of interest

International groups compete in Les Grand Feux Loto-Québec, the summertime fireworks competition

in Vieux-Québec. One highlight is the Parade of Giants, where enormous puppets walk alongside tiny companions, all in period costume. (Worth a search for photos online!) A new theme is chosen every year to illuminate that particular facet of history. Visit www.nouvellefrance.qc.ca or call ② **866/391-3383** or 418/694-3311. Four days in mid-August.

Festibière de Québec. A mug and tokens open up a world of beer at this annual festival. Taste the local and international goods from microbreweries, pubs, and cider houses. Giant hot dogs and *poutine* can fill your belly in between the suds. Believe it or not, education is a key component, with speakers lined up to talk history, the brewing process, distribution, and marketing. More modest events are also in fall and winter. Visit www.festibieredequebec.com or call ② **418/948-1166.** Four days in mid-August.

Bordeaux Wine Festival. This increasingly popular bi-annual festival pours the best from Bordeaux and also features workshops and local foods. Visit **www.ville.quebec.qc.ca/en/bordeaux**. This is an every-other-year event, and the next takes place over three days in late August 2017.

SEPTEMBER

Festival de Magie de Québec. Get out the top hats, and hide the rabbits! More than 40 free magic shows and workshops take place during this St-Roch festival. A few years ago, escape artist Simon Pérusse extricated himself from a straight jacket while hanging upside down from a crane. For details, visit **www.festivaldemagie.ca**. Held late August to early September (Labour Day weekend).

Fête Arc-en-Ciel. Québec City's 5-day gay-pride fest attracts thousands of people to Place d'Youville and St-Roch. Drag shows, movies, happy hours, and dance parties are all part of the mix. For details, visit www.arcencielquebec.ca or call ② **418/809-3383**. Held late August to early September (Labour Day weekend).

Grand Prix Cyclistes. The world's top cycling teams (as in the same guys in the Tour de France) spend 1 day competing in Québec and then head to Montréal for a race there. Both races are held on city streets (routes can be found online) and are free to spectators. The teams arrive a few days prior and can be spotted on training rides or

having a bite at local restaurants. Visit www.
gpcqm.ca or call (C) **450/671-9090** for more
information. Mid-September.

OCTOBER

Québec International Jazz Festival. This
festival, steadily growing acclaim, celebrates
its 10th edition 2016 by featuring more than
80 shows at venues ranging from large to
intimate. For details, visit www.jazzaquebec.
ca or call (C) **418/977-9455**. Held mid-
October to early November.

NOVEMBER & DECEMBER

German Christmas Market. A small
wooden village of shops sprouts up near

City Hall to kick off the holiday season.
Expect roasted chestnuts, grilled sausages,
and holiday handicrafts. Check out www.
noelallemandquebec.com for details or call
(C) **418/262-4106**. Held late November to
mid-December.

Festi Lumière. Decorative lights, an outdoor fireplace, and fun events for kids draw
visitors to the Aquarium's annual winter celebration. For details, visit www.aquarium
duquebec.com or call (C) **866/659-5264**.
Held late-December to early March.

THE PERFORMING ARTS

Circus

For a summer night full of acrobatic wonder, catch the Québec troupe **Flip
FabriQue** (www.flipfabrique.com), at the Agora amphitheater in Lower
Town. Seats are free and allocated on a first-come, first-serve basis. This
troupe steps into the enormous shoes left by Cirque du Soleil after it gave
Québec City many years of waterfront entertainment.

Cirque du Soleil got its start just outside of Québec City and has a history
of creating free public performances for major celebrations such as the 450th
anniversary of Jaques Cartier's discovery of Canada (in 1984) or the 400th
anniversary of the founding of Québec City (in 2008). As of 2015, the troupe's
nearest performances take place at the Amphithéâtre Cogeco in Trois-
Rivières, about half-way between (126 km/78 miles) from Québec City and
Montréal. To confirm dates or buy tickets, visit **www.cirquedusoleil.com**.

Classical Music, Opera & Dance

The region's premier classical groups are **Orchestre Symphonique de Québec** (www.osq.org; (C) **877/643-8131** or 418/643-5598), Canada's oldest symphony, which performs at the Grand Théâtre de Québec (see below), and **Les
Violons du Roy** (www.violonsduroy.com; (C) **418/692-3026**), a string orchestra that is celebrating its 32nd year. It features a core group of 15 musicians
and performs at the centrally located Palais Montcalm (see below). The
notable **Opéra de Québec** (www.operadequebec.qc.ca; (C) **877/643-8131**) is
also in its 32nd year and hosts the annual **Festival d'opéra de Québec** from
late July to early August.

Concert Halls & Performance Venues

Many of the city's churches host sacred and secular music concerts, as well as
special Christmas festivities. A number of outdoor amphitheaters around town

have full summer schedules. Look for posters on outdoor kiosks around the city and check with the tourist office (p. 174) for listings.

ExpoCité   About a 10-minute drive northwest of Parliament Hill, this expo center is designed for major gatherings. The complex includes the brand new Le Centre Vidéotron, which can seat more than 20,000 and is home to the Remparts, a popular junior hockey team. The site's array of buildings also hosts events such as monster truck extravaganzas, boxing matches, and occasional rock shows. At some point in 2017, it may also be the new location for the permanent farmer's market, currently in Vieux-Port (p. 176). 250 boul. Wilfrid-Hamel (ExpoCité), north of St-Roch. www.expocite.com. © **888/866-3976** or 418/691-7110.

Grand Théâtre de Québec ★★   Classical music concerts, opera, dance, jazz, klezmer, and theatrical productions are presented in two halls. Visiting conductors, orchestras, and dance companies perform here, in addition to resident companies such as the Orchestre Symphonique de Québec and Opéra de Québec. 269 boul. René-Lévesque est (near av. Turnbull), Parliament Hill. www.grandtheatre.qc.ca. © **877/643-8131** or 418/643-8131.

Le Capitole ★   Big musical productions such as *Sweeney Todd* and *The Beatles Story*, along with live musical performances, keep this historic 1,262-seat theater on Place d'Youville buzzing along (productions are in French). More intimate shows are put on in the attached Le Cabaret du Capitole. 972 rue St-Jean (at Place d'Youville), Parliament Hill. www.lecapitole.com. © **800/261-9903** or 418/694-4444.

Palais Montcalm ★   Renovations have made this venue bigger and more modern, and it's now a hub of the city's cultural community. The main performance space seats 979 and presents a mix of dance programs, plays, and classical music concerts. More intimate recitals happen in a 125-seat cafe-theater. 995 Place d'Youville (near Porte St-Jean), Parliament Hill. www.palaismontcalm. ca. © **877/641-6040** or 418/641-6040.

BARS & NIGHTCLUBS

In addition to regular bars and nightclubs, look for *boîtes à chansons* (literally, "boxes with songs"), which are small clubs that feature casual evenings of music from singer-songwriters. They're a regional specialty and popular throughout Québec.

Vieux-Québec: Haute-Ville (Upper Town)

Le Jazz Bar ★   A recent renovation spruced up this corner spot with floor-to-ceiling windows overlooking the bustle of Upper Town. Situated within the historic Hotel Clarendon, jazz duos and trios play on Friday and Saturday nights starting at 9pm for a cover charge. You can order nibbles off a bar menu, and a decent cocktail, if you like. 57 rue Sainte-Anne (at rue des Jardins). www.hotelclarendon.com/jazz-bar-en. © **888/222-3304.**

Pub St-Alexandre ★ Roomy and sophisticated, this is one of the best-looking bars in town. It's done in British-pub style: polished mahogany, exposed brick, and a working fireplace that's particularly comforting during the 8 cold months of the year. Bartenders serve more than 50 single-malt scotches and 250 beers, along with hearty bar food (*croque monsieur,* steak-and-kidney pie, fish and chips). Check the schedule for the occasional live music—rock, blues, jazz, or Irish. 1087 rue St-Jean (near rue St-Stanislas). www.pubstalexandre.com. ✆ **418/694-0015.**

1608 Wine & Cheese Bar ★★ This is a modern re-interpretation of what once was an elegant room inside Québec's magical castle, the hotel Château Frontenac (p. 186). Pull up a chair to the semi-circular bar at 1608 and you're assured a fancy pour (and outstanding locally-made cheese), among the well-heeled, even if you're not staying the night. Free valet parking may be all the encouragement you need. Château Frontenac, 1 rue des Carrières. www.fairmont.com/frontenac-quebec/dining. ✆ **418/692-3861.**

Vieux-Québec: Basse-Ville (Lower Town)

Le Pape-Georges ★ This cozy bar in a nearly 350-year-old stone-and-beamed room features *chanson* (a French-cabaret singing style), along with other music, weekend nights at 10pm (and Thurs in summer). Light fare is available, along with the requisite adult beverages (the bar's motto: "Save water; drink wine!"). 8 rue Cul-de-Sac (near boul. Champlain). www.papegeorges.ca. ✆ **418/692-1320.**

SSS ★ SSS may be the only lounge and restaurant in Vieux-Québec that adopts the slick, bigger-city approach of sounding its techno beats onto the sidewalk to lure cocktail seekers. Owned by the same team behind the upscale restaurant **Toast!** (p. 205), SSS offers gourmet Québécois comfort foods—pulled pork poutine, "mini pogo of piglet," aka hot dogs, etc. Guests can opt for entrees or appetizers, dining room or bar. On busy nights, a snack menu kicks in after 10:30pm (and on busy afternoons 2–5pm). 71 rue St-Paul (near rue Sault-au-Matelot). www.restaurantsss.com. ✆ **418/692-1991.**

Théâtre Petit-Champlain ★ Québécois and French singers alternate with jazz and blues groups in this roomy cafe and theater in Lower Town. Performances take place most Thursdays through Saturdays at 8pm. Tickets run about C$20 to C$50. The pretty outdoor patio is perfect for preshow drinks. 68 rue du Petit-Champlain (near the funiculaire). www.theatrepetitchamplain.com. ✆ **418/692-2631.**

Parliament Hill (on or Near Grande-Allée)

Ciel! Bistro-Bar★★ Finally the rotating restaurant atop l'Hôtel Le Concorde Québec has a bar! If the weather is right, the views are astonishing (and constantly changing; the motion sensitive need not apply). Take the lobby elevator all the way up to a twilight cocktail (the bar area is open daily 11:30am to midnight), a romantic dinner, or a sun-lit brunch on Saturday and

DANCE, dance, DANCE!

The Parliament Hill neighborhood, on or near Grande-Allée, has the city's highest concentration of dance clubs. **Dagobert Night Club,** 600 Grande-Allée est (www.dagobert.ca; ☎ **418/522-0393**) imports DJs from Montréal and as far away as the U.K. and is a rite of passage for many locals or others just of age who pack the 1,000-person patio. Just across the street is **Maurice Night Club,** 575 Grande-Allée est (www.mauricenightclub.com; ☎ **418/647-2000**), a converted mansion with a couple of bars (an older crowd gravitates toward its **Charlotte Lounge**). The nearby **Savini,** 680 Grande-Allée est (www.savini.ca; ☎ **418/647-4747**), a self-dubbed *"vinothèque,"* combines wine, hostesses in teeny dresses, and nightly DJs. It's also a fine spot for late-night pizza or salad. Catering mostly to gay and lesbian clientele, **Le Drague Cabaret Club,** 815 rue St-Augustin (www.ledrague.com; ☎ **418/649-7212**), or "the Drag," features two dance floors and a cabaret with drag shows on Thursday, Friday, and Sunday nights. It's located just off rue St-Jean in the Faubourg St-Jean neighborhood, within walking distance of the other clubs.

Sunday. As this is under the same umbrella as stalwart restaurants Le Cochon Dingue and **Café Du Monde** (p. 206) the menu is reliable. 1225 Cours du Général-de Montcalm (at Grande-Allée on 28th floor inside L'Hôtel Le Concorde Québec). www.cielbistrobar.com. ☎ **418/640-5802.**

La Ninkasi du Faubourg With a tagline *"bières et culture,"* Ninkasi features almost all Québécois wine and spirits, including 40 local microbrews. In warm months, you can savor your wine on an outdoor terrace. Ninkasi is open daily from 1pm to 3am. 811 rue St-Jean (1 block west of av. Honoré-Mercier). www.laninkasi.ca. ☎ **418/529-8538.**

Le Sacrilège Open daily from noon to 3am, this bar is all *terrasse* (or terrace). It's a fine place for a pint on a chilly day, too. But if it's just warm enough (and for the Québécois it nearly always is), friends will nestle into a spot within the walled courtyard and let the night (or day) go by. 447 rue St-Jean (near rue Scott). www.lesacrilege.com. ☎ **418/649-1985.**

St-Roch

La Barberie Microbrasserie Coopérative de travail ★★ There's no better spot to hang out on a sunny afternoon with a carousel of house-made microbrews than in La Barberie's beer garden. Get there early on weekends because seats go fast and stay occupied. This place is so laid back that midweek you can bring your lunch and heat it up on the premises. 310 rue St-Roch (at rue de la Reine). www.labarberie.com. ☎ **418/522-4373.**

Le Cercle ★★★ A unique gallery-bar-resto-concert venue, this spot in St-Roch can be a go-to for excellent wines, small plates (p. 208), good music, and eclectic, slightly avant-garde entertainment. 228 rue St-Joseph est (near rue Caron). www.le-cercle.ca. ☎ **418/948-8648.**

QUÉBEC CITY WALKING TOURS

T he many pleasures of walking in picturesque French Québec are easily comparable to walking in similar *quartiers* in northern European cities. Stone houses rub shoulders with each other, carriage wheels creak behind muscular horses, sunlight filters through leafy canopies, drinkers and diners lounge in sidewalk cafes, childish shrieks of laughter echo down cobblestone streets. Not common to other cities, however, is the bewitching vista of river and mountains that the higher elevations bestow.

In winter especially, Vieux-Québec takes on a Dickensian quality, with a lamp glow flickering behind curtains of falling snow. The man who should know—Charles Dickens himself—described the city as having "splendid views which burst upon the eye at every turn."

WALKING TOUR 1: UPPER TOWN (VIEUX-QUÉBEC: HAUTE-VILLE)

START:	**Château Frontenac, the castlelike hotel that dominates the city**
FINISH:	**Hôtel du Parlement, on Grande-Allée, just outside the walls**
TIME:	**2 to 3 hours, depending on whether you take all the optional diversions**
BEST TIMES:	**Anytime, although early morning when the streets are emptier is most atmospheric, and the best time to take unobstructed photographs**
WORST TIMES:	**During a major festival or inclement weather**

Fortress walls surround the Upper Town (Haute-Ville) of Old Québec (Vieux-Québec). This section of the city overlooks the St. Lawrence River and includes much of what makes Québec so beloved. Buildings and compounds along this tour have been carefully preserved, and most are at least a century old. *Start:* At the grand Château Frontenac, the visual heart of the city.

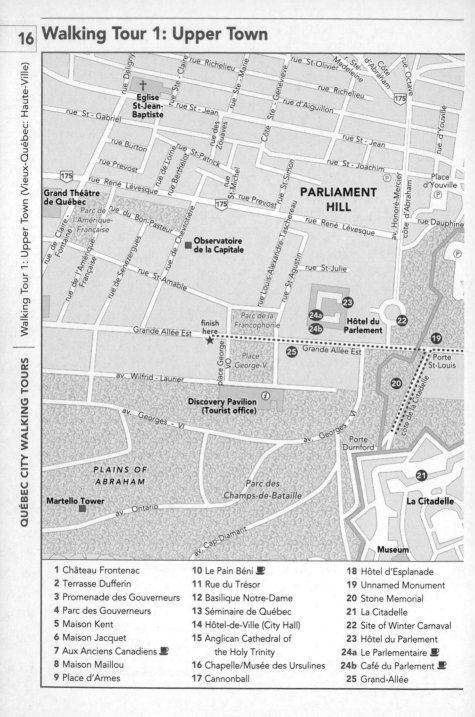

1 Château Frontenac
2 Terrasse Dufferin
3 Promenade des Gouverneurs
4 Parc des Gouverneurs
5 Maison Kent
6 Maison Jacquet
7 Aux Anciens Canadiens 🍴
8 Maison Maillou
9 Place d'Armes

10 Le Pain Béni 🍴
11 Rue du Trésor
12 Basilique Notre-Dame
13 Séminaire de Québec
14 Hôtel-de-Ville (City Hall)
15 Anglican Cathedral of
    the Holy Trinity
16 Chapelle/Musée des Ursulines
17 Cannonball

18 Hôtel d'Esplanade
19 Unnamed Monument
20 Stone Memorial
21 La Citadelle
22 Site of Winter Carnaval
23 Hôtel du Parlement
24a Le Parlementaire 🍴
24b Café du Parlement 🍴
25 Grand-Allée

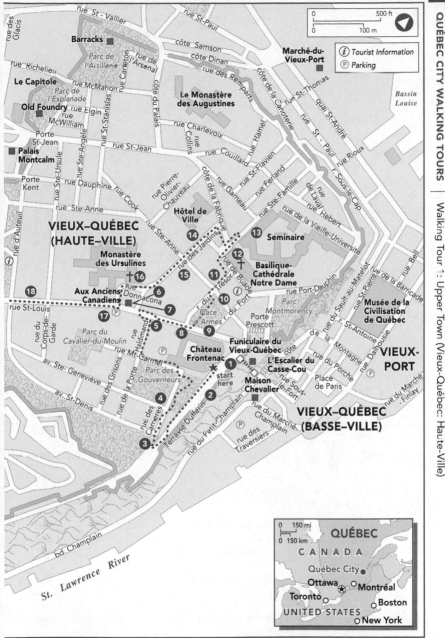

rue des Glacis

rue St-Vallier

rue St-Paul

Barracks

côte Samson

côte Dinan

Marché-du-Vieux-Port

rue Richelieu

Parc de l'Artillerie

rue de l'Arsenal

rue des Remparts

ⓘ *Tourist Information*

Ⓟ *Parking*

0   500 ft
0   100 m

Le Capitole

rue McMahon

Parc de l'Esplanade

Old Foundry

rue Elgin

rue McWilliam

rue Carleton

côte du Palais

Le Monastère des Augustines

côte de la Canoterie

rue St-Thomas

quai St-André

rue St - Paul

Bassin Louise

Porte St-Jean

rue St-Stanislas

rue Ste-Angèle

rue St-Jean

rue Charlevoix

rue Collins

rue Couillard

rue Hamel

rue St-Flavien

rue Ferland

r. Sous-le-Cap

rue Rioux

Palais Montcalm

Porte Kent

rue Ste-Ursule

rue Dauphine

rue Cook

rue Pierre-Olivier-Chauveau

côte de la Fabrique

rue Garneau

rue Ste-Famille

rue de Laval

rue Hébert

rue de la Barricade

rue Ste-Anne

rue Ste-Anne

Hôtel de Ville

rue des Jardins

rue de la Vieille-Université

rue St-Pierre

rue de la Barricade

rue Bell

VIEUX–QUÉBEC (HAUTE–VILLE)

⑭

⑬ **Seminaire**

Monastère des Ursulines

✝⑯

⑮

⑫ ✝

⑪

Basilique-Cathédrale Notre Dame

ⓘ

rue du Fort

Parc Montmorency

rue Port-Dauphin

rue du Sault-au-Matelot

rue St-Antoine

Musée de la Civilisation de Québec

⑱

Aux Anciens Canadiens

rue Donnacona

⑥

⑩

rue du Trésor

rue de Buade

ⓘ rue St-Louis

⑰ Ⓟ

⑦

Place d'Armes

Porte Prescott

de la Montagne

rue Dalhousie

VIEUX–PORT

rue du Corps-de-Garde

Parc du Cavalier-du-Moulin

rue Haldimand

⑤

⑧

⑨

Château Frontenac

Funiculaire du Vieux-Québec

rue du Porche

Ⓟ

Place de Paris

av. Ste-Geneviève

rue Mt-Carmel

Parc des Gouverneurs

★ ①

start here

L'Escalier du Casse-Cou

rue Sous-le-Fort

rue du Marché - Finlay

av. St-Denis

rue de la Porte

rue des Grisons

④

② ③

Ⓟ

Maison Chevalier

rue du Marché Champlain

VIEUX–QUÉBEC (BASSE–VILLE)

rue des Carrières

Terrasse Dufferin

rue du Petit-Champlain

rue des Traversiers

bd. Champlain

St. Lawrence River

0   150 mi
0   150 km

QUÉBEC

CANADA

Québec City ●

Ottawa ⊛   ○ **Montréal**

Toronto ○   ○ **Boston**

UNITED STATES   ○ **New York**

1 Château Frontenac

It's not hard to see why this is reportedly the most photographed hotel in the world. A copper roof only needs replacing every 100 years, and this one just came due. A major, multimillion-dollar renovation project wrapped in 2014 and transformed this "castle" inside and out. When you gaze up toward its spires, imagine that more than 36 tons (about 80,000 lb.) of new chocolate-brown metal were needed to alter the tableau. It will take another 2 decades to oxidize the refurbished areas into a distinctive green patina. The original section of the famous edifice that defines the Québec City skyline

Québec City's iconic Château Frontenac

was built as a hotel from 1892 to 1893 by the Canadian Pacific Railway Company. Known locally as "the Château," the hotel today has 611 rooms (p. 186).

Walk around to the river side of the Château, where there is a grand boardwalk called:

2 Terrasse Dufferin

With its green-and-white-topped gazebos in warm months, this boardwalk promenade looks much as it did 100 years ago, when ladies with parasols and gentlemen with top hats strolled along it on sunny afternoons. It offers vistas of river, watercraft, and distant mountains, and is particularly romantic at sunset.

Walk south on Terrasse Dufferin, past the Château. If you're in the mood for some exercise, go to the end of the boardwalk and continue up the stairs—all 310 of them— walking south along the:

3 Promenade des Gouverneurs

This walkway was renovated skirts the sheer cliff wall, climbing up and up past Québec's military **Citadelle** (p. 219), a fort built by the British army between 1820 and 1850 that remains an active military garrison. The promenade/staircase ends at the grassy **Parc des Champs-de-Bataille** (p. 228), about 15 minutes away. If you go to the end, return back to Terrasse Dufferin to continue the stroll.

Walk back on the terrace as far as the battery of old (but not original) cannons on the left, which set up as they were in the old days. Climb the stairs toward the obelisk into the:

4 Parc des Gouverneurs

Just southwest of the Château Frontenac, this park stands on the site of the mansion built to house the French governors of Québec. The mansion burned in 1834, and the ruins lie buried under the great bulk of the Château. B&Bs and small hotels now border the park on two sides.

The **obelisk monument** is dedicated to both generals in the momentous battle of September 13, 1759, when Britain's General James Wolfe and France's Louis-Joseph, marquis de Montcalm, fought for what would be the ultimate destiny of Québec (and, quite possibly, all of North America). The French were defeated, and both generals died. Wolfe, wounded in the fighting, lived only long enough to hear of England's victory. Montcalm died a few hours after Wolfe. Told that he was mortally wounded, Montcalm replied, "All the better. I will not see the English in Québec."

Walk up rue Mont-Carmel, which runs between the park and Château Frontenac. Turn right onto rue Haldimand. At the next corner, rue St-Louis, stands a white house with blue trim. This is:

5 Maison Kent

Built in 1648, this might be Québec's oldest building. It's most famous for being the building in which France signed the capitulation to the British forces. Its name comes from the duke of Kent, Queen Victoria's father. He lived here for a few years at the end of the 18th century, just before he married Victoria's mother in an arranged liaison. His true love, it is said, was with him in Maison Kent. Today, the building houses France's consulate general.

To the left and diagonally across from Maison Kent, at rue St-Louis and rue des Jardins, is:

6 Maison Jacquet

This small, white dwelling with crimson roof and trim dates from 1677 and now houses a popular restaurant called **Aux Anciens Canadiens** (p. 197). Among the oldest houses in the province, it has sheltered some prominent Québécois, including Philippe Aubert de Gaspé, the author of *Aux Anciens Canadiens,* which recounts Québec's history and folklore. He lived here from 1815 to 1824.

7 Aux Anciens Canadiens 🍴

Try Québécois home cooking right here at the restaurant named for de Gaspé's book at 34 rue St-Louis. Consider caribou in blueberry-wine sauce or Québec meat pie, and don't pass up the maple sugar pie with cream. See p. 197.

Leaving the restaurant, turn back toward Maison Kent (toward the river) and walk along rue St-Louis to no. 17:

8 Maison Maillou

This house's foundations date from 1736, but the house was enlarged in 1799 and restored in 1959. It's best seen from the opposite side of the street. Maison Maillou was built as an elegant luxury home and later served as headquarters of militias and armies. Note the metal shutters used to thwart weather and unfriendly fire.

Continue on rue St-Louis to arrive at the central plaza called:

9 Place d'Armes

This plaza was once the military parade ground outside the governors' mansion (which no longer exists). In the small park at the center is the fountain **Monument to the Faith,** which recalls the arrival of the Recollet monks from France in 1615. France's king granted them a large plot of land in 1681 on which to build their church and monastery.

Facing the square is the **monument to Samuel de Champlain,** who founded Québec in 1608. Created by French artist Paul Chevré and architect Paul Le Cardonnel, the statue has stood here since 1898. Its pedestal is made from stone that was also used in the Arc de Triomphe and Sacré-Coeur Basilica in Paris.

Near the Champlain statue is the diamond-shaped **UNESCO monument** designating Québec City as a World Heritage Site, a rare distinction. Installed in 1986, the monument is made of bronze, granite, and glass.

The city's major **tourist information center** faces the plaza, at 12 rue Ste-Anne.

10 Le Pain Béni ☕

This is one option in a part of town that's great for sitting and watching the world go by. Grab a sidewalk table and enjoy something to drink or eat on the first-floor of Auberge Place d'Armes at 24 rue Ste-Anne (p. 200).

Just adjacent to Le Pain Béni is the narrow pedestrian lane called:

11 Rue du Trésor

Artists (or their representatives) hang their prints and paintings of Québec scenes on both sides of the walkway. In decent weather, it's busy with browsers and sellers. Most prices are within the means of the average visitor, but don't be shy about bargaining for a better deal.

Follow rue du Trésor down to rue Buade and turn left. On the right, at the corner of rue Ste-Famille is the:

12 Basilique Notre-Dame

The basilica's golden interior is ornate and its air rich with the scent of burning candles. Many artworks remain from the time of the French regime. The chancel lamp was a gift from Louis XIV, and the crypt is the final resting place for most of Québec's bishops. The basilica dates back to 1647 and has suffered a tumultuous history of bombardment and reconstruction; see p. 217 for more information, including the celebration of the parish's 350th anniversary.

As you exit the basilica, turn a sharp right to enter the grounds and, a few steps in, the all-white inner courtyard of the historic:

13 Séminaire de Québec

Founded in 1663 by North America's first bishop, Bishop Laval, this seminary had grown into Laval University by 1852 and priests are still in residence here. During summer, tours given by **Musée de l'Amérique**

Rue du Trésor is an outdoor art gallery featuring local artists.

Francophone (based inside the seminary's grounds), pass by some of the seminary's buildings, which reveal lavish decorations of stone, tile, and brass. See p. 220.

Head back to the basilica. Directly across the small park from the church is:

14 Hôtel-de-Ville (City Hall)

The park next to City Hall is often converted into an outdoor event space in summer, especially during the **Festival d'Été** (Summer Festival; p. 237) when it is used for concerts and other staged programs or for the **German Christmas Market** (p. 239), when it is transformed into a winter village of old.

As you face City Hall, the tall building to the left is **Édifice Price, the** Old City's tallest building at 18 stories. It was built in 1929 in Art Deco style with geometric motifs and a steepled copper roof. When it was built, it inadvertently gave a bird's-eye view into the adjacent Ursuline Convent, and a "view tax" had to be paid to the nuns to appease them. It is dramatically lit at night.

Facing the front of Hôtel-de-Ville, walk left on rue des Jardins toward Édifice Price. On your left, you'll pass a small statue celebrating the city's connections to *le cirque* and its performers. Cross over rue Ste-Anne. On the left are the spires of the:

15 Anglican Cathedral of the Holy Trinity

Modeled after London's St-Martin-in-the-Fields, this building dates from 1804 and was the first Anglican cathedral to be built outside the British Isles. The interior is simple, but spacious and bright, with pews of solid

English oak from the Royal Windsor forest and a latticed ceiling with a gilded-chain motif. Lucky visitors may happen upon an organ recital or choral rehearsal.

One block up rue des Jardins, turn right at the small square (triangle shaped, actually) and go a few more steps to 12 rue Donnacona, the:

16 Chapelle/Musée des Ursulines

Handiwork by Ursuline nuns from the 17th, 18th, and 19th centuries is on display here, along with Amerindian crafts and a cape that was made for Marie de l'Incarnation, a founder of the convent, when she left for New France in 1639.

Peek into the restored chapel if it's open. The tomb of Marie de l'Incarnation is here. She was beatified by Pope John Paul II in 1980. Two richly decorated altarpieces, created by sculptor Pierre-Noël Levasseur between 1726 and 1736, are also worth a look.

From the museum, turn right on rue Donnacona to walk past the **Ursuline Convent,** originally built in 1642. The present complex is actually a succession of different buildings added and repaired at various times until 1836, as frequent fires took their toll. A statue of Marie is outside. The convent is now a private girls' school and not open to the public.

Continue left up the hill along rue du Parloir to rue St-Louis. Turn right. At the next block, rue du Corps-de-Garde, note the tree on the left side of the street with a:

17 Cannonball

One story about the cannonball lodged in the base of this tree trunk says that it landed here during the Battle of Québec in 1759 and, over the

years, became firmly embraced by the tree. Another story says it was placed here on purpose to keep the wheels of horse-drawn carriages from bumping the tree when making tight turns.

Continue along rue St-Louis another 2 blocks to rue d'Auteuil. The house on the right corner is:

18 Hôtel d'Esplanade

Notice that stone blocks many of the windows in this façade facing rue St-Louis. This is because houses were once taxed by the number of windows they had, and the frugal homeowner found this way to get around the law—even though it cut down on his view.

An 18th-century cannonball lodged in the base of a tree

Continue straight on rue St-Louis toward the Porte St-Louis, a gate in the walls. Before the gate on the right is the Esplanade powder magazine, part of the old fortifications. Just before the gate is an:

19 Unnamed Monument

This monument commemorates the 1943 meeting in Québec of U.S. President Franklin D. Roosevelt and British Prime Minister Winston Churchill. It remains a soft-pedaled reminder to French Québécois that it was the English-speaking nations that rid France of the Nazis.

Just across the street from the monument is a small road, Côte de la Citadelle, that leads to La Citadelle. Walk up that road. On the right are headquarters and barracks of a militia district, arranged around an inner court. Near its entrance is a:

20 Stone Memorial

This marks the resting place of 13 soldiers of General Richard Montgomery's American army, felled in the unsuccessful assault on Québec in 1775. Obviously, the conflicts that swirled for centuries around who would ultimately rule Québec didn't end with the British victory after its 1759 battle with French troops.

Continue up the hill to:

21 La Citadelle

The impressive star-shaped fortress just beyond view keeps watch from a commanding position on a grassy plateau 108m (354 ft.) above the banks of the St. Lawrence. It took 30 years to complete, by which time it had become obsolete. Since 1920, the Citadelle has been the home of the French-speaking **Royal 22e Régiment,** which fought in both world wars and in Korea. A museum dedicated to the regiment's 100-year history was significantly expanded in 2014. With good timing and weather, it's possible to watch a **Changing of the Guard** ceremony, or (as it's called) "beating the retreat." See p. 219 for more details.

Return to rue St-Louis and turn left to pass through Porte St-Louis, which was built in 1873 on the site of a gate dating from 1692. Here, the street broadens to become Grande-Allée. To the right is a park that runs alongside the city walls.

22 Site of Winter Carnaval

One of the most captivating events on the Canadian calendar, the 17-day **Carnaval de Québec** happens every February and includes outdoor games, snow tubing, dogsled races, canoe races along the St. Lawrence River, night parades, and more. A palace of snow and ice rises on this spot just outside the city walls, with ice sculptures throughout the field. Colorfully clad Québécois come to admire the palace and dance the nights away at outdoor parties. On the left side of Grande-Allée, a carnival park of games, food, and music is set up on Parc des Champs-de-Bataille. For an instant pick-me-up during the cold winter festival, try to find the Carnaval's signature drink, the caribou, which is an elixir of sherry, port wine, and hard liquors. See p. 235 for more about the festivities.

Across the street from the park, on your right, stands the province of Québec's stately:

23 Hôtel du Parlement

Constructed in 1884, this government building houses what Québécois call their "National Assembly" (note the use of the word "national" and not "provincial").

The massive fountain in front of the building, **La Fontaine de Tourny,** was commissioned by the mayor of Bordeaux, France, in 1857. Sculptor Mathurin Moreau created the dreamlike figures on the fountain's base.

In the sumptuous Parliament chambers, the fleur-de-lis symbol and the initials VR (for Victoria Regina) are reminders of Québec's dual heritage. If the crown on top is lit, Parliament is in session. Along the exterior façade are 22 bronze statues of prominent figures in Québec's tumultuous history.

Guided tours are available weekdays year-round from 9am to 4:15pm, plus weekends in summer from 10am to 4:15pm. See p. 222 for more information.

24 Le Parlementaire & Café du Parlement 🍵

Le Parlementaire restaurant (✆ **418/643-6640**), in the Hôtel du Parlement (p. 222) at 1045 rue des Parlementaires, is done up in regal Beaux Arts decor and open to the public (as well as parliamentarians and visiting dignitaries) for breakfast and lunch Monday through Friday most of the year. The more casual **Café du Parlement** (✆ **418/643-5529**) has eat-in or takeout options in biodegradable containers, and is located on the ground floor. Or mosey on down Grande-Allée to find plenty of other options.

Continue down:

25 Grand-Allée

Just past Hôtel du Parlement is a park called Place George-V, and behind the park are the charred remains of the **1885 Armory.** A major visual icon and home to the country's oldest French-Canadian regiment, the Armory was all but destroyed in an April 2008 fire. The stone façade still stands. The destruction was a huge blow to the city. A contract to restore the historically significant structure began in 2015 and is expected to finish in 2017.

To the left of the Armory is a building that houses the **Discovery Pavilion** (p. 230), where a multimedia exhibit called "Battles: 1759–1760" is presented.

After the park, you'll see that cafes, restaurants, and bars line the street on both sides. This strip really gets jumping at night, particularly in the complex that includes **Maurice Night Club** and **Charlotte Lounge** (p. 242), at no. 575.

One food possibility is **Chez Ashton,** at 640 Grande-Allée est. The Québec fast-food restaurant makes what many consider the town's best *poutine*—French fries with cheese curds and brown gravy.

Further up Grande-Allée, inside l'Hôtel Le Concorde Québec and up to the 28th floor is **Ciel! Bistro-Bar** (p. 241), a rotating bar and restaurant with a 360-degree view of the province's stunning landscape.

The city bus along Grande-Allée can return you to the Old City, or turn left on Place Montcalm and enter the **Parc des Champs-de-Bataille** (Battlefields Park; p. 228) at the Joan of Arc Garden. If you turn left in the park and continue along its boulevards and footpaths, you'll end up at the Citadelle. If you turn right, you'll reach the **Musée National des Beaux-Arts du Québec** (p. 223).

WALKING TOUR 2: # LOWER TOWN (VIEUX-QUÉBEC: BASSE-VILLE & VIEUX-PORT)

START: **Either in Upper Town at Terrasse Dufferin, the boardwalk in front of Château Frontenac, or if you're already in Lower Town, at the *funiculaire* (the cable car that connects the upper and lower parts of the Old City)**

FINISH: **Place-Royale, the restored central square of Lower Town**

TIME: **1½ hours**

BEST TIMES: **Anytime during the day. Early morning lets you soak up the visual history, though shops won't be open**

WORST TIMES: **Very late at night, inclement weather**

The Lower Town (Basse-Ville) part of Old Québec (Vieux-Québec) encompasses the city's oldest residential area—now flush with boutique hotels, high-end restaurants, and touristy shops—and Vieux-Port, the old port district. The impressive Musée de la Civilisation is here; if you have time, you may want to pause from the tour for a visit. We start at the cliff-side elevator *(funiculaire)* that connects Upper and Lower towns.

If you're in Upper Town, descend to Lower Town by one of two options:

1 Funiculaire (Option A)

This cable car's upper terminus is on Terrasse Dufferin near the Château Frontenac. As the car descends the steep slope, its glass front provides a broad view of Basse-Ville (Lower Town).

Or, if you prefer a more active means of descent, use the stairs to the left of the *funiculaire*, the:

2 L'Éscalier du Casse-Cou (Option B)

"Breakneck Stairs" is the self-explanatory name given to this stairway (although truth be told, they're not *that* harrowing anymore). Stairs have been in place here since the settlement began. In 1698, the town council had to forbid citizens from taking their animals up and down the stairway.

Both Breakneck Stairs and the *funiculaire* arrive at the intersection of rues Petit-Champlain and Sous-le-Fort. Look at the building from which the *funiculaire* passengers exit:

3 Maison Louis Jolliet

This building is now the *funiculaire*'s lower terminus and full of tourist trinkets and gewgaws, but it has an auspicious pedigree. It was built in 1683 and was home to Louis Jolliet, the Québec-born explorer who, along with a priest, Jacques Marquette, was the first person of European parentage to explore the Mississippi River's upper reaches.

Walk down the pretty little street here:

4 Rue du Petit-Champlain

Allegedly North America's oldest street, this pedestrian-only lane swarms with restaurantgoers, cafe sitters, strolling couples, and gaggles of schoolchildren in the warm months. Some shops listed in the "Shopping in Lower Town" section of chapter 14 are here. In winter, it's a snowy wonderland, with ice statues and twinkling white lights.

5 Le Lapin Sauté 🍴

Though it's early in the stroll, this street has so many eating and shopping options that you might want to pause for a while. Look for the sign with the flying rabbits for **Le Lapin Sauté,** 52 rue du Petit-Champlain, a country-cozy bistro with hearty food (where prices are steep but the quality reliable). A lovely terrace overlooks Parc Félix-Leclerc and, in the warm months, street musicians serenade.

At the end of Petit-Champlain, turn left onto boulevard Champlain. A lighthouse from the Gaspé Peninsula used to stand across the street, but it has returned to its original home, leaving just an anchor and cannons to stand guard (rather forlornly) over the river.

Follow the street's curve; this block offers pleasant boutiques and cafes. At the corner is the crimson-roofed:

6 Maison Chevalier

Dating from 1752, this was once the home of merchant Jean-Baptiste Chevalier. Note the wealth of windows, more than 30 in front-facing sections alone. In 1763, the house sold at auction to ship owner Jean-Louis Frémont, the grandfather of Virginia-born John Charles Frémont. John Charles went on to become an American explorer, soldier, and politician who was the first Republican Party candidate for the office of President of the United States.

The Chevalier House sold in 1806 to an Englishman, who in turn rented it to a hotelier, who transformed it into an inn. In 1960, the Québec government restored the house, and it became a museum about 5 years later. It's overseen by the **Musée de la Civilisation,** which mounts temporary exhibitions. Entrance fees and hours are listed on p. 211.

Just past the maison's front door, turn left and walk up the short block of rue Notre-Dame, a carefully restored street of stone and brick buildings. (Just ahead is Place-Royale. If you opt to see the next stop, the Royal Battery, you'll return to this spot and continue on rue Notre-Dame in the same direction.) A cozy *boîte à chansons* (small

QUÉBEC CITY WALKING TOURS | Walking Tour 2: Lower Town (Vieux-Québec: Basse-Ville & Vieux-Port)

254

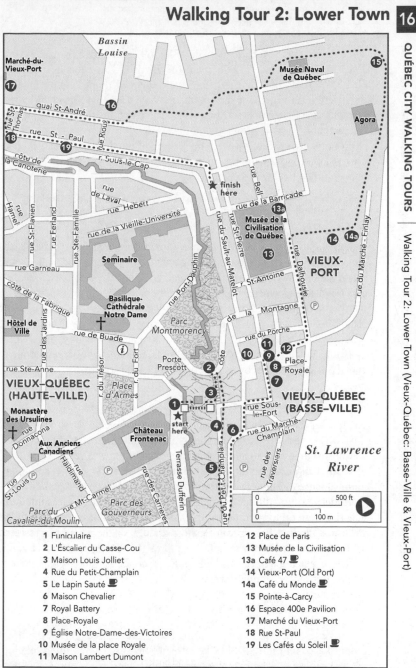

1 Funiculaire
2 L'Éscalier du Casse-Cou
3 Maison Louis Jolliet
4 Rue du Petit-Champlain
5 Le Lapin Sauté
6 Maison Chevalier
7 Royal Battery
8 Place-Royale
9 Église Notre-Dame-des-Victoires
10 Musée de la place Royale
11 Maison Lambert Dumont

12 Place de Paris
13 Musée de la Civilisation
13a Café 47
14 Vieux-Port (Old Port)
14a Café du Monde
15 Pointe-à-Carcy
16 Espace 400e Pavilion
17 Marché du Vieux-Port
18 Rue St-Paul
19 Les Cafés du Soleil

club with live music) called Le Papes-Georges is just around the corner at 8 rue Cul-De-Sac. Turn right at Sous-le-Fort and walk 1 block to the:

7 Royal Battery

The French erected fortifications here in 1691 and added the cannons in 1712 to defend Lower Town from the British. The cannons got their chance in 1759, but the English victory silenced them, and eventually, they were left to rust. Sunken foundations were all that remained by the turn of the 20th century, and when the time came for restorations, it had to be rebuilt from the ground up.

From the Royal Battery, walk back up rue Sous-le-Fort. This is a good photo opportunity, with the imposing Château Frontenac on the cliff above framed between ancient houses.

Turn right on rue Notre-Dame. Half a block up the grade is the heart of Basse-Ville, the small:

8 Place-Royale

Occupying the center of New France's first permanent colony, this small and still very much European-feeling enclosed square served as the town marketplace. It went into decline around 1860 and, by 1950, had become a derelict, run-down part of town. Today, it has been restored to very nearly recapture its historic appearance. The prominent bust is of Louis XIV, the Sun King, a gift from the city of Paris in 1928. The striking 17th- and 18th-century houses once belonged to wealthy merchants. Note the ladders on some of the steep roofs, used to fight fire and remove snow. See p. 214 for more information about the square.

Facing directly onto the square is:

9 Église Notre-Dame-des-Victoires

Named for French naval victories over the British in 1690 and 1711, Québec's oldest stone church was built in 1688 after a massive Lower Town fire destroyed 55 homes in 1682. The church was restored in 1763 after its partial destruction by the British in the 1759 siege. The white-and-gold interior has a few murky paintings and a large model boat suspended from the ceiling, a votive offering brought by early settlers to ensure safe voyages. On the walls, small prints depict the stages of the Passion. The church is open to visitors daily 9:30am to 5pm May to late June and until 8:30pm from late June through early September. The rest of the year it's open only for celebrations, concerts, and special events. See p. 218 for more information.

Walk straight across the plaza, passing the:

10 Musée de la place Royale

For decades, this space was nothing but a propped-up façade with an empty lot behind it, but it has been rebuilt to serve as an interpretation center with shows and exhibitions about this district's history; it's good for kids, as well as adults (p. 215).

At the corner on the right is the:

11 Maison Lambert Dumont

This building now houses Geomania, a store selling rocks and crystals. In earlier years, though, it was home to the Dumont family and one of several residences in the square. To the right as you're facing it once stood a hotel where U.S. President William Taft would stay as he headed north to vacation in the picturesque Charlevoix region.

Walk about 15m (49 ft.) past the last building on your left and turn around; the entire end of that building is an amusing *trompe l'oeil* mural of streets and houses, and depictions of citizens from the earliest colonial days to the present. Have your photo taken here—nearly everyone does!

Return to Place-Royale and head left toward the water, down two small sets of stairs to the:

12 Place de Paris

This plaza contains a discordantly bland white sculpture that resembles three stacked Rubik's Cubes. It's called *Dialogue avec L'Histoire* and was a gift from the city of Paris in 1987.

Continue ahead to rue Dalhousie, a main street for cars, and turn left. Another option, not on the walking tour map, is to cross the street toward the Vieux-Port (Old Port), turn left to follow the waterfront pedestrian and bike path, and continue the walking tour at stop 14 (below). Otherwise, a few short blocks up rue Dalhousie on the left is the:

13 Musée de la Civilisation

This wonderful museum may be housed in a lackluster gray-block building, but there is nothing plain about it once you enter. Spacious and airy, with ingeniously arranged multidimensional exhibits, it's one of Canada's most innovative museums. If you don't have time to visit now, put it at the top of your must-see list for later. See p. 211.

13a Café 47 ☕

If you're doing this stroll in the colder months, you might want to head indoors at this point. **Café 47** is up two flights of stairs inside the **Musée de la Civilisation,** where a few choice indoor tables overlook the river. Or, if it's warm enough, take a table on the terrace. Café 47 serves a cafeteria-style menu Tuesday to Sunday from 10am to 4:30pm and a bistro menu, including wine and beer, from 11:30am to 2pm. To continue the tour, head back to rue Dalhousie and cross over toward Terminal de Croisières to the waterfront.

From the museum, head across the parking lot to the river and turn left at the water's edge, also called:

14 Vieux-Port (Old Port)

In the 17th century, this 29-hectare (72-acre) riverfront area was the port of call for European ships bringing supplies and settlers to the new colony. With the decline of shipping by the early 20th century, the port fell into precipitous decline. But since the mid-1980s, it has experienced a rebirth, becoming the summer destination for international cruise ships. It got additional sprucing up for Québec's 400th anniversary in 2008.

Continue along the river's promenade, just behind the Terminal de Croisières, the cruise terminal, is:

14a Café du Monde 🍴

Another dining option awaits right on the harbor: **Café du Monde,** at 84 rue Dalhousie (but visible from the waterfront), offers traditional French cuisine in a fun-for-all atmosphere (p. 206).

With Café du Monde behind you, turn left to return to the waterfront, until you pass the Agora, an outdoor theater, and behind it, the city's Customs House, built between 1830 and 1839. To your right is the small landscaped:

15 Pointe-à-Carcy

The bronze statue of a sailor here is a memorial to Canadian merchant seamen who lost their lives in World War II. From the point, you can look out across Louise Basin to the Bunge of Canada grain elevator that stores wheat, barley, corn, and soybean crops that are produced in western Canada before they are shipped to Europe. The silos made up a massive "screen" upon which the nightly **"Image Mill"** show was projected on summer nights from 2008 through 2014.

Follow the walkway left from Pointe-à-Carcy along the Louise Basin. You'll pass the **Musée Naval de Québec,** which chronicles the birth of the Canadian Navy and the military support provided by ships via the St. Lawrence, including supply and troop delivery to battles on the Plains of Abraham. For details visit www.navalmuseumofquebec.com or call 📞 **418/694-5387.** In the warm months, you can board a scenic river cruise here.

At the end of the basin, take a short jog left, and then right to stay along the water's edge. Up ahead on the left is a modern glass building, the:

16 Espace 400e Pavilion

This modern building was the central location for Québec's 400th-anniversary celebrations in 2008. It now hosts temporary exhibitions or events such as the **Festibière de Québec** (Québec Beer Festival; p. 238).

From the pavilion, continue on the pedestrian path 1 block to:

17 Marché du Vieux-Port

This colorful market at 160 quai St-André has jaunty teal-blue roofs and, in summer, rows and rows of booths heaped with fresh fruits and vegetables, regional wines and ciders, pâtés, jams, cheeses, chocolates, fresh fish and meat, handicrafts, and soaps. Cafes and kiosks offer options for a meal or sweet treat (p. 216).

As you approach, you'll see, down the street, the city's grand train station, designed in 1916 by New York architect Bruce Price. He designed the Château Frontenac in 1893 and used his signature copper-turned-green spires here, too.

Leaving the market, cross rue St-André at the light and walk a short block to:

18 Rue St-Paul

Turn left onto this street, which is home to galleries, craft shops, and about a half-dozen antiques stores. They include **La Nouvelle France Antiquités** (no. 225), which sells antiques with a mid-century flair, and **Les Antiquités Bolduc** (no. 89), which has old fashioned photos, porcelain figures, antique lamps, and the like. Rue St-Paul manages to maintain a sense of unspoiled neighborhood.

19 Les Cafés du Soleil ☕

Les Cafés du Soleil, at 143 rue St-Paul, is one of the few options in Lower Town for a coffee and croissant (and mercifully both are excellent). Pull up a cafe chair and sip from a real mug or take it to go and meander along Lower Town's pretty streets. For those that find that their Lower Town hotel doesn't offer (acceptable) coffee—this may became your go-to morning spot.

From here, return to the heart of Lower Town—Place-Royale and the *funiculaire*—by turning right off rue St-Paul onto either rue du Sault-au-Matelot or the parallel rue St-Pierre. Both are quiet streets with galleries and restaurants.

DAY TRIPS FROM QUÉBEC CITY

17

Forests, mountains, waterfalls, and other natural treasures surround Québec City and can be reached in less than a few hours' drive—it's easy to spend a whole day, or weekend, if you wish. Bucolic **Île d'Orléans,** over a bridge just outside the city, is an unspoiled mini-oasis with farms, orchards, maple groves, and 18th- and 19th-century houses. The **waterfalls of Montmorency** make for dazzling fun, especially in the spring, when winter thaws make them thunder. **Le Massif** is a top destination for downhill sports enthusiasts, especially after a fresh snowfall.

You can easily combine the second Day Trip, to Montmorency Falls, with the first or third Day Trips to Île d'Orléans or Le Massif. The waterfalls are along the highway just across from Île d'Orléans and on the way north to Le Massif.

TOURING QUÉBEC'S BREADBASKET: ÎLE D'ORLÉANS ★★★

16km (10 miles) NE of Québec City

Isolated from the mainland until 1935, the only way to get to the scenic, rolling hills of this little island in eyesight from the city used to by boat (in summer) or over the ice in sleighs (in winter). The highway bridge built that year has allowed the island's fertile fields to become Québec City's primary market garden. During harvest periods, fruits and vegetables are picked fresh on the farms and trucked in daily. The island produces artisanal cheeses, ciders (both alcoholic and non), wines, and microbrews, and proudly promotes agritourism for visitors. In warmer months, visitors go for the day or for extended sojourns.

Île d'Orléans was first inhabited by First Nations people, and then settled by the French as one of their initial outposts of New France in the 17th century. (Jacques Cartier landed here in 1535 and first named the island Bacchus, in celebration of its many grapevines, but renamed it later to honor the duke of Orléans.) The island has six tiny villages, originally established as parishes, and each has a church as its focal point. Some are made of stone and date from the days of the French regime; with fewer than a dozen such churches left in all of the province of Québec, this is a particular point of pride for the islanders. Notable, too, are the many red-roofed homes.

The ideal time to visit is when crops are in harvest and sold at roadside stands. In mid-July, hand-painted signs posted by the main road announce FRAISES: CUEILLIR VOUS-MÉME (STRAWBERRIES: YOU PICK 'EM). The same invitation to pick your own, or sample various forms of cider, is offered during apple season, August through October. Other seasonal highlights include the visit of thousands of migrating snow geese, ducks, and Canada geese in April and May and again in late October. It's a spectacular sight when they launch in flapping hordes so thick that they almost blot out the sun.

Essentials

GETTING THERE

BY CAR   Get on Autoroute 440 east, in the direction of Ste-Anne-de-Beaupré. In about 15 minutes, the Île d'Orléans bridge will be on your right. Take exit 325. If you'd like to hire a guide, **Maple Leaf Guide Services** (www.stfe.ca; ✆ **877/622-3677** or 418/622-3677) can provide one in your car or theirs.

BY BUS   Old Québec Tours, which also goes by the name **Dupont,** (www. toursvieuxquebec.com; ✆ **800/267-8687** or 418/664-0460), offers a 4½-hour "countryside" tour that, in addition to Île d'Orléans, includes a visit to the Montmorency Falls (p. 264) and the Basilica of Sainte-Anne-de-Beaupré.

BY BIKE   Biking over the bridge is not recommended, given the bridge's narrow and precarious pedestrian sidewalk. Cyclists who arrive with their bikes on the back of their cars can park at the tourist office for a small fee, or in many of the parking lots of the island's churches for free. To rent a bike, **Ecolocyclo,** 517 chemin Royal in St-Pierre (www.ecolocyclo.net; ✆ **418/828-0370**), is open 10am to 6pm daily late-June to early September and on the weekends (or weekdays on-call) late-May to early-June and mid-September to mid-October.

VISITOR INFORMATION

After arriving on the island, turn right on Route 368 east toward Ste-Pétronille. The **Bureau d'Accueil Touristique,** or Tourist Information Center (www. tourisme.iledorleans.com; ✆ **866/941-9411** or 418/828-9411), is in the house on the right corner at 490 côte du Pont. Pick up the useful map that shows most of the farms and restaurants or rent an audioguide. The bureau is open daily from about 9am to 5pm, with longer hours in the peak summer months and somewhat shorter hours in winter. Note that many attractions are closed or have limited hours from October through May.

Driving the Island's Perimeter

A coast-hugging road—Route 368, also called chemin Royal and, in a few stretches, chemin de Bout-de-l'Île—circles the island, which is 34km (21 miles) long and 8km (5 miles) wide. It's possible to make a circuit of Île d'Orléans by car in a half-day, but you can justify a full day if you eat a good meal, visit an orchard or cheese-making facility, or just skip stones at the edge of the river. We suggest making a **counter-clockwise circuit** on Route 368, starting with Ste-Pétronille, only 3km (1¾ miles) after turning right from the bridge. You'll get the flavor of the island more quickly and will pass by some of our favorite sights sooner. If you're strapped for time, loop around as far as St-Jean, and then drive across the island on the pastoral route du Mitan ("Middle Road"). You'll get back to the bridge by turning left onto Route 368.

Where to Eat & Stay along Chemin Royal

If you're hungry when you arrive, **Ste-Pétronille,** the first village on the driving tour, was a top vacation destination for the Québécois at the end of the 19th century and is known for its Victorian inn and restaurant, **La Goéliche,** 22 chemin du Quai (www.goeliche.ca; ✆ **888/511-2248** or 418/828-2248). All rooms face the water, and first-floor units have small terraces. Nonguests can come for breakfast, lunch, or dinner, or simply for the view of the mighty St. Lawrence. For a more modest snack, the nearby **Chocolaterie de l'Île d'Orléans,** 150 chemin du Bout-de-l'Île (www.chocolaterieorleans.com; ✆ **800/363-2252** or 418/828-2252), serves sandwiches, quiche, and pizza and specializes in homemade chocolates and ice cream.

You might time your trip to plan a meal at **Le Moulin de St-Laurent** (www.moulinstlaurent.qc.ca; ✆ **888/629-3888** or 418/829-3888) at 754 chemin Royal in the village of St-Laurent. It is one of Île d'Orléans's most romantic restaurants. It's housed in a flourmill that operated from 1720 to 1928. From June through August, lunch (11:30am–2:30pm) and dinner (5:30–8:30pm) are served daily; hours vary in May, September, and October. Call to confirm hours and to make reservations.

Take note of the *cabanes à sucre* (sugar shacks) that pop up in spring. These rustic cabins offer the family-style meals traditionally served while the sap is running. A typical menu includes pea soup, ham, and stack of pancakes drenched in maple syrup. You'll pass other restaurants and places for nibbles during the drive. Some are noted in the text below.

The village of **St-Jean,** at about the halfway point on the long south-eastern side of the island, was home to sea captains—that might be why the houses in the village appear more luxurious than others on the island. The creamy-yellow "Scottish brick" in the façades of several of the homes was ballast in boats that came over from Europe and was considered a sign of luxury and wealth. The village **church** was built in 1734, and the walled **cemetery** is the final resting place of many fishermen and seafarers. **Manoir Mauvide-Genest,** 1451 chemin Royal (www.manoirmauvidegenest.com; ✆ **418/829-2630**), was the manor home of a French surgeon who settled here in 1720 and went on to become one of New France's leading figures. The building, open daily 10am to 5pm in high season and on Fridays, Saturdays, and Sundays in May, September and October, is filled with authentic and reproduction furnishings and is classified as a historic monument. Heading east from here, you may be able

Street numbers on the ring road called chemin Royal start anew in each village. That means that as you loop around the perimeter of Île d'Orléans, you could pass a no. 1000 chemin Royal in one stretch and then another no. 1000 chemin Royal a few minutes later. Be sure that you know not just the number of your destination, but also which *village* it's in.

to smell cinnamon rolls fresh out the oven at **La Boulange,** 2001 chemin Royal (www.laboulange.ca; © **418/829-3162**). Across the street and through the church parking lot, steps lead to a picturesque spot where striated rocks line the St. Lawrence.

It's here in St-Jean that you can drive straight across the island on route du Mitan ("Middle Road"). This is a scenic road for a quick detour into the countryside, too.

Potatoes and leeks are grown at the island's most northeastern tip, which lead some to dub **St-François** "the village of vichyssoise." The St. Lawrence River is 10 times wider here than when it flows past Québec City and can be viewed especially well from the town's **observation tower,** in the rest area you'll pass on your right. After you've looped around the island's northern edge, the road stops being Route 368 east and becomes Route 368 west.

The next little village, **Ste-Famille,** was founded in 1661 and is the island's oldest parish. Just as you enter the village, you will pass 10 agritourism spots in quick order, including **Les Fromages de l'Îsle d'Orléans,** 4696 chemin Royal (www.fromagesdeliledorleans.com; © **418/829-0177**), an artisanal dairy that makes a 17th century–style cheese called Paillasson. The village's **Parc des Ancêtres** is a riverside green space with picnic tables. Sharing the same parking lot is **Pub le Mitan,** 3887 chemin Royal (www.microorleans. com; © **418/829-0408**), a microbrewery with a deck that overlooks the river, recommended more for its brews and views than its food.

When you cross into **St-Pierre,** you're nearly back to where you started. If you haven't stopped at any orchards yet, visit **Bilodeau,** 2200 chemin Royal (www.cidreriebilodeau.qc.ca; © **418/828-9316**). It produces some of Île d'Orléans's regular ciders and *cidre de glace,* a sweet wine made from apples left on the trees until after the first frost. Another wine option here is the appealing **Cassis Monna et Filles,** 721 chemin Royal (www.cassismonna. com; © **418/828-2525**). Black currants, or *gadelle noire,* are grown here, and a chic shop features a display on how the berries are harvested and transformed into Crème de Cassis, the key element to a Kir cocktail. St-Pierre's central attraction is its original church at 1249 chemin Royal, the island's oldest (1717). Services are no longer held here, but a large **handicraft shop** with crafts made by local artisans is in the back, behind the altar. The shop is open most days from May to October (© **418/828-9824**).

VISITING MONTMORENCY FALLS ★★

11km (6¾ miles) NE of Québec City

Back on the mainland, the impressive Montmorency Falls are visible from Autoroute 440 and act as a hub for outdoor activity in all seasons. You can view the waterfalls from the bottom, from the top, from paths along the side, and even from above, on a bridge that crosses them. At 83m (272 ft.) tall, they're 30m (98 ft.) higher than Niagara Falls—a boast no visitor is spared. These falls, however, are far narrower. They were named by Samuel de Champlain for his patron, the duke of Montmorency, to whom he dedicated his voyage of 1603. The yellow cast of the falls comes from the high iron content of the riverbed. On summer nights, the plunging water and its surrounding cove is illuminated and the falls host Québec City's fireworks competition, **Les Grand Feux Loto-Québec** (p. 237).

Winter brings a particularly impressive sight: The freezing spray sent up by crashing water builds a mountain of white ice at the base, nicknamed *pain de sucre* (sugarloaf). It grows as high as 30m (98 ft.). It attracts ice climbers, and those of us that simply prefer to observe.

Essentials

GETTING THERE

BY CAR   Take Autoroute 440 east out of Québec City. After 10 minutes, watch for exit 325 for the falls and the parking lot. If you miss the exit, you'll see the falls on your left and will be able to make a legal U-turn.

BY BUS   **Old Québec Tours,** which also goes by the name **Dupont** (www.toursvieuxquebec.com; ℰ **800/267-8687** or 418/664-0460), offers tours to the falls.

BY TRAIN   From mid-June to mid-October, Montmorency Falls is the Québec City departure point (or arrival point) for the **Charlevoix Light Rail Transit** (**LRT;** operated by Réseau Charlevoix, www.reseaucharlevoix.com; ℰ **844/737-3282**), a scenic, two-car train that transports passengers along the river's edge between the falls and the Charlevoix region, including Baie-Saint-Paul and La Malbaie. The ski resort Le Massif is located just south of Baie-Saint-Paul (see below). Advance purchase or reservations are strongly recommended. Adult round-trip tickets from the falls to Baie-Saint-Paul are C$70. For an additional C$5.35, you can reserve a riverside seat.

VISITOR INFORMATION

The address for the falls is 5300 boul. Ste-Anne in Québec City. Visitors can access the falls year-round. The cable car charges per person or family and operates daily from May to October. Visit www.parcdelachutemontmorency.com or call ℰ **844/522-4883** or 418/663-3330 for rates, hours, and other park activities.

Montmorency Falls are taller than Niagara Falls

PARKING

All three of the parking areas charge fees—at the base of the cable car at the bottom of the falls, at Manoir Montmorency at the top of the falls, and at Boischatel, northeast of the falls. Rates depend on season, vehicle size, and in some cases, number of passengers.

Viewing the Falls

You have several choices for viewing the 83m (272-ft.) falls. A path from the lower parking area leads to the base of the falls, where the water comes crashing down. The view is spectacular from here in all seasons. Stairs ascend from here to the top, 487 in sum, with viewing platforms along the way. At the top, a footbridge spans the water where it flows over the cliff. If you don't want to walk to the top, a cable car runs from the parking lot to a terminal alongside the falls, with a pathway that leads close to the water's edge. (Round-trip tickets are around C$14 for adults, C$7 for kids 6–17.) At that top terminal is **Manoir Montmorency,** a villa that contains an interpretation center, gift shop, ice cream and refreshments stand, cafe, and a restaurant—open hours vary seasonally, and meals are typically offered from 11:30am to 3pm. Be sure to confirm hours in advance. The dining room and porch have a side view of the falls; reservations are suggested. In winter, you can rent snowshoes here.

For visitors who want to combine a little rock climbing with a little hiking, the Boischatel fault has three **via ferrata circuits.** Anchored by a safety tether, visitors are led on group hikes by a professional guide along the cliffs with aerial views of the cove that surrounds the falls. The beginner route, for ages 8 and up, is 200m (656 ft.) long and takes just over an hour to complete; the intermediate option, for ages 12 and up, is 60m (197 ft.) longer and takes 2½ hours. The third option combines via ferrata with a **zip line tour** (also available separately) that takes just over 2 hours and is appropriate for ages 14 and up. Fees range from C$16-C$48.

Where to Eat

In addition to the restaurant at Manoir Montmorency (above), picnicking is a good option, though you may want to buy your victuals in Québec City. The falls are surrounded by the provincial **Parc de la Chute-Montmorency,** where visitors can take in the view. The grounds are accessible year-round and include hiking trails, playgrounds, and historic guided tours.

SKIING AT LE MASSIF ★★

75km (46 miles) NE of Québec City

Le Massif, the area's most dramatic ski mountain, is in Petite-Rivière-St-François, about 1 hour drive from Québec City. Fans of the mountain wax rhapsodic over its Zen qualities, including quiet ski lifts, healthy food options, and runs that give the illusion of heading directly into the icy and expansive St. Lawrence River. Le Massif claims the highest vertical east of the Canadian Rockies with 52 trails, including one that's 5.1km (3.2 miles).

Le Massif is in the heart of the **Charlevoix region,** where the stunning expanse of the river, high-end inns, and a wide variety of outdoor activities, including whale-watching in summer and fall, invite an overnight stay. Check www.tourisme-charlevoix.com for possible accommodations.

Cirque du Soleil co-founder Daniel Gauthier owns Le Massif and has been working for years to develop both the ski operations and the outlying area. The most recent addition includes the urban-meets-rural **Hôtel La Ferme** (the farm), in Baie-St-Paul. With an air of simple elegance, the outcrop of buildings are arranged like a traditional farm and cater to the thrifty (dorm room housing starts at C$85 per night) to the sophisticated (loft rooms with balconies start at C$379). Two restaurants and an outdoor Nordic spa make La Ferme a destination unto itself. Gauthier calls the region "a place where tranquility and energy coexist in perfect harmony." That's true. He also says that development is necessary for the long-term survival of his mountain. That may be true, too. Whether he'll achieve the second without soiling the first is the essential question. Locals are watching with great interest and more than a little nervousness.

Essentials
GETTING THERE
BY CAR   Take Autoroute 440 east toward Sainte-Anne-de-Beaupré, continue on 138 east for about 45km (28 miles), turn right at sign for **Le Massif.** The ride to Le Massif takes just over 1 hour.

The ski slopes of Le Massif have an enchanting view over the frozen Saint Lawrence River.

BY CARPOOL   Eco-responsible or exceptionally outgoing travelers can find a carpool via **Allo Stop** (www.allostop-quebec.com).

BY BUS   Le Massif offers round-trip ski **bus shuttles** that depart from the shopping complex Place Ste-Foy and the Place d'Armes near Château Frontenac for C$26. Book seats by calling ℭ **800/267-8687** or 418/664-0460.

BY TRAIN   While the Charlevoix LRT (see "Visiting Montmorency Falls," above) does stop at Baie-Saint-Paul, it currently only runs from summer to early fall. (It may be cold in Québec but the snow never lasts that long!)

VISITOR INFORMATION
Le Massif de Charlevoix (www.lemassif.com; ℭ 877/536-2774 or 418/632-5876) is a growing resort complex that includes the mountain, the Charlevoix LRT (operated by Réseau Charlevoix), and Hôtel La Ferme, located in Baie-St-Paul. Representatives or the website can answer your questions to help plan a stay. You can also check **www.tourisme-charlevoix.com**, an official tourism site for the region, and **www.quebecregion.com**, the Québec City Tourism's website. The mountain is typically open early December through early April from 8:30am to 4pm on weekends and 9am to 4pm (sometimes earlier) on weekdays.

Check **www.lemassif.com** for the current year's pricing. There are full- and half-day rates for adults, seniors, and children of different ages, and no fee for children 6 and under.

PARKING
Parking lots are at both the summit chalet and the mountain's base.

Another Local Mountain

Those interested in more downhill fun will also want to be aware of **Parc du Mont Ste-Anne** (www.mont-sainte-anne. com; ℭ **888/827-4579**), which is closer to Québec City: 42km (26 miles) northeast. In winter, it's the area's busiest ski mountain, with an 800m-high (2,625-ft.) peak.

Hitting the Summit (Then the Base)

Unlike most ski mountains, at **Le Massif** it's most common to park at the summit (as opposed to the base), snap on the skis or board, and descend. *La Jean-Noël* is the easiest trail down. Le Massif's terrain covers 164 hectares (406 acres) with more than half the trails categorized as black diamond or expert. The five lifts and two gondolas can handle 10,060 riders per hour. Snowfall is greatest, on average, in December and February, with a typical annual base of 645cm (21.2 ft). There's a terrain park and the national alpine downhill training center, boasting one of the three toughest trails on the women's downhill World Cup circuit.

Another option is **rodeling** with sleds on wooden rails. Packages include transport from the summit chalet to a dedicated trail, sled and helmet rentals, a 7.5km (4.6 mile) guided descent, and a return gondola ride to the summit. Lessons in skiing, snowboarding, and telemark are also available onsite.

Where to Eat

Amenities are limited to what's offered at Le Massif's base and the summit chalet, where you'll find a cafeteria and **Pub Le Coteilleux.** Depending on how urgently you want to get your feet up, or in a hot tub, a sprinkling of restaurants are in the neighboring villages, including the quaint town of Petite-Rivière-Saint-François, along rue Principale, the more scenic way back to Québec. This river-hugging road can be treacherous depending on the weather. Many more dining choices are along 138 west, especially in Beaupré.

PLANNING YOUR TRIP TO MONTRÉAL & QUÉBEC CITY

The province of Québec is immense: It's physically the largest province in the second-largest country in the world (after Russia); covers an area more than three times the size of France; and stretches from the northern borders of New York, Vermont, and New Hampshire up almost to the Arctic Circle.

That said, most of the region's population lives in the stretch just immediately north of the U.S. border. The greater Montréal metropolitan area is home to nearly half of the province's population. Québec City lies just 263km (163 miles) northeast of Montréal, commanding a stunning location on the rim of a promontory overlooking the St. Lawrence River, which is at its narrowest here. Most of the province's developed resort and scenic areas lie within a 3-hour drive of either city. For the specifics on getting to both Montréal and Québec City, see chapters 4 and 11, respectively.

[FastFACTS] MONTRÉAL & QUÉBEC CITY

American Automobile Association (AAA) Members of **AAA** are covered by the **Canadian Automobile Association (CAA)** while traveling in Canada. Bring your membership card and proof of insurance. The 24-hour hotline for emergency assistance is ℭ **800/222-4357.** The AAA card also provides discounts at a wide variety of hotels and restaurants in the province of Québec. Visit **www. caaquebec.com** for more information.

Area Codes The Montréal area codes are **514** and **438,** and the Québec City area codes are **418** and **581.** Outside of Montréal, the area codes are **450, 579, 819,** and **873.** You always need to dial the three-digit area code in addition to the seven-digit number. Numbers that begin with **800, 866, 877, 888,** or **855** are free to call from both Canada and the U.S.

ATMs ATMs (*guichet automatique*) are practically everywhere, including bank lobbies, shopping centers, bars, and gas stations. Machines in banks don't typically charge user fees if they are affiliated with your banking institution back home, but ask your bank to make sure. Elsewhere, ATMs are notorious for charging high flat rates to withdraw cash; C$5 on a minimum withdrawal of C$20 is not uncommon. Many institutions (and some taxis) now also accept payment by bank card. Most machines in Canada only allow a four-digit PIN, so check with your bank beforehand and change your PIN if it has five- or six-digits. Also, as in other countries, it's common to be charged fees when withdrawing from ATMs.

Business Hours Most stores in the province are open from 9 or 10am until 5 or 6pm Monday through Wednesday, 9 or 10am to 9pm on Thursday and Friday, 9 or 10am to 5 or 6pm on Saturday, and Sunday from noon to 5pm. **Banks** are usually open Monday through Friday from 8 or 9am to 4pm and usually closed for the entire weekend (although some are open Sat and even Sun). **Post office** hours vary wildly by location, but are generally open from 9:30am to 5:30pm on weekdays. Some are open 9:30am to 5pm on Saturdays, and most are closed on Sundays. While many **restaurants** are open all day between meals, some shut down between lunch and dinner. Most restaurants serve until 9:30 or 10pm.

Bars normally stay open until 3am, while some "after-hours" clubs open when other clubs are closing and keep people dancing until noon.

Car Rental Terms, cars, and prices for car rentals are similar to those in the rest of North America and Europe, and all the major companies operate in the province. At the Montréal-Trudeau Airport, for instance, car rental agencies include **Avis, Budget,** and **Hertz.** Major car rental companies also have offices in the central tourist areas of downtown Montréal and Québec City.

Québec province mandates that residents have radial snow tires on their cars in winter, from mid-December until March 15. Rental-car agencies are required to provide snow tires on car rentals during that period, and many charge an extra, nonnegotiable fee. The minimum driving age is 16 in Québec, but some car rental companies will not rent to people under 25. Others charge higher rates for drivers under the age of 21.

Cellphones See "Mobile Phones," later in this section.

Crime See "Safety," later in this section.

Customs International visitors can expect at least a probing question or two at the border or airport. Normal baggage and personal possessions should be no problem, but plants, animals, fireworks, and weapons are

among the items that may be prohibited or require additional documents before they're allowed in. For specific information about Canadian rules, check with the **Canada Border Services Agency** (www.cbsa-asfc. gc.ca; ✆ **506/636-5064** from outside the country or 800/461-9999 within Canada). Search for "bsf5082" to get a full list of visitor information.

Tobacco and alcoholic beverages face strict import restrictions: Individuals 18 years or older are allowed to bring in 200 cigarettes, 50 cigars, or 200 grams of tobacco; and only one of the following amounts of alcohol: 1.14 liters of liquor, 1.5 liters of wine, or 8.5 liters of beer (24 12-ounce cans or bottles). Additional amounts face hefty taxes. Possession of a car radar detector is prohibited, whether or not it is connected. Police officers can confiscate it and fines may run as high as C$650. Visitors can temporarily bring recreational vehicles, such as snowmobiles, boats, and trailers, as well as outboard motors, for personal use.

If you're traveling with expensive items, such as laptops or musical equipment, consider registering them before you leave your country to avoid challenges at the border on your return.

For information on what you're allowed to bring home, contact one of the following agencies:

U.S. Citizens: U.S. Customs & Border Protection (CBP), 1300 Pennsylvania Ave., NW, Washington, DC 20229 (www.cbp.gov; ℂ 877/227-5511).

U.K. Citizens: www.hmrc.gov.uk or ℂ 0800/595-000.

Australian Citizens: Australian Customs Service, Customs House, 5 Constitution Avenue, Canberra City, ACT 2601 (www.customs.gov.au; ℂ 1300/363-263 or 612/9313-3010 from outside Australia).

New Zealand Citizens: New Zealand Customs, the Customhouse, 1 Hinemoa Street, Harbour Quays, P.O. Box 2218, Wellington, 6140 (www.customs.govt.nz; ℂ 0800/428-786 or 649/927-8036 from outside New Zealand).

Doctors See the "Fast Facts" sections of chapters 4 and 11.

Drinking Laws The legal drinking age in the province is 18. All hard liquor and spirits in Québec are sold through official government stores operated by the Québec Société des Alcools (look for maroon signs with the acronym SAQ). Wine and beer are available in grocery and convenience stores, called *dépanneurs.* Bars can pour drinks as late as 3am, but often stay open later.

Penalties for drunk driving in Canada are heavy. Provisions instituted in 2008 include higher mandatory penalties, such as a minimum fine of C$1,000 and 1 to 3 years driving prohibition for a convicted first offense, and for a second offense, a minimum of 30 days in jail and 3 to 5 years probation. Drivers caught under the influence face a maximum life sentence if they cause death, and a maximum 10-year sentence and possible lifetime ban on driving if they cause bodily harm. Learn more at **www.saaq.gouv.qc.ca/en**.

Driving Rules All international drivers must carry a **valid driver's license** from their country of residence. A U.S. license is sufficient as long as you are a visitor and actually are a U.S. resident. A U.K. license is sufficient, as well.

In Canada, highway distances and speed limits are given in kilometers (km). The highway speed limit is 100kmph (62 mph). Buckle up or face a stiff penalty for neglecting to wear your seatbelt. Radar detectors are prohibited in the province of Québec. They can be confiscated, even if they're not being used.

Electricity Both the U.S. and Canada use 110 to 120 volts AC (60 cycles), compared to the 220 to 240 volts AC (50 cycles) used in most of Europe, Australia, and New Zealand. If your small appliances use 220 to 240 volts, you'll need a 110-volt transformer and a plug adapter with two flat parallel pins to operate them in Canada. They can be difficult to find in Canada, so bring one with you.

Embassies & Consulates Embassies are located in Ottawa, Canada's capital. Consulate offices are throughout the Canadian provinces, including Québec. The U.S. Embassy information line is ℂ **613/688-5335** or 613/238-5335 for after-hours emergencies. The U.S. consulate in Montréal is at 315 Place d'Youville Ste. 500 (ℂ **514/398-9695**) but visitors must first check in at 1155 Rue St-Alexandre; non-emergency American citizen services are provided here by appointment only. The U.S. consulate in Québec City is on Jardin des Gouverneurs at 2 rue de la Terrasse-Dufferin (ℂ **418/692-2095**).

The U.K. consulate for the province is in Montréal at 2000 McGill College Ave., Ste. 1940 (ℂ **514/866-5863**). For contact information for other embassies and consulates, search for "foreign representatives in Canada" at www.international.gc.ca.

Emergencies Dial ℂ **911** for police, firefighters, or an ambulance.

Family Travel Montréal and Québec City offer an abundance of family-oriented activities. Many of them are outdoors, even in winter. Water sports, river cruises, fort climbing, and fireworks displays are among summer's many attractions, with dog sledding and skiing the top choices in snowy months. Québec City's walls and fortifications are fodder for imagining the days of knights and princesses. In both cities, many museums make special efforts to address children's interests and enthusiasms.

PLANNING YOUR TRIP TO MONTRÉAL & QUÉBEC CITY | Family Travel

We try to include kid-friendly accommodations, restaurants, and attractions throughout this guide, but also, see "Especially for Kids" in chapter 7 on p. 128 and in chapter 14 on p. 233. See "Travelers With Wheelchairs, Strollers, or Restricted Mobility" later in this chapter for more about getting around.

Children who speak French or are learning French might like a guidebook of their own. The fun *Mon Premier Guide de Voyage au Québec* has 112 pages of photos, miniassays, and activities for kids age 6 to 12. You can find it in provincial bookshops.

Gasoline Gasoline in Canada is sold by the liter; 3.78 liters equals 1 gallon. At press time, the average price of a liter in Montréal and Québec costs approximately C$1.12, the equivalent of about US$4.25 per gallon.

Health Canada has a state-run health system, and Québec hospitals are modern and decently equipped, with well-trained staffs. You are unlikely to get sick from Canada's food or water.

In general, Canadians who reside outside the province of Québec are covered by an interprovincial agreement, which allows them to present their own province's health card (for example, OHIP card in Ontario) and have their health services covered by direct billing. In some cases, however, services must be paid for upfront and

patients must seek reimbursement from their home province.

Medical treatment in Canada isn't free for foreigners, and doctors and hospitals will make you pay at the time of service. See "Insurance" below for suggestions about medical insurance.

Familiar over-the-counter medicines are widely available in Canada. If there is a possibility that you will run out of prescribed medicines during your visit, take along a prescription from your doctor. Have the generic name of prescription medicines in case a local pharmacist is unfamiliar with the brand name. Pack medications in your carry-on luggage and have them in their original containers with pharmacy labels—otherwise, they may not make it through airport security. If you're entering Canada with syringes used for medical reasons, bring a medical certificate that shows they are for medical use and be sure to declare them to Canadian Customs officials.

If you suffer from a chronic illness, consult your doctor before departure.

Hospitals In Montréal, see "Fast Facts" in chapter 4; in Québec City, see "Fast Facts" in chapter 11.

Insurance U.S. health plans (including Medicare and Medicaid) do not generally provide coverage in Canada, and the ones that do often require you to pay for services upfront and reimburse you only after

you return home. As a safety net, you may want to buy travel medical insurance. Travelers from the U.K. should carry their European Health Insurance Card (EHIC) as proof of entitlement to free/reduced cost medical treatment abroad (go to www.nhs.uk and search for EHIC; ℂ **0845/606-2030**). Always seek out a policy with a reputable insurance company for repatriation costs, lost money, baggage, or cancellation, and travel insurance.

Internet Access & Wi-Fi Nearly all hotels and *auberges*, as well as most cafes, offer Wi-Fi. Some hotels still offer high-speed Internet access through cable connections. Except at the larger hotels, Wi-Fi is generally free. Many hotels maintain business centers with computers for use by guests or outsiders, or at least have one computer available for guest use. Again, except at the larger hotels, this access is often free. This is your best bet for Internet access if you're traveling without a laptop or mobile device with Wi-Fi.

Language Canada is officially bilingual, but the province of Québec has laws that make French mandatory in signage. About 65% of Montréal's population has French as its first language (and about 95% of Québec City's population does). An estimated four out of five Francophones (French speakers) speak at least some English. Hotel desk staff, sales clerks, and telephone operators nearly always greet people initially in French, but usually switch to English quickly, if necessary. Outside of Montréal, visitors are more likely to encounter residents who don't speak English. If smiles and sign language don't work, look around for a young person—most of them study English in school.

Legal Aid If you are arrested, your country's embassy or consulate can provide the names of lawyers who speak English. See "Embassies & Consulates" above for more information.

LGBT Travelers The province of Québec is a destination for international gay travelers. Gay life here is generally open and accepted (gay marriage is legal throughout the province), and gay travelers are heavily marketed to. Travelers will often find the rainbow flag prominently displayed on the doors and websites of hotels and restaurants.

The **Tourisme Montréal** website, www.tourisme-montreal.org, has a "Gay and Lesbian" option under "What To Do" that lists gay-friendly accommodations, events, websites for LGBT meet-ups, and more. Of several local publications, the most thorough is *Fugues* (www.fugues.com), which lists events and gay-friendly lodgings, clubs, saunas, and other resources. Free copies are available at tourist offices and in racks around the city.

In Montréal, many gay and lesbian travelers head straight to the **Gay Village** (also known simply as "the Village"), a neighborhood east of downtown located primarily along rue Ste-Catherine est between rue St-Hubert and rue Papineau. See p. 141 for more about this neighborhood. As the Tourisme Montréal website says, "Rainbow columns on a subway station entrance? I've got a feeling we're not in Kansas anymore!" The Village is action central on any night, but it especially picks up during **Montréal Pride** (www.fiertemontreal pride.com) in August and the **Black & Blue Festival** (www.bbcm.org) in October, which is one of the world's largest circuit parties, with a week of entertainment and club dancing.

The **Village Tourism Information Centre**, 1307 rue Ste-Catherine est (℡ 888/647-2247), is open June to August from noon to 6pm (days vary; call in advance) and has information about everything from wine bars to yoga classes. It's operated by the **Québec Gay Chamber of Commerce** (www.ccgq.ca).

In Québec City, the gay community is much smaller. Geographically, it's centered in Upper Town just outside the city walls, on rue St-Jean and the parallel rue d'Aiguillon, starting from where they cross rue St-Augustin and heading west. **Le Drague Cabaret Club,** 815 rue St-Augustin (www. ledrague.com; ℡ 418/649-7212), or "the Drag," is a

central gathering place with a cabaret and two dance rooms. Over Labour Day weekend, Québec City hosts a 5-day gay-pride fest, **Fête Arc-en-Ciel** (www. arcencielquebec.ca), which attracts thousands of people.

Mail All mail sent through **Canada Post** (www.canada-post.ca; ℡ 866/607-6301) must bear Canadian stamps. That might seem obvious, but apparently a large number of U.S. visitors use U.S. stamps. A letter or postcard to the U.S. costs C$1.20. A letter or postcard to anywhere else outside of Canada costs C$2.50. A letter to a Canadian address costs C85¢. **FedEx** (www.fedex.com/ca; ℡ 800/463-3339) offers service from Canada and lists locations at its website.

Medical Requirements Also, see "Health." Unless you're arriving from an area known to be suffering from an epidemic (particularly cholera or yellow fever), inoculations or vaccinations are not required for entry into Canada.

Mobile Phones Cellphone service is good in Québec cities and sometimes spotty in areas beyond city borders. Cellphone service is widely available throughout the regions mentioned in this book.

Visitors from the U.S. should be able to get roaming service or a short-term international data plan that allows them to use their cellphones in Canada. Some wireless companies let customers adjust their plans to get cheaper rates while traveling. Ask your provider for options. Europeans and most Australians are on the GSM (Global System for Mobile Communications) network with removable plastic SIM cards in their phones. Call your wireless provider for information about traveling. You may be able to purchase pay-as-you-go SIM cards in Canada with local providers such as Rogers (www.rogers.com). Since Canadian mobile service carriers use the same formats as in the United States, American travelers can simply contact their mobile carrier to adjust their plan for service in Canada. It will cost a bit more, but it's simple and easy.

If you end up traveling with a phone that doesn't get reception, **prepaid phone services** are an option. With **OneSuite.com** (www.onesuite.com), for instance, you prepay an

online account for as little as US$10. You can then dial a toll-free or local access number (from, say, a hotel phone), enter your PIN, and then dial the number you're calling. Calls from Canada to mainland U.S. cost just US2.5¢ to US3.5¢ per minute. Some hotels charge for local and even toll-free calls, so check before dialing.

Cheaper still are calls conducted online. **Skype** (www.skype.com) allows you to make international calls from your laptop or via its smartphone app. Calls to people who also have the program on their computers are free. You can call people who don't have the service, although modest fees apply.

Money & Costs Frommer's lists exact prices in the local currency. The currency conversions provided were correct at press time. However, rates fluctuate, so before departing consult a currency exchange website

such as **www.oanda.com/ currency/converter** to check up-to-the-minute rates.

Beware of hidden credit card fees while traveling. Check with your credit or debit card issuer to see what fees, if any, will be charged for overseas transactions.

Canadian currency comes in denominations of dollars and cents. Bills—C$5, C$10, C$20, C$50, and C$100— are all the same size but different colors. Coins include small change (C5¢, C10¢, and C25¢) as well as C$1 and C$2 coins. The gold-colored C$1 coin is nicknamed a "loonie" because of the image of a loon on one side. It replaced the C$1 bill, which was phased out in the late 1980s. The C$2 coin is sometimes called a "toonie." Canada began phasing out its penny in 2013 and pennies are no longer in circulation.

THE VALUE OF CANADIAN DOLLAR VS. OTHER POPULAR CURRENCIES

Can$	Aus$	Euro (€)	NZ$	UK£	US$
C$1	A$0.98	€0.74	NZ$1.06	£0.53	$0.79

WHAT THINGS COST IN MONTRÉAL & QUÉBEC CITY · C$

	C$
Taxi from the airport to downtown Montréal	43.00
Taxi from the airport to downtown Québec City	34.00
Double room, moderate	from 160.00
Double room, inexpensive	from 100.00
Three-course dinner for one without wine, moderate	25.00
Bottle of beer	2.00–4.00
Cup of coffee	2.00
1 liter of premium gas	1.12
Admission to most museums	10.00–20.00
Admission to most national parks	Free

Newspapers & Magazines The *Globe and Mail* (www.theglobeandmail.com) is the national English-language paper. *La Presse* (www.cyberpresse.ca/actualites/regional/montreal) is the leading French-language newspaper. A sister publication, *Le Soleil* (www.cyberpresse.ca/le-soleil), is published in Québec City. Montréal's primary English-language newspaper is the *Montréal Gazette* (www.montrealgazette.com). Most large newsstands and shops in larger hotels carry the *New York Times, Wall Street Journal*, and *International New York Times* (formerly *International Herald Tribune*.)

Packing Montréal and Québec City have four distinct seasons: winter, from November to April; spring, from April to June; summer, from June to September; and autumn, from September to November. Pack light, breathable fabrics in warmer months, and warm layers in colder ones. For more, see the box, "Bracing for the Canadian Winter," on p. 38.

Passports For country-specific passport information, contact the following agencies:

For Residents of Australia Contact the Australian **Passport Information Service.** Visit www.passports.gov.au or call ℂ **131-232.**

For Residents of Ireland Contact the **Passport Office,** Frederick Buildings, Molesworth Street, Dublin 2

(www.dfa.ie; ℂ **01/671-1633).**

For Residents of New Zealand Contact the **Passports Office,** Department of Internal Affairs, Level 3, 109 Featherston Street, P.O. Box 1568, Wellington 6011 (www.passports.govt.nz; ℂ **0800/22-50-50** in New Zealand or 04/463-9360).

For Residents of the United Kingdom Visit your nearest passport office, major post office, or travel agency, or contact the **Identity and Passport Service (IPS),** 4th Floor, Peel Building, 2 Marsham Street, London, SW1P 4DF (www.ips.gov.uk; ℂ **0300/222-0000**).

For Residents of the United States To find your regional passport office, check the **U.S. State Department website** (http://travel.state.gov) or call the **National Passport Information Center** (ℂ **877/487-2778**) for automated information.

Petrol Please see "Gasoline," earlier in this chapter.

Police Dial ℂ **911** for police, firefighters, or an ambulance.

Safety Montréal and Québec City are extremely safe cities, and far safer than their U.S. or European counterparts of similar size. Still, common sense insists that visitors stay alert and observe the usual urban precautions. It's best to stay out of parks at night and to take a taxi when returning from a late dinner or nightclub.

Québec is one of Canada's more liberal provinces.

Mass demonstrations are rare and political violence is unusual. Tolerance of others is a Canadian characteristic, and it's highly unlikely that visitors of ethnic, religious, or racial minorities will encounter even mild forms of discrimination. That applies to sexual orientation, as well, especially in Montréal, which has one of the largest and most visible gay communities in North America.

Senior Travel Mention the fact that you're a senior citizen when you make your travel reservations. Many Québec hotels offer discounts for older travelers. Throughout the province, theaters, museums, and other attractions offer reduced admission to people as young as 60.

Many reliable agencies and organizations target the 50-plus market. **Road Scholar,** run by Elderhostel, Inc. (www.roadscholar.org; ℂ **800/454-5768**) arranges worldwide study programs for those aged 55 and older, and offers a variety of trips to Québec City and Montréal.

Smoking Smoking was banned in the province's bars, restaurants, clubs, casinos, and some other public spaces in 2006. Most inns and hotels are now entirely smoke-free as well. Check before you book if you're looking for a room in which you can smoke.

Taxes Most goods and services in Canada are taxed 5% by the federal government (the GST/TPS) and 9.975% by the province of Québec (the TVQ). In Montréal, hotel bills have an additional 3.5% accommodations tax. A Foreign Convention and Tour Incentive Program provides limited rebates on the GST for services used during foreign conventions held in Canada, for nonresident exhibitors, and for the short-term accommodations portion of tour packages for nonresident individuals and tour operators. Details are at **www.cra-arc.gc.ca/visitors**.

Telephones The Canadian telephone system, operated by Bell Canada, closely resembles the U.S. model. All **operators speak English and French,** and they respond in the appropriate language as soon as callers speak to them. In Canada, dial ✆ **0** to reach an operator. When making a **local call** within the province of Québec, you must dial the area code before the seven-digit number.

Phone numbers that begin with 800, 888, 877, and 866 are **toll-free.** That means they're free to call within Canada and from the U.S. You need to dial 1 first.

Remember that both local and long-distance calls usually cost more from hotels—sometimes a lot more, so check before dialing. Some hotels charge for all calls, including toll-free ones.

To call the province of Québec from the U.S.: Simply dial 1, then the three-digit area code, then the seven-digit number. *Example:* To call the

Infotouriste Centre in Montréal, dial 1-514-873-2015.

To call Québec from the U.K./Ireland/Australia/New Zealand: Dial the international access code 00 (from Australia, 0011), then the Canadian country code 1, then the area code, and then the seven-digit number. *Example:* To call the Infotouriste Centre in Montréal, dial 00-1-514-873-2015.

To call the U.S. from Québec: Simply dial 1, then the three-digit area code and seven-digit number.

To call the U.K./Ireland/Australia/New Zealand from Québec: Dial 011, then the country code (U.K. 44, Ireland 353, Australia 61, New Zealand 64), then the number.

For **directory information,** dial ✆ **411**.

Time Montréal and Québec City are in the Eastern Standard Time (EST) zone, that is, 5 hours behind Greenwich Mean Time (GMT). Canada has six primary time zones: For example, when it's 9am in Vancouver, British Columbia (Pacific Time), it's 10am in Calgary, Alberta (Mountain Time), 11am in Winnipeg, Manitoba (Central Time), noon in Montréal and Québec City, Québec (Eastern Time), 1pm in Halifax, Nova Scotia (Atlantic Time), 1:30pm in St. John's, Newfoundland (Newfoundland Time), 5pm in London, U.K. (GMT), and 2am the next day in Sydney, Australia.

Daylight saving time (summer time) is in effect from the second Sunday in March

to the first Sunday in November. Daylight saving time moves the clock 1 hour ahead of standard time.

Tipping Local tipping practices are similar to those in large Western cities. In hotels, tip bellhops C$1 per bag and tip the chamber staff C$3 to C$5 per day. Tip the doorman or concierge a few dollars only if he or she has provided you with some specific service (for example, calling a cab for you or obtaining difficult-to-get theater tickets). Tip the valet-parking attendant C$2 to C$3 every time you get your car. In restaurants, bars, and nightclubs, tip waiters 15% to 20% of the check, tip checkroom attendants C$1 per garment, and tip valet-parking attendants C$1 per vehicle. Other service personnel: Tip taxi drivers 15% of the fare, tip skycaps at airports C$1 per bag, and tip hairdressers, barbers, and estheticians 15% to 20%.

Toilets You won't find public toilets on the streets in Montréal or Québec City, but they can be found in tourist offices, museums, railway and bus stations, service stations, and large shopping complexes. Restaurants and bars in heavily visited areas often reserve their restrooms for patrons.

Travelers With Wheelchairs, Strollers, or Restricted Mobility Québec regulations regarding wheelchair accessibility are similar to those in the U.S. and the rest of Canada, including requirements for curb cuts, entrance ramps, designated parking spaces, and specially equipped bathrooms. That said, while the more modern parts of the cities are fully wheelchair accessible, access to the restaurants and inns housed in 18th- and 19th-century buildings, especially in Vieux-Montréal and Québec City, is often difficult or impossible. Montréal's underground Métro system has only eight stations with elevators; the rest have escalators or just stairs.

Information on accessibility of specific accommodations and tourists sites is online at **www.bonjour quebec.com**, the official website of the Québec government. Search for "Kéroul," the organization that Tourisme Québec collaborates with to update the database. Kéroul also provides information at its own websites, **www.keroul. qc.ca** and **www.laroute accessible.com**.

Visas For citizens of many countries, including the U.S., U.K., Ireland, Australia, and New Zealand, only a passport is required to visit Canada for up to 90 days; no visas or proof of vaccinations are necessary. For the most up-to-date list of visitor visa exemptions, visit **Citizenship and Immigration Canada** at **www. cic.gc.ca**.

Visitor Information In Montréal, see chapter 4; in Québec City, see chapter 11.

Water Tap water is safe to drink. See "Health," earlier in this section.

Wi-Fi See "Internet & Wi-Fi," earlier in this section.

Women Travelers Montréal and Québec City are generally safe cities for female adults. Do exercise caution, however, especially when walking alone at night.

Index

General Index

A

B

C

D

Photo Credits